Principles of
Knowledge
Management

Principles of Knowledge Management

Theory, Practice, and Cases

Elie Geisler and Nilmini Wickramasinghe

Routledge
Taylor & Francis Group

LONDON AND NEW YORK

First published 2009 by M.E. Sharpe

Published 2015 by Routledge
2 Park Square, Milton Park, Abingdon, Oxon OX14 4RN
711 Third Avenue, New York, NY, 10017, USA

Routledge is an imprint of the Taylor & Francis Group, an informa business

Library of Congress Cataloging-in-Publication Data

Geisler, Eliezer, 1942–
  Principles of knowledge management : theory, practices, and cases / Elie Geisler and Nilmini Wickramasinghe.
    p. cm.
  ISBN 978-0-7656-1322-6 (pbk. : alk. paper)
  1. Knowledge management. 2. Knowledge management—Case studies. 3. Management information systems. 4. Management information systems—Case studies. I. Wickramasinghe, Nilmini. II. Title.

HD30.2.G446 2008
658.4'038—dc22

ISBN 13: 9780765613226 (pbk)

This book is dedicated to my grandchildren:
Tyler, Max, Jack, Grace, and Shani.

Elie Geisler

This book is dedicated to my parents.

Nilmini Wickramasinghe

Contents

Acknowledgments

In the development of this book we have benefited from inputs and insights from many people. We wish to thank them and acknowledge their contributions. We thank Eric Valentine for his encouragement and help throughout the project. We also thank Lynn Taylor and Katie Corasaniti at M.E. Sharpe for their editorial assistance and support. We thank our graduate students, Manjari Sharda and Meghna Gandhi, for their assistance in data collection, literature searches, and analysis. We also are indebted to the contributors of the cases in Part IV of this book. We particularly owe a debt of gratitude to Janet Goranson, who worked with us throughout the preparation of the manuscript; her insights and continuous support were critical to this work.

Introduction

This is a book written by two authors from two distinct disciplinary perspectives who wanted to compose a different type of textbook on knowledge management (KM). Nilmini Wickramasinghe is trained in the discipline of information systems. Her interests thus led her almost directly into the new area of KM. Elie Geisler comes from the discipline of organizational behavior and theory. His interests in the workings of research, development, and technology organizations also led him into the new field of knowledge workers, knowledge economy, and KM.

These uniquely diverse academic backgrounds have resulted in a distinct partnership that has produced a textbook relatively free of the biases encountered in a new area such as KM. We were able to combine our interests and expertise in the preparation of a textbook that addresses the *knowledge* component as well as the *management* aspects of this emerging field of study.

This book is about the conceptual nature of KM and its applications—as illustrated in several cases. The book contains four parts. Part I examines the fundamentals of KM. In this part we review the current concepts of the structure of KM and the processes by which KM is diffused in human organizations. We have added to this discussion our own ideas and frameworks resulting from research we have been conducting over the decade.

In Part II we address the structure, attributes, and processes of the knowledge-based enterprise. In particular, we focus on the design and implementation of knowledge management systems (KMS). We draw in this part from our previous experience in research and consulting to explain the factors that impinge upon success or failure in the adoption and implementation of KMS in the private as well as the public sectors.

In Part III, a unique contribution we bring to this nascent field of KM, we address the issues of measuring the outcomes, impacts, and benefits of KMS. We also offer a discussion of the KM audit in light of recent legislation about the flow of information and knowledge in organizations.

We also explore what the future holds for KM and KMS. We address the current perspectives of scholars and managers—some who discount KM as a fad and others who contend that this is the way the future is shaped in organizational life.

We complement the book with eight cases. These are drawn from the literature and our practical experiences with organizations in several sectors and industries. The cases are provided as illustrations, not as a deterministic approach to what is right and wrong in the analysis of KM.

AUDIENCES FOR THIS BOOK

This is a textbook for undergraduate and graduate courses in KM and KMS. Instructors who teach these courses will be able to select this book as their main text or as an auxiliary book of cases. The book also is intended to be a resource for a much broader segment of undergraduate and graduate students, such as those in business administration, management of information systems, communications, public administration, management of technology, and economics.

SPECIAL FEATURES

Four features make this book unique among KM texts currently in the market. First, this book has original cases, designed to illustrate the learning objectives of the text. Second, the book offers a new conceptual approach to the nature and utilization of knowledge and KM. In addition to simply describing the current state of the art, this book advances a new approach that we developed.

The third feature of this book is its combination of the varied backgrounds and disciplinary expertise of its authors. The conjoining of the information systems and organizational analysis skills of the authors forms a powerful cooperation in the preparation of this unique textbook.

Finally, the fourth special feature is the extended discussion of metrics and measurement issues and techniques of KM and KMS. This feature provides students and scholars with a unique and hitherto unavailable text addressing metrics beyond the traditional ones of benchmarking, balanced scorecards, and assessments of quality.

PART I

FUNDAMENTALS OF KNOWLEDGE MANAGEMENT

1 What Is Knowledge Management?

KEY LEARNING OUTCOMES

You will know you have mastered the material in this chapter when you can define and explain the following:

1. Knowledge management's importance in today's knowledge economy.
2. What knowledge management means.
3. The challenges and drivers for knowledge management.
4. The evolution of the study of knowledge management.

As we move into the twenty-first century, the need for rapid access to relevant knowledge has never been greater. The business world is increasingly competitive, and the demand for innovative products and services is enormous. In this century of creativity and ideas, the most valuable resources available to any organizations are human skills, expertise, and relationships. Knowledge management (KM) is about capitalizing on these precious assets in a systematic fashion. Most companies do not capitalize on the wealth of expertise in the form of knowledge scattered across their levels nor maximize the use of information and data, coupled with the potential of people's skills, competencies, ideas, intuition, commitment, and motivation. In today's economy, knowledge is people, money, leverage, learning, flexibility, power, and competitive advantage. Knowledge is more relevant to sustained business than capital, labor, or land. Nevertheless, it remains the most neglected asset and so KM has developed as the combination of business strategies, processes, tools, and techniques needed to address this void in organizations.

In this chapter we introduce the concept of KM. We highlight the need for it and define what it is and is not. As we shall find in further chapters, knowledge is not a simple construct to define; thus it should come as no surprise that the concept of KM is equally difficult to pin down. In this chapter we emphasize the need for a holistic approach to KM. We also discuss the evolution of KM: how it has come to be the discipline it is today. In doing so, we highlight the challenges of KM, the major drivers, and the KM strategies, process tools, and techniques that are difficult to embrace and yet so beneficial. This chapter serves as an overview of the KM area of research and practice. Subsequent chapters will then drill down into these various components in more detail.

WHAT IS KNOWLEDGE MANAGEMENT?

KM is quickly gaining recognition as a key determinant of value in the marketplace, organizational success, and competitive edge. Today, companies compete not only on the basis of product, service, and operational superiority, but also through the enhanced management of their corporate memory and intellectual assets. They are beginning to realize that their edge lies in how they manage the efficient flow and transfer of knowledge across the organization. A report, "Knowledge Management Software Market Forecast," estimated that the total KM software market would reach $30 billion by 2015. A review of the business literature reveals many definitions of KM posited by various researchers and practitioners. A few of these definitions are described below:

> According to the Gartner Group, knowledge management is a discipline that promotes an integrated approach to identifying, managing, and sharing all of an enterprise's information needs. These information assets may include databases, documents, policies, and procedures as well as previously unarticulated expertise and experience resident in individual workers. (Lee 2000)
>
> Knowledge management is an intelligent process by which raw data is gathered and transformed into information elements. These information elements are assembled and organized into context-relevant structures that represent knowledge. (Onge 2001)
>
> KM is a formal process that engages an organization's people, processes, and technology in a solution that captures knowledge and delivers it to the right people at the right time. (Duffy 2001)
>
> Arthur Andersen defined KM as the discipline of enabling individuals in an organization to collectively acquire, share, and leverage knowledge to achieve business objectives. (Duffy 2001)

KM for the organization, then, consists of the ability to gain knowledge from its own experience and from the experience of others and to judiciously apply that knowledge in fulfilling the mission of the organization (Figure 1.1). These activities are executed by marrying technology, organizational structures, and cognitive-based strategies to raise the yield of existing knowledge and produce new knowledge. Critical in this endeavor is the enhancement of various cognitive systems (organizations, humans, computers, or joint human-computer systems) in acquiring, storing, and utilizing knowledge for learning, problem solving, and decision making (Skyrme 1991).

The common factor in all the definitions is the recognition of the enormous value that human resources contribute to the knowledge of an organization. Regarding knowledge creation, organizations have information about products, services, and

Figure 1.1 **What Is KM? Some Definitions**

- KM is a discipline that promotes an integrated approach to identifying, managing, and sharing all of the enterprise's information needs. (Gartner Group)
- KM is an intelligent process by which raw data is gathered and transformed into information elements . . . these are assembled and organized into context-relevant structures that represent knowledge. (Onge 2001)
- KM is a formal process that engages an organization's people, processes, and technology in a solution that captures knowledge and delivers it to the right people at the right time. (Duffy 2001)
- KM is the discipline of enabling individuals in an organization to collectively acquire, share, and leverage knowledge to achieve business objectives. (Arthur Andersen/Accenture)
- KM is the management of intellectual capital in the interests of the enterprise. (Hoffman 1998)
- KM is the concept under which information is turned into actionable knowledge and made available effortlessly in a usable form to the people who can apply it. (*Information Week* 2003)

processes stored in various systems such as databases, file servers, Web pages, e-mails, and enterprise resource planning (ERP). If all this information is stored centrally and is accessible to all the employees in the form of knowledge, it will not only reduce the time employees spend searching for data to make better business decisions throughout the enterprise, but also provide decision makers with more time for innovation and creativity. Organizations need to create enterprise information portals of knowledge that store a wide variety of structured and unstructured data sources in the form of knowledge so that knowledge will be accessible to all employees through easy Web-based interfaces. Information centers, market intelligence, and learning are converging to form KM functions (Drucker 1999; Hansen and Oetinger 2001).

DESCRIPTIONS OF KNOWLEDGE MANAGEMENT AND SOME IMPLICATIONS FOR ENTERPRISES

As described above by various authors, KM is a multidisciplinary approach that takes a comprehensive, systematic view of the information assets of an organization by identifying, capturing, collecting, organizing, indexing, storing, integrating, retrieving, and sharing them. Such assets include explicit knowledge, such as databases, documents, environmental knowledge, policies, procedures, and organizational culture, as well as the tacit knowledge of the organization's employees, their expertise, and their practical work experience. Further, KM strives to make the collective knowledge, information, and experience of the organization available to individual employees for their use and to motivate them to contribute their knowledge to the collective assets (Figure 1.2).

KM has two primary facets: (1) planning, capturing, organizing, interconnecting, and providing access to organizational intellectual capital through such intellectual technologies as document markup, thesaurus construction, or need analysis; and (2) directing or supervising such assets and those who are involved in these processes. These facets may be integrated into a single role or divided among several roles in an organization (Drucker 1988; Ellerman 1999; Granstrand 2000).

Organizations collect data about customers, products, suppliers, and transactions through their transactional operational systems. This information is stored in many formats, both structured (databases, ERP systems, etc.) and unstructured (document and content management, groupware, e-mail, and other forms of interpersonal communication) (Clegg 1999; Davenport and Prusak 1998). KM transforms this information into knowledge. KM is an intelligent process by which raw data are gathered and transformed into information elements. In KM, data residing in an organization's datasets, file servers, Web pages, e-mails, ERP, and customer relationship management (CRM) systems from all structured and unstructured data sources are integrated to a single enterprise information portal (EIP) that can be accessed through a usually personalized, Web-based interface. KM is the process through which organizations generate value from their intellectual and knowledge-based assets. Most often, generating value from such assets involves sharing them among employees, departments, and even with other companies in an effort to devise best practices. KM involves the creation, dissemination, and utilization of knowledge. While KM is often facilitated by information technology (IT), technology by itself is not synonymous with KM (Becker 1993; Ellinger et al. 1999; Gupta et al. 2004).

KM helps an organization gain insight and understanding from its own experience. Specific KM activities focus the organization on acquiring, storing, and using knowledge for such things as problem solving, dynamic learning, strategic planning, and decision making. KM also protects intellectual assets from decay, adds to firm intelligence, and provides increased flexibility. Therefore, KM is the management of the organization toward the continuous renewal of the organizational knowledge base—this means, for example, creating supportive organizational structures, facilitating organizational members, and putting IT instruments with emphasis on teamwork and diffusion of knowledge (as, e.g., groupware) into place. KM complements and enhances other organizational initiatives such as total quality management (TQM), business process reengineering (BPR), and organizational learning, providing a new and urgent focus to sustain competitive position.

Figure 1.2 **Some Descriptions of KM**

- KM is a multidisciplinary approach that takes a comprehensive, systematic view to the information assets of an organization by identifying, capturing, collecting, organizing, indexing, storing, integrating, retrieving, and sharing them. Such assets include: (1) explicit knowledge, such as databases, documents, environmental knowledge, policies, procedures, and organizational culture; and (2) the tacit knowledge of the organization's employees, their expertise, and their practical work experience.
- KM has two facets: (1) planning, capturing, organizing, interconnecting, and providing access to organizational intellectual capital through such intellectual technologies as document markup, thesaurus construction, and needs analysis; and (2) directing or supervising such assets and those that are involved in these processes.
- KM is the process through which organizations generate value from their intellectual and knowledge-based assets. Most often, generating value from such assets involves sharing them among employees, departments, and even with other companies in an effort to devise the best practices. KM involves the creation, dissemination, and utilization of knowledge. While KM often is facilitated by information technology, technology by itself is not synonymous with KM.
- KM helps an organization gain insight and understanding from its own experience. Specific KM activities focus the organization on acquiring, storing, and using knowledge for such things as problem solving, dynamic learning, strategic planning, and decision making.
- KM complements and enhances other organizational initiatives such as total quality management, business process reengineering, and organizational learning, providing a new and urgent focus to sustain competitive position.

EVOLUTION OF THE STUDY OF KNOWLEDGE MANAGEMENT

The history of KM is not clear and linear in its development since the field has evolved from so many different disciplines and domains (Figure 1.3). A number of management theorists have contributed to the evolution of KM as it stands today, among them Peter Drucker, Paul Strassmann, and Peter Senge in the United States. In particular, Drucker and Strassmann have stressed the growing importance of information and explicit knowledge as organizational resources, while Senge has focused on the "learning organization," a cultural dimension of managing knowledge. Leonard-Barton's case study of Chaparral Steel, a company that has had an effective KM strategy in place since the mid-1970s, inspired the research documented in her book *Wellsprings of Knowledge: Building and Sustaining Sources of Innovation* (1995). Everett Rogers's work at Stanford in the diffusion of innovation and Thomas Allen's research at MIT in information and technology transfer, both of which date from the late 1970s, also have contributed to our understanding of how knowledge is produced, used, and diffused within organizations.

By the mid-1980s, the importance of knowledge as a competitive asset was apparent, even though classical economic theory still ignored knowledge as an asset and most organizations still lacked strategies and methods for managing it. Recognition of the growing importance of organizational knowledge was accompanied by a need to deal with exponential increases in the amount of available knowledge and the increased complexity of both products and processes (Carrillo 1998; Davis and Botkin 1994; Malhotra 2001). The computer technology that contributed so heavily to this "information overload" now started to become part of the solution in a variety of domains. Doug Engelbart's augment (for "augmenting human intelligence"), introduced in 1978, was an early hypertext/groupware application capable of interfacing with other applications and systems. Rob Acksyn's and Don McCracken's Knowledge Management System, an open, distributed hypermedia tool, is another notable example (Ives et al. 1998).

The 1980s also saw the development of systems for managing knowledge that relied on work done in artificial intelligence and expert systems, giving us such terms as *knowledge acquisition*, *knowledge engineering*, *knowledge-based systems*, and *computer-based ontologies*. The term *knowledge management* finally came into being in the business community during this decade. To provide a technological base for managing knowledge, in 1989 a consortium of U.S. companies started the Initiative for Managing Knowledge Assets. Articles dealing with KM began appearing in journals such as *Sloan Management Review*, *Organizational Science*, and *Harvard Business Review*, and the first books on organizational learning and KM were published (for example, Senge's *The Fifth Discipline* and Sakaiya's *The Knowledge Value Revolution*). By 1990, a number of management consulting firms had begun in-house KM programs, and several well-known U.S., European, and Japanese firms had instituted focused KM programs.

KM was introduced in the popular press in 1991, when Tom Stewart published "Brainpower" in *Fortune* magazine. Perhaps the most widely read work to date is Ikujiro Nonaka and Hirotaka Takeuchi's *The Knowledge-Creating Company:*

How Japanese Companies Create the Dynamics of Innovation (1995). By the mid-1990s, KM initiatives were flourishing, thanks in part to the Internet. The International Knowledge Management Network (IKMN), begun in Europe in 1989, went online in 1994 and was soon joined by the U.S.-based Knowledge Management Forum and other KM-related groups and publications. The number of KM-based conferences and seminars is growing as organizations focus on managing and leveraging explicit and tacit knowledge resources to achieve competitive advantage.

In 1994 the IKMN published the results of a KM survey conducted among European firms, and in 1995 the European Community began offering funding for KM-related projects through the ESPRIT program. KM, which appears to offer a highly desirable alternative to less successful TQM and BPR initiatives, has become big business for such major international consulting firms as Ernst & Young Cap Gemini, Accenture (formerly Andersen Consulting), and Booz-Allen & Hamilton (Lesser et al. 2000; Moore 2000; O'Dell 1996). In addition, a number of professional organizations interested in such related areas as benchmarking, best practices, risk management, and change management are exploring the relationship of KM to their areas of special expertise (Lipnack and Stamps 2000).

During the 1970s and 1980s, data collection was a large part of companies' practices of accumulating client information. Companies used relational databases along with other application software packages to record customer or product-related data. Companies used many disparate operational systems for the data collection and compilation. As a result, organizations were flooded with information. At this stage, organizations used IT mainly for recording data to answer the question "What happened?" The systems of this phase were termed report-oriented systems (Croasdell 2001; Holt et al. 2000; Levine 2001).

Although organizations successfully implemented systems for the "What happened?" phase, the lack of an integrated one-source databank meant that the data recorded in reporting systems was not very useful for introspection analysis. So the companies started looking for a system that could help them analyze "Why did it happen?" This question required drilling beneath the numbers on a report to slice-and-dice data at a detailed level. For this requirement, in the late 1990s companies began to use data warehousing to consolidate information from disparate operational systems into one source for reliable and accessible information. *Data warehousing* is a generic term for the system for storing, retrieving, and managing large amounts of any type of data. Many organizations had implemented systems that were matured enough to give "Why did it happen?" analysis, but as global competition grew fiercer, organizations started looking for technologies that could help them examine still another question, "What will happen?" The data placed inside warehouse systems, coupled with data mining techniques, could predict future trends and behaviors, allowing companies to make proactive, knowledge-driven decisions (Bacon and Fitzgerald 2001; Mahe and Rieu 1998; Malhotra 2000).

Many business leaders then started demanding technologies that could help them answer the questions "What is happening?" and "What do I want to happen?" To answer these questions, the new technologies had to be fully integrated with people

Figure 1.3 **The Evolution of KM**

- The field of KM has evolved from many different disciplines and conceptual domains.
- By the mid-1980s, the importance of KM as a competitive asset was apparent.
- Classical economic theory has generally underestimated knowledge as an asset, and most organizations still lack adequate strategies and methods for managing it.
- Starting in the 1980s, a continuing trend in the development of systems for managing knowledge has emerged from work done in artificial intelligence and expert systems.
- Since the mid-1990s, the Internet has allowed KM initiatives to flourish.

and processes. "What is happening?" means to support day-to-day operations and decisions; data warehouse are updated continuously on a real-time, online basis. "What do I want to happen?" means that systems are fully automated to provide self-service to the users, such as customer-relationship management (Nonaka 1991).

WHY IS KNOWLEDGE MANAGEMENT DIFFICULT?

There are many problems associated with identifying knowledge assets and being able to use them and manage them in an efficient, cost-effective manner. Enterprises need to:

- establish an enterprise-wide vocabulary to ensure that the knowledge is correctly understood (Skyrme and Amidon 1997);
- be able to identify, model, and explicitly represent their knowledge;
- share and reuse their knowledge among differing applications for various types of users; this implies being able to share existing knowledge sources and also future ones (Skyrme 1991; Simon 1999); and
- create a culture that encourages knowledge sharing (Rubenstein and Geisler 2003).

Knowledge engineering methods and tools have come a long way toward addressing the use of an organization's knowledge assets. They provide disciplined approaches to designing and building knowledge-based applications. There are tools to support the capture, modeling, validation, verification, and maintenance of the knowledge in these applications. However, these tools do not extend to supporting the processes for managing knowledge at all levels within the organization (Silver 2000).

At the strategic level, the organization needs to be able to analyze and plan its business in terms of the knowledge it currently has and the knowledge it needs for future business processes. At the tactical level, the organization is concerned with identifying and formalizing existing knowledge, acquiring new knowledge for future use, archiving it in organizational memories, and creating systems that enable effective and efficient application of the knowledge within the organization. At the operational level, knowledge is used in everyday practice by professional personnel who need access to the right knowledge, at the right time, in the right location (Orlikowski and Barley 2001; Sharma and Gupta 2001).

KM is a difficult hurdle for organizations to overcome for two main reasons. First, in order to be able to absorb the application of KM, the organization and its management need to experience almost a paradigm shift. KM is more than information, so to manage it requires a new conceptual framework of the role of knowledge as a strategic asset with competitive attributes.

Second, the tools and methods of applying KM in organizational processes require a transition to a mode of integration with the *strategic* aspects of organizational policies and market perspective (Phillips and Vollmer 2000; Roberts 2000). Such a transition is a difficult exercise, involving a different view of the organization and the role it plays in its relevant environment (Orlikowski and Hofman 1997; Thorne and Smith 2000).

To overcome these two formidable barriers, modern organizations have to merge or integrate both the strategic and the operational levels of KM. Simply implementing the tools and techniques of KM is hardly enough to make KM an organizational reality, let alone a successful event (Popper and Lipshitz 2000; Sharma et al. 2004). Hence, the complexity of KM is inherent in the two aspects of its organizational usage: as a strategic as well as a tactical instrument of competitive assets. Failure in either of these two levels of organizational penetration will hinder the success of the entire system (Stewart 1997).

SIGNIFICANCE OF KNOWLEDGE MANAGEMENT SYSTEMS

In essence, KM tools and technologies are the systems that integrate various legacy systems, databases, ERP systems, and data warehouses to help organizations answer all these questions: "What happened?" "Why did it happen?" "What will happen?" "What is happening?" and "What do I want to happen?" Integrating all these with advanced decision support and online, real-time events improves customer interactions, encourages customer loyalty, and is instrumental in the success and survival of the organization. KM solutions are often integrated in an emerging environment known as EIP. The rates of change and improvements in technology enablers have made KM more feasible today than at any previous time.

To serve customers well and remain in business, companies need, at the very least, to reduce their cycle times, operate with minimum fixed assets and overhead (people, inventory, and facilities), shorten product development time, improve customer service, empower employees, innovate and deliver high-quality products, enhance flexibility and adaptation, capture information, create knowledge, share, and learn. None of this is possible without a continual focus on the creation, updating, availability, quality, and use of knowledge by all employees and teams, at work and in the marketplace (Wickramasinghe et al. 2004).

Many enterprises do not "know what they know." Such a situation can lead to duplication of effort throughout an organization. Any company that can figure out how to give its people the organizational knowledge they need—at the point and time needed—can position itself to compete effectively and succeed quickly. Many companies have vital knowledge resting with one individual and do little to make the knowledge more generally available. Many companies are unaware of their own knowledge base, and evidence has shown that knowledge is often lost from a company through employee attrition or related cost-saving measures. The enterprise that harnesses its intellectual capital can apply that asset to its business challenges and opportunities (Stewart 1997; Stratigos 2001).

Computers and communications systems are good at capturing, transforming, and distributing highly structured knowledge that changes rapidly. Some companies are using analysis, planning, and computer-supported work systems to radically improve decision making, resource allocation, management systems, and access and to promulgate process know-how and overall performance as a way to develop core strategic competencies. Any organization can effectively use KM to develop and improve its control and effectiveness.

The value of KM relates directly to the effectiveness with which the managed knowledge enables the members of the organization to deal with today's situations and effectively envision and create their future. Without on-demand access to managed knowledge, every situation is addressed based on what each individual or group brings to the situation. With on-demand access to managed knowledge, every situation is addressed with the sum total of everything anyone in the organization has ever learned about a situation of a similar nature. Which approach would make a more effective organization?

WHAT CONSTITUTES INTELLECTUAL OR KNOWLEDGE-BASED ASSETS?

Not all information is valuable. Therefore, it is up to individual companies to determine what information qualifies as intellectual and knowledge-based assets. In general, however, intellectual and knowledge-based assets fall into one of two categories: explicit or tacit. Explicit assets include patents, trademarks, business plans, marketing research, and customer lists. As a general rule, explicit knowledge consists of anything that can be documented, archived, and codified, often with the help of IT. Much harder to grasp is the concept of tacit knowledge—the know-how contained in people's heads. The challenge inherent in tacit knowledge is figuring out how to recognize, generate, share, and manage it. While IT in the form of e-mail, groupware, instant messaging, and related technologies can facilitate the dissemination of tacit knowledge, identifying tacit knowledge in the first place is a major hurdle for most organizations.

SOME BENEFITS FROM KNOWLEDGE MANAGEMENT

Some benefits of KM correlate directly to bottom-line savings, while others are more difficult to quantify. In today's information-driven economy, companies uncover the most opportunities—and ultimately derive the most value—from intellectual rather than physical assets. To get the most value from a company's intellectual assets, KM practitioners maintain that knowledge must be shared and serve as the foundation for collaboration. Yet improving collaboration is not an end in itself; without an overarching business context, KM is meaningless at best and harmful at worst. Consequently, an effective KM program should help a company do one or more of the following:

- Foster innovation by encouraging the free flow of ideas.
- Improve customer service by streamlining response time.
- Boost revenues by getting products and services to market faster.
- Enhance employee retention rates by recognizing the value of employees' knowledge and rewarding them for it.
- Streamline operations and reduce costs by eliminating redundant or unnecessary processes.

These are the most prevalent examples. A creative approach to KM can result in improved efficiency, higher productivity, and increased revenues in practically any business functions. Other benefits and their metrics are further described in Part III.

WHAT ARE THE CHALLENGES OF KNOWLEDGE MANAGEMENT?

Embracing KM and implementing any KM initiative is a very challenging endeavor. It is useful to divide these challenges into the following seven categories.

Getting Employees on Board

The major problems that occur in KM usually result because companies ignore people and cultural issues. In an environment where an individual's knowledge is valued and rewarded, establishing a culture that recognizes tacit knowledge and encourages employees to share it is critical. The need to sell the KM concept to employees should not be underestimated; after all, in many cases, employees are being asked to surrender their knowledge and experience—the very traits that make them valuable as individuals.

One way companies motivate employees to participate in KM is by creating an incentive program. However, then there is the danger that employees will participate solely to earn incentives, without regard to the quality or relevance of the information they contribute. The best KM efforts are as transparent to employees' workflow as possible. Ideally, participation in KM should be its own reward. If KM does not make life easier for employees, it will fail (Rubenstein and Geisler 2003).

Refusing to Allow Technology to Dictate Knowledge Management

KM is not a technology-based concept. Organizations should not allow themselves to be duped by software vendors touting their all-inclusive KM solutions. Companies that implement a centralized database system, electronic message board, Web portal, or any other collaborative tool in the hope of establishing a KM program are wasting both their time and their money. While technology can support KM, it is not the starting point of a KM program. KM decisions should be based primarily on who (people), what (knowledge), and why (business objective and processes), while how (technology) should be addressed last.

Having a Specific Business Goal

A KM program should not be divorced from a business goal. While sharing best practices is a commendable idea, there must be an underlying business reason to do so. Without a solid business case, KM is a futile exercise. This challenge is closely related to the need to interpret the strategic and operational practices of KM in the organization.

Having a Dynamic, Not Static, Approach to Knowledge Management

As with many physical assets, the value of knowledge can erode over time. Since knowledge can get stale fast, the content in a KM program should be constantly updated, amended, and deleted. The relevance of knowledge at any given time changes, as do the skills of employees. Therefore, there is no endpoint to a KM program. Like product development, marketing, and R&D, KM is a constantly evolving business practice.

Identifying the Correct Information to Turn Into Usable Knowledge

Companies using KM diligently need to be on the lookout for information overload. Quantity rarely equals quality. Indeed, the point of a KM program is to identify and disseminate knowledge gems from a sea of information.

Identifying Who Should Lead Knowledge Management Efforts

Since KM is not only a technology-based concept but also a business practice, enterprise-wide KM efforts should not be led by the chief information officer (CIO), although the CIO is a suitable choice to lead KM efforts within the IT department. Some companies have dedicated KM staff headed by a chief knowledge officer or other high-profile executive. Other companies rely on an executive sponsor in the functional area where KM is implemented. For a more extensive discussion of such issues of implementation, see Rubenstein and Geisler (2003).

Identifying Technologies to Support Knowledge Management

KM tools run the gamut from standard, off-the-shelf e-mail packages to sophisticated collaboration tools designed specifically to support community building and identity. Generally, tools fall into one or more of the following categories: knowledge repositories, expertise access tools, e-learning applications, discussion and chat technologies, synchronous interaction tools, and search and data mining tools.

BUSINESS DRIVERS OF KNOWLEDGE MANAGEMENT

There are three business drivers for the fast growth of the KM movement:

1. The shrinking cycle time for competency-base renewal, driven by the rate of industrial innovation.
2. The urge to value intellectual capital, driven by the growing economic weight of intangible assets and exasperated by an unprecedented wave of mergers, acquisitions, and alliances.
3. The pressure for most organizations to cope with a massive flood of unstructured information.

Driver One: Obsolescence Rate of the Competency Base

The first economic driver in the emergence of KM has to do with the growing speed at which the know-how embodied in the workforce—that is, the competency base of an organization—loses currency. This is obviously related to the shortening lifetime of technologies and the need of employees to acquire new skills. But it is also related to the entirely new portfolio of competencies that the knowledge worker requires in order to develop lifelong employability.

Given this new demand for lifelong learning, companies need not only to develop a new training infrastructure, but also to redefine the relationship between learning and work. While the education establishment is giving way to an alternative training system composed of corporate universities, adult learning centers, and online services, the meaning of training at work is shifting from a support function to the very essence of business development. Hence, establishing what employees have to do in order to add maximum value, what they have to learn, how they can do it well and quickly, and how it can be transferred to the right processes and have an impact on business results is a major managerial challenge for today's organizations. This need has sparked the learning industry as one of the fastest growing in the service sector.

Even if there is a growing culture about learning in organizations, this youngest child of the KM family still has to mature. To begin with, it has to reconcile the new and powerful business motivations with existing understanding (i.e., scientific theories) about human learning. Indeed, the prevailing discourse and practice about organizational learning has been influenced more by some parallel disciplines, such as systems theory, than by learning theory founded on empirical studies. Once both ends—the pragmatic forces driving innovation on learning management and the wealth of understanding resulting from more than a century of experimental and theoretical work—meet, the field might multiply its impact.

Driver Two: Weight of Intangible Assets in a Company's Market Value

A second business driver is the need to account for the value of intangible assets. Two converging forces have fueled such need. One is the growing differential between the book value of a public company and the market value of its stock price. The signs are so compelling that many people actually equate such differential with the very definition of intellectual capital. Another urge to value intangible assets comes from the recent wave of mergers, acquisitions, and alliances—the largest in history. From this need to determine the value of intangible capital relative to the total value of a company have sprung efforts to determine the magic formula, sort of an intellectual gold rush.

Most of those intellectual gold diggers might be looking at the wrong side of the river. So long as the question remains "How do I determine the financial base of my intellectual assets?" the likely answer will be some artifact to establish an indirect correspondence between heterogeneous classes of entities—oranges and apples. Perhaps, when the search involves not just accounting for but developing a consolidated capital base and, therefore, a value-based KM strategy, the value of intellectual assets will be fully determined.

Then companies might start looking for a homogeneous value frame for all forms of capital and their rules of correspondence. In order to do that, business leaders will have to come to terms with the tenets of measurement and value theories, again, an encounter between pragmatic business vigor and existing human understanding.

Driver Three: Efficiency Pressures to Cope With Massive Information

The third business driver constitutes the need of individuals and organizations to cope effectively with an overwhelming flood of data. Inefficiencies associated with poor information acquisition, indexing, recording, storage, retrieval, transfer, and so on are huge. The much debated "productivity paradox" in the U.S. economy (relating higher investment in IT technology with relatively poorer results) has less to do with hardware reliability than with lack of process capability.

Hence, a third child of the KM dynasty was quick to be born in response to such pressure: software companies, aware of the demand for systems capable of delivering integrated information management rather than mere data processing, began notably during 1997 to relabel existing or in-development products as "KM solutions." Not surprisingly, most of them are the same old data warehouses, yellow pages, document taxonomies, and the like. Again, the solution is unlikely because the question is wrong. Most of these products are based on an attempt to build powerful enough data superstructures. This is understandable when the chief knowledge officer is seen as a projection of a high-end CIO. But no matter how large, no matter how complex, current information systems cannot deliver the foundations for KM.

The main constraint of IT in dealing with KM matters is the very concept of knowledge that prevails in the IT industry. Knowledge is very extensively regarded as "content" and, therefore, treated as "object." Knowledge is seldom seen as a human act, an event, a happening. Taken as content, it is void of agent and context (human and cultural factors) and remains a computer operation; hence, the prevailing role of information systems in current "KM solutions."

Sure, those packages can be customized, but they are still only subordinated to a given structure. Until "KM solutions" depart from business processes and incorporate tools that leverage process capacity, they will remain unfulfilled promises. Some companies prefer to emphasize basic KM operations—notably document handling, collaborative teamwork, and basic forms of knowledge visualization—and design flexible environments with a low learning threshold. Rather than offering the ubiquitous "KM solution," they are developing platforms where proper KM strategies

Figure 1.4   **Key Business Drivers of KM**

- The shrinking cycle time for competency-based renewal, driven by the rate of industrial innovation. Too much innovation and an avalanche of knowledge produced make it essential to keep KM vigilant and current.
- The urge to value intellectual capital, driven by the growing economic weight of intangible assets and animated by the wave of mergers, acquisitions, and alliances. Firms are beginning to understand how valuable knowledge is to their success, so any strategic changes will necessitate paying attention to KM.
- Organizations now have an improved tool kit of methods and techniques to build and manipulate KM systems.

can be built within the organization. Yet with so many efforts going on, innovative platforms designed to leverage KM agents in their value contexts may be showing up any time now (Figure 1.4).

KNOWLEDGE MANAGEMENT: A CROSS-DISCIPLINARY DOMAIN

Figure 1.5 encapsulates what this thing called KM really is and its complex structure. From this figure we can see the many facets of KM, which include people components, technology components, and process components. Any effective KM initiative must consider *all* these facets. In the following chapters we shall drill down to uncover and reveal the key issues in each of these areas. Figure 1.5, then, provides the holistic perspective of KM and serves as the road map of the KM terrain that we shall be covering in the rest of the book.

A REVIEW OF THE DISCIPLINES OF KNOWLEDGE MANAGEMENT

Any discussion of KM should highlight the multidisciplinary nature of this emerging field. Figure 1.5 shows the interaction of organization, business, and technological infrastructures with the strategy of implementing KM in the organizational context. This complex architecture requires an array of disciplines and technologies, including organization science, strategic management, cognitive sciences, and information technology. Such an understanding will enable organizations to gain a broad perspective about KM and thereby ultimately construct appropriate and effective KM initiatives.

In the section below, we list and briefly describe the major disciplines employed in the design and implementation of KM:

- *Cognitive science.* Insights from *how* we learn and know will certainly improve tools and techniques for gathering and transferring knowledge.
- *Expert systems, artificial intelligence, and knowledge base management systems (KBMS).* AI and related technologies have acquired an undeserved reputation of having failed to meet their own and the marketplace's high expectations. In fact, these technologies continue to be applied widely, and the lessons practitioners have learned are directly applicable to KM.

Figure 1.5 **Schematic View of the Key Components of KM**

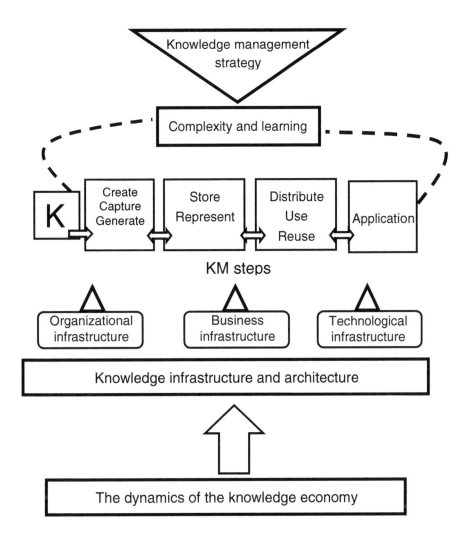

- *Computer-supported collaborative work (groupware).* In Europe, the term *KM* is almost synonymous with *groupware* . . . and therefore with Lotus Notes. Sharing and collaboration are clearly vital to organizational KM—with or without supporting technology.
- *Library and information science.* We take it for granted that card catalogs in libraries will help us find the right book when we need it. The body of research and practice in classification and knowledge organization that makes libraries work will be even more vital as businesses are inundated by information. Tools for thesaurus construction and controlled vocabularies are already helping employees manage knowledge.

- *Technical writing.* Also underappreciated—even sneered at—as a professional activity, technical writing (often referred to by its practitioners as technical communication) forms a body of theory and practice that is directly relevant to effective representation and transfer of knowledge.
- *Document management.* Originally concerned primarily with managing the accessibility of images, document management has moved on to making content accessible and reusable at the component level. Early recognition of the need to associate "meta-information" with each document object prefigures document management technology's growing role in KM activities.
- *Decision support systems.* According to Daniel J. Power, "Researchers working on Decision Support Systems have brought together insights from the fields of cognitive sciences, management sciences, computer sciences, operations research, and systems engineering in order to produce computerized artifacts for helping knowledge workers in their performance of cognitive tasks and to integrate such artifacts within the decision-making processes of modern organizations."
- *Semantic networks.* Semantic networks are formed from ideas and typed relationships among them—a sort of "hypertext without the content" but with far more systematic structure according to meaning. Often applied in such arcane tasks as textual analysis, semantic nets are now in use in mainstream professional applications, including medicine, to represent domain knowledge in an explicit way that can be shared.
- *Relational and object databases.* Although relational databases are currently used primarily as tools for managing structured data, while object-oriented databases are considered more appropriate for unstructured content, organizations have only begun to apply the models on which they are founded for representing and managing knowledge resources.
- *Simulation.* KM expert Karl-Erik Sveiby suggests "simulation" as a component technology of KM, referring to "computer simulations, manual simulations as well as role plays and micro arenas for testing out skills."[1]
- *Organizational science.* The science of managing organizations increasingly deals with the need to manage knowledge—often explicitly. It is not a surprise that the American Management Association's APQC has sponsored major KM events.

At the beginning of the twenty-first century, when businesses face an overwhelming amount of information and perhaps lack sufficient resources or understanding to manage all of it, KM is critically important. The basic yet important components, terms, and concepts associated with KM have been presented in this chapter. In addition, we have tried to chart the evolution of KM as a discipline and underscore its multidisciplinary nature. KM is not easy to embrace, but by grappling with this complex and dynamic discipline, organizations will be richly rewarded. Indeed, in today's knowledge economy, KM is becoming a competitive necessity rather than a competitive choice, and thus it is prudent for all organizations to embrace appropriate KM initiatives.

LEARNING OUTCOMES

- There is a host of definitions of KM. Among them: KM is a discipline; KM is an intelligent process; KM is a formal process that engages people, processes, and technology.
- KM is difficult to implement because both the strategic and the operational aspects of KM need to be present in the organization.
- The key business drivers of KM are the avalanche of information and knowledge in the current knowledge economy, and the increasing tools and techniques to manage knowledge and to measure its value to the organization.

DISCUSSION QUESTONS

1. Why is KM so important to organizations in today's knowledge economy?
2. What are the key business drivers of KM?
3. What are the major challenges to the implementation of KM in organizations?

NOTE

1. Personal communication.

2 Conceptual Foundations of Knowledge

KEY LEARNING OUTCOMES

You will know you have mastered the material in this chapter when you can define and explain the following:

1. The timeline of knowledge management evolution.
2. The traditional data to knowledge management flow.
3. The historical development from data crunching to information management.
4. How knowledge progresses: The evolutionary and cumulative models.

In the last decade of the twentieth century a newly discovered field of academic interest emerged: knowledge management (KM). It was first described as a *process* by which an organization handles its intellectual assets and is able to utilize them for the purpose of learning (Senge 1990) and improved performance (Schwartz 2006). This area of intellectual exploration and business interest seems to have erupted on both the academic and business landscape. With a peculiar velocity, the conception and methods of KM invaded the discourse on the type and use of organizational assets for the new century (Davenport and Prusak 1998).

WHAT PROMPTED THE SURGE IN KNOWLEDGE MANAGEMENT

Why the surge in the attention given to KM by both academics and industry practitioners? There are at least two plausible explanations. The first is the progression from information systems, technology, and telecommunication. In hindsight, such progression may seem a natural phenomenon that could perhaps have been predicted (Prusak 1997; Tallman and Phene 2007). The rapid development of information technology (IT) and its proliferation in the business environment reached some kind of maturation in the mid-1990s. In particular, information systems migrated from the backrooms of business companies (as processors of accounting and payroll functions) to the front offices. In this move the information system became an aid to the managerial functions of marketing, production, and even strategic planning (Baskerville and Dulipovici 2006; Tordoir 1995). When this transformation of information systems and technology became the norm rather than the exception in the corporate world, an increasing number of managers began to identify opportunities for the exchange of knowledge and the potential for even more functions for the systems they had installed throughout the corporation (Smith et al. 2006; White 2002).

Although there has been little empirical evidence to show, without reservation, that information technologies indeed contributed to the corporate economic bottom line, managers felt the need to justify the enormous expense in IT over the previous four decades. One such justification was the potential of IT to mature, evolve, and migrate into more complex and sophisticated systems of knowledge (Geisler 1999, 2007). The idea was to have a natural progression of these systems into the allure of systems of *knowledge*, which would impact the entire enterprise and perhaps be more amenable to measures of cost-effectiveness.

This corporate perspective was reinforced by hopeful voices from the academic community focusing on the flow from databases to information systems to, finally, maturation into systems of knowledge. Scholars and executives had reinforced each other's similar positions with an indelible trust in the power of technology to assist in the generation and utilization of systems that would manage human and organizational knowledge (Dalkir 2005; Foray 2004).

A second plausible explanation is the role played by the aftermath of three phenomena: the effort of reengineering corporate America, globalization and outsourcing, and the emergence of the Internet as a business technological tool.

The early 1990s witnessed the emergence and decline of the massive effort of reengineering conducted by corporations from many sectors of the economy (Hammer and Champy 1993). The concept of reengineering called for a total transformation of processes within the corporation by utilizing information technology as an instrument for increased efficiency of the transformed processes. The massive restructuring of corporate processes led to the downsizing of many vital corporate functions and units and, inevitably, to a massive hemorrhage of knowledgeable people. This outcome, of course, contributed to reduced costs and to some increased efficiencies and elimination of redundancies. But the loss of so many employees and what they knew, and the heralded role of IT as the key facilitator of reengineering, ultimately led company executives to look for alternative means of preserving knowledge—with the help of IT or its successor: KM (Geisler 1997, 2007).

In parallel, the business community also witnessed the phenomena of globalization and outsourcing of many corporate functions to less expensive suppliers, even in other countries. The movement to outsource was not confined to manufacturing but extended also to services and administrative functions, such as customer relations. In some cases, even research and development—long considered core activities in the corporation—were outsourced to cheaper providers and contractors.

Information and telecommunication followed by KM became the key factors that corporations employed to justify their outsourcing in the global economy. These factors explained how the outsourced activities could be carried out over such geographical distances. Understandably, as companies outsourced an increasing number of functions, they ceased to employ specialists in these areas, thus losing the knowledge these employees possessed. The necessary knowledge (on how to do what, when, and how well) was now embedded in the people in the outsourced organizations, many of whom resided and worked halfway across the globe. The need to maintain a core of knowledge in the corporation had become a crucial and an urgent mandate for the global company (Alavi and Leidner 2001; Argyris 2004).

The third phenomenon was the emergence of the Internet as a corporate or business tool. Executives now believed that this massive interactive system of accumulated information also contained knowledge essential for the success and survival of their enterprises. However, since this system was outside the boundaries of their organization and widely available on a global scale, they recognized the need to construct a knowledge system of their own that would have the ability to interact with the Internet (von Krogh et al. 2000).

These drivers or motivators were the background phenomena that not only provided managers with the rationale to engage in KM, but also offered the instruments and the technology with which to "join the club" in the KM movement. What remained to be done was to determine how and how far each organization would proceed (Nonaka and Takeuchi 1995).

THE FUSION OF KNOWLEDGE AND MANAGEMENT

Simply recognizing that knowledge is important and that there are antecedents that require its collection is not enough. There are several types of knowledge in the corporate environment as well as in any other organization, such as not-for-profit and government institutions. The main categories are *technical* and *managerial* or *administrative* knowledge. Technical knowledge is generally confined to the technological units such as the research and development (R&D) and new product development (NPD) departments. Managerial knowledge is embedded in the executives who manage the organization (Geisler 1999, 2006).

With the proliferation of the academic study of management and organizational analysis, there emerged the need to cultivate and to increase the stock of what managers know about how to run their organizations. In the last half of the twentieth century there was a tremendous growth in the number of business schools at universities worldwide. In the United States, this trend was also accompanied by a rapid growth in academic research and peer-reviewed journals covering all aspects of management and business. We estimate that between 1970 and 2000 there was a twenty-fold growth in the number of scientific journals in business and management, and a twofold increase in the number of business programs at both the undergraduate and the graduate levels.

Such an accumulation of knowledge invariably caused the fusion of the practicing managers with the emerging state of knowledge (Table 2.1). Increasingly, the ranks of middle management were now occupied by graduates of business schools, armed with the now ubiquitous degree of Master of Business Administration (MBA). By design, this was a cadre of knowledgeable, self-assured, and competent managers.

Table 2.1

A Brief View of the Development of KM

1960s	1970s	1980s	1990s	2000
Powerful business computers Proliferation of business schools	New crop of MBAs Development of knowledge about firms and management	Personal computers Emergence of the World Wide Web	Accumulation of research findings Use of Internet in business Emergence of KM as a discipline	Development of KM models Increased activity in KM

They aptly defied the old conventions. They employed quantitative tools and based their corporate decisions on careful analysis of key dimensions of their organization. They employed like-minded consultants and happily invested in technology, primarily in information and telecommunication technologies.

It was only a matter of time before this new breed of managers arrived at the inevitable conclusion that knowledge was an essential tool in their success and in the discharge of their executive functions.

ACADEMIA AND BUSINESS: THE MAKING OF A PARTNERSHIP

Traditionally, the academic world or university-based research is the initiator of new explanations into challenging topics of corporate life, performance, and processes. With the proliferation of university programs in business and management came a parallel, dramatic growth in knowledge in the form of theories, models, concepts, and operational techniques—all on how organizations are formed, how they operate, and how they can be made more successful (Dessler 2003; Kaplan and Norton 1996).

A similar crop of a more practical type of knowledge appeared in the form of a flurry of books written by academics, consultants, and retired executives. These books provided examples from successful companies such as Starbucks (Michelli 2006) and a host of other tidbits and advice based on the best practices of successful corporations (Chesbrough 2006; Collins 2001).

The findings from rigorous academic research and the practical advice from practitioners coalesced to form the knowledge base coveted by practicing managers. They clearly understood that there is a method to corporate success and that common elements control their own processes and exercise of their managerial functions as well as those of other managers in the same industry and even in unrelated industries. The phenomenon of management (including marketing, finance, production, project management, and strategic management) has finally come of age in the form of a knowledge base generated by scholars and researchers and translated into language and methods to be fully utilized by the practicing manager who is battling everyday threats in the corporate trenches (Laudon and Laudon 1999).

The inevitable outcome was the growing respect that managers bestowed upon such streams of knowledge. Thus, when academic researchers began to stratify and to gather such knowledge in systems that allowed for codification, transfer, and utilization (at least in theory), corporate managers joined in this endeavor to form the collaboration that became the nascent field of knowledge management.

FROM DATA TO KNOWLEDGE: THE CONVENTIONAL APPROACH

The traditional model of the data-to-knowledge continuum incorporates the history of the development of KM. In Figure 2.1 we show the flow from data management, which intensified in the 1950s and 1960s, to the information age and finally the current period of KM.

In the period following World War II, the surge of computers and their use in business applications had been focused on "crunching" massive amounts of data. The emphasis was on the backroom operations of the enterprise—organizational functions such as payroll, accounts payable and receivables, various accounting functions, and maintaining databases of employees, vendors, and customers. The inevitable outcome was the generation of what became known as *information*, and the period from the 1960s to the 1990s now was aptly named the Information Age. This much-loaded descriptor of the era did not necessarily mean that much new information was being created. Rather, the magnanimous epithet described the sudden surge in the ability of organizations to collect, store, and manipulate inordinately vast amounts of data relevant to the discharge of their functions—all with speed and accuracy hitherto unimaginable.

An illustrative product of the era was Moore's Law, proposed by Gordon Moore in 1965. Moore was a cofounder of Intel Corporation. His law stated that the power of computing would double every eighteen months. Later he added the notion that as computing power increases, the cost of such computing is reduced. Moore's observation puts into perspective the rapid rise in computing power since the 1960s when International Business Machines (IBM) introduced its 360 computers.

FROM INFORMATION MANAGEMENT TO KNOWLEDGE SYSTEMS

The more data management functions became computerized and the more powerful computing capabilities became, the more organizations discovered new applications for this magnificent technology. As computers in corporations became ubiquitous, especially after the introduction in the 1980s of personal computers, the focus on backroom operations started to diminish and further uses for computers began to emerge in the managerial and strategic functions of corporations (Anand et al. 2007).

Another factor that greatly contributed to the shift from backroom operations to front office, managerial, and strategic applications of information systems was the development of increasingly sophisticated computer programming—software. Since the 1980s there has been a dramatic evolution in the software industry. The rise in computing power at much reduced costs when combined with powerful programs has created a distinctive watershed of applications in the executive functions of corporations and in the overall strategic management of organizations (Patmayakuni et al. 2007).

Figure 2.1   **The Traditional Data-Information Knowledge-Wisdom Continuum**

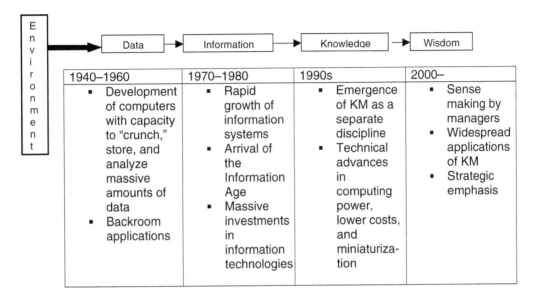

	1940–1960	1970–1980	1990s	2000–
	• Development of computers with capacity to "crunch," store, and analyze massive amounts of data • Backroom applications	• Rapid growth of information systems • Arrival of the Information Age • Massive investments in information technologies	• Emergence of KM as a separate discipline • Technical advances in computing power, lower costs, and miniaturization	• Sense making by managers • Widespread applications of KM • Strategic emphasis

The focus was no longer on data crunching or the manipulation of information. The new trend, begun in the 1990s, was toward nonstandardized information, later termed organizational knowledge (Choo 1998; Wiig 1993). There was also a corresponding rise in *integration* activities by an array of corporate consultants and by organizations striving to make sense of the avalanche of new ITs, sophisticated software, and complex systems that began to overwhelm the traditional basic functions such as marketing, manufacturing, and interactions with customers, suppliers, and regulators (Geisler 2005; Weick 2001).

These powerful trends and processes quickly led to the emergence of chunks of information that were, to a degree, more than just data or information. These "quanta" of information looked more and more like *knowledge* and were indeed classified as such. Soon enough there were attempts to conceptualize this trend by pointing to the continuum data → information → knowledge. This continuum, however, denotes a *historical* rather than a *conceptual* development. There was hardly any quantum change from data to information, or from information to knowledge (Laudon and Laudon 1999). So the conventional approach, which assumes a continuum from data to knowledge, cannot effectively demonstrate the true conceptual transformation. This conventional approach conjures the movement from the use of computers and IT to "data-chunking" to the more sophisticated realm of managerial decision making and strategic analysis—hence to working with knowledge (Wilson 2002).

DEFINITIONS OF KNOWLEDGE

In Chapter 1 we advanced some definitions of KM. But this chapter examines the continuum from data to knowledge and the role that knowledge plays in the historical progress we described in Table 2.1 and Figure 2.1.

Knowledge has been defined primarily with respect to its utilization within a given scheme, platform, or functional framework. Davenport and Prusak (1998) define knowledge as "framed experiences, values, contextual information, and expert insight that provides a framework for evaluating and incorporating new experiences and information." On the other hand, Nonaka and Takeuchi, in their pioneering book *The Knowledge-Creating Company* (1995, 79), define knowledge as "a dynamic human process of justifying personal belief towards the truth."

A working definition of knowledge will equate this notion with understanding, wisdom, awareness of the world, transformed information, and any other metaphor for the concept of "knowing." In some cultures and languages there are several words that describe knowledge. In Hebrew, for example, knowledge is often referred to as *hochma* (wisdom), *bina* (intelligence), *daat* (knowledge), *yeda* (precise knowledge), and *havane* (understanding). The word *daat* also means "opinion": those who know express their reasoned opinion. Similarly, the Greeks distinguished between *episteme* (knowledge) derived from *epistanai* (to understand) and *logos* (wisdom manifested in the universe through reason and order). The term *episteme* (and subsequently *epistemology*) is derived from the combination of the terms *epi* and *histanai*, meaning the understanding or study of the foundations of a phenomenon and its boundaries—that is, its structural form. This examination of the meanings of knowledge in these ancient cultures—meanings that we still apply today—reveals that throughout the ages "knowledge" has been defined as the human ability to understand the world we inhabit and to discern the foundations, reason, processes, and limits or boundaries of our existence.

Yet none of the acceptable definitions provides an undisputed description of what truly constitutes human knowledge (and by extension organizational knowledge). Geisler (2006) proposes a codification of knowledge similar to the Dewey system used in library science. The system would codify knowledge according to (1) source, (2) structure, (3) robustness and meaning, and (4) relevance and applicability of the "nuggets" of knowledge. These are also classified by purpose (what the nugget of knowledge is for), structure (how nuggets are designed and what they contain), and function (what the nuggets of knowledge do). Geisler's framework breaks the notion of knowledge down to its component of a "nugget," further defined as the carrier of the knowledge, usually in the form of statements.

Much of the KM literature reveals widespread uniformity on the paucity of the inherent descriptive power of current definitions of knowledge. A common classification is the differentiation between *tacit* and *explicit* knowledge, proposed by Polanyi (1966) and Nonaka and Takeuchi (1995). This distinction is discussed in Chapter 3.

LEARNING OUTCOMES

- How knowledge progresses from data and information.
- KM in organizations emerged from the initial backroom applications of computers and information science to the limelight of strategic planning and problem solving.

- The field of KM still lacks a concise definition of what precisely constitutes knowledge.

DISCUSSION QUESTIONS

1. What is knowledge and why is it so difficult to define?
2. What prompted the surge in KM since the 1980s?
3. How did academia and business join to develop the field of KM?

3 The Tacit Dimension and the Models of Knowledge and Knowledge Management

KEY LEARNING OUTCOMES

You will know you have mastered the material in this chapter when you can define and explain the following:

1. The nature of tacit knowledge.
2. How knowledge is structured.
3. How knowledge progresses.

THE DUALITY OF KNOWLEDGE

The notion that we know more than we express is hardly new. Philosophers have explored this dichotomy in their quest for understanding how human knowledge is structured and how it is exhibited in what people do and how they behave.

On the European continent, the movement of the Enlightenment produced philosophers who are commonly called rationalists. René Descartes (1596–1650), Baruch Spinoza (1632–1677), and Gottfried Leibnitz (1646–1716) are the most famous and influential rationalists. They believed that the human mind knows the external world by the application of rational processes and does not necessarily need experience to promote rational thinking.

A contrasting avenue of philosophical exploration into the nature of human knowledge was opened by a group of scholars known as empiricists, many of who were British. They believed that knowledge is based on experience and on human ability to sense the external world and to capture its reality as well as humanly possible. The empiricists, beginning with John Locke (1632–1704), believed that there are no preconceived ideas, so that the individual mind is an empty platform with the uncanny ability to observe and to process human experiences, transforming them into knowledge. Extended to political theory, this concept meant that there is no such truth as the "divine right" of kings, nor preexisting major differences among human beings, and that all humans are somewhat equal players in the search for knowledge.

George Berkeley (1685–1753) was a member of the Scottish clergy. He forcefully rejected Locke's far-reaching distinction between ideas and the reality of the empirical universe. He then argued that knowledge is made of the *ideas* that human beings create in their minds about the world around them. The empirical world is therefore irrelevant to the human mind, because the mind can deal only with the ideas it forms by itself. Berkeley's views are termed idealism, due to his belief that the empirical world exists only in the sense that the human mind perceives it as such. Therefore, people cannot know what exists or what is true; their knowledge of the world is only what they perceive of it.

These scholars were primarily concerned with how knowledge is formed in the human mind. They did not necessarily investigate the form taken by knowledge itself. However, they did explore the possibility that there is a duality of knowledge: experience versus ideas, or what the mind knows versus what people experience because of such knowledge.

DAVID HUME AND IMMANUEL KANT

David Hume (1711–1776) was, like Berkeley, born in Scotland. He spent a good portion of his adult life in France, where he was exposed to the ideas of the French humanists Rousseau and Voltaire. Hume's conception of human knowledge became a mix of the British sense of skepticism and the Continental embrace of the ideas of the Enlightenment (Geisler 2007a; Humphrey 1992). Hume argued that knowledge is merely the manifestation of human experience. He distinguished between "impressions," which are experiences received from the senses, and "ideas," which are the next step of generating knowledge—by building upon the impressions people already possess.

Immanuel Kant (1724–1804) was a professor of philosophy at the University of Königsberg in Germany. He undertook the monumental task of attempting to reconcile between the rationalists and the empiricists. To accomplish this, he proposed a synthesis of the basic notions of the two divergent schools.

Kant distinguished between the mental processes of "perception" and "thinking." Perception is the mode by which people process sensorial inputs. Thinking is the way in which people compose complex concepts. Perceptions are assessed by the use of the criteria of time and space and what Kant described as priori categories. Resorting to the categories allows humans to perceive the external world and make sense of its reality. Kant also suggested that the human mind forms abstract notions ("ideas") as the result of logical inference.

Kant's influence on the modern philosophy of knowledge includes his impact on Marx, Hegel, Hayek, and even Karl Popper. He offered a viable explanation of how knowledge is created in the human mind, while encompassing both the empiricist and the rationalist/idealist approaches. Moreover, Kant's platform approaches the dichotomy between what we know and how we express such knowledge and how we share and exchange it.

Table 3.1

Evolution of the Duality of Knowledge in Philosophy

Knowledge scholars	Key concepts	Contribution to notion of duality of knowledge

John Locke
George Berkeley
David Hume
	Knowledge is mortal ideas
	Impressions as a result of senses
	    and ideas derived from them
		Dichotomy between
		    cognitive processes and
		    the physical universe

Immanuel Kant	Perception and thinking
	A priori mind categories
	Abstract notions in the mind
		Duality of notions in
		    perception and mental
		    reasoning

Bertrand Russell
Alfred North Whitehead
Ludwig Wittgenstein
Willard Quine
Noam Chomsky
	Propositions describe reality
	Correspondence between logic of
	    language and the universe
	Knowledge sharing depends on
	    linguistic skills
		Distinction between what
		    humans know and
		    how they are able to
		    share and communicate
		    knowledge

Linguistic Approaches to Knowledge

A more recent school of the philosophy of knowledge includes various scholars of the twentieth century. This school included Ludwig Wittgenstein (1889–1951), Bertrand Russell (1872–1970), Willard Quine (1908–2000), and Noam Chomsky (1928–). The key argument of this school was that knowledge is a reflection or manifestation of the use of knowledge. These scholars believed that language could be reduced to basic propositions that thus describe the empirical world. Therefore, there is a strong correspondence between the logic of the structure of language and the empirical world—so that when humans describe the world with words, the words are meaningful, allowing people to interact with others and to exchange knowledge. Chomsky, of the Massachusetts Institute of Technology, emphasized the distinction between the knowledge of language skills and the ways in which humans make use of such skills in cognition and in their knowledge of the physical universe, as well as in exchanging such knowledge (Chomsky 2006). This distinction is a strong lead into the dichotomy between tacit and explicit forms of human knowledge.

Table 3.1 summarizes the key concepts discussed above and their contributions to the duality of knowledge as tacit and explicit. The table also shows the evolution of these key concepts, constantly approaching the current view that some or much of human knowledge is tacit and difficult to share and exchange.

If exchanging what we know with others depends on the use of linguistic skills, then we, as humans, are able to share what we know only in proportion to how well we master the linguistic skills with which we are endowed. Hence, there will be a great deal of knowledge that we possess but cannot share with others, nor can they share with us.

The Tacit and Explicit Dimensions

The question that emerges from the previous section is this: Can we improve the exchange of knowledge if we improve our language skills? This question may be expanded: If we improve *any* communications skills (such as human-machine or machine-machine), can we thus improve our exchange of knowledge?

TACIT KNOWLEDGE

The answers to such questions have occupied the attention of knowledge management (KM) scholars ever since Polanyi (1966) proposed the duality of tacit versus explicit knowledge. Michael Polanyi argued that the human mind contains much more knowledge than people are able to share with the outside world—or to make explicit. *Tacit* knowledge is usually defined as abilities, expertise, and conceptual thinking. The attribute of *tacitness* refers not only to what is known but also to the knower. Following in the footsteps of the linguistics scholars, for example, will suggest that tacit knowledge is the portion of what people know that has not yet been exchanged or that cannot be exchanged.

Some knowers have more facility than others to share and to diffuse what they know. Perhaps they have better mastery of language skills or are better able to articulate their knowledge via other tools of human communication and interaction.

Nonaka and Takeuchi (1995) propose a different perspective for the definition of tacit knowledge. They advance the Japanese cultural traditions of management as an example of the interaction between tacit and explicit knowledge. They define tacit knowledge as "knowledge of experience of the body," "simultaneous knowledge (here and now)," and "analog knowledge (practice)." These types of tacit knowledge are subjective, hence embedded in the knower's mind and not yet expressed as explicit knowledge.

But what is this elusive entity we call "tacit knowledge"? Tacit knowledge can be categorized as skills, mental perspectives of the world, and higher-order reasoning. This means that we harbor in our mind a combination of knowledge gained from experience and our ability to rationalize, to reason, and to understand ourselves and our surroundings (Geisler 2007c). As we peruse the literature, we find several descriptors—conceptual and operational—that offer a glimpse into the forms in which such knowledge may appear. Table 3.2 shows the common descriptors and the purposes of the knowledge they refer to.

Interesting examples of the types of tacit knowledge put such knowledge into context. Skills or expertise in mastering tools or technological artifacts range from "knowing" how to ride a bicycle to flying a space shuttle. Expertise may be even more complex, such as knowing how to surgically remove a brain tumor. Skill at riding a bicycle requires rudimentary principles of balance and the use of physical abilities. Complex brain surgery employs expertise and abilities gained over a very prolonged period of learning and experimenting with such a skill.

Mental perspectives such as concepts and ideas are another grouping of tacit knowledge. Here we "know" how and why certain phenomena happen in ourselves and in the world around us. We form opinions, define conditions, provide answers to queries that routinely pop up in our mind: how and why things are the way they are. We have knowledge about physical phenomena such as the seasons of the year. Finally, we conjure in our mind more complex aspects of tacit knowledge. We engen-

Table 3.2

Descriptors of What Constitutes Tacit Knowledge

Groups or categories	Descriptors	Purpose (What is the knowledge for?)
Skills, expertise, crafts, and abilities	How to; know-how Mastering tools and techniques Mastering routine tasks in the environment	Survival Competitiveness Performance
Nuggets: Mental perspectives	Concepts Ideas Formulations Statements of facts Action items Opinions Conditions Answers to queries	Fulfillment of human curiosity and quest for knowledge Solving routine problems and overcoming simple barriers
Higher-order intelligence: Understanding and reasoning	Conjectures Lessons Warnings Synthetic logic Solutions Mental models	Solving complex problems Planning and forecasting Better understanding of the individual and the universe

der conjectures, develop solutions to problems, and create reasoned understanding of our reality. In this category we "know" by making conjectures about our place in the universe and about such higher-order notions as justice, freedom, and the future (Geisler 2007b).

The categories in Table 3.2 are not necessarily hierarchical, so that higher-order reasoning depends on skills and mental perspectives. All three categories of tacit knowledge may occur simultaneously. At present there is no consensus on how these categories interact or how they seem to interdepend.

EXPLICIT KNOWLEDGE: CONVERSION AND TRANSFORMATION OF TACIT KNOWLEDGE

Nonaka and Takeuchi (1995, 61) define *explicit* knowledge as "knowledge of rationality," "sequential knowledge" (there and then), and "digital knowledge" (theory). They emphasize that explicit knowledge "is about past events or objects . . . and is oriented toward a context-free theory." Explicit knowledge is therefore the declarative or the externalized form of tacit knowledge. Other definitions suggest such attributes of explicitness as ability to share, disseminate, reapply, teach, and transfer what people know (Dalkir 2005). There is, therefore, a convergence of the conceptions of knowledge as a reflection of language and communication skills (Chomsky 2006) and as a set of interconnected "nuggets" or statements depicting the physical and mental worlds of the knower (Rubenstein and Geisler 2003).

Table 3.3

Conversion and Transformation of Tacit Knowledge Into Explicit Knowledge: A Summary of the Literature

Conceptual frameworks	Authors
Socialization: from individual to individual	Nonaka and Takeuchi (1995)
Externalization: conceptual knowledge	Nonaka and Takeuchi (1995)
From "describing" to "doing"	Wickramasinghe and von Lubitz (2007)
From physical "facts" to "mental skills"	Wickramasinghe and von Lubitz (2007)

Applications	Models/Tools/Instruments
Physical transfer	Documents, video, films, records
Mental transfer	Mentoring, consulting, experts, debriefing, story-telling
Individual level	Direct contact
Group and organizational levels	Reports, evaluations, rules, procedures, policies, codes, lessons, best practices, principles, structure, and architecture

However, the key question then remains: How do we convert and transform *tacit* into *explicit* knowledge? Table 3.3 summarizes the literature on the models and processing of such transfer and conversion phenomena. The table depicts the conceptual frameworks proposed by various scholars and the array of applications, models, and tools in use or suggested.

Geisler (2007c) has identified a variety of mechanisms, tools, or instruments used to transfer tacit knowledge from individuals to other individuals and organizations. These mechanisms, shown in Table 3.3, are like the traditional means by which people communicate. So what is different about knowledge? Are we simply referring to the *content* of what is being communicated and exchanged as "knowledge," whereas we traditionally referred to such content as the "message" being communicated?

To an extent that we refrain from a more precise definition of what constitutes knowledge, there is little conceptual or operational difference between the attributes of communication theory and the transfer and sharing of tacit knowledge (Geisler 2006; Lynn-Fink and Bourne 2007).

Explicit knowledge, therefore, may be roughly defined as the knowledge that is now in the public domain. This knowledge can now be accessed and possessed by all who have the necessary mental and physical tools and capabilities. Physical tools include electrical and electronic devices (computers, telecommunication technology) as well as documents and similar written recording devices (Wilbanks 2007).

EXAMPLES OF TACIT AND EXPLICIT KNOWLEDGE

Military combat pilots who return from their missions are required to undergo lengthy, exhaustive sessions of "debriefing." They are asked to describe in very specific detail the particulars of their flight, their combat mission, and the outcomes of this event. In addition to an avalanche of facts, the pilots are asked about their impressions, lessons learned, and similar cognitive processes that may be defined as tacit knowledge. The debriefing officers attempt to extract the knowledge that the pilots have embedded in their minds—immediately after their extraordinary experience and before such mental processes begin to decay and forgetfulness sets in. The results of these debriefing sessions are compiled into "lessons learned" to be used by future pilots. These lessons become explicit knowledge, now embedded in the organization's records, training manuals, and documents that serve as inputs to policy and decision making and as background material for historians.

Not every individual or organization so methodically extracts tacit knowledge to be converted into explicit knowledge. Managers in work organizations possess vast amounts of tacit knowledge. From their experience, these managers "know" how their and other organizations work. They "know" how other managers think and how the market for their products or services reacts and what factors drive such behaviors. Some of this knowledge is shared with others by means of mentoring activities, but much of it is lost when the manager retires or otherwise leaves the organization. In Chapter 7 we expand this discussion to include the role that knowledge management systems (KMS) may play in preserving such knowledge.

THE COGNITIVE MODELS: THE RIFT WITH INFORMATION SYSTEMS

Perhaps the most salient contribution of KM to the understanding of how organizations produce and share knowledge has been the introduction of cognitive models as the key variable in the exploration of this phenomenon. Earlier models emphasized *information* and its processes, flow, and utilization in human and organizational contexts.

The advent of cognitive models has introduced the "knower" as the prime carrier of knowledge. Earlier, information had been considered the unit of analysis, and its flow and processes had been viewed as the mainstay of human communication. In the early days of the nascent field of KM, the definition of knowledge became a mere extension of data and information, as shown in Table 2.2 in Chapter 2. Information was generally defined as a "message" whereas knowledge (in the continuum from data to wisdom) was viewed as "contextual information." This meant that knowledge is a hybrid notion, as Davenport and Prusak (1998, 2) had suggested. Knowledge, they proposed, is "a third mix of framed experiences, values, contextual information, and expert insight . . . it originates and is applied in the mind of the knowers."

Here is the point of departure: knowledge changed from a complex form of *information* to a uniquely defined form of human capability. And as we show later in this and the next chapters, the distinguishing of knowledge from information also applies to the concept and organizational formats of KMS (Boudreau and Ramstad 2007).

SPIRAL AND SENSE-MAKING MODELS OF KNOWLEDGE

Several cognitive models have been proposed. Nonaka and Takeuchi (1995), for example, advance the model of knowledge spiral, in which tacit knowledge is transformed and systematized by organizations in a dynamic, nonsequential process.

Largely, this model assumes that knowledge, albeit tacit knowledge is a uniquely definable entity, different from information. Although Nonaka and Takeuchi go as far as defining the types of knowledge (e.g., operational, systematic, sympathized, and conceptual), they stop short of an in-depth definition of what knowledge is and how it is structured in a format definitely distinct from information.

Based in large measure on the work of Herbert Simon and Karl Weick, the cognitive model of knowledge as sense making has emerged. This model is anchored in the proposition that knowledge processes involve the conversion of individual knowledge into organizational knowledge animated by logical underpinnings. That is, when individuals develop knowledge in their work organizations, they do so systematically, with specific objectives in mind and according to a well-defined process.

Thus, the creation of knowledge in organizations is a thoughtful event. Members of the organization collect, absorb, and coalesce information from their external universe, then convert this modified platform of information into knowledge. In Nonaka and Takeuchi's "spiral model," individuals transfer knowledge to an ever-growing network of communities, groups, departments, and large organizations. This spiral effect of knowledge creation is filled with feedback, for as the knowledge base thus created grows, so do the interactions that fine-tune and further expand the knowledge base.

Karl Weick (2001) argues that members of an organization strive to make sense of their surroundings and of organizational events and phenomena they experience. His model has four stages or processes. The first is *ecological change*, in which the flow of information from outside the organization is disturbed. This leads to a dramatic increase in the importance that organizational members now give to the analysis of their relevant organizational environment. They wish to make sense of the disruption of information, to understand what happened and why, and to rely on a logical construction of their universe.

The second process is *enactment*, in which members of the organization reconstruct and configure their environment in their effort to make sense of all that has occurred. This process leads to *selection,* when members choose a course of action to learn from their action, followed by the *retention* phase, in which these lessons are institutionalized.

Chun Wei Choo (2005) proposes a model in which organizational members extract information from their external environment. By making sense of such a flow of information, they create knowledge, which becomes useful input for decision making and goal-directed behavior. The emphasis in this type of model of knowledge is the logical processing of information and its transformation, selection, and integration into the organization's processes by applying cognitive mechanisms of logical thinking, sense making, and rational procedures.

Cognitive models introduced the role of the knower, rationality, and the interaction between individuals and their organizations into the analysis of the flow from tacit to explicit forms of knowledge. However, these models relied on the exchange between knowers and their environment in which information is captured by the individual to be transformed into knowledge. This invariably led to the rift between information and knowledge.

Table 3.4

Contributions of Cognitive Models of Knowledge to the Rift Between Knowledge and Information Systems

Cognitive model	Contributions
Knowledge spiral (e.g., Nonaka and Takeuchi 1995)	How tacit knowledge becomes explicit How tacit and explicit knowledge are exchanged, converted, and used
Sense making (e.g., Choo 2005; Weick 2001)	How people make sense flows of experiences How external inputs become meaningful and are shared with others
Semantic networks and organizational knowledge systems (e.g., Wiig 1993)	How people organize their mental models How people store knowledge as semantic networks How people selectively share and convert tacit knowledge to explicit knowledge

The Rift With Information Systems and the Emergence of Knowledge Systems

In Chapter 2 we described the change process from information to knowledge. With the advent of the cognitive models of knowledge and KM, there emerged the need to establish KM or knowledge systems as a disciplinary area and as a concept and entity separate and different from information and information systems. The chain from data to knowledge and wisdom was no longer valid. Knowledge was no longer the extension or transformation of information by a knower.

There emerged a need to view knowledge as a separate entity, an independent concept with its own structure and applications in human organizations (Geisler 2006; Weinberger, 2007). By and large, knowledge scholars began to consider knowledge as a subject separated from information. The main body of research examined the diffusion of knowledge in organizations, its adoption, usage, and the contributions of knowledge systems to the organizational goals, processes, and outcomes.

However, little attention was given to a better understanding of knowledge as a unique unit of analysis, independently of the concept of information. To some extent, the separation of knowledge from information systems is not yet complete (Geisler 2007a; Zuboff 1989).

The conception of knowledge and knowledge systems outside the realm of information science and information systems is not just a minor semantic distinction. Increasingly scholars see a major conceptual differentiation between what constitutes knowledge and what constitutes information.

Table 3.4 shows the contributions of cognitive models of knowledge to the process of distinguishing knowledge and knowledge systems as a unique notion. The cumulative contributions of the cognitive models have supported the accelerated process of the conceptual separation of knowledge from information.

A model connecting the cognitive structure with organizational attributes was proposed by Karl Wiig (1993). The model suggests that people store knowledge in their minds as semantic networks that in turn describe mental or tacit perspectives of experience. These networks are then selectively transformed into usable knowledge that is needed to accomplish organizational functions and tasks. Wiig (2004) also proposed a taxonomy of knowledge forms or modalities: public, shared, and personal. The *public* modality of knowledge is coded and accessible. The *shared* is coded yet inaccessible (such as the knowledge embedded in technologies and information systems and services). The *personal* mode of knowledge is uncoded and inaccessible. This last mode is similar to procedural knowledge. Wiig's taxonomy is also similar to Geisler's (2006) taxonomy of format, content, and purpose.

As much as these cognitive models attempted to describe the mental structure and the organizational use of knowledge systems, they fell short of addressing the nature or basic structure of knowledge. To this end we proceed in the following section.

THE STRUCTURE OF KNOWLEDGE

What is knowledge? The literature has identified two major types: *tacit* or mental models of what constitutes knowledge, and *organizational* or shared, explicit, or public knowledge. Figure 3.1 shows the intersection of the two types of conceptual frameworks. The middle area is the "region of transformation," where the exchange between the two frameworks occurs and where individuals share their knowledge with others in the organization (Wiig 2004).

Figure 3.2 extends this framework and depicts the modes or instruments by which the cognitive/personal and the organizational models of knowledge are structured (Stankovsky 2005). This figure provides examples of the *conduits* of knowledge, where knowledge is deposited, and how it is transacted among knowers (Geisler 2007c).

Knowledge is therefore structured along the lines of the mental models of individuals and their externalization via organizational conduits—as shown in Figure 3.2. In the organization, knowledge can be carved in marble, written on paper, and, more recently, stored in a computer. The knowledge (facts, ideas, or rules) is preserved in forms—including language, pictorial representation, and mathematical and other symbols—that are intelligible to other (present and future) members of the organization. Organizational records come in many forms and are stored as harbingers of knowledge.

HOW KNOWLEDGE PROGRESSES: THE EVOLUTIONARY MODEL

How knowledge progresses is a key issue in our attempts to understand the phenomenon of knowledge. As we explain in Part II of this book, knowledge has increasingly gained a major role in the social, political, and economic world.

First, the rate of *production* of human knowledge (both technical and administrative) has been accelerating almost without precedent in human history. People produce and store today, and every day, more knowledge than their ancestors achieved in thirty-five centuries of recorded history.

Secondly, humans have developed the means, tools, instruments, machines, and modes of communication, storage, and transfer of knowledge to an extent unforeseen

Figure 3.1 **Major Types of Knowledge**

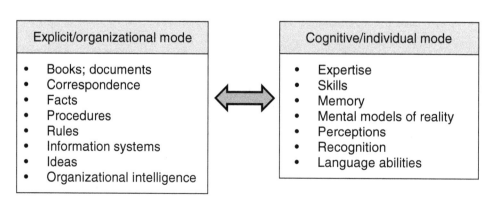

Cognitive/
tacit/
individual
knowledge

Explicit/
organizational
knowledge

Region of transformation:
the intersection of the individual
and organizational knowledge
frameworks

Figure 3.2 **Illustrative Components and Conduits of the Structure of Knowledge**

Explicit/organizational mode	Cognitive/individual mode
• Books; documents • Correspondence • Facts • Procedures • Rules • Information systems • Ideas • Organizational intelligence	• Expertise • Skills • Memory • Mental models of reality • Perceptions • Recognition • Language abilities

Figure 3.3   **Stages in the Evolutionary Epistemology Model of Knowledge**

1. Genetic adaptation
2. Non-mnemonic problem solving
3. Vicarious locomotive devices
4. Instinct
5. Habit
6. Visually supported thought
7. Mnemonically supported thought
8. Socially vicarious explorations
9. Language
10. Cultural accumulation
11. Science

Figure 3.4   **Seven Reasons Why Human and Social/Organizational Knowledge Is Not Evolutionary**

1. Knowledge is not reifiable to the extent that it is driven to propagation and survival through reproducibility.
2. Knowledge is not led to extinction.
3. Knowledge may reappear in cycles.
4. There is no need for diversity for knowledge to be selected.
5. Transfer processes via the concept of the meme are at best fuzzy.
6. Social knowledge is linked to social events; hence its existence depends on the event.
7. Knowledge is linked to higher-order constructs, concepts, and notions.

a century ago. People now have the ability to process more knowledge than ever before in human history. They are also able to have such knowledge embedded in the products and services of the global economy. Knowledge is thus exchanged and transacted worldwide, without frontiers, to the point where it is becoming an internationally traded *commodity*.

So how does knowledge progress? How do humans add to their stock of what they know? How do they feed this insatiable appetite for knowledge that the current society and economy have come to possess?

The model of evolutionary growth of knowledge has gained some acceptance in recent years. Starting with Sir Karl Popper (1972), the notion of "evolutionary epistemology" has gained widespread acceptance among scholars interested in the nature and progress of human knowledge. Popper was mostly interested in the epistemology of scientific inquiry. He argues that science progresses by applying the test of refutability to scientific theories. This test consists of empirical verification, so it resembles the process of natural selection in the world of biology—hence the link to the theory of evolution.

Donald Campbell (1974) extended Popper's model by arguing that human knowledge progresses within a hierarchical process containing eleven steps or stages. This process, according to Campbell, exhibits the attributes of evolutionary progression found in biological phenomena. The eleven stages, shown in Figure 3.3, are a mix of uses and functions that knowledge seems to perform in the quest for survival of the fittest. Yet some steps are skills (e.g., language, problem solving) whereas other steps are biological processes (e.g., genetic adaptation). None of this mixed bag of attributes provides an element in the definition of knowledge as a unique entity or construct (Ter Hark 2004).

There are two principles that guide evolutionary epistemology. The first is *blind variation and selective retention*. This principle is applied in the early stages of the process, in which "good" or useful knowledge is retained and "bad" knowledge is discarded. The second principle involves *vicarious selection*, in which knowledge may be selected or refuted according to whether it "fits" the stock of knowledge already in existence. These principles guide the selection of which knowledge should and will be retained. This means that when entities (individuals or organizations) add "good" knowledge to their stock, they are now better able to survive and to compete. The ultimate step in the hierarchy of the steps is *science*, which invokes the most complex and sophisticated procedure for acceptance of knowledge (Radnitzky 1987; Wuketitis 1983).

Geisler (2001) has challenged the evolutionary model of knowledge. He offers seven reasons why knowledge, particularly human and social knowledge, is not evolutionary. The reasons are shown in Figure 3.4.

ACTOR-NETWORK THEORY AND KNOWLEDGE MANAGEMENT

Organizational knowledge can exist at the confluence of people, processes, and technology. The challenge when embarking upon a suitable KM initiative is to be able to effectively and systematically capture, store, use, and distribute this knowledge. Thus it is imperative to use a robust and appropriate framework or analytic lens that not only facilitates the identification of the multifaceted knowledge components but also enables the efficient, systematic capture of this knowledge. Actor-network theory (ANT) presents itself as a useful framework.

BACKGROUND OF ACTOR-NETWORK THEORY

ANT was developed primarily by a British sociologist, John Law, and two French scholars, Bruno Latour and Michel Callon. ANT is an interdisciplinary approach to social sciences and technology studies that provides a material-semiotic framework for describing the ordering of scientific, technological, social, and organizational processes or events (Latour 2005). ANT developed around problems associated with attempts to handle sociotechnical "imbroglios" by regarding the world as heterogeneous (Chagani 1998). Examples include electric cars (Callon et al. 1986), supersonic aircraft (Law and Callon 1988), Portuguese navigation (Law et al. 1987), the domestication of scallops in Brittany (Callon and Law 1986), Kodak and the mass market for amateur photography (Latour and Law 1991), and a new railway system in Paris (Latour 1996). ANT has also been applied to information systems research by Tatnall (Tatnall et al. 2003) and Gliding (Tatnall and Gliding 1999) after its extensive use in geographical systems analysis, continuing through its peak in the 1990s. The utilization of heterogeneous entities (Bijker et al. 1987) regards the questions "Is it social?" or "Is it technical?" as missing the point; instead, the question should be "Is this association stronger or weaker than that one?" (Latour and Elliott 1988).

Although labeled a theory, ANT is not a theory in a social-theory sense nor does it try to explain the behavior of social actors. ANT is rather a framework based upon an array of concepts. It is based upon the idea that human and nonhuman objects and subjects are treated according to the same *principle of generalized symmetry* and integrated into the same conceptual framework.

CONCEPTS OF ACTOR-NETWORK THEORY

The critical concepts of ANT that are important for considering Picture Archiving and Communication System (PACS) implementation include the actors or actants, the heterogeneous network, the tokens or quasi objects, punctualization, the obligatory passage point, and the concept of irreversibility (Walsham 1997).

Actors or Actants

Typically, actors are the participants in the network, including both human and non-human objects and/or subjects. In ANT, the extent of a network is determined by actors that are able to make their presence *individually felt* (Law et al. 1987) by other actors. However, in order to avoid the strong bias toward interpreting the word *actor* to mean only a human being, the neologism *actant* is commonly used to refer to both human and nonhuman actors. Examples include humans (medical practitioners, x-ray technicians, medical administrators, etc.), electronic instruments, technical artifacts, and graphical representations.

Heterogeneous Network

The heterogeneous network is a network of aligned interests formed by the actors. This network of materially heterogeneous actors is put together by a great deal of work that both shapes those various social and nonsocial elements and "disciplines" them so they work together instead of "making off on their own" (Latour 2005, 62). For example, sixteenth-century Portuguese navigation successfully combined improved sailing vessels, the magnetic compass, knowledge of trade winds, and a new method for the astronomical determination of latitude. The result was a "durable network" capable of resisting hostile forces including currents, winds, and Muslim navigators (Law and Hassard 1999).

ANT claims that, in principle, all actors, whether human or nonhuman, have equal importance and that the differences between such actors, their characteristics, and their relative importance are all generated within a web of relations. The power of an actor emerges out of the effect of a network of relations.

Tokens or Quasi Objects

Tokens or quasi objects are the success outcomes or functioning of the actors that is passed onto the other actors within the network. As the token is increasingly transmitted or passed through the network, it becomes increasingly punctualized and reified. When the token is decreasingly transmitted or when an actor fails to transmit the token (e.g., the oil pump breaks), punctualization and reification are decreased as well.

Punctualization

Punctualization is similar to the concept of abstraction in object-oriented programming. A combination of actors can be viewed together as one single actor. These subactors are hidden from the normal view. This concept is referred to as punctualization or formation of a black box. An incorrect or failed passage of a token to an actor will result in the breakdown of a network (Callon et al. 1986) and a need to open the lid of the box to look inside at the whole network of other complex associations. When the network breaks down, it results in breakdown of punctualization, allowing the viewers to view the subactors of the actor. This concept is referred to as depunctualization. For example, an automobile is generally considered as one unit. Only when it breaks down is it seen as a combination of many machine parts. It is only when a universal joint wears out that the car owner needs to know that it is an important part of the transmission.

Obligatory Passage Point

The obligatory passage point (OPP) broadly refers to a situation that has to occur in order for all the actors to satisfy the interests that have been attributed to them by the focal actor. The focal actor defines the OPP through which the other actors must pass and by which the focal actor becomes indispensable (Callon and Law 1986).

Irreversibility

According to Callon and Law (1986), the degree of irreversibility depends on (1) the extent to which it is subsequently impossible to go back to a point where that translation was only one among others and (2) the extent to which it shapes and determines subsequent translations.

STAGES OF ACTOR-NETWORK THEORY

ANT takes into account the dynamic nature of interactions over time (Callon and Law 1986). This is done through the stages of inscription and translation. Translation can be further broken down into five substages: problematization, interessement, enrollment, mobilization of allies, and framing.

Inscription

Latour (1988) describes inscription as a process of creating technical artifacts that ensure the protection of an actor's interests.

Inscriptions (including texts, but also images of many sorts, databases, and the like) are central to knowledge work. Some say that texts (such as journal articles, conference papers and presentations, grant proposals, and patents) are among the major, if not the major, products of scientific work. Inscriptions make actions at a distance possible by stabilizing work in such a way that it can travel across space and time and be combined with other work.

Texts are also central to the process of gaining credibility. They carry work to other people and institutions. They attempt to present work in such a way that its meaning and significance are irrefutable. And texts are where authors establish equivalences among problems, which Callon et al. (1986) identify as a major strategy of enrolling others. An important part of the standard journal article or grant application, for example, is to say, in essence, "If you are interested in X (major issue), you must be interested in Y."

Translation

Translation is the central concept of ANT. Translation (Law 1992) can be defined as "the means by which one entity gives a role to others" (Singleton and Michael 1993). The stage of translation can also be regarded as a stage of negotiation. After the actor-network is actually created, there will, of course, be several actors. For the purpose of clarity and simplicity, a powerful and/or primary actor will translate other actors' interests into his own by negotiating with them. This is the stage where all the actors come to an agreement to determine whether the network should be built and defended. Callon and Law (1986) defines five important substages of translation: problematization, interessement, enrollment, mobilization of allies, and framing.

Problematization is the first stage of translation, where the problem that needs to be solved is identified. The actors and their interests are also identified and framed. For each group of actors with similar interests, a primary actor is chosen as the head of the group. This primary actor establishes itself as the OPP between the other actors and the network, rendering it indispensable. All the other actors must then accept the particular viewpoint of this actor.

Interessement is the second stage of translation, where the primary actor identified in the first stage works to convince other actors that the roles defined by it are acceptable and feasible and to negotiate their terms of involvement. It thus works toward getting the actors interested in the network.

The third stage of translation, *enrollment,* is the stage of acceptance by the actors of roles defined by the primary actor in the prior stages. The actors accept their roles and interests in this stage.

The *mobilization of allies* involves a reexamination of the primary actors to evaluate whether they represent the actors of their respective groups. Do they accurately represent the masses? If they do, then the enrollment becomes active support.

Framing, the final stage, provides the stabilization of the network. As the key issues and debates get resolved within the network, technologies can become stabilized over time.

ADOPTION OF ACTOR-NETWORK THEORY TO KNOWLEDGE MANAGMENT

In order to fully appreciate the benefit of incorporating an ANT perspective into any KM initiative, it is first necessary to revisit the knowledge construct itself.

An extensive review of the KM literature suggests "there has been very little research on how to successfully develop and implement KM solutions" (Massey et al. 2002, 271). Furthermore, it appears that currently there is little, if any, research on how to actualize the knowledge spiral and thereby facilitate the creation of new knowledge, a significant component within any successful KM solution. In addition, a study by Alavi and Leidner (2001, 117) suggests "that considering the flexibility of modern IT, other forms . . . of knowledge creation can be enhanced through the use of various forms of information systems." The collective message of these findings indicates the need for a more rigorous use of ITs and techniques in facilitating successful KM initiatives, especially knowledge creation or acquisition. To do this successfully, however, organizations need a robust and suitable framework such as ANT. However, to understand the true power of ANT in this context, it is first necessary to understand the predominant knowledge creation approaches—that is, the people-centric and the technology-centric perspectives.

In the recent past, two conceptual streams of thought have emerged that describe knowledge creation either as a people- or technology-centric process (Wickramasinghe 2006). The former is represented by different models (Newell et al. 2002; Wickramasinghe 2006) (Table 3.5), while the latter has a more monolithic nature.

Nonaka's *people-centric knowledge spiral* (Nonaka 1994; Nonaka and Nishiguchi 2001) is the most widely used framework for knowledge creation. Employing ideas of Polanyi (1966), it views knowledge as an object existing in two forms: explicit or factual knowledge (i.e., "know-what") and tacit or experiential knowledge (i.e., "know-how"). Nonaka's model underscores the dynamic nature of knowledge and the continuous conversion of existing tacit knowledge into new explicit knowledge and vice versa—that is, a "knowledge spiral." Nonaka identifies four principal forms of such conversion:

- *socialization* (tacit to tacit knowledge): usually occurs through apprenticeship-type relations where the teacher or master passes the skill to the apprentice;
- *combination* (explicit to explicit knowledge): formal learning of facts;
- *externalization* (tacit to explicit knowledge): articulation of nuances;
- *internalization* (explicit to tacit knowledge): associating newly acquired facts to enrich preexisting expertise and skills.

Spender's *people-centric model* (Newell et al. 2002) recognizes the existence of both explicit and implicit knowledge in an individual and social sense. Spender's definition of implicit knowledge corresponds with Nonaka's tacit knowledge (although Nonaka does not differentiate between individual and social dimensions of knowledge).

Blackler's *people-centric approach* (Newell et al. 2002) emphasizes that knowledge can exist in several, almost "physiological" forms (encoded, embedded, embodied, encultured, embrained) that span the continuum of tacit (embrained) to explicit (encoded) knowledge. The embedded, embodied, and encultured types of knowledge combine varying degrees of tacit (implicit) and explicit knowledge, serving as transitional links between the two extremes. A very important derivative of Blackler's analysis that highlights the connection between knowledge and organizational processes is the clear indication that different types of organizations require different types of knowledge.

Table 3.5

People-Centric Perspectives of Knowledge Creation

Theory	Explanation of knowledge creation
Nonaka's knowledge spiral (Nonaka 1994; Nonaka and Nishiguchi 2001)	Two types of knowledge • tacit • explicit Creation of knowledge results from spiraling between four main conversions, transforming • extant explicit knowledge into new explicit knowledge (transformation) • extant tacit knowledge into new tacit knowledge (socialization) • extant explicit knowledge into new tacit knowledge (internalization) • extant tacit knowledge into new explicit knowledge (externalization)
Spender (Newell et al. 2002)	Two types of knowledge • explicit • implicit (similar to tacit as described by Nonaka) Two levels of knowledge creation • individual • social
Blackler (Newell et al. 2002)	Five "physiological" forms of knowledge that make up a continuum • encoded (similar to explicit) • embedded (combination of explicit and tacit/implicit) • embodied (combination of explicit and tacit/implicit) • encultured (combination of explicit and tacit/implicit) • embrained (similar to tacit/implicit)

In contrast, the *technology-centric* approach derives new knowledge using "mechanistic" methods such as knowledge discovery in databases (KDD)—data mining is probably the most commonly employed method. KDD focuses on how data are transformed into knowledge by identifying valid, novel, potentially useful, and ultimately understandable patterns within data sets that would remain opaque without purposeful extraction and analysis (Adriaans and Zantinge 1996; Wickramasinghe 2006). Consequently, KDD-based creation of knowledge depends on providing common (superior) structure to often widely dispersed data sets.

STEPS IN DATA MINING

The following steps are typically undertaken in data mining (Wickramasinghe 2006). These steps are iterative, with the process moving backward whenever it is required to do so.

1. Develop an understanding of the application, of the relevant prior knowledge, and of the end user's goals.

2. Create a target data set to be used for discovery.
3. Clean and preprocess the data (including handling missing data fields, noise in the data, accounting for time series, and known changes).
4. Reduce the number of variables and find invariant representations of the data, if possible.
5. Choose the data-mining task (classification, regression, clustering, etc.).
6. Choose the data-mining algorithm.
7. Search for patterns of interest (this is the actual data mining).
8. Interpret the patterns mined. If necessary, iterate any steps 1 through 7.
9. Consolidate the knowledge discovered, prepare reports, and then use and reuse the newly created knowledge.

Figure 3.5 is a generic representation of a typical knowledge discovery process. A data-mining project usually starts with data collection or data selection, covering almost all steps (described above and illustrated in Figure 3.5) in the KDD process. In this respect, the first three steps of the KDD process (selection, preprocessing, and transformation) are considered exploratory data mining, whereas the last two steps (data mining and interpretation or evaluation) in the KDD process are considered predictive data mining. The primary objectives of data mining, in practice, tend to be description (performed by exploratory data mining) and prediction (performed by predictive data mining). Description focuses on finding human-interpretable patterns describing the data, while prediction involves using some observations and attributes to predict unknown or future values of other attributes of interest. The relative importance of description and prediction for particular data mining applications can vary considerably. The descriptive and predictive tasks are carried out by applying different machine learning, artificial intelligence, and statistical algorithms.

A major goal of exploratory data mining is data cleaning and understanding. Some of the data operations undertaken during exploratory data mining are sampling, partitioning, charting, graphing, associating, clustering, transforming, filtering, and imputing. Predictive data mining, which deals with future values of variables, utilizes many algorithms, including regression, decision trees, and neural networks. Predictive data mining also involves an assessment step that compares the effectiveness of different models according to many performance metrics.

Figure 3.5 shows an integrated view of the knowledge discovery process, the evolution of knowledge from data to information to knowledge, and the types of data mining (exploratory and predictive) and their interrelationships. In this one figure, we capture all the major aspects connected with data mining and, by so doing, emphasize the integral role of data mining in knowledge management.

TYPES OF KNOWLEDGE

In addition to the two major perspectives pertaining to knowledge creation, it is also important to note that knowledge is not a homogeneous construct. As with many concepts in organizational theory, the existence of duality as discussed by Orlikowski

Figure 3.5 **Integrated View of the Knowledge Discovery Process**

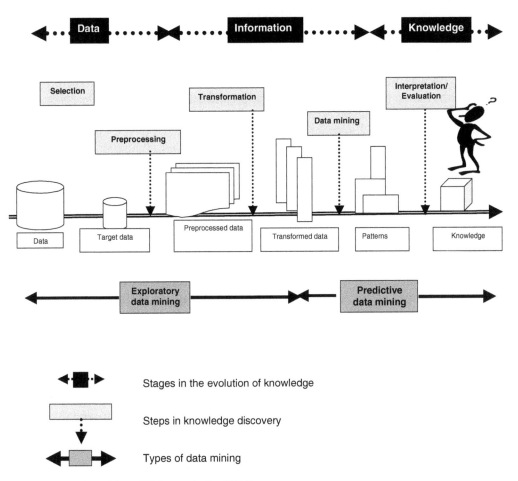

Source: Adapted from Wickramasinghe (2006).

(1992) applies to the examination of the types of knowledge and even the processes of KM with their four discrete but continuously evolving steps. Traditionally, researchers turn to Burrell and Morgan's well-established framework of objective and subjective characterizations. A more recent approach is Deetz's four discourses of organizational inquiry bounded by the dimensions of consensus/dissensus and emergent/a priori (Schultze and Leidner 2002). In trying to manage knowledge, it is necessary to first understand the duality of knowledge—its objective and subjective components as well as its consensus/dissensus dimensions. Specifically, knowledge can exist as an object in essentially two forms: explicit or factual knowledge and tacit or "know how" knowledge. It is well established that while both types of knowledge are important, tacit knowledge is more difficult to identify and thus manage (Wickramasinghe 2006).

Of equal importance, though perhaps less well defined, knowledge also has a subjective component and can be viewed as an ongoing phenomenon, being shaped by the social practices of communities (Boland and Tenkasi 1995). The objective elements of knowledge can be thought of as primarily having an impact on process, while the subjective elements typically impact innovation. Enabling and enhancing both effective and efficient processes as well as the functions of supporting and fostering innovation are key concerns of KM. Thus, there exists an interesting duality in KM that some have called a contradiction and others describe as the *loose-tight* nature of KM (Wickramasinghe 2006).

KM is both loose and tight because of the need to recognize and draw upon two distinct philosophical perspectives—the Lockean/Leibnitzian stream and the Hegelian/Kantian stream. Models of convergence and compliance representing the tight side are grounded in a Lockean/Leibnitzian tradition. These models are essential to provide the information-processing aspects of KM, most notably by enabling efficiencies of scale and scope and thus supporting the objective view of KM. In contrast, the *loose* side provides agility and flexibility in the Hegelian/Kantian tradition. Such models recognize the importance of the divergence of meaning that is essential to support the sense-making, subjective view of KM.

Finally, it is important to stress that organizational knowledge is not static; rather it changes and evolves during the lifetime of an organization. Furthermore, it is possible to transform one form of knowledge into another—that is, to transform tacit knowledge into explicit and vice versa or transform subjective knowledge into objective knowledge. This process of transforming one form of knowledge into another is known as the knowledge spiral (Nonaka 1994). Naturally, this does not imply that one form of knowledge is necessarily transformed 100 percent into another form of knowledge. According to Nonaka, there are four possibilities: (1) tacit to tacit knowledge transformation usually occurs through apprenticeship-type relations where the teacher or master passes on the skill to the apprentice; (2) explicit to explicit knowledge transformation usually occurs via formal learning of facts; (3) tacit to explicit knowledge transformation usually occurs when there is an articulation of nuances; for example, if an expert surgeon is asked why he performs a particular surgical procedure in a certain manner, his articulation of the steps makes his tacit knowledge explicit; (4) explicit to tacit knowledge transformation usually occurs when explicit knowledge is internalized and can then be used to broaden, reframe, and extend a person's tacit knowledge. Integral to these transformations of knowledge through the knowledge spiral is that new knowledge is being continuously created, thus potentially bringing many benefits to organizations. By transforming tacit knowledge to explicit knowledge, for example, an organization is able to capture the expertise of particular individuals, thus expanding the organizational memory and also allowing single loop and double loop organizational learning to take place (Wickramasinghe 2006).

Given that ANT acknowledges technology and people perspectives in its definition of actants and that ANT is a dynamic, not static, framework, it does lend itself most suitably to be used as an analytic lens to frame any KM initiative. We illustrate this with Figure 3.6 and Table 3.6. Specifically, Figure 3.6 provides the key dimensions of a generic KM initiative. Table 3.6 maps these into an ANT context.

Figure 3.6 **KM: Key Dimensions**

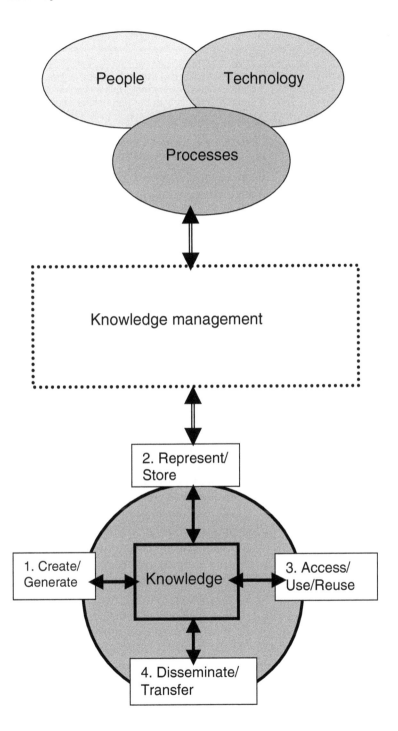

Table 3.6

Mapping a KM Initiative With the Stages of ANT

Stage	KM initiative
Inscription	From the specific KM initiative; e.g., if a groupware system is implemented to facilitate knowledge sharing, this system would define specific steps for how the actors interact with the technology and each other.
Translation	New and augmented roles result.
Problematization	Problem to be resolved, usually a critical decision to be made and the need to access germane knowledge.
Interessement	Roles are renegotiated with the implementation of the KM initiative.
Enrollment	Roles slowly become accepted as the KM initiative evolves and becomes familiar.
Mobilization of allies	All actants start to embrace the new KM initiative.
Framing	The KM initiative is now part of the dynamics and operations of the organization.

CRITICISM OF ANT

Before concluding, and for completeness, we note that while there are many positive aspects of ANT, it has often also been criticized. Much of the criticism of ANT is aimed at its principle of generalized symmetry, which treats both human and nonhuman objects alike. A commonly held view is that people are fundamentally different from nonhuman objects (Collins, Yearley, and Pickering 1992). Critics opine that there is a brave new world coming that involves more and more interaction between machines and humans, who may reach the point of becoming cyborgs—a world that humans should resist rather than celebrate. ANT, the critics claim, dehumanizes humans by treating human and nonhuman actors alike. However, although only humans can purposely act, their actions are strongly influenced by nonhuman actors. In addition, bringing nonhuman actors into the picture helps ANT avoid the exaggerated and highly criticized epistemological relativism that is often associated with constructivist theories, especially those inspired by the sociology of scientific knowledge.

Callon and Latour appear to opine that two actors can be made dissociable only if they are made one. Their ideas and interests must be equivalent and the actor who holds the equivalences holds the secret of power. Although the sociology of translation unleashes a good deal of theoretical energy in modeling how subjects constitute each other, the question of how the subject constitutes itself is hardly touched upon by the developers of ANT. Abramson (1998) suggests working through the sociology of translation to sketch out a model of power that would retain the model of centers and peripheries but see them as constituted in and through networks, so that they are not concrete, immutable centers nor ever-relegated peripheries, but fluid and always engaged in the struggle to retain their position as points of obligatory passage for the networks in whose names they speak (Latour and Law 1991).

Another criticism is that ANT fails to provide explanations for the dynamic restructuring of networks. The concept of punctualization is not clearly explained. Questions remain: How can an actor be simultaneously an actor and a network? How far does this interpretation iterate before a stable network becomes too complex to even comprehend? ANT portrays successful networks as those that are stable and have good translation. However, how can it be finally determined if the network is ever stable?

Callon and Latour explain this concept of punctualization using macro- and micro-actors. The difference between macro-actors and micro-actors is size, not kind. Macro-actors can be thought of as assemblages of micro-actors, with some actors aggregating, or translating, the wills of others through a process of enrollment; micro-actors in these assemblages include humans, mediated texts, technical artifacts, money, or anything else that can be inscribed in the project of the macro-actor. Macro-actors are therefore to be thought of as networks that grow and shrink through processes of translation. A successful translation generates a shared space, aligning actors and points of view. In order to grow, an actor must enroll other wills by translating what they want and by reifying this translation in such a way that none of them can desire anything else any longer (Callon and Latour 1981).

ANT has also been criticized as amoral. Bijker has responded to this criticism by stating that the amorality of ANT is not a necessity. Moral and political positions are possible, but one must first describe the network before taking such positions. It is also said that ANT fails to take account of the effects that technology can have on those who are not part of the network that produces it, and that it therefore fails to support value judgments concerning the desirability or undesirability of such effects. ANT is also criticized for its disinclination (or inability) to make contributions to debates about policy for technology and science.

In 1997, after having devoted much of his writing during the decade to developing ANT with colleagues such as Michael Callon and Madeline Akrich, Latour declared the end of the ANT in his contribution to the "Actor-Network and After" workshop. Latour left little doubt about its demise: "There are four things that do not work with actor-network theory; the word actor, the word network, the word theory, and the hyphen! Four nails in the coffin." In a later book, *Reassembling the Social: An Introduction to Actor-Network Theory* (2005), however, Latour reversed his view, accepting the wide use of the term. He also remarked that he had been helpfully reminded that the ANT acronym "was perfectly fit for a blind, myopic, workaholic, trail-sniffing, and collective traveler" (the ant)—qualitative hallmarks of actor-network epistemology. Latour's argument is that things have been changing dramatically and hence there needs to be continuous rediscovery and revision to the earlier processes. Although the theory was designed to meet these goals, it needs continuous revision to meet current challenges and requirements. Latour believes that the basic theory is still the most apt methodology to explain sociological change. He draws a decent analogy between his theory and that of a military officer who continuously revises his strategy to fight the enemy.

CONCLUSIONS

Despite these criticisms of ANT, we claim that it is one of the most appropriate, powerful tools for analyzing very complex dynamic systems. In particular, it helps us in gauging the dynamic expansion of a network as well as the power factors within the network. Modern organizations are complex and today's environment is dynamic. Such a context requires multiple actors working toward the common good and effecting superior decisions. To achieve this goal, it is vital that organizations embrace the tools, techniques, and tactics of KM. To ensure that a KM initiative is successful and realizes its true potential, we recommend that such an initiative incorporate the power of ANT as an analytic lens.

LEARNING OUTCOMES

- What is the nature of tacit and explicit forms of knowledge?
- How knowledge is structured. What are the various models of knowledge creation?
- The rift between knowledge and information systems.
- Is knowledge evolutionary? The elements of evolutionary epistemology and its criticism.
- What is ANT and how is it useful for KM?
- What are the criticisms of ANT?
- Do these criticisms affect the usefulness of ANT for KM?

DISCUSSION QUESTIONS

1. What are the key differences between the tacit and explicit forms of knowledge?
2. What is the nature of the rift or distinction between knowledge systems and information systems?
3. Is knowledge evolutionary? What are the pros and cons of evolutionary epistemology?
4. What are the different knowledge creation frameworks?
5. What are the steps in the knowledge discovery process?
6. What is the concept of the knowledge spiral and why might ANT be helpful?
7. Are there any problems with ANT? Why and when might it be unsuitable?

4 The Alternative Model of Knowledge
Cumulation and Progress

KEY LEARNING OUTCOMES

*You will know you have mastered the material in this chapter
when you can define and explain the following:*

1. The issue of the unit of analysis of knowledge.
2. Nuggets and memes.
3. The cumulation model.
4. The role of managerial cognition.
5. Fusion of knowledge and management.

THE ALTERNATIVE MODEL

A key issue in knowledge management (KM) that was not resolved by knowledge scholars such as Nonaka, Van Groug, Polanyi, and Davenport is the elemental form of knowledge, or the basic unit of what constitutes human and, by extension, organizational knowledge (Geisler 2007). The current literature on KM treats the notion of "knowledge" as a given entity, in many ways considered indivisible.

Indeed, the comparison of this notion with the atom as a basic unit of matter is very relevant. KM scholars have distinguished between tacit and explicit knowledge, but stopped short of delving into the "atom" of knowledge to explore its constituent elements. In the example of subatomic structure there are three parts—the proton, the electron, and the neutron. We might even suggest that the comparison with nuclear physics also extends to the distinction between tacit and explicit knowledge. These differences are similar to those between quantum mechanics (which applies to subatomic particles) and general relativity (which applies to larger physical entities). The laws for each type of matter are different, and the phenomena themselves are different (Frappaolo 2006).

Hence, there emerged two types of definitions of what constitutes knowledge, according to the categories of tacit and explicit. The types of knowledge are notions as different as the distinction of the two categories.

EXPLICIT KNOWLEDGE AND THE NOTION OF "NUGGETS"

The search for the basic unit of knowledge has led to the generation of structural units of what constitutes explicit knowledge (Rubenstein and Geisler 2003). This effort also includes an examination of the differences between the notions of "knowledge" and "to know." The "knower" is the repository of "knowledge" with the ability to share, export, and diffuse such knowledge to others (von Krogh et al. 2000).

The unit of knowledge that is exported by the knower, thus becoming explicit, has been characterized as a *nugget*. Rubenstein and Geisler (2003) define a nugget as the basic unit that carries or contains knowledge. They distinguish between "intellectual" nuggets, "supernuggets," and "nugget events." Figure 4.1 shows some attributes of these types of nuggets.

Nuggets are compound statements describing what people know. Some nuggets are in the form of causal statements, denoting knowledge of cause and effect. Other nuggets are statements or propositions that describe concepts, formulas, constructs, ideas, and notions: some in correlation to each other, some simply as descriptors of

Figure 4.1   **Attributes of Types of Nuggets**

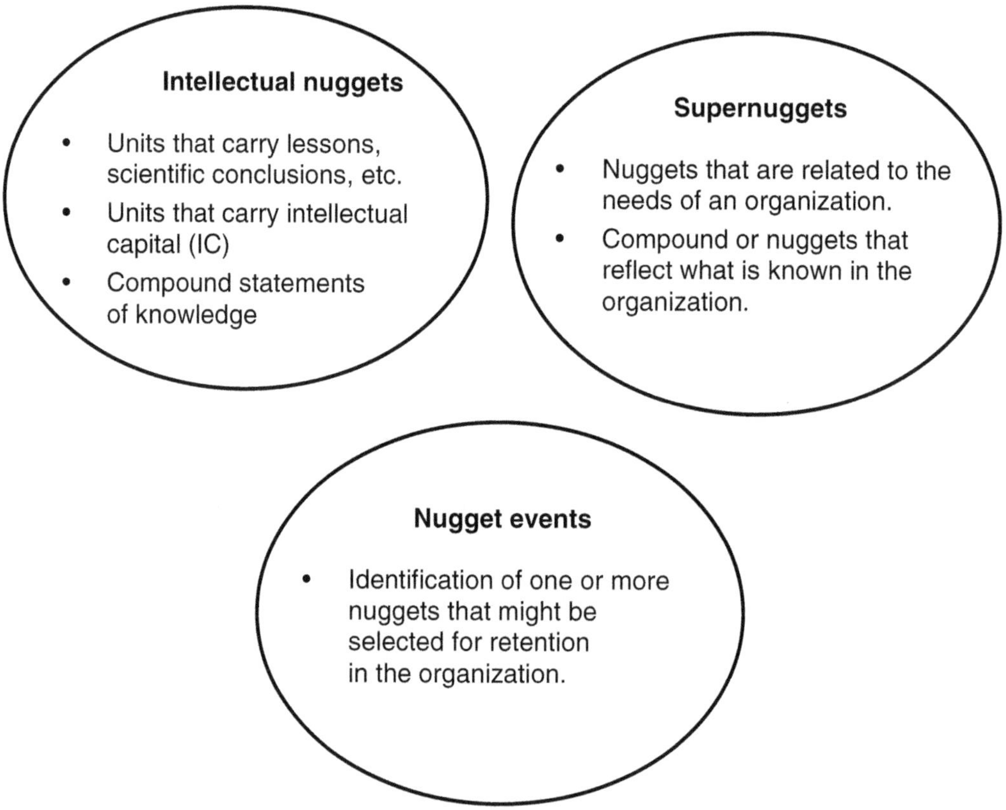

Figure 4.2 **Examples of Nuggets of Knowledge**

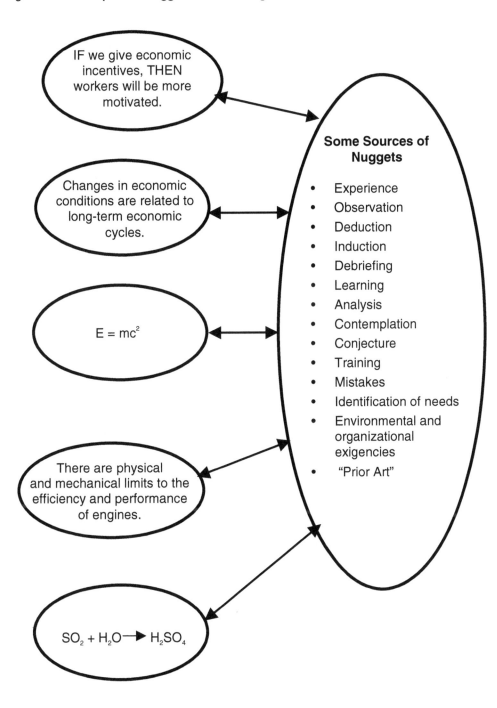

what a person knows. Nuggets utilize language to put together a form of expression of knowledge that can be shared, diffused, collected, stored, and utilized by individuals and organizations.

Nuggets allow people to share explicit knowledge. They are tools that facilitate the creation and transaction in knowledge among individuals and in a more structured way within their organizations (Ichijo and Nonaka 2006). Nuggets are the mechanism by which semantics and knowledge are integrated to allow for interpersonal and organizational exchanges. Figure 4.2 (see page 55) shows examples of nuggets.

In summary, nuggets are not the basic *units* of knowledge. Rather, they are the vehicles or instruments by which knowledge is carried. The transformation of knowledge into the linguistic format of the nugget is the process by which individuals and organizations transact. There is no inherent requirement that these nuggets are the "true" representation or description of reality (Geisler 2007). These nuggets are merely the vehicles that transport knowledge so people can communicate their knowledge to others.

EXPLICIT KNOWLEDGE AND THE NOTION OF "MEME"

In the search for the structure of what knowledge is, there was a movement to explore unity in the elements of this phenomenon. Edward Wilson (1998) coined the term *consilience* as the phenomenon in which causal explanations that are obtained from facts in one scientific discipline can be implemented in other disciplinary areas. Examples are intersects between biology, social sciences, and environmental sciences. Wilson argues that the unity of human learning is also reflected in the coevolution of genetics, social sciences, and human culture.

Such coevolution of diverse scientific phenomena and the quest for unity of knowledge provide a solid platform for the search for a basic unit of knowledge. The argument seems to be that if knowledge is essentially the same across scientific disciplines and human intellectual pursuits, then there must be an elemental structure of knowledge.

An analogy would be the physical world. If all that exists in the world is matter, then there must be a unifying element that is basic to the structure of *all* matter in existence. Even though matter exhibits itself in different forms, the basic structure (i.e., atoms and subatomic particles) is essentially the same. The recent exploration of string theory adds to the strength of the analogy, in that the search for the building blocks of matter simply goes ever deeper to even more elemental structures.

Richard Dawkins (1978) of Oxford University coined the term *meme*. Dawkins believed that there exists a fundamental element of human culture, similar to the biological gene, and that such an element is transformed via processes that are similar to biological replication and genetics. He also suggested that these "memes" are carriers of information or knowledge (as genes carry biological attributes) and that these memes evolve—by learning and adaptation—as do biological processes of replication and evolution (Brodie 1996). Memes, therefore, carry ideas, notions, and concepts such as civilization, freedom, and justice—just as genes carry the characteristics of biological entities (Blackmore and Dawkins 1999).

The notion of memes indeed proliferated beyond the confines of Oxford University. In 1997 scholars working in this field founded an electronic journal, *The Journal of Memetics: Evolutionary Models of Information Transmission.* Memetics became a new disciplinary area. Brodie (1996), Lynch (1998), and Aunger (2002) have presented a more elaborate framework of memetics as the science that explores memes as cultural replications that evolve by processes of variation and selection. As in the propagation of viral epidemics, a single source (meme) can replicate and engender a pandemic in the cultural world of ideas (Aunger 2000).

Distin (2004, 13) even argues that human beings are not simply "meme machines," but intelligent and purposeful creatures. She advances the notion of "cultural DNA" by which our cultural knowledge evolves in the confluence of the replication of cultural components (Figure 4.3) *and* the conscious push of the intellectual products of human creativity.

Figure 4.3 **Memetics: Transmission and Replication of Cultural Knowledge**

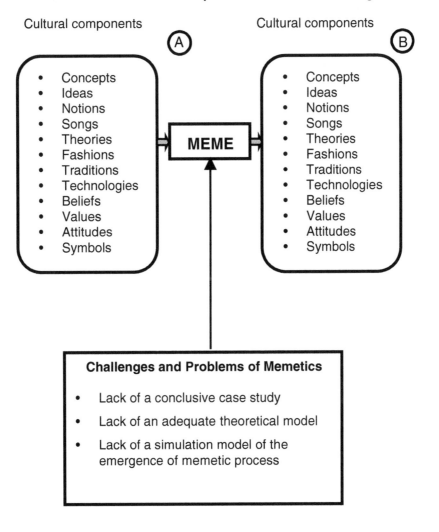

CRITIQUE OF MEMETICS

The *Journal of Memetics* defines the field as the investigation of "the evolutionary mechanisms that determine the propagation of information within a population of human, animal, or artificial agents" (www.jom-einit.org). The emphasis of this field is not the propagation or the structure of knowledge, but the evolutionary progress of human culture. Nonetheless, the progress of human knowledge is captured within the models of memetics, since memes are proposed as carriers and replicators of elements of human knowledge (Aunger 2002).

In a powerful critique of memetics that appeared in this journal, Edmonds (2002) advances three challenges to the new scientific field (see Figure 4.3). The first calls for the emergence of a conclusive case in which there is a description of a replicator of a cultural component. Edmunds argues that such a mechanism must be a physical rather than a cognitive entity (similar to DNA, for example, with its physical existence outside the human mind). Edmunds also argues that the field needs a theoretical model that will explain why the human brain, defined by some memeticists as the host or carrier of memes for cultural evolution, would engage in such an altruistic effort when it is "a costly organization in biological terms." Third, Edmunds challenges memetics to produce a simulation that would model how memes are diffused in viral-like propagation within a given population of human beings. He compares such a simulation to the simulation of how life would spring from the chemical reactions of inanimate materials and elements.

Memetics can also be criticized for its lack of measures of the content of memes as containers of knowledge. Memes may be viewed as the vehicles of distribution and diffusion of ideas, or the ideas themselves, but perhaps not both. Ideas do propagate and add to the portfolio of human culture. However memes are defined, they basically remain semantic representations of ideas and concepts. Memeticists simply reify them by endowing these linguistic statements with the characteristics of a separate existence. Memes are thus considered to have a life of their own (similar to microbes and viruses) with the innate abilities to replicate and propagate in the environment of human minds (Geisler 2007; Lynch 1998).

THE BASIC STRUCTURE OF KNOWLEDGE

The recurrent question in the study of knowledge and knowledge systems is this: What is the basic structure of knowledge? This is a quest for the fundamental elements that compose what we call *knowledge*. The contributions of the Japanese school to this quest provide a model of the exchange mechanisms between tacit and explicit forms of knowledge (Ichijo and Nonaka 2006; Nonaka and Takeuchi 1995). Other contributions to this quest define knowledge in terms of skills, ideas, and nuggets.

But the quest for a basic unit of knowledge and its fundamental components seems to be yet unanswered. Geisler (2007) proposes a model of the structure of knowledge that shifts the exploration to the cognitive aspects of human knowledge. He argues that the fundamental building blocks of knowledge are the cognitive compilations of sensorial inputs. In this model, knowledge is formed when sensorial inputs from the

Figure 4.4 **Sensorial Inputs and Their Attributes**

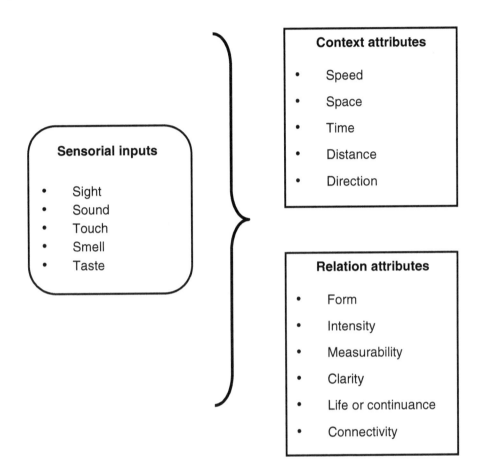

five human senses are collected in the mind. Figure 4.4 shows the characteristics of these sensorial inputs and the framework in which they are brought together.

In this model, the inputs from the five senses are conjoined in the mind. The differences or *intervals* in their appearance in the mind allow for their integration into a meaningful unit. The conjoining of sight and sound allows for the determination of the space and time of the source of these inputs, its distance from the knower, and the speed of its movement as well as the direction of the movement. Geisler argues that such conjoining occurs by trial and error and that experiences tend to verify or to refute the meaning derived from the congregation of sensorial inputs. The more these experiences accumulate in the mind, the higher the probability that the conjoining of sensorial inputs will generate knowledge that can withstand the test of subsequent experiences.

The key notion in this model of the structure of knowledge is the definition of the basic elements that compose the concept of knowledge and the claim that such fundamental elements do exist and that they can be traced to sensorial inputs. This is a reductionist approach to the phenomenon of knowledge; it resembles the exploration of subatomic particles. In this model, therefore, knowledge is not simply the entity that ontologically appears in the form of nuggets, skills, experiences, and the like. Rather, there is an attempt to delve *inside* the atom, or inside the *construct* of knowledge, to determine its fundamental components.

If knowledge is different from information, then there must be something that engenders such differences. The elements that make up these differences must be distinct from those that make up information—that is, language and semiotics. Therefore, knowledge would have to be a *cognitive* phenomenon. Hence, to "know" would mean to be part of a cognitive process. Knowledge and the knower thus meld, and knowledge would now be defined as *tacit* knowledge. Such a model would then have to explain and define the nature of *explicit* knowledge and perhaps also the nature of consciousness (Thompson and Madigan 2007).

THE PRINCIPLE OF CLUSTERING AND THE NOTION OF "KANE"

Geisler (2007) has proposed the notion of KANE as the basic structural unit of knowledge. KANE is the acronym for Knowledge Basic Unit of Existence. In this model of a basic unit of measurement of knowledge, the KANE is the initial clustering of sensorial inputs into a meaningful entity (Figure 4.5). The KANE is defined as the first registry of contested sensorial inputs, so that, upon their clustering, these inputs now form a perceptible union, which can be stored in memory and is already different from the simple set of sensorial inputs, which may be entering the mind through the senses.

Geisler (2007) also suggests that knowledge progresses by means of the process of *continuous cumulation*. This cumulation hypothesis proposes that knowledge progresses as additions to the stock of what a person knows. As KANEs are formed

Figure 4.5   **KANE: The Principle of Clustering of Knowledge**

$$K = C3$$

$$K = \text{Knowledge}$$

$$C3 = C1 \rightarrow C2 \rightarrow C3$$

in which

$$C1 = \text{clustering}$$

$$C2 = \text{comparing}$$

$$C3 = \text{conceptualizing}$$

in the mind, they are continually added to the platform of knowledge. Therefore, knowledge progresses by the incremental additions of units of knowledge, in a process bounded only by the physical constraints of the mind—similar to the limits imposed on computers by the size of the central processing unit.

The additive characteristics of the cumulative nature of knowledge also help to explain issues related to the increasing complexity of the portfolio of knowledge. Cumulation creates different architectures or structures of sediments of knowledge. This may be compared with a wall constructed with bricks of different sizes and color. Using such bricks in a random manner will result in different shapes and designs of the wall.

Geisler (2007) lists several advantages of the model of continuous cumulation. First, he suggests that the cumulation model best explains declarative memory (Tulving and Schachter 1990). This is the part of memory where a person assembles all the knowledge gained from childhood. Second, cumulation of knowledge explains how humans learn and the role of obsolescence in the exercise of their skills. The knowledge people accumulate allows them to exist and survive as social beings. The larger this portfolio of knowledge, the higher is the likelihood that it will contain knowledge that is useful for existence and even survival.

Primarily proponents of the school of evolutionary epistemology had challenged a model of cumulation as a descriptor of the progress by human knowledge. However, the cumulation model also benefits from the notion of clustering of sensorial inputs into the basic unit of KANE. Such congruence in the parts of the model and the consistency in proposing clustering as the key mechanism for the formation of increasingly complex frameworks of knowledge may perhaps provide added resiliency to the model in the face of its critics.

TOWARD ORGANIZATIONAL KNOWLEDGE: THE FUSION OF KNOWLEDGE AND MANAGEMENT

As we strive to generate a model of knowledge creation and its progress, it has become evident that, although humans garner knowledge about themselves as individuals and their individual surroundings, they also exist in social networks and communities. Armed with the ability to share and to diffuse knowledge, human beings form organizations that benefit from such exchange and the buildup of pools of knowledge (Frappaolo 2006). A good part of the knowledge that individuals generate and store is shared with others in the community. This is the role that *explicit* knowledge seems to play in the ability of people to codify and diffuse what they know to their social and economic organizations (Frydman and Goldberg 2007).

Codified knowledge is assembled and stored in organizations, providing a source of knowledge to organizational members. There are several purposes for the creation of such knowledge systems. We explore them in the following chapters. Geisler (2006), for example, identifies three purposes for organizational knowledge: (1) useful (survival and growth), (2) hedonistic (pleasure in gaining knowledge), and (3) systemic (increasing the stock of knowledge for additional usages).

As knowledge is transferred from individuals to the organizational or institutional setting, there is a fusion of knowledge: as a cognitive phenomenon, knowledge resides in the individual, but management of the knowledge is transacted in the organization. Once the knowledge falls within the organizational framework, the members of the organization need to manage such transactions and to ensure that they take place in an effective manner. The following chapters address the issues of management of knowledge and knowledge systems.

Learning Outcomes

- What is the unit of analysis of knowledge?
- What are nuggets and memes?
- What is the cummulation model of the progress of knowledge?
- What are the arguments in support and against this model?
- What is the role of managerial cognition and what is its relationship to the cummulation model?
- How do knowledge and management fuse or combine?

Discussion Questions

1. How would you define the unit of analysis of knowledge?
2. Do you accept the arguments for the existence of nuggets, and for the existence of memes?
3. What is your opinion of the criticisms of memes and Memetics?
4. What is the cummulation model and how do you compare it with other models of the progress of knowledge, such as evolutionary epistemology?
5. How would you define managerial cognition and what are the empirical implications of this framework?
6. Is managerial cognition different from other forms of human cognition? If so, how? Please be specific in your rationale and answer.

PART II

THE KNOWLEDGE-BASED ENTERPRISE
IMPLEMENTATION OF KNOWLEDGE AND KNOWLEDGE MANAGEMENT SYSTEMS

In Part II of this book we introduce the knowledge-based enterprise. This is a new form of organization, born in the latter years of the twentieth century, and rapidly becoming the standard form of the twenty-first century. We also introduce the notions and processes of the implementation of knowledge and knowledge management systems in this type of organization.

The knowledge-based enterprise relies on a sound and adequate knowledge system. In the several years since these notions have appeared in the academic as well as the popular press, "knowledge-based enterprise" and the "knowledge economy" have become "clichés." Although they describe real phenomena of the final decade of the twentieth and the beginning of the twenty-first centuries, there is a growing trend of viewing these notions as a broad description of modern organizations.

In effect, the knowledge-based economy and the knowledge-based enterprise are more focused concepts, designed to describe and explain the role that knowledge currently plays in the life, success, and survival of the contemporary enterprise. In this part of the book we discuss what has become the crucial role of knowledge in today's and (without a doubt) tomorrow's enterprises. But, all depends on the effective implementation of a knowledge system in the organization—and this is a complex, complicated, and uncertain process. This part of the book offers a simplified yet comprehensive analysis of this process.

5 The Networked Knowledge Economy

KEY LEARNING OUTCOMES

You will know you have mastered the material in this chapter when you can define and explain the following:

1. The networked knowledge economy.
2. How the knowledge economy is different from the old economy.
3. The key elements of today's knowledge economy.
4. Why the knowledge economy is so significant in this century.

Toward the end of the twentieth century, public policies for science, technology, and innovation attracted increased attention as a result of claims that knowledge-intensive industries were now at the core of growth and that the world was entering a completely new form of "knowledge society." For the previous 200 years, neoclassical economics had recognized only two key factors of production: labor and capital. Today, at the beginning of the twenty-first century, this phenomenon is changing: information and knowledge are replacing capital and energy as the primary wealth-creating assets, just as capital and energy replaced land and labor 200 years ago. In addition, technological developments in the twentieth century have transformed most wealth-creating work from physically based to knowledge-based, thereby making technology and knowledge the key factors of production. With the increased mobility of information and the global workforce, knowledge and expertise can be transported instantaneously around the world, and any advantage gained by one company can be eliminated by competitive improvements overnight. In such an environment, the only sustainable comparative advantage a company can enjoy is its process of innovation—combining market and technology know-how with the creative talents of knowledge workers to solve a constant stream of competitive problems—coupled with its ability to derive value from information. Welcome to the *knowledge economy*, where the growing codification of knowledge and its transmission through communications and computer networks have led to the emerging "information society" or "Information Age" (Benhabib and Spiegel 1994; Cameron 1996).

The Information Age has had a dramatic effect on businesses as well as on people's lifestyles. Globalization, rapid technological change, and the importance of knowledge in gaining and sustaining competitive advantage characterize today's Information Age. For a long time, economists identified capital, labor, and natural resources as the essential ingredients for economic enterprise. The new economy of the twenty-first century, however, is increasingly based on knowledge (Gagnon 2007; Westland 2006).

In this chapter we shall discuss the key elements of today's knowledge economy and its significance for businesses in this century. We also will describe the Information Age and provide a brief historical outline of the major transitions from the Agrarian Age to the Information Age.

HISTORICAL PERSPECTIVE: FROM AGRARIAN AGE TO INFORMATION AGE

Over the last 5,000 years, human history has moved from the Stone Age to the Agrarian Age (or agricultural economy), the Industrial Age (or industrial economy), and now the Information Age (or knowledge economy). In the past, the transition from one epoch to the next occurred slowly, unfolding over many generations. The first hunting-and-gathering economies lasted hundreds of thousands of years. Then came the Agrarian Age, which dominated for 10,000 years. In the Agrarian Age, society was basically divided into two classes: the landowners and the people who worked on the land (the serfs). Wealth was generated through agriculture.

When the Industrial Age arrived, everything changed; it was no longer agriculture that generated most of the wealth, but manufacturing. Suddenly, land was no longer the key to wealth. Business acumen and factories created a new class of wealthy person: the self-made business owner. A factory occupied far less land than a sheep farm or a wheat farm and in addition generated more relative wealth (Agion et al. 1998; Mansell and Wehn 1998). However, it still required enormous capital to build a factory and start a business. The industrial era reigned from the 1760s in Britain to the 1950s in the United States, when manufacturing began shrinking as a percentage of the U.S. economy.

Toward the end of the twentieth century came the Internet and World Wide Web. Coupled with this technology revolution was the phenomenon of globalization. This in turn led to a population explosion in cyberspace, with recent estimates indicating that more than 700 million people worldwide use the Internet frequently for their day-to-day activities. The birth of the Information Age changed everything again. Factories (or real estate) were no longer necessary to run a business since anyone with a Web site could start a business—the dot-com phenomenon. The barriers to wealth that existed in the Agrarian Age and the Industrial Age were completely gone or significantly reduced, with people who could never have dreamed of owning their own business now making millions from their computer (Barro and Sala-Martin 1995; Braim 1998).

Figure 5.1 **Descriptions of Key Economies**

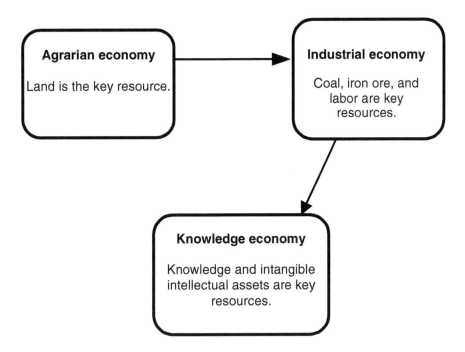

The Industrial Age was about centralization and control. In contrast, the Information Age is about decentralization and no or little control—no government or media magnate controls the Internet. This is the crucial thing to understand about the Information Age. The Information Age also has created a new language, with words like *microprocessors*, *operating systems*, and *graphical user interfaces*. Today, these terms are as familiar as *assembly line* and *mass production*, key terms of the Industrial Age. Integral to the Information Age is new technology and fast access to information, which are transforming the business landscape. Figure 5.1 summarizes the key economic distinctions between the Agrarian Age, the Industrial Age, and the Information Age.

OLD ECONOMY VERSUS NEW ECONOMY

The twenty-first–century economy is increasingly based on knowledge and information. Knowledge is now recognized as the driver of productivity and economic growth, leading to a new focus on the role of information, technology, and learning in economic performance. The term *knowledge-based economy* stems from this fuller recognition of the role of knowledge and technology in economic growth. Knowledge, as embodied in human beings (as *human capital*) and in technology, has always been central to economic development. However, only over the last few years has its relative importance been recognized and emphasized as a driver of fast economic growth (Bassi 1997; Foray and Lundvall 1996; Johnston and Blumentritt 1998).

Figure 5.2   **Old Versus New Economics**

- The economics is not of scarcity, but rather of abundance. Unlike most resources that are depleted when used, information and knowledge can be shared and actually grow through application.
- The effect of location is diminished. Using appropriate technology and methods, virtual marketplaces and virtual organizations can be created that offer the benefits of speed and agility, round-the-clock operation, and global research.
- Laws, barriers, and taxes are difficult to apply solely on a national basis. Knowledge and information "leak" to where demand is highest and barriers are lowest.
- Knowledge-enhanced products or services can command price premiums over comparable products with low embedded knowledge or knowledge intensity.
- Pricing and value depends heavily on context. Thus the same information or knowledge can have vastly different values to different people at different times.
- Knowledge when locked into systems or processes has higher inherent value than when it can walk out the door in people's heads.
- Human capital—competencies—is a key component of value in a knowledge-based company, yet few companies report competency levels in annual reports. In contrast, downsizing is often seen as a positive, cost-cutting measure.
- In the new economy, success and survival depend upon organizational capabilities such as speed, responsiveness, agility, learning capacity, and employee competence.

In recent years, business executives have recognized the role of technology, information, innovation, and creativity in expanding economic potential. The modern economy is based on intangibles—the exploitation of ideas rather than material things. Many new terms have been coined for this new economy, such as *knowledge-based economy*, *borderless economy*, *weightless economy*, and *digital economy*. A unique and curious feature of this new economy is that it seems to defy the basic economic law of scarcity; that is, if a physical object is sold, the seller ceases to own it, but when an idea is sold in the new economy, the seller still possesses it and can sell it over and over again. Hence, the wealth-increasing potential of a single idea or the knowledge it contains is enormous (Rubenstein and Geisler 2003; Spath et al. 2007). Figure 5.2 summarizes the old versus the new economies.

THE ESSENTIALS OF THE KNOWLEDGE-BASED ECONOMY

There are many points of view concerning what the knowledge economy is. Some argue that we have a knowledge economy because knowledge is more important than before as an input "sidelining both capital and labor," as Peter Drucker (1999, 26) has often expressed. Others argue that the knowledge economy is one where knowledge is more important as a product than it has been. There is also discussion about whether the knowledge economy is a new phenomenon or whether it has always existed—the old wine in new bottles debate. Despite the current hype, the idea of a knowledge economy is not in itself an entirely new concept. Knowledge and its uses have always been a critical ingredient of economic success, and knowledge as a construct has been at the root of numerous philosophical debates throughout the ages. However, recent times have seen the importance of knowledge increase. Why?

The world has seen rapid globalization of economic activity, enormous increases in the output of science and technology, and massive growth in the importance of networks and connectivity—all driven by knowledge and its use. In fact, in this emerging economy, knowledge has become the key driver of economic competitiveness and success: it has added massive value to economic production through increases in productivity and the application of new technologies and new ideas—in the form of both new inventions and new applications of existing knowledge. This in turn has brought about revolutionary change to virtually all markets and sectors. In short, the knowledge economy is an economy that creates, disseminates, and uses knowledge to enhance its growth and competitiveness. The emergence of the knowledge economy can be characterized by the increasing role of knowledge as a factor of production and its impact on skills, learning, organization, and innovation. Ultimately, knowledge has become the only key to achieving a sustainable competitive advantage (Beal 2000; Churchman 1971; Kelly 1997; Spath et al. 2007).

WHAT THE KNOWLEDGE ECONOMY IS AND IS NOT

It is a common misconception that the knowledge economy is inevitably about high-tech or information technology (IT). However, the application of new techniques to subsistence farming can increase yields significantly; the use of information and logistical services can allow traditional craft sectors to serve much wider markets than before; the application of environmental technologies and practices can bring the green revolution to developing countries. These are all examples of the knowledge economy in low-tech action. Therefore, the crucial question is how can any economy use appropriate knowledge to improve its productivity and increase welfare. The creation of new knowledge can be relevant in all circumstances—not just in leading-edge scientific discoveries, but more often in straightforward new ideas about how to do simple things better (Sveiby 1997; Tapscott 1997).

The commonly held notion that a knowledge economy is a services economy is also dangerously misleading. As information and knowledge add value to basic products, manufacturing and services are becoming increasingly integrated into complex chains of creation, production, and distribution. At the core of the economy are goods-producing industries linked into value chains, which see inputs coming from knowledge-based business services and goods-related construction and energy industries, and outputs going to goods-related distribution service industries. Industries concerned with the creation, production, and distribution of goods (including manufacturing) remain at the heart of the economy.

The basic enabler in this entire process is actually education, which encourages learning and the exploration of new knowledge, with information and communication technologies (ICTs) providing the mechanisms to exchange knowledge and to reduce the transaction costs associated with the communication and exchange of knowledge. Many advanced and developing economies have already successfully transitioned to an active knowledge-based economy (Diaz and Federico 1970; Lundvall and Johnson 1994).

In the knowledge-based economy, knowledge drives profits for the organizations for gaining and sustaining competitive advantage. Intellectual capital (i.e., employees, their knowledge of products and services, and their creativity and innovation) is a crucial source of knowledge assets. The knowledge-based economy is about adding ideas to products and turning new ideas into new products. Realizing the importance of knowledge assets, many companies have changed their traditional organization's structures. The traditional command-and-control model of management is rapidly being replaced by decentralized teams of individuals motivated by their ownership in the companies.

Perhaps the most dramatic evolution in business over the past decade is the dawn of the new economy. The velocity and dynamic nature of the new marketplace has created a competitive incentive among many companies to consolidate and reconcile their knowledge assets as a means of creating value that is sustainable over time. In order to achieve competitive sustainability, many firms are launching extensive knowledge management efforts. To compete effectively, firms must leverage their existing knowledge and create new knowledge that favorably positions them in their chosen markets (OECD 1996; Porter 1990; Wade 1990).

The new structure of this economy is emerging from the convergence of computing, communications, and content. Products are becoming digital and markets are becoming electronic. Information in all its forms becomes digital. In the old economy, information flow was physical: cash, checks, invoices, bills, reports, face-to-face meetings, analog telephone calls, radio or television transmissions, and so on. A company's assets were also physical: real estate, facilities, plants, office buildings, and inventory.

The knowledge-based economy is based on the application of human know-how to everything that companies produce. Human expertise and ideas create more and more of the economy's added value. The knowledge content of products and services is growing significantly as consumer ideas, information, and technology become part of products. In the new economy, the key assets of the organization are intellectual assets in the form of information, information processing, and knowledge. A hallmark of the new knowledge economy is the ability of organizations to realize economic value from their collection of knowledge assets as well as their assets of information, production distribution, and affiliation. Figure 5.3 summarizes the various notions of the knowledge economy.

Figure 5.3   **A Summary of the Notions of the Knowledge Economy**

- The term *knowledge-based economy*, coined by the Organization for Cooperation and Development, is defined as "directly based on the production, distribution, and use of knowledge and information." (OECD 1996)
- In the knowledge economy, comparative advantage is less a function of natural resources and capital-labor ratios, and more a function of technology and skills.
- The knowledge economy is a process whereby a state or country takes knowledge and converts it into economic gains and welfare improvement.
- KM defines the tools, techniques, and processes used to achieve the goals of the knowledge economy.

ELEMENTS OF THE NEW ECONOMY

Relationships with trading partners, customers and suppliers, distribution networks, intellectual property, patents, image, and so on are all elements of a knowledge economy. These elements represent intellectual capital. Becoming a knowledge-based economy means using knowledge as a core resource for adding value. Organizations have to integrate and leverage intellectual capital in order to participate in the knowledge-based economy (Figure 5.4).

This reality of the new economy presents major challenges to enterprises. Not many enterprises are currently geared to cope with the demands of high-speed operations and high demands of customers. The following business practices are crucial for the success of enterprises in this new economy (Blundell et al. 1995; Westland 2006).

DIGITIZATION

In the old economy, information was analog or physical. In the new economy, information is in digital form. Digital information combining with digital networks for communication has opened a new world of opportunities. Today, vast amounts of information can be squeezed or transmitted at high speed. The Internet is a critical component of the emerging digital economy. In the old economy, the key driver of economic growth was mechanization of production, particularly in manufacturing and agriculture. In the new economy, the key driver will be digitization (using digital information technologies to produce goods and services), particularly using the Internet and other information technologies. The information technology revolution, which was a key spark to ignite the knowledge economy as the discovery of electricity was the key spark to ignite the shift to the industrial economy, is transforming virtually all industries and is central to increased economic efficiency and productivity, higher standards of living, and greater personal empowerment (Baskerville and Smithson 1995).

VIRTUALIZATION AND MOLECULARIZATION

As information shifts from analog to digital, physical things can become virtual—changing the metabolism of the economy, the types of institutions and relationships possible, and the nature of economic activity itself. The industrial hierarchy and economy is giving way to molecular organizations and economic structures. The new enterprise has a molecular structure, and knowledge workers (a human molecule) function as a business unit.

INTEGRATION

The new economy is a networked economy integrating various components such as people, organizations, products, and processes. The new technology networks enable small companies to overcome the main advantage of large companies—economies of scale and access to resources. This network economy is beginning to break down walls among companies—suppliers, customers, and competitors. To conduct business in worldwide markets requires firms to have alliances, collaborations, and integration of business processes with partners. In the new economy, no single firm can do everything. Delivering products and services at efficient costs and time requires a number of firms to come together and integrate their operations (International Labor Organization 2001).

Changes are occurring throughout the world as the economic base moves toward a greater dependence on knowledge and technology. Many nations are improving the knowledge-based economy by promoting and supporting enterprises with necessary infrastructures. Enterprises are embracing alliance and cooperation in order to succeed based on knowledge sharing, as knowledge is becoming the key component for a firm's success (Romer 1990).

SPEED

Responsiveness is the key in e-commerce (electronic commerce) and e-business (electronic business) and is a prime driver of today's knowledge-based economy. Speed, speed, and more speed are central to the knowledge-based economy. Large enterprises can afford to make large investments in technology. These investments enable them to move quickly in targeting new classes of customers. On the other hand, small to medium-sized enterprises can rarely afford to make similar investments. These enterprises must therefore continuously analyze existing market conditions in order to quickly identify and embrace viable emerging opportunities (Sugasawa and Shantha 1999).

GLOBAL DOMAIN

The development of information technology and the vast increases in productivity are only one side of the new economy; the other side is the globalization of markets. Countries now compete with each other for talent as well as for customers. The new technologies provide companies with global markets. Organizations can identify customer segments in many countries and deliver products and services twenty-four hours a day. There are no boundaries for markets or trade.

INTELLECTUAL CAPITALISM

Information and communication technologies are playing a pivotal role in the emergence of intellectual capitalism. The capital of the traditional economy is now being transformed into a new form that can be called intellectual capitalism. In broad terms, intellectual capitalism can be interpreted as resulting from a confluence of a capitalist economy and a knowledge economy in which intellectual capital is dominant (Turpin and Xielin 2000).

KNOWLEDGE ASSETS

A firm's knowledge assets are found primarily in the creativity of its knowledge workers combined with technological and market know-how. Knowledge is embodied in

Figure 5.4 **Elements of the Knowledge Economy**

- Digitization
- Virtualization and molecularization
- Integration
- Speed
- Global domain
- Intellectual capitalism
- Knowledge assets
- Innovations

human beings as human capital, so the success or otherwise of a knowledge-driven economy is based on the capacity of those operating within it to learn. The generation and exploitation of knowledge is now the predominant factor in the creation of wealth. Individuals must acquire and maintain relevant skills. In a successful knowledge economy, businesses as well as individuals must invest in learning. Organizational learning is about the acquisition and effective dissemination and sharing of various types of knowledge, expertise, and experience. As the economy has become increasingly volatile and knowledge-based, success for people, organizations, and entire communities is determined more than ever by the ability to learn and adapt. Society in today's new economy is based around learning and the acquisition of skills, ensuring that the benefits of innovation and change are spread broadly so that all citizens, including those not yet engaged in or benefiting from the new economy, have access to the tools and resources they need to get ahead and stay ahead (United States Department of Commerce 1998).

INNOVATIONS

In the new economy, technology is not just the tool for automation of processes; it is the catalyst for profound change throughout the economy and society. Technological innovation has now become central to survival and growth. In the old economy, information was a scarce resource to which few had access. In the new economy, constant innovations in ever-cheaper information technologies have enabled increasingly ubiquitous access to information, giving individuals greater power to make informed choices. Innovation plays a central role in productivity growth in the new economy. Innovation and productivity are the prerequisites for higher wages and expanded opportunities for workers. However, innovation and change can be disruptive, leading to industrial and economic restructuring in cities and sometimes entire regions, which in turn upsets traditional ways of doing things, making some skills obsolete.

FROM THE PRODUCTION ECONOMY TO THE KNOWLEDGE-BASED ECONOMY

In a production economy (P-economy), land, labor, and capital are the three essentials of production. In the new K-economy, knowledge falls into two key categories as follows: (1) technology, data, and procedures belonging to a firm, such as copyrights

Figure 5.5   **From the P-Economy to the K-Economy**

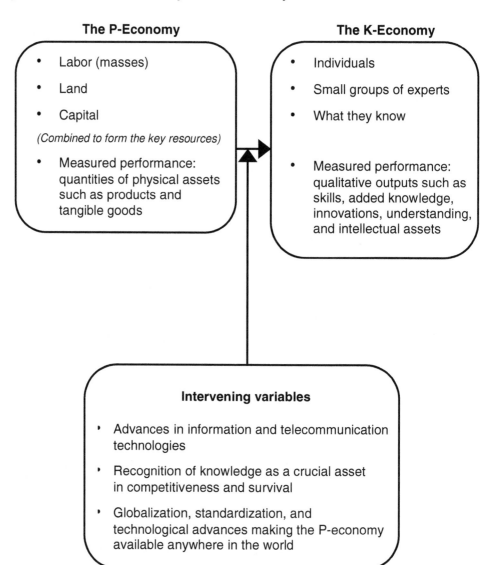

and patents, computer software, databases, networks, and organizational structures, and (2) the human capital of a company. Although ownership may differ, the point to note is that both types of knowledge ultimately depend on people. As the well-respected philosopher C.W. Churchman (1971, 10) notes, "To conceive of knowledge as a collection of information seems to rob the concept of all of its life . . . knowledge resides in the user and not in the collection. It is how the user reacts to a collection of information that matters." Churchman is clearly underscoring the importance of people in the process of knowledge: its acquisition, creation, use, and reuse. What this means it that the K-economy will be a people-powered economy. People will be the company's and the country's biggest assets. People skills, combined with their knowledge, creativity, and ideas, will determine whether a company or a country remains at the cutting edge or languishes in the backwater.

Although knowledge, creativity, and ideas can determine the growth of the economy, the corporation, and the individual, it would be wrong to assume that the K-economy is limited to involvement in computers as well as information and communication technology (ICT). The K-economy also necessitates the development of new tools, new marketing strategies, and new corporate structures that will enable employees to work more efficiently, utilize their knowledge, and empower them in their jobs. Similarly, by enabling a company to cut costs, increase marketing opportunities, and reduce bureaucratic red tape, the K-economy should enhance corporate competitiveness (Rubenstein and Geisler 2003).

Figure 5.5 shows the transition from the P-economy to the K-economy. There were at least three intervening variables that made possible this transition. The first was the tremendous advances in ICT. But there was also a rapidly growing recognition by senior managers in business and government organizations that knowledge is a critical asset for their strategic well being. We emphasize this notion several times in this book because this recognition was a fundamental change in executive perception that made knowledge management possible in the contemporary economy (Westland 2006).

The economic and social phenomena of globalization, standardization, and technological advances also contributed to the transition. Manufacturing and related activities, which depended on the synergetic combination of labor and capital, could now be successfully implemented in hitherto underdeveloped economies. Such integration from the developed to the less developed countries has created a unique opportunity for the more advanced economies to devote their resources to the new area of intellectual development.

Hence, there emerged a situation whereby the *pull* of the intellectual capabilities of the highly skilled workforce combined with the *push* from an economic system denuded of its traditional means of production to open new opportunities for innovation and achievement.

HOW TO CREATE AN ADEQUATE ENVIRONMENT FOR THE KNOWLEDGE ECONOMY

The following three approaches can be used to create the appropriate environment for the knowledge economy:

- Creating a society of skilled, flexible, and creative people with opportunities for quality education and lifelong learning available to all, and a flexible and appropriate mix of public and private funding.
- Building a dynamic information infrastructure that fosters a variety of efficient, competitive information and communications services and tools available to all sectors of society. This includes not only high-end ICTs such as the Internet and

mobile telephony, but also other elements of an information-rich society such as radio, television, and other media and computers and other devices for storing, processing, and using information.

• Creating an efficient innovation system that would bring together firms, science and research centers, universities, think tanks, and other organizations that can tap into and contribute to the growing stock of global knowledge, adapt it to local needs, and use it to create new products, services, and ways of doing business.

CREATING KNOWLEDGE-BASED ORGANIZATIONS

Creating knowledge-based organizations is not an easy exercise, as organizations have to overcome tremendous hurdles in bringing disparate enterprise data sources into a cohesive data warehouse and knowledge management systems. The following activities need to be considered.

ENABLE WIDESPREAD ACCESS OF ICTs

As information technology becomes an increasingly important driver of the new economy (and a determinant of workers' skill requirements) and an increasingly vital tool for accessing information and participating in the new economy, widespread access is essential. Public libraries, schools, job centers, community centers, and all regions of the nation must be connected to the Internet, and individuals must have the skills they need to use these technologies.

DEVELOP LEARNING APPROACHES

The implication of the knowledge economy is that organizations give prime importance to learning and knowledge creation. There are two kinds of knowledge: (1) tacit knowledge, which is gained from experience rather than instilled by formal education and training, and (2) explicit knowledge, which is structured and well documented. In the knowledge economy, tacit knowledge is as important as formal, codified, structured, and explicit knowledge.

In order to take advantage of the knowledge economy, organizations need to become learning organizations. Learning means not only using new technologies to access global knowledge, but also using them to communicate with other people about innovation. In the learning economy, individuals, firms, and countries will be able to create wealth in proportion to their capacity to learn and share innovation. Formal education, too, needs to focus less on passing on information and more on teaching people how to learn and think.

CREATE A CONTINUOUS CYCLE OF DISCOVERY AND DISSEMINATION

Organization learning must be continuous. Organizational learning is the process by which organizations acquire tacit knowledge and experience. Such knowledge is unlikely to be available in codified form, so it cannot be acquired by formal education and training. Instead, it requires a continuous cycle of discovery, dissemination, and the emergence of shared understandings. Successful firms give priority to the need to build a learning capacity, incorporating continuous improvement mechanisms within the organization.

REALIZE THE IMPORTANCE OF INTELLECTUAL CAPITAL

To become knowledge-driven, companies must learn how to recognize changes in intellectual capital that affect the worth of their business and ultimately their balance sheets. A firm's intellectual capital—employees' knowledge, brainpower, know-how, and processes, as well as their ability to continuously improve those processes—is a source of competitive advantage. In the knowledge-based economy, the intangible values of a firm's intellectual capital far outweigh the tangible values of its physical assets, such as buildings or equipment. The physical assets of a firm such as Yahoo, for example, are a tiny proportion of its market capitalization. The difference is its intellectual capital.

FOCUS ON INNOVATION AND KNOWLEDGE NETWORKS

The knowledge economy increasingly relies on the creation, diffusion, and use of knowledge. Hence the success of enterprises and of national economies as a whole will become more reliant upon their effectiveness in gathering, absorbing, and utilizing knowledge, as well as in its creation. A knowledge economy is, in effect, a hierarchy of networks driven by the acceleration of the rate of change and the rate of learning, where the opportunity and capability to get access to and join knowledge-intensive and learning-intensive relations determines the socioeconomic position of individuals and firms. Companies must become learning organizations, continuously adapting management, organization, and skills to accommodate new technologies and grasp new opportunities. They will be increasingly joined in networks, where interactive learning involving creators, producers, and users in experimentation and exchange of information drives innovation. This can only occur given increased attention to the development of knowledge networks (Spath et al. 2007).

INVEST IN KNOWLEDGE AND SKILLS

To spur innovation and equip citizens to succeed in the new economy, government should invest more in the knowledge infrastructure of the twenty-first century: world-class education, training and lifelong learning, science, technology, technology standards, and other intangible public goods. These are the essential drivers of economic progress today. In the new knowledge-based economy, more than two-thirds of economic growth stems from technological innovation. But the knowledge economy is not only about expanding the frontiers of knowledge; it is also about more effective use and implementation of all kinds of knowledge in all kinds of economic activity. In short, competitive success stems from the capacity to innovate. Moreover, skills and learning not only drive economic growth, but also increasingly determine individual opportunity. Investments in education and training, including science and engineering education, are critical to ensuring that companies have the skilled workers they need to be productive and that workers have the skills they need to navigate, adapt, and prosper in the new economy.

CREATE LEARNING ORGANIZATIONS AND INNOVATION SYSTEMS

In a knowledge organization, firms search for linkages to promote interfirm, interactive learning and for outside partners and networks to provide complementary assets. These relationships help firms spread the costs and risks associated with innovation, gain access to new research results, acquire key technological components, and share assets in manufacturing, marketing, and distribution. As they develop new products and processes, firms must determine which activities they will undertake individually; which they must undertake in collaboration with other firms, universities, or research institutions; and which they must undertake with the support of government. Innovation is thus the result of numerous interactions between actors and institutions, which together form an innovation system (Rubenstein and Geisler 2003).

REPLACE BUREAUCRACIES WITH NETWORKS

Organizations should become as fast, responsive, and flexible as the economy and society with which they interact. The new model of managing should be decentralized, nonbureaucratic, catalytic, results-oriented, and empowering. Procedurally, organizations should use information technologies to fundamentally reengineer their processes, providing and improving a wide array of services, increasing efficiency, and cutting costs.

In the old economy, bureaucracy was the characteristic structure of organizations. In the new economy, boundaries of all sorts have blurred. In what has been described as "co-opetition," companies are entering into partnerships and alliances of all forms. Direct competitors in one market may well collaborate on research and development in another market. The collaborative network model requires organizations to relax their often overly rigid bureaucratic program controls and instead rely on incentives, information sharing, competition, and accountability to achieve goals.

THE IMPACT OF THE INTERNET AND OTHER INFORMATION AND COMMUNICATION TECHNOLOGIES ON THE KNOWLEDGE ECONOMY

The impact of the Internet and other ICTs on economic activity is just beginning. ICTs are affecting every single aspect of business. Billions of dollars of the sale and purchase of goods and services are conducted with the help of the Internet and ICTs. Roboticization and computerization are increasingly automating manufacturing and reducing the availability of traditional jobs. Teleworking is growing in size and scope. The Internet is clearly provoking a massive revolution in business, causing companies to reflect on how they can change their infrastructure. The Internet is also decreasing the cost of interactions. Further, the Internet is shrinking time and distance, allowing companies to bring their customers and suppliers inside their business, and creating shared efficiencies and greater loyalty. All the Fortune 500 companies today have a Web site and rely heavily on the Internet as the core element in their strategy. Some companies known as "pure net play" or "dot-com" companies conduct their entire business operation using the Internet, sometimes becoming much bigger than the top Fortune companies. Consider the market valuation of Yahoo, which is about six times greater than that of the *New York Times*. Yahoo, which has no physical distribution system and can update information in real time around the clock, is quickly changing the rules about how information is disseminated around the world. The world, in particular the business world, has been utterly transformed by the Internet.

We believe that in the future the Internet and other ICTs will transform the nature of economic structures through new concepts of e-business. Learning communities of all sizes will grow in concept and participation. The focus of education will shift from content of standard knowledge to connection of diverse ideas. The Internet will allow self-motivated, individualized instruction, emphasizing broad-based application of multimedia as a key learning tool. As a result of the impact of these trends on economic activity, the concept of economic development and the role of the local economic developer will broaden. While continuing to recruit workers and improve a community's educational system, an economic developer will need to work differently to create new capacities for the new knowledge economy.

THE ROLE OF INFORMATION AND COMMUNICATION TECHNOLOGIES IN IMPROVING VALUE CHAINS

A key impact of the technology revolution is the possibility of improving the value chain of an organization and/or the value stream for an industry using ICTs. We shall now discuss the key issues to consider in order to realize these benefits.

ORGANIZATIONAL STRUCTURE

ICTs are transforming organizational structures as well as business processes. They facilitate flatter hierarchies, reduce resource costs by shortening management chains, and break down organizational boundaries between customers and suppliers.

For example, many companies have introduced "virtual team working" worldwide, using the Internet and video conferencing technology. By breaking down hierarchical, functional, and geographical barriers, this strategy has greatly increased their speed of decision making.

SUPPLIER RELATIONS

The Internet gives access to a global pool of suppliers, allowing significant purchasing savings. In addition, e-communication with suppliers drives down the cost of the procurement process. Many companies worldwide are closing their people-intensive purchasing system and changing to technology-based e-procurement systems. The

Internet has thus helped companies save time, effort, and millions of dollars. Many researchers conclude that companies could cut costs by 20 percent by purchasing materials through e-procurement systems and could reduce the time to issue a request for quotation from seven days to two hours.

OPERATIONS

Computer-aided design and manufacturing improve quality, speed up production cycles, and reduce time-to-market for new product developments. Many companies are now linked with their partners through intranets and/or extranets, using computer-aided design to work together in real time. This technology helps them to reduce time delays, hold lower inventories, and create real-time-based enterprises.

MARKETING AND SALES

A digital shop front is much cheaper to maintain than a physical one. The cost to a bank of a funds transfer over the counter is one dollar—but only one cent over the Internet. A Web site allows even the smallest company to operate as an open-all-hours, global business. Many companies today offer secure online ordering from their Web site, increasing turnover enormously, with new orders flooding in from around the world.

DISTRIBUTION

Use of ICTs dramatically reduces the time needed to process orders (by as much as 50 to 90 percent for most firms according to an OECD study). Further, ICTs reduce the need for stock holding. OECD studies estimate that e-commerce means an overall inventory reduction in the United States of $250 to $350 billion (a 20 to 25 percent reduction in current levels).

AFTER-SALES CARE

Use of "smart databases" plus twenty-four–hour access via the Internet enables a better tailored, faster, and more convenient customer care service. Self-service technologies and online ordering, together with e-mail, database technology, electronic accounting procedures, and video conferencing, enable companies to provide a twenty-four–hour interactive customer service.

DRIVERS OF THE KNOWLEDGE ECONOMY

As we show in Figure 5.5, the knowledge economy is emerging from two defining forces: the rise in the *knowledge intensity* of economic activities and the increasing *globalization* of economic affairs. The combined forces of the IT revolution and the increasing pace of technological change are driving the rise in knowledge intensity. We discuss these issues under the following subheadings.

GLOBALIZATION

The other main driver of the emerging knowledge economy is the rapid globalization of economic activities. While there have been other periods of relative openness in the world economy, the pace and extent of the current phase of globalization is without precedent. With the advent of ICTs, the vision of perfect competition is becoming a reality. Consumers can now find out the prices offered by all vendors for any product. Competition is fostered by the increasing size of the market opened up by these technologies. Products with a high knowledge component generate higher returns and a greater growth potential. Competition and innovation go hand in hand.

INFORMATION OR KNOWLEDGE INTENSITY

Efficient production relies on information and know-how; over 70 percent of workers in developed economies are either information or knowledge workers. Many workers use their heads more than their hands. Idea-driven innovation cycles in the knowledge economy determine an economy's position in the global hierarchy. The more innovative and intelligent a business location is, the higher its rank in the ladder of global investment.

NETWORKING AND CONNECTIVITY

Information and communication technologies are the main drivers of the knowledge economy. ICTs are best regarded as the facilitators of knowledge creation in innovative societies. Today, goods and services can be developed, bought, sold, and, in many cases, even delivered over electronic networks. Electronic commerce offers many advantages in cost savings, efficiencies, and market reach over traditional physical methods.

KNOWLEDGE, SKILLS, AND LEARNING

Information and communication technologies have greatly reduced the cost and increased the capacity of organizations to codify knowledge and process and communicate information. In doing so, they have created opportunity for organizations to create a repository of knowledge, skills, and learning. Machines replaced labor in the industrial era, IT will be the locus of codified knowledge in the knowledge economy, and work in the knowledge economy will increasingly demand uniquely human (tacit) skills—such as conceptual and interpersonal management and communication skills.

BEYOND THE KNOWLEDGE ECONOMY

The twenty-first–century economy is all about deploying and obtaining maximum advantage from human and intellectual assets. The knowledge-based economy places great importance on the diffusion and use of information and knowledge as well as its creation. The success of enterprises and of national economies as a whole is ever more reliant upon their effectiveness in gathering and utilizing knowledge. In the first phase of the Information Age, horizontal processes have significantly overshadowed the basic vertical choices of functions, geographies, markets, and products. These include reengineering, supply-chain management, and customer-relationship management. Though it is still too soon to predict the next phase, the changes in management style and organization already are pointing toward the following shifts:

- From linear to network
- From hierarchy to network
- From integrated to distributed
- From independent to interdependent
- From mergers to alliances

Based on these changes, it is easy to conclude that the business of the future will be networked, distributed, interdependent, and built on alliances. In the decade ahead, the telecommunications infrastructure (both wired and wireless) will become much stronger worldwide, and many new computing platforms and operating systems probably will emerge. With these changes, information is likely to migrate from commodity to utility.

In the last ten years, the Internet has become an essential and growing part of everyday life in many societies. In the course of one generation, beginning in the 1970s, the world entered the Information Age. It was an age dominated by the transmission, processing, and use of information and knowledge in private life as well as in education and work. The framework of information and knowledge is driven by information and communication technology, which includes computers, network infrastructures, and, more recently, mobile communication. Knowledge, and the ability to create, access, and use it effectively, has long been a tool of innovation, competition, and economic success and a key driver of economic and social development. Yet several dramatic changes in recent years have fundamentally increased the importance of knowledge and the competitive edge that it gives to those who harness it quickly and effectively. The ability to process and transmit information, globally and instantaneously, has increased exponentially per unit of cost in recent years due to the combined effect of advances in computing (microprocessor) speed, competition, innovation, and lower costs in global communications networks.

Networks and geographical clusters of firms are a particularly important feature of the knowledge economy. Firms find it increasingly necessary to work with other firms and institutions in technology-based alliances because of the rising cost, increasing complexity, and widening scope of technology.

Many firms are becoming multitechnology corporations locating around centers of excellence in different countries. Despite improved capability in global communication, firms increasingly co-locate because it is the only effective way to share understanding (tacit knowledge). Consequently, skills and lifestyle are becoming increasingly important location factors. The innovation system and its "knowledge distribution power" are critically important in the knowledge economy. Learning is increasingly central for both people and organizations. Learning organizations are increasingly networked knowledge-based organizations.

LEARNING OUTCOMES

- Advances in information technologies, globalization, and recognition by managers that knowledge has become a crucial resource and organizational asset primarily drove the transition from the traditional economy to the knowledge economy.
- The knowledge economy is digital, virtual, molecularized, and integrated. It is also speedier than traditional economic systems, has a global reach, relies on intellectual assets, and is highly innovative.

DISCUSSION QUESTIONS

1. What are the key characteristics of the knowledge economy, and how does it differ from production economies?
2. What was the process of transition from the P-economy to the K-economy? Describe the drivers of the transition and the intervening variables.
3. What are the factors necessary for the creation of knowledge-based organizations?

6 The Knowledge-Based Enterprise

KEY LEARNING OUTCOMES

You will know you have mastered the material in this chapter when you can define and explain the following:

1. The attributes of the knowledge-based enterprise.
2. How the knowledge-based enterprise is different from other forms of organizations.
3. The characteristics of the structure and key processes of the knowledge-based enterprise.

In the previous chapter we identified some key attributes of knowledge and its structure. We also defined the knowledge-based economy. If indeed knowledge is becoming the key asset of the current and future organization, it is essential to define and carefully examine the organizational setting within which the phenomenon is taking place. The processes by which knowledge is captured, stored, manipulated, and diffused occur within the contemporary enterprise, including businesses, government organizations, and not-for-profit enterprises (Chatzkel 2003).

In this chapter we encounter the nature of the knowledge-based enterprise (KBE). We will identify the processes needed for the KBE to absorb, implement, and use knowledge. How does the KBE exercise its strategic management and its human resources management? What makes the KBE different from other types of organizations? We also will examine the emergence of the new executive role of chief knowledge officer (CKO).

Knowledge-based organizations are the vehicle through which knowledge is distributed and shared in the society and the economy. These KBEs are the contemporary workplaces where individuals and groups congregate and conduct their labor and their business activities, thus exchanging their knowledge. Within these KBEs emerge knowledge systems, which serve as the mechanisms for transacting in knowledge as the new form of competitive asset in organizations.

CHARACTERISTICS OF KNOWLEDGE-BASED ENTERPRISES

What exactly are KBEs? How different or similar are they to other, more traditional organizations? It is reasonable to assume that even before the 1990s, organizations transacted in knowledge and that knowledge played an important role in their survival and market competitiveness. What then made the difference and allowed us to identify this special type of organization we now call the KBE?

The state of the literature presently offers little help in our understanding of this process. Fuller (2002), for example, provides a comprehensive description of the historical, social, economic, and organizational antecedents of knowledge management (KM). The development of this discipline is undoubtedly very closely tied to the emergence of the KBE, at least in a form that promotes a better definition of such organizations as based on knowledge rather than on capital or labor (Groff and Jones 2003; Hildreth and Kimble 1999).

The picture that emerges from the literature on KM suggests that the KBE is a type of organization designed to support a flow of knowledge and transactions in knowledge with fewer constraints than in traditional organizations (Bahrami and Evans 2004; Stewart 2003). The main driver for such a flexible structure seems to be the need of the enterprise to innovate in order to survive and compete effectively in the contemporary environment (Leonard-Barton 1998; Tissen et al. 2000).

Figure 6.1 shows the key characteristics of the KBE. These are attributes fostered by the highly volatile environment that today's enterprises have to face. Knowledge thus becomes a modus operandi of these enterprises, allowing them to compete in this volatility. The question remains: Is this type of enterprise a result of the emerging role of knowledge, or is the role of knowledge in such a structure enhanced to an extent that allows the enterprise to survive?

The characteristics of the KBE give a picture of an organization that recognizes the role of knowledge and creates mechanisms to allow it to flourish and to be transacted with relative ease. In response to the exigencies of the highly volatile environment of today's enterprises, the KBE is, by and large, a flexible, open system in search of better ways to transact with its relevant and increasingly changing environment. This mode of structure and operations defines an organization that is able to adapt to frequent changes in its relevant environment. As the world becomes smaller and more accessible and as information and telecommunication technologies are drastically improved, an organization wishing to remain competitive must rely on a nonrigid framework and on mechanisms to absorb and utilize knowledge (Aguayo 2004; Andriessen 2003; Schwartz 2006).

The KBE is also characterized by its unique culture and the perspective of its senior managers. In order to compete and to survive, the culture of a KBE must encourage and promote the unrestrained flow of knowledge. In practice, this entails the removal of barriers to such a flow and the favoring of incentives to the creation, import, and exchange of knowledge. Successful KBEs seem to have a culture that supports knowledge exchange in a very broad manner, not necessarily for selected types of knowledge or for specific and well-defined objectives (King 2007; Stankovsky 2005).

Figure 6.1 **Characteristics of the KBE**

Current Key Environmental Attributes

- High volatility
- Globalization
- Increased outsourcing
- Decline of role of manufacturing
- Emergence of enterprise information systems
- Increased role and capabilities of communications and computing technologies

Some Characteristics of the KBE

- Flexible structure
- Informal processes
- Enhanced communication network
- Culture favoring the transaction and exchange of knowledge
- Senior management cognizant of the key role of knowledge and supportive of its applications in the enterprise
- Structures and processes devised to transact in knowledge, such as cooperation, joint ventures, and exchanges of personnel with other enterprises
- Knowledge considered a key strategic asset of the enterprise

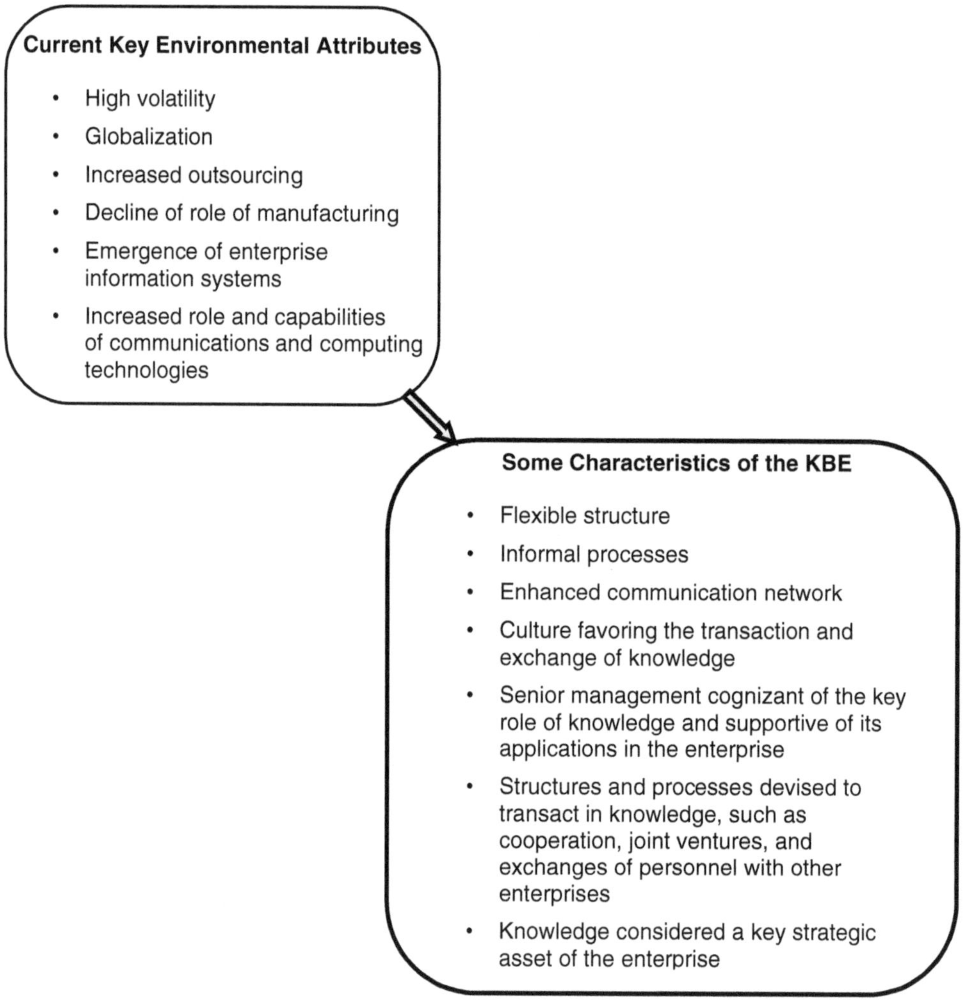

KNOWLEDGE-BASED ENTERPRISES VERSUS RESEARCH AND DEVELOPMENT AND TECHNOLOGY ORGANIZATIONS

There are many similarities between KBEs and organizations primarily engaged in research and development (R&D) and technology in general. These technology-based organizations have been intensely studied since the 1950s. The characteristics of these organizations are similar to those we identify in Figure 6.1 for KBEs (Thamhain 2005). They include senior management support, a propensity for flexibility and agility, a structure and processes that are conducive to innovation, and a culture that promotes KM and the management of technology (Ettlie 2000; Rubenstein 1989).

What is then the similarity between the R&D/technology-based organization and the KBE, and what is the meaning of this similarity? It is a known fact that researchers who studied R&D and technology management have naturally migrated to the study of KM (Leonard and Swap 2005; Wickramasinghe and von Lubitz 2007). Some scholars have considered knowledge to be a form of technology and believe that the role of knowledge and its value as a crucial asset for the enterprise equals that of technology. It may also be possible that the variables and frameworks of KM systems in the KBE are modeled after those developed earlier for technology-based organizations (Geisler 2008; Kendal and Creen 2006; Nissen 2006).

Many of the KBEs recently studied are also technology-based organizations. In their quest for dynamics, agility, and competitive position in rapidly changing markets, these organizations need timely and varied inputs of knowledge (Colling and Dankbaar 2003; Harris 2005). It therefore stands to reason that enterprises engaged in transactions in a technology-based environment will also be highly preoccupied with the knowledge they possess. These enterprises have been transacting in knowledge for many years, but only recently have researchers been able to conceptually (and empirically) identify and attempt to model this phenomenon.

In other words, we have not suddenly discovered the knowledge-based enterprise. To a large extent it has always existed—albeit under the radar of management researchers, since the focus of their studies was the *technology*-based enterprise, which had always existed in a volatile environment of discovery and innovation (Burgelman et al. 2003).

As organizations that emphasize innovation, mobility, and adaptation to changing market conditions, KBEs are a new and different form that describes the technology-based organization. This new description emphasizes a different aspect of the competitive key asset of the enterprise: knowledge. In this sense, it is no longer sufficient for the enterprise to control its technological resources. It now behooves the enterprise to also manage its knowledge in order to compete, prosper, and survive (Colling and Dankbaar 2003).

THE KNOWLEDGE-BASED ENTERPRISE: STRATEGIC MANAGEMENT AND COMPETITIVENESS

The KBE resorts to the asset of the knowledge it possesses in order to achieve desired competitive position in the marketplace (Fuller 2002). In its quest for a strategic positioning in a volatile environment, the KBE monitors its relevant environment and searches for knowledge of different types from the various entities upon which it depends or which influence its existence (Burgelman et al. 2003).

Figure 6.2 shows the six types of entities that the KBE monitors and from which it absorbs the knowledge it needs for survival and growth. The figure also shows the attributes that a KBE must possess so it can indeed process such inputs of knowledge.

Figure 6.2   **How the KBE Monitors Knowledge in Its Environment**

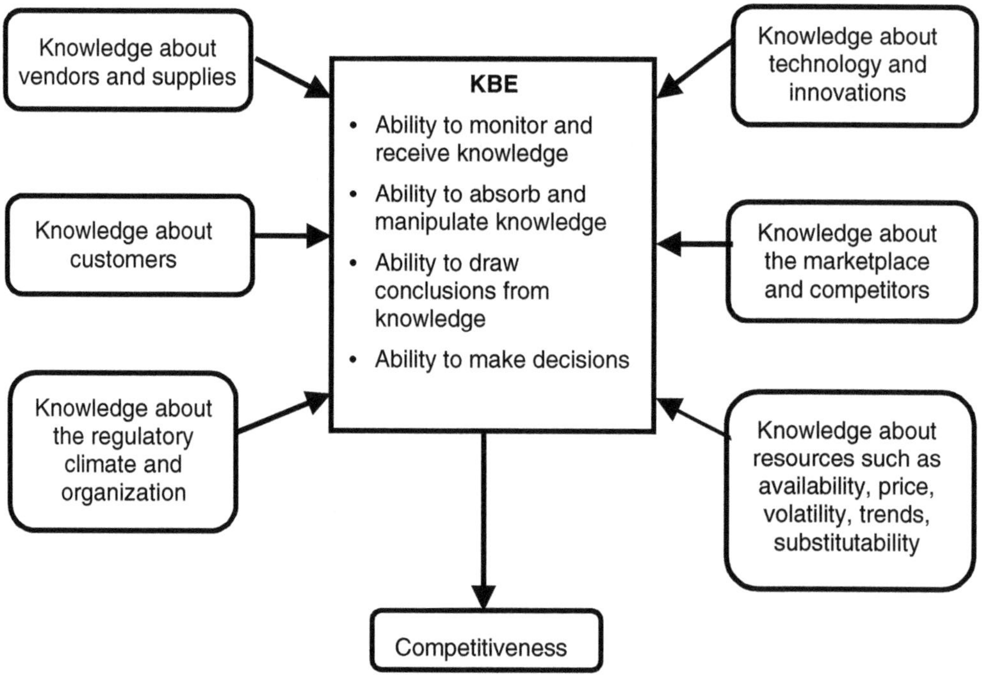

KNOWLEDGE ABOUT SUPPLIES

The KBE monitors its vendors and suppliers. It needs knowledge about the following aspects of its supplier base:

1. What fluctuations are there in the health of key suppliers, such as rate of deliveries and the general health of the corporation?
2. Are alternative suppliers available and competent?
3. What are the possibilities of joint effort and collaboration with suppliers in research, development, innovation, and production?
4. What are the economic and financial considerations in regard to suppliers, such as cost, cost-efficiencies, and comparison with alternatives?
5. Are suppliers delivering adequate quality? What are the barriers to their performance if the quality of deliveries is not in the acceptable range?
6. What is the value to the organization of various strategies, such as retaining the vendor or supplier, expanding the relationship with the vendor or supplier, terminating the relationship, or substituting another vendor or supplier?
7. What is the relationship, what are the correlations, and what are the particular values accrued to the organization's knowledge base from the various vendors and suppliers, and how will trends in their relative growth influence the future stream of knowledge they currently provide?

KNOWLEDGE ABOUT CUSTOMERS

1. What is the composition of the customer base; what are the various segments to which the organization markets or caters?
2. What are the trends in these segments? Are they on a growth or contrition pattern? Are their tastes or preferences changing, and if so, in which direction and by how much?
3. What is customers' level of satisfaction with the products or services they receive from the organization? What are the fluctuations in this level of satisfaction? Are such fluctuations within acceptable benchmarks or standards? If they are not, what conclusion can be drawn?
4. What variables drive the satisfaction or dissatisfaction of the customer base? Is such sentiment anchored in basic issues, such as product design, or in less fundamental problems, such as one-time delivery tardiness?
5. Has such knowledge about the sentiments and reactions of the customer been absorbed in the enterprise? Has it been presented to senior management? Has such sentiment resulted in loss of sales, decline in market share, or wholesale migration of customers to competitors?

KNOWLEDGE ABOUT REGULATORS

The more complex the environment of the KBE, the more it will be the target of regulators. These usually include safety regulations, environmental protection regulations, information flow and protection (such as HIPPA in the health care industry), and transparency in reporting and corporate ethics (such as the Sarbanes-Oxley Act and the European Union's Global Reporting Initiative). These regulatory and procedural requirements are particularly crucial for KBEs, which must closely monitor changes and updates in the regulatory climate and in the specific regulations. More specifically, these organizations will procure and collect knowledge to answer the following questions:

1. What are the most recent changes in regulations, rules, procedures, and legal challenges that are relevant to the enterprise?
2. What are the implications of these changes for the enterprise, such as added cost, human resources, need for specialized skills, and focus and attention of senior management?
3. What is the level of compliance maintained by the enterprise with the various types of regulatory requirements? How would changes in compliance affect the enterprise? For example, will increased compliance result in added prestige and customers? Would reduction in compliance trigger legal challenges and social discomfort in the industry and the market? What might be the financial and legal implications of such actions on the part of the enterprise?
4. What is the degree of relevance, accuracy, and connectivity of knowledge collected by the enterprise on the regulatory climate and on specific regulatory bodies and their activities?

KNOWLEDGE ABOUT TECHNOLOGY AND INNOVATION

The KBE is largely defined as an organization that transacts in knowledge as a producer, seller, or transformer of knowledge (Brown 2001). Since knowledge is found in the relevant environment of the enterprise and transported to it in order to enhance competitiveness in the volatile environment, technological innovation would be considered a key instrument in achieving this strategic advantage. This is particularly true in technology-based enterprises (Tsoukas 1996).

KBEs need to maintain a very current position on monitoring developments in technology and innovation in their environment. Enterprises that transact in knowledge as a key strategic resource must be constantly aware of developments that might transform the balance of demand and supply in their industry or affect their products and services.

Consider, for example, a company manufacturing and selling a sophisticated medical system. The system is based on a given technological innovation that the company had devised and in which it has intellectual property rights. The technology relies on optical processes. Consider now that a small company is innovating a new technology based on electromagnetic field instead of optical processes. This innovation, once commercialized, may result in new, perhaps improved and more versatile medical systems. Unless our focal company is aptly aware of this innovation and its potential repercussion in the industry, the company may well face challenges with dire consequences to its position in the marketplace. The enterprise would therefore need to monitor the following types of knowledge and associated issues:

1. What is the state of technology in the key technologies embedded in the enterprise's line of products and services?
2. Who are the key players in the industry who are engaged in R&D and new product development in these technologies? What has been their progress? What are the prospects (probabilities) of technical *and* commercial success in any of their relevant projects?
3. What does the enterprise know to date about alternative technologies to those currently being used in its line of products or services? What are the financial and organizational implications of the possibility of implementing these alternatives? What are the economic and other implications (including risk) of *not* implementing alternative technologies?
4. What might be the learning curves for updating, modernizing, and expanding the current technologies in the enterprise's products and services?
5. What are the contributions of existing technologies owned by the enterprise to the state of innovation of the enterprise? What is missing, if any, in this relationship? What changes need to be made? Are the enterprise and its senior managers aware of these circumstances? (Anand et al. 2007)
6. What are the contributions of the existing stock of technologies (and perhaps also knowledge about developments in technology and innovations in the marketplace) to the strategic position of the enterprise, to its planning, and to its constituents?

KNOWLEDGE ABOUT THE MARKETPLACE AND COMPETITORS

All organizations, especially those depending on knowledge or working within a volatile environment, must be well aware of the characteristics and trends in their marketplace (Hansen et al. 1999). They need knowledge that will allow them to confront competitive challenges by providing answers to the following questions:

1. What are the trends in the marketplace? How are the competitors doing? Have there been changes in the composition of the market share among competitors? If so, what kind of changes and what are their significance and implications for the enterprise?
2. What are the current and prospective innovations in products and services that competitors are launching or preparing to launch in the marketplace?
3. How prepared is the enterprise to confront and respond to changes in the marketplace? Does the enterprise possess the necessary tools, such as adequate planning, slack resources, and executive acumen, to compete effectively in a volatile marketplace?

KNOWLEDGE ABOUT RESOURCES

The KBE depends on a steady input of resources and their effective application to achieve organizational goals (Anand et al. 2007). The resource-based view of the firm is a model that provides a strategic perspective of the enterprise by emphasizing its ability to procure and utilize the resources it needs (Ketchen et al. 2007).

The KBE is particularly dependent upon knowledge about the resources it needs to maintain the level and quality of the skills required for effective transactions in knowledge. This means that the enterprise must monitor its relevant environment for knowledge about the availability, cost, volatility, trends, and substitutability of its knowledge-based resources (Martin 2007; Sutcliffe and Weber 2003). The following queries must therefore be answered:

1. Are resources such as export workers (knowledge workers) available, affordable, and possessing of the skills and knowledge currently needed or planned by the enterprise?
2. Is there a plan of action to prepare, train, and absorb such knowledge-based human resources? Are there currently, or in planning, cooperative programs with colleges and universities? Are there now, or in planning, programs of internal updating and development of knowledge-based human resources? Are there now, or in planning, any incentives, grants, or specific programs to encourage knowledge workers to improve and to update their skills?
3. Are there programs in place or in planning to recruit, train, and update managers at all levels?
4. What is the state of monitoring resources, such as knowledge? Are the systems or programs that the enterprise currently utilizes an effective tool in procuring knowledge? Are there problems in connectivity or other technological

barriers to the ability of the enterprise to access knowledge systems in other organizations in its environment?

5. Are there procedures and standards in place or in planning to attain possible substitutes for the resources that the enterprise needs but cannot access or implement? In particular, this refers to substitutes for knowledge-based resources.

CAPABILITIES OF THE KNOWLEDGE-BASED ENTERPRISE

Armed with the various types of knowledge described in Figure 6.2 and listed above, the KBE must be able to absorb and analyze this knowledge in order to draw conclusions and provide useful input to its decision-making process, hence to its competitiveness (Cohen 2006). These capabilities of the KBE are themselves dependent on the effectiveness of the monitoring and procurement of knowledge from the environment.

The KBE is thus engaged in an ongoing process of transacting in knowledge as a critical resource that fuels its internal capabilities to continue to transact in knowledge and to accomplish its organizational objectives. For the KBE, therefore, knowledge is more than simply one type of resource that complements other inputs in the discharge of the goals of the enterprise. Rather, knowledge for the KBE represents the lifeblood of its existence. Knowledge animates its processes, constitutes its learning processes, and supports its functioning as a viable enterprise (Starbuck 1992).

THE ROLE OF MANAGEMENT IN THE KNOWLEDGE-BASED ENTERPRISE

Managing an organization in a volatile market environment is a difficult task (Narayanan 2001). It is even more arduous in the KBE (Poston and Speier 2005). The role of management, both at the middle and senior levels, is extremely complex, due to a combination of factors. These drivers of managerial roles and tasks in the KBE are shown in Figure 6.3. The figure is an extension of Figure 6.2 on page 88, in which we showed how the KBE monitors its environment.

Managers in the KBE have the role of *arbiters* on the type of knowledge to be gathered by the organization. They decide what categories of knowledge should be pursued and from which sources they should be procured. This is a complex and critical role, primarily because it determines the knowledge base that the organization will henceforth possess and from which it will extract what it needs for the strategic management of its future (Allen 2003; Kaplan and Norton 2004).

Managers in the KBE also have the role of *integrators* of the knowledge being gathered from the external environment of the organization. They decide on how the various knowledge bases are to be compiled and integrated into a useful system. They also decide on the establishment of a knowledge management system (KMS), particularly by selecting the type of functions this system will perform and its relation to the mission, strategic goals, and key activities of the enterprise (Yeh and Lung-Hung 2007).

Once knowledge is codified and stored in the KMS, managers need to *interpret*

Figure 6.3 **Managerial Roles and Tasks in the KBE**

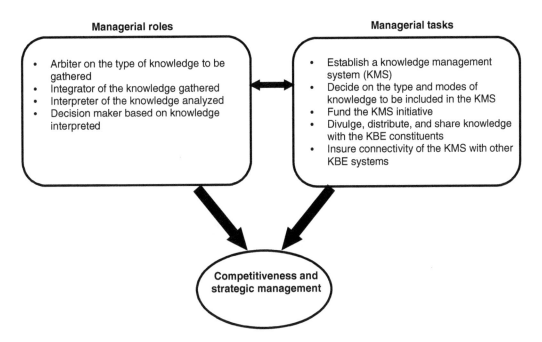

what is known by the enterprise. This also includes the knowledge that is embedded in the individual members of the enterprise. Managers are called upon to "make sense" of the knowledge thus accumulated and to draw useful conclusions (Southon et al. 2002). This is a complex process that requires managers not only to understand the organizational phenomena that such knowledge indicates, but also to possess a measure of intuition and creativity (Kaplan and Norton 2004).

The interpretation of knowledge by managers is a process anchored in the complexities of strategic management. Managers interpret the "vision" of the enterprise and its strategic objectives. From these broad assessments, they determine the meaning to be extracted from the knowledge base of the enterprise (Schilling 2006). To accomplish such a complex process, firms need adequate organizational frameworks and linkages in which strategies can be interpreted and successfully implemented by lower levels of managers. We discuss some of these issues in Chapters 8 and 9.

Managers in the KBE also channel the knowledge they interpret into their *decision-making* processes. This role is crucial in ascertaining that the enterprise functions properly and that the decisions made at all levels are based on knowledge about phenomena both inside the enterprise and in its external environment (Lehr and Rice 2002).

THE EMERGENCE OF THE CHIEF KNOWLEDGE OFFICER

In recent years some enterprises have introduced the managerial roles of CKO and chief learning officer (CLO). These positions are designed to foster the use of knowledge

Figure 6.4   **The Role of the CKO**

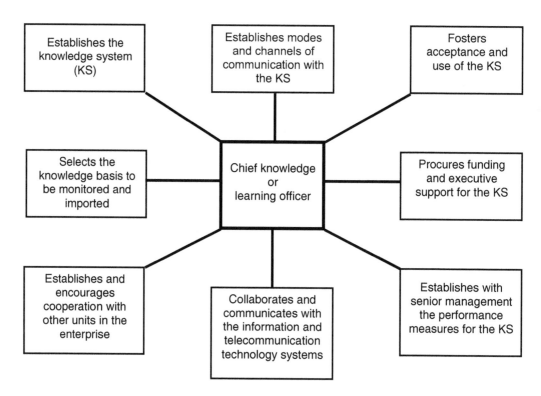

systems in KBEs and to provide legitimacy and organizational support for the role that KM plays in the strategic management of the enterprise (Kerfoot 2006).

A much-heralded example is the case of Jack Welch, the former chief executive officer of General Electric. Welch credited much of his success to his ability to promote KM as an integral component of his leadership in the company (Lakshman 2005). This and other success stories of the role of CKO have added support to a growing belief that this new organizational position is rapidly spreading across corporations (Pearce and Manz 2005).

THE ROLE OF THE CHIEF KNOWLEDGE OFFICER

Figure 6.4 shows the different aspects of the role of the CKO in the KBE. This figure is a more detailed version of Figure 6.3. It lists the more focused functions of the manager who is charged with the knowledge base of the enterprise and with the learning that is derived from such a system of knowledge.

The CKO position in the KBE involves all aspects of the knowledge system and the KMS in the organization. The CKO (at least in theory) is responsible for the establishment of these systems, their operation, and their performance. This entails a complex array of decisions and judgment calls about the nature of the knowledge to be transacted in the organization and the modes, methods, and channels used in such transactions.

The CKO is also considered the CLO. This aspect of the position includes the responsibility for drawing conclusions from the knowledge transacted by and within the enterprise and for the distribution of such conclusions and lessons throughout the organization. It behooves the CKO (or CLO) to negotiate not only the knowledge system itself, but also the organizational hurdles to its successful utilization and distribution among the critical units in the enterprise.

IS THE CHIEF KNOWLEDGE OFFICER DIFFERENT FROM THE CHIEF INFORMATION OFFICER?

Another responsibility of the CKO in the KBE is the overall management of the knowledge systems (or KMS), including the utilization of the knowledge. In this the CKO differs substantially from the traditional chief information officer (CIO). The emphasis on content, in addition to the technical composition of the system, endows the CKO with ownership over the content.

CIOs generally manage the information system and are in charge of its technical foundations and the smooth operation of its components. Their areas of responsibility are focused on the technology and the channels through which information flows in the enterprise, but not on the content of the information flow. In one financial institution, for example, the CIO engaged information consultants to design and implement a management information system. After several months, the CIO opted to replace the consultants with an in-house group. He explained his action by stating "the information systems consultants lacked basic understanding of what kind of information will flow through the system. They are not financial people."[1] This statement clearly reveals the distinction between the *technology* and the *content*.

But such a distinction is difficult to maintain in a knowledge system. Since such systems are in their infancy and firms still lack adequate experience with their application in the organization, it is therefore left to the CKO to initiate and plan not only the technical composition of a knowledge system but also to influence the content of the transactions within the system. Does this make the CKO an expert on all matters and organizational functions in which knowledge is transacted? Clearly, this is not the case. The CKO serves as a facilitator in the management of organizational knowledge (Grant 1996). Unlike the technical focus of the CIO, the CKO is instrumental in establishing the knowledge system and is also responsible for facilitating its utilization. This broadening of the CKO role (as compared with the CIO) contributes to the difficulties that the CKO encounters when it is time to assess the performance and successful application of the knowledge system.

CRITICAL SUCCESS FACTORS IN THE PERFORMANCE OF THE CHIEF KNOWLEDGE OFFICER

The CKO's performance is assessed by the enterprise along four key dimensions. These are shown in Figure 6.5. The dimensions cover the spectrum of the roles that

Figure 6.5   **Critical Success Factors of the CKO**

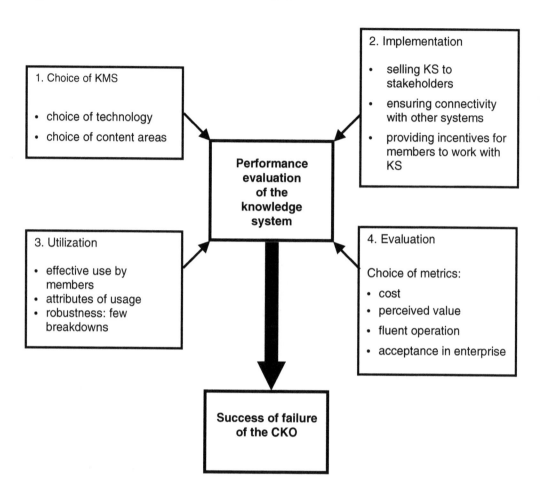

the CKO plays (listed in Figure 6.4), from the establishment of the knowledge system all the way to its utilization by management.

CHOICE OF THE SYSTEM

The first critical success factor is the *choice of the system.* This is usually a difficult endeavor, for the CKO has to decide or at least be instrumental in the selection of the technology as well as the content areas for the knowledge to be transacted by the system. Poor choices may only be evident or measurable down the line, after the system has been installed and in operation. Failure to make the correct choice or even to make a flawless choice will impact negatively on the assessment of the CKO's performance.

IMPLEMENTATION OF THE SYSTEM

The *implementation* of the system is another critical success factor. The CKO must sell the system to the various stakeholders, successfully connect the system to other systems in the enterprise, and provide effective incentives for potential users.

Each of these variables represents a major undertaking on the part of the CKO. Failure in any one of these actions may hinder the successful implementation of a knowledge system (Rubenstein and Geisler 2003). As with the initial choice of a system, in these variables much depends on the cooperation and support of other parties, such as senior and middle management. Much also depends on the willingness of organizational members to accept a knowledge system and to participate in it (by depositing knowledge and extracting knowledge they need for their functioning within the enterprise).

UTILIZATION OF THE SYSTEM

The third success factor is the *utilization* of the knowledge system. The CKO is evaluated on the basis of how well the system has been utilized by organizational stakeholders (Herschel and Nemati 2000). This factor largely depends on how members of the enterprise use the system. It also depends on the various attributes of usage, such as inputs versus outputs of knowledge deposited and extracted, number of searches per time period, and the robustness of the system. If the technology holds with few malfunctions and breakdowns, and if organizational members indeed use the system, there is a good chance that the CKO will be positively assessed on the basis of this factor.

EVALUATION

Finally, the CKO will be assessed by the choice of metrics agreed upon between the CKO and the KBE. The metrics may include cost, value from the system as perceived by users and management, how well the system operates, and how the system was accepted by users. These and other metrics are described in Part III of this book.

THE THEORY AND THE REALITY

The prevailing wisdom in the literature stresses the need for a CKO and exalts the benefits that a knowledge system offers the KBE. There is also widespread agreement among writers that the CKO has a solid platform from which to operate and achieve success. In practice, however, the reality is different and less optimistic.

DeSouza and Raider (2006) have described the phenomenon whereby organizations cut costs by eliminating or cutting back on the efforts of the CKO within the enterprise. They argue that organizations view knowledge management as a luxury and thus feel justified in discontinuing the KM effort whenever economic conditions are in decline in the enterprise.

The reality of KM and the role of the CKO seem quite different from the promis-

Figure 6.6   **Factors Contributing to Lack of Success of CKOs and Knowledge Systems**

- CKOs lack clear and measurable outcomes.
- CKOs are responsible for content as well as technology, which makes it difficult for them to control.
- CKOs success factors are linked to the success of the knowledge system, which may be beyond their personal reach and control.
- CKOs take ownership of the knowledge system, and then frequently move to other functions or organizations, thus contributing to a general lack of procedures and continuity in institutionalizing the KM effort.
- CKOs generally fail to "sell" the knowledge effort as crucial for the survival of the enterprise.
- CKOs usually agree to a biased, even wrong set of performance and success metrics.

ing scenario of the CKO as a key official in the KBE. Several factors may explain the discrepancy between the crucial role that we believe the CKO plays in the enterprise and the reality of the lack of measurable successes of CKOs (Rubenstein and Geisler 2003; Zack 2003). Figure 6.6 lists some of the salient reasons for such lack of success.

As we see in Figure 6.6, the lack of success in the performance of many CKOs is due to a combination of two sets of variables. The first is the nature of the knowledge system. It involves the mix of technology and content, which both have to be well chosen and well implemented. It also involves human nature: organizational members may at best ignore the knowledge system and, in the worst case, even reject it by not depositing their knowledge into the system and by not using it as frequently as managers would wish or predict. The result is a negative impression of the CKO.

The second set of variables is the inability of some CKOs to market their system to their stakeholders. Part of the problem is the fuzzy nature of knowledge and the difficulties in defining and measuring value from knowledge in a manner that will convince stakeholders and make the knowledge system an attractive organizational asset.

In summary, the KBE depends for its strategic success on its knowledge system and its CKO. In reality, however, several factors we discussed in this chapter seem to interfere with the smooth operation of a knowledge system. In essence, regardless of how successful the knowledge system and the CKO are in the enterprise, almost all the members of the organization are increasingly becoming *knowledge workers*. They are discussed in Chapter 7.

LEARNING OUTCOMES

- The KBE depends on the existence of shared knowledge in the organization in the form of a knowledge system, administered by the CKO or a similar position.
- Although CKOs are crucial to the strategic survival of the KBE, in reality many organizations underestimate their value and in rough economic times tend to downsize or even eliminate the position.

DISCUSSION QUESTIONS

1. What are the key attributes of the KBE, and how is this enterprise different from other organizations?
2. What are the mechanisms by which the KBE manages its strategic objectives and its internal processes? List and discuss three such mechanisms.
3. Why is there a distinction between the theory that CKOs are crucial to the KBE and the reality whereby CKOs have a high rate of failure and are not adequately assessed by their organizations?

NOTE

1. Personal communication.

Knowledge Workers

7 The Management of Human Capital

KEY LEARNING OUTCOMES

*You will know you have mastered the material in this chapter
when you can define and explain the following:*

1. The nature of human capital.
2. Knowledge workers and the creation of wealth.
3. How we manage knowledge workers.

It would be presumptuous on our part to declare that we just invented the notion of knowledge workers and human capital. This concept has long been the topic of research in the areas of research and development (R&D) and technology management (Badawy 1982; Carayannis 2001; Rubenstein 1989). Scholars researching the processes of research, development, innovation, and technology have long recognized the special functions of scientists and engineers and the role they play in technology-based organizations.

These early studies recognized the value of the human input into the R&D and innovation process and hence the value to the enterprise. It became abundantly clear that scientists and engineers represent a highly skilled workforce and that what they know (rather than financial capital or other types of workforces) constitutes the core of the enterprise and its competitive position in the marketplace (Abbott 1988). Even before the ubiquitous appearance of the term *knowledge workers*, scholars who studied scientists and engineers had identified their knowledge as human capital. The pioneering work of Ralph Katz (1988, 2003) explored the management of knowledge in the innovative organization. This was thought to be accomplished via such processes as technology transfer and the management of technical communication between individuals and within the framework of innovative project teams.

These early scholars devised several concepts, such as "professionals," "technology-based human resources," and "innovative work teams," to identify the phenomenon of human capital in the technology organization. These key concepts described the processes by which expert workers in science and engineering contributed to innovation, new products and services, and hence to the performance and success of the enterprise (Cano and Cano 2006; Mello 2002).

CONTRIBUTIONS OF EARLY RESEARCH

The management of R&D and technology workers was a prolific area of study from the 1980s to the mid-1990s. In Figure 7.1 we attempt to summarize the salient findings from this extensive body of research.

Figure 7.1 **Contributions of Research on R&D/Technology Workers to the Study of Knowledge Workers**

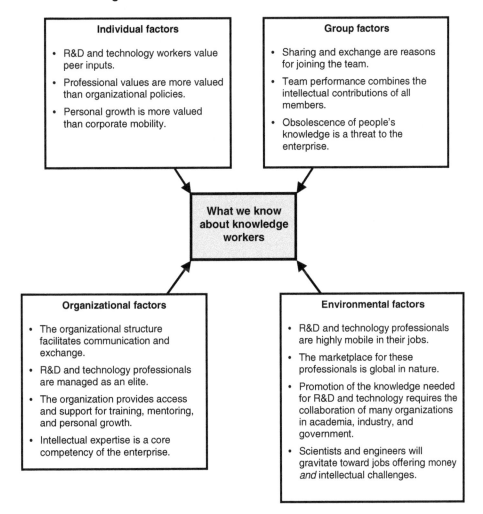

INDIVIDUAL FACTORS

The early literature produced several findings concerning the personal attributes of R&D and technology professionals. These professionals view their peers (both inside and outside their organization) as their core group that inspires them and whose norms and requirements they adopt and satisfy. This early research also revealed that these science and technology professionals place substantial value on their personal and intellectual growth, often at the expense of the needs and policies of their own organizations, particularly when their need for power collides with organizational policies. These professionals look to their peers in the profession for guidance and support. Thus, professional organizations are a critical resource for scientists and engineers (Angle 1989; Cortada 1998; Quinn et al. 1997).

TEAMWORK FACTORS

Prior research has found that science and technology professionals join work groups and remain as members when they can share and exchange knowledge (Bahrami and Evans 1997). In addition, team performance is closely tied to the intellectual contributions of the members. In these instances, the performance of the group depends less on the resources available (such as capital, equipment, and facilities) than on the level of knowledge and intellectual abilities and skills exhibited by the members of the group.

Technological obsolescence—that is, the process by which team members lose current knowledge in their area of expertise—is a real threat to the team and to the enterprise. It takes a long time for facilities and equipment to become outdated, so the consequences can be forecast and a solution planned well ahead. The obsolescence of group members, however, occurs relatively quickly, is difficult to predict accurately, and has devastating impacts on the team's performance (Badawy 1982; Rubenstein 1989).

ORGANIZATIONAL FACTORS

For R&D and technology professionals to succeed, prior research has found that structural and process variables have to be aligned for their benefit. They need a flexible organizational structure and support from senior management. They perform best in an organizational climate that fosters innovation, creativity, and risk taking. They respond to effort in mentoring, training, and personal growth (Barthelme et al. 1998; Connell and Crawford 2007).

ENVIRONMENTAL FACTORS

Prior research on workers in R&D and technology organizations suggested that these workers belong to a national as well as global network of peers. This network provides professional guidance in the discourse of methodologies, ethical behavior, and conduct as well as a forum for the exchange of ideas. Professional organizations constitute the operational institutions of the network.

Scientists and engineers consider this network and its associations as their global marketplace, so these professionals are much more marketable than any other group of workers in history. The global characteristics of the network of peers erase many of the limitations imposed by regional or natural boundaries, political or economic systems, and geographic distances.

Moreover, scientists and engineers may feel some conflict between their allegiance to the organization that employs them and the requirements of the professional organization to which they belong. When rules, procedures, or ethical issues are in conflict between the two organizations, scientists and engineers are caught in the middle and have to resolve this conflict—sometimes painfully (Badawy 1982; Gould 2006).

In summary, previous research has improved our understanding of how science and technology professionals (who transact in knowledge) behave and what factors impinge upon their performance. Two key findings that emerged from this body of research focused on the unique features of this group of workers and the crucial role they play in the competitiveness of the enterprise. It became very clear that this unique class of professional workers obey a different set of rules and are affected by a different set of influences than previous groups of workers in the industrial society. They are highly educated, highly trained, and highly motivated. They have a global network of peers; their "workers' union" is not limited to the workplace or to employees with a specific set of skills, but includes a worldwide network of all science and technology professionals.

THE NATURE OF HUMAN CAPITAL AND INTELLECTUAL ASSETS

In most organizations, the cost of human resources is at least 40 percent of the organization's expenses. With the advent of the host of highly educated workers, the cost of this segment of human resources began to escalate. Many organizations soon discovered that the cost of their talented people was driving the total cost of their human resources far beyond the 50 percent mark (Fitz-enz 2000; Flamholtz 1985).

The cost of the new breed of human resources was only one side of the phenomenon. As the economic burden of the knowledge-intensive workers increased, so did their value and appreciation over time. This meant that a new method had emerged for the evaluation of human resources as an organizational asset of economic value (Alverson 2004; Leydesdorff 2006).

In the past, the value of human resources has been focused on their ability to perform work, operate the equipment, manage and direct groups of employees, and perform the necessary jobs of manufacturing, selling, and accounting. Armed with basic skills, these workers received specialized training from their organizations. This training was targeted to the needs of the enterprise. Although some skills thus acquired could be transportable to other organizations of a similar nature, much of the training was aimed at industry- and company-specific goals and requirements (Scarborough 1999).

The new breed of workers is evaluated by what they *know,* rather than by what they can *do* for the organization. They operate as individual (and aggregated as teams) knowledge bases. So as the stock of their knowledge increases, so does their value

Figure 7.2   **The Notion of Human Capital as Intellectual Asset in Work Organizations**

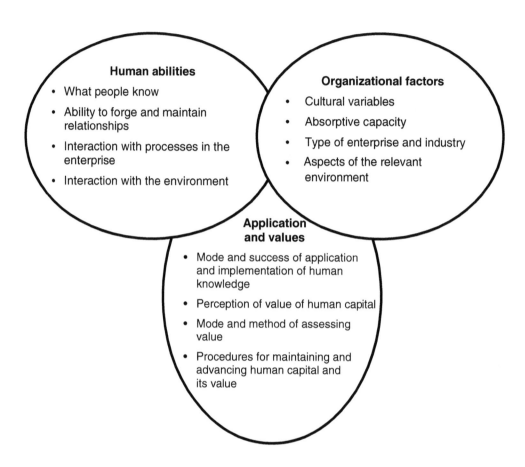

to their workplace. Human capital therefore means the extent to which these workers possess intellectual capacity and the knowledge base necessary to survive and successfully perform in a contemporary business environment characterized by agility, high mobility, and hypercompetition (Hamel 2007; Senge 1990).

The notion of human capital is composed of three building blocks, as shown in Figure 7.2.

HUMAN ABILITIES

This component of human capital involves the set of abilities that is peculiar to knowledge workers. The human intellectual asset includes not only what organizational members know, but also how they are able to forge and maintain relationship with others, within and outside the enterprise (Bryan and Joyce 2007). In addition, these workers also possess the ability to interact successfully with the internal processes of the organization and with relevant elements in its external environment (Davenport 2005; Huselid et al. 2005).

In practical terms, this means that knowledge workers are able to be an integral part of organizational processes, such as decision making, communication, and change. They are able to exercise their knowledge within the boundaries of what the organization can and cannot do, and to perform within parameters of what is generally expected of any members of their enterprise (Nag et al. 2007).

Because knowledge workers are different from other workers due to their talent and special skills, their successful integration in the enterprise requires the ability to function alongside other members of the organization (Horibe 1999). In essence, all the different abilities shown in Figure 7.2 are needed to account for a well-rounded human asset who can provide value to the enterprise (Amar 2001).

ORGANIZATIONAL FACTORS

Human capital exists within a complex web of organizational variables. Foremost among them is the *culture* of the organization. This concept of culture includes not only the perceptions of the value of intellectual contribution, but also the sum total of rites, rituals, symbols, and traditions that animate an organization. There is a reciprocal relationship between the culture and the knowledge workers in the knowledge-based enterprise.

First, there is the impact of existing cultural variables on human intellectual assets. The rules and regulations and the incentives and disincentives imposed by the enterprise affect the composition of its human capital, the workers' performance, and their loyalty to the organization (Ong and Lai 2007). For example, a Chicago-based company, Beatrice Foods, was well known for its dairy products. Its internal culture discounted the development of human and knowledge assets, allocating minimum resources for travel and personnel enrichment. Although the company had been profitable, it no longer exists as an independent enterprise. Conversely, 3M of Minneapolis has forged a culture that fosters creativity, new product development, internal venturing, and the growth and enrichment of its human assets.

Second, there is the impact of knowledge workers on the culture of the organization. The process by which the organization influences the workers may soon be modified so that the very presence and actions of knowledge workers will create a culture that is more amenable to their needs (Huang et al. 2007). Bell and Howell Corporation is an interesting example. When Donald Frey became chief executive officer in 1971, the company was predominantly a manufacturing enterprise. Among its leading products were motion picture cameras, copier-duplicators, and even a zoom lens system for the *Surveyor* spacecraft. In his seventeen years as chief executive, Frey radically transformed the company into a supplier of online information services, data processing services, and other professional, scientific, and technical services. This transition from a manufacturing firm to a highly sophisticated information services company has created a new culture in the company. Driven by the new cadre of knowledge workers, the current culture is much friendlier to its intellectual assets.

ABSORPTIVE CAPACITY

Cohen and Levinthal (1990) coined the notion of the "absorptive capacity" of organizations. They defined it as the ability of an enterprise to identify knowledge in its relevant environment, import and absorb it into its processes, and apply it as needed to obtain and maintain strategic competitiveness. Such absorptive capacity is predicated upon the combined performance of knowledge workers. Their contributions to the strategic aims of the enterprise make up their value as intellectual assets. Simply put, these workers know how to absorb and apply knowledge, hence to make the enterprise a competitive player in its industry (Tallman and Phene 2007).

The more knowledge workers absorb and apply knowledge, the more they add value to the organization. Their intellectual abilities and contributions thus become invaluable assets to the enterprise. It then behooves the organization to create a culture that welcomes and rewards these workers, ensuring that they will perform successfully, wish to remain, and encourage other workers like them to join in and add to the value of the enterprise (Roos 1998; Sveiby 1997).

APPLICATION AND VALUE

The value of intellectual assets can materialize only when they are successfully applied in organizational settings (Boudreau and Ramstad 2007; Lord and Farrington 2006). The success of this process depends on the perception in the enterprise of what constitutes value and how intellectual assets are included in such definitions. We have already learned from previous studies of R&D workers (scientists and engineers) that their success depends, among other factors, on the procedures and the climate in the organization for maintaining these human assets and advancing their intellectual growth and the stock of their knowledge (Ravn 2004).

In summary, intellectual assets are composed of the abilities of workers, combined with a supportive culture and the absorptive capacity of the organization. The third component of what constitutes intellectual assets is the organization's internal environment, within which the abilities of these workers can be successfully applied so as to generate value to the enterprise (Jones and Schilling 2000).

MANAGEMENT AS INTELLECTUAL ASSETS

The discussion up to this point has dealt with the broad issue of knowledge workers as human capital and intellectual assets. But prior research on managers of R&D has shown that the difficulties of managing this unique group of employees energize a unique type of manager who is also an intellectual asset to the organization (Davenport and Prusak 2003).

In order to manage this type of human capital, managers at all levels of the hierarchy must develop abilities that exceed those of traditional managers (Katz, 2003; Werr and Stjernberg 2003). Figure 7.3 shows this set of unique attributes of these managers.

Figure 7.3   **Managers as Intellectual Assets in the KBE**

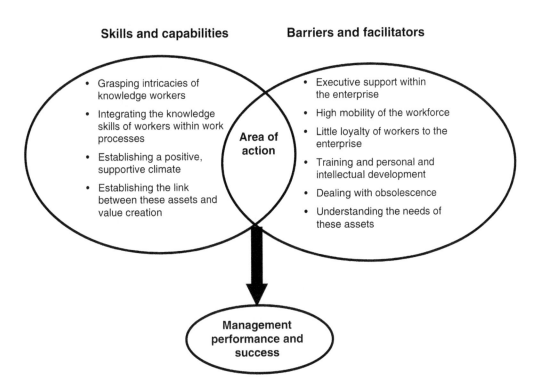

SKILLS AND CAPABILITIES

Managers need the skill to understand the special attributes and unique needs of their human capital. Knowledge workers are increasingly becoming independent contractors, selling their expertise to the higher or better bidder in the global marketplace (Euker 2007; Katz 1988). Members of this new group of knowledge-based employees will work during their career for five to ten organizations, whereas the previous generations worked for one or two organizations. These knowledge-based employees exhibit little commitment to their current workplace and are constantly open to offers from other potential employers.

Given this change in the rules of the game, managers of this unique cadre must be able to understand what motivates these knowledge workers and how to meet their needs and expectations. These workers do not need machines to perform their job or to move to another employer. They carry their assets and capabilities in their heads, so they can quickly move to another employer anywhere in the world. The challenge for present and future managers is how to deal with these workers, how to appeal to them, and how to ensure that they will stay and perform (Hildreth and Kimble 2002; Sensiper 1998).

Besides being able to grasp the special nature of their knowledge workers, managers themselves need a certain level of intellectual competence that allows them to ask relevant questions, make sensible decisions, and understand the tasks performed by these workers. They need to be educated and insightful, with some technical knowledge and a solid behavioral and managerial know-how that facilitates their successful interaction with their subordinates. Finally, they need some kind of a knowledge system to support them in their complex task of managing their intellectual assets.

Fitz-enz (2000) suggests an integrated, six-point model describing the human capital in the enterprise. His model shows six interconnected tasks that are continuously conducted: planning, retaining, developing, acquiring, maintaining, and evaluating. To monitor this scheme, he proposes a scorecard based on such variables as cost, time, quantity, level of error, and reaction to the finding. Thus, for each function, managers can assess how well the enterprise is doing at any given time.

During the shortage of nursing personnel in the early years of the twenty-first century, one large urban hospital attempted to fill vacant positions with independent contractors: registered nurses who worked for a private company and were dispatched as needed to the various departments of the hospital. This scheme proved very costly. The hospital then applied a scheme similar to that proposed by Fitz-enz. Reassessing its policy toward the nursing staff, the hospital developed a comprehensive plan that focused not only on hiring (acquiring) but also on retaining, developing, and maintaining its existing nursing personnel.

RELATING INTELLECTUAL ASSETS TO THE CREATION OF VALUE IN THE ENTERPRISE

How do we link the functioning of intellectual assets to the creation of value and ultimately wealth in the enterprise? There are two models that can assist us in this task.

THE STRUCTURAL MODEL

The first is a structural model of *contextual hierarchy* in which we relate the activities of human capital to the enterprise-wide activities that are known to generate value. Figure 7.4 shows the schematic description of this model.

This contextual hierarchy model is a composite of the model of actors transacting in knowledge (Geisler 2007) and the pathway model suggested by Fitz-enz (2000). As shown in Figure 7.4, the model contains three levels of actors. The first is the *generators* of knowledge. These are the people, teams, and units who form the human capital. They generate and compile knowledge on and through their jobs, tasks, and interests in the enterprise. Next, these actors transfer what they know, sharing it with people, groups, and units who can now adopt, adapt, implement, and use this knowledge. They are the *users* and *transformers* of knowledge.

For example, knowledge about the thermal characteristics of materials and knowledge about customers' preferences may be shared with the research, production, and marketing departments of a maker of machinery such as automobiles, airplanes, or

Figure 7.4 **A Contextual Hierarchy Model of the Relation of Intellectual Assets to Creation of Value in the Enterprise**

Beneficiaries of knowledge

- People, teams, and units who benefit from knowledge and create economic and other value based on such contributions

Users and transformers of knowledge

- People, teams, and units who share, transfer, transmit, and exchange knowledge
- People, teams, and units who adopt, adapt, use, and implement knowledge

Generators of knowledge

- People, teams, and units who procure, generate, and assemble knowledge
- Knowledge created for functions, processes, products, and services
- Knowledge created to forge relationships, contacts, and collaborations

consumer electronics. These departments use knowledge to conduct their operation, to make products and services, and to sell and distribute them. The knowledge they receive and utilize comes from all sources within the enterprise and includes knowledge about technical, administrative, and market variables. The users and transformers sort through the knowledge, adopting and utilizing whatever they believe will be of most use to them.

The third group, at the enterprise level, is composed of the *beneficiaries* of the knowledge. They are first and foremost the enterprise, which benefits from the achievement of its goals, such as sales, profits, strategic market positioning, and growth (Miller et al. 2007). The difficult task is to show the link between how users and transformers adopt and use knowledge to achieve their goals and how their work creates the ultimate benefits that accrue to the enterprise.

An interesting illustration is the knowledge about the behavior of customers and the marketplace that is shared by various sources within the enterprise and that helps the sales and customer service units to perform their tasks. This successful application of knowledge may be shown to directly impact the levels of sales and revenue as measured at the level of the enterprise. Moreover, the more complex the marketplace, the more the functional departments need varied knowledge to perform their tasks with a high probability of success.

THE PROCESS MODEL

A different model that links the generation of knowledge to the creation of value and ultimately the creation of wealth by the enterprise is the process model. Figure 7.5 depicts the key elements of this model. The figure is based on the models suggested by Geisler (2000) and Rubenstein (1989).

This model is predicated upon the succession of outputs produced by each of the components in the model. The generators of knowledge create a host of outputs that are then transferred to users within the enterprise and shared with them. These outputs include solutions to problems, prior experience on what works and why, and methods, techniques, and models. These are some of the formats in which knowledge is presented, packaged, and shared by its generators. The transfer processes may include personal communication, memoranda, reports and papers, formulas, and demonstrations.

The users produce outputs such as cost cutting, increased productivity and efficiency, reduced barriers to innovation, and improved decision processes. These outputs are then transferred to the beneficiaries, who in turn apply them to their processes and tasks. The results are in the form of outputs such as improved market share, better regulatory compliance, and improved competitiveness in the marketplace.

A major urban hospital having problems with regulatory changes provides a good example of the use of knowledge outputs. Faced with a new set of regulations on the distribution of patient information, the hospital found itself breaking the new laws on a massive scale. The Health Insurance Portability and Accountability (HIPAA) Act of 1996 prohibited certain manipulation, disposal, and sharing of patient information. Even with guidance from the hospital's legal team, the caregivers were unaware that several traditional practices were inherently noncompliant with the regulations. Compliance was restored thanks to a continuous flow of knowledge, based on personal experiences and lessons from other health care delivery organizations, that was shared by caregivers at all levels, resulting in managerial action and the institution of rules and standards within the hospital—hence ensuring compliance.

Figure 7.5 **A Process Model of the Relation of Intellectual Assets to Creation of Value in the Enterprise**

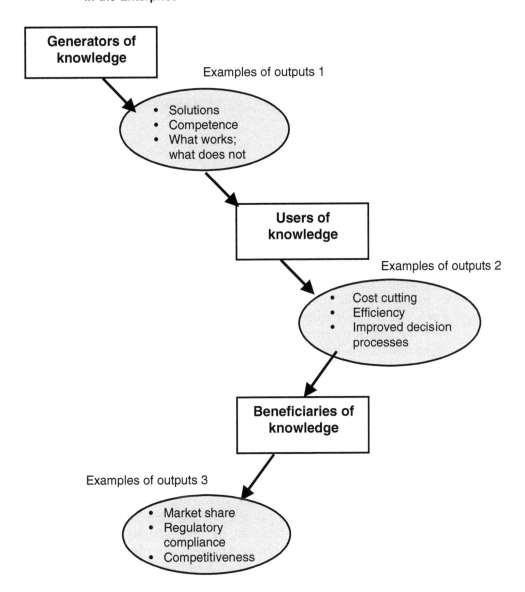

THE ROLE OF TEAMS IN THE CREATION OF VALUE

The sharing of knowledge among actors at the various levels and functional units of the enterprise depends on two key components. The first is the existence of teams of knowledge workers, within and between units. The second is the existence of a shared platform on which these workers can transact, exchange what they know, and collaborate (Horibe 1999; Jones and Schilling 2000).

Knowledge transfer and sharing occurs more successfully when teams of workers are involved. Research on R&D performance has shown that the combined power of team members far outweighs the performance of the individual (Badawy 1982; Katz 2003). When knowledge workers perform within work groups, they achieve a positive exchange of knowledge, developing innovative ways to share what they know and to transfer the integrated outputs of the team to other constituents in the enterprise. However, in order to do so, team members must share a common platform that allows them to interact and to intelligently exchange knowledge. This includes the ability to converse and to transact in knowledge.

BARRIERS TO TEAM PERFORMANCE

There are at least four categories of barriers to the exchange of knowledge within and between teams. Table 7.1 lists these categories.

Organizational or unit cultural barriers are those factors embedded in the norms, procedures, and practices of behavior, and the attitudes of individuals and groups toward knowledge and its management. When there is lack of group cohesion and the cultural characteristics are not particularly favorable to the exchange of knowledge, teams may be reluctant to share and to transact in what they know. They may, for example, prefer to keep such knowledge to themselves in order to maintain their power or independence as a group.

Disciplinary differences include "silo"-type isolation of particular groups who share the values, terminology, and modes of thinking and acting that are characteristic of a discipline or profession. For example, engineers and lawyers might form distinct groups, with few incentives to depart from their magnificent isolation within their silos.

An illustrative case of a government organization responsible for both scientific knowledge and the preparation of regulations demonstrates the power of silos and isolation. The scientific branch of the agency produced results that were routinely transferred to the regulatory branch, but with little explanation, few details, and a convoluted scientific and technical jargon. Lacking adequate knowledge, the regulatory branch had to consistently interpret the knowledge thus received. Although this regulatory branch resorted to the help of scientific consultants in order to understand what their technical colleagues were doing, there was still a considerable lag between what the scientists provided and what the regulators believed they knew.

The type of knowledge and the weaknesses in the platform are also barriers to intra- and interteam exchange of knowledge (Davenport and Prusak 2003). Problems such as breakdowns in communication networks and the relative inability of individuals to share their tacit knowledge are example of these barriers.

In summary, these barriers are hardly unique to the exchange of knowledge within and between teams. They have, for example, been previously identified in the interface between teams in R&D and teams in manufacturing, design, and marketing (Rubenstein 1989). It seems to us that the *content* of what is being shared or transferred is of less importance than the actual *activity* of exchange, transfer, and sharing. However, the reality of intra- and intergroup exchange is that strong barriers inhibit the seamless flow of whatever is being shared, whether technology, scientific findings, or knowledge.

Table 7.1

Barriers to the Exchange of Knowledge Within and Between Teams

Categories	Barriers
Organizational and unit culture	Lack of group cohesion Norms, procedures, and organizational practices Structural inhibitors and process inefficiencies
Disciplinary and professional differences	Lack of common terminology, concepts, and interchange "Silo" effect of disciplinary isolation
Type of knowledge	Tacit versus explicit knowledge Function and purpose of knowledge
Weaknesses in the platform	Breakdowns in communication patterns and networks Problems with mission, purpose, and leadership

How to Overcome the Barriers

There is no magic that would allow managers to run flawless and seamless exchanges of knowledge within and between work teams (Boudreau and Ramstad 2007; Davenport 2005; Sensiper 1998). The best solution seems to be focusing on each category of barriers with specific answers to ameliorate or alleviate the underlying conditions that seem to generate or encourage these barriers.

For example, managers have been somewhat successful in overcoming professional silos by encouraging and supporting cross-disciplinary teams who work together from the very beginning. Other solutions are fostering group cohesion and providing strong support from senior managers to the transfer of knowledge activities in the organization—with adequate incentives and a strong cultural message. These are certainly not simple or easy measures and they do not guarantee success. But they are a good starting point for managerial attempts to overcome barriers to the exchange of knowledge.

Knowledge Workers and Knowledge Management Systems

The connection between knowledge workers and the knowledge management system (KMS) is threefold. First, knowledge workers are the primary *suppliers* of knowledge to these systems. Second, knowledge workers are the main *users* of the KMS. Third, knowledge workers, in conjunction with the KMS, are the new type of asset of the contemporary (and future) enterprise. This third point means that knowledge systems are the institutionalized version of the knowledge workers (Cortada 1998; Tallman and Phene 2007).

In much of the literature on knowledge management (KM), the tendency has been to examine these two phenomena independently. Figure 7.6 shows this trend and the intersection of the two areas of study.

In Chapter 8 we focus on the design and implementation of the KMS in the enterprise. Knowledge workers represent a crucial element in the functioning of the KMS and its success or failure. In fact, many of the barriers to the exchange of knowledge

Figure 7.6   **Interfaces Between Knowledge Workers and KMS**

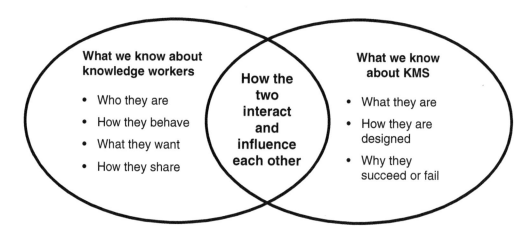

among individuals and teams are also prime drivers of the KMS and largely responsible for its success or failure. It is therefore very important to understand how knowledge workers and the systems that organizations create to transact in knowledge are intertwined and how they impact each other.

The Greatest Generation

The contemporary workforce, in general, and the knowledge-based workforce, in particular, are composed of four intermingled demographic segments. The oldest is the generation of workers born between 1900 and 1945. Increasingly in retirement, this group, described by Tom Brokaw (2004) as "the greatest generation," bravely introduced communication technologies, nuclear power, and military as well as commercial aviation. This generation is responsible for such innovations as computers, composite materials, radar, television, jet propulsion, antibiotics, xerography, magnetic tape, and, perhaps above all, the proliferation of postsecondary education and the dissemination of scientific knowledge as a government-sponsored right that is affordable and widely available to all (Geisler 2001).

Before the arrival of this generation, higher education was the destination of the privileged. Science and technology were conducted mostly in small-scale endeavors. This generation changed the fabric of the production of knowledge and its modes of dissemination, in part by creating hundreds, perhaps thousands, of new universities and colleges worldwide. Massive public funds were directed toward the establishment of local, national, and international networks of institutions that produce and disseminate knowledge. Public funds also supported large-scale scientific and technical programs and projects aimed at the exploration of the planet: space, the oceans, climate, the subatomic world, management and the social sciences, and the environment. By introducing the computer between 1940 and 1960, this generation in effect heralded the revolution in information and telecommunication technologies.

Although this generation is rapidly disappearing or well into retirement, it has left an indelible mark upon contemporary society and economy. Its contributions to science, technology, and knowledge paved the way for the revolutionary achievements of the generation that followed: the baby boomers.

THE BOOMERS

Born between 1946 and 1964, the baby boomers—about 80 million of them—represent about 28 percent of the adult population in the United States. They are believed to hold 60 percent of the wealth in the United States and 80 percent in the United Kingdom.

This generation brought about enormous changes in the social, political, and technological fabric of the world. The boomers continued the work of their predecessors by extending and greatly improving upon the tremendous contributions they inherited. The boomer generation introduced cellular phones, the Internet, and numerous other advances in information and telecommunication technology. Defying convention, the boomers transformed technology and knowledge to the point where they became the norm, the standard, and the driving forces of contemporary society and economy.

Because the "greatest generation" had established the infrastructure for the knowledge society and the knowledge economy, the boomers became the first generation in the workplace to actually earn the title "knowledge workers." The boomers supported the creation of organizational platforms for research, development, innovation, and knowledge as well as a host of incentives for workers whose assets focused on knowledge. They also fostered the high regard that science, technology, and knowledge enjoy in the population.

THE GEN-XERS

The third demographic segment is Generation X. These are workers born between 1965 and 1980. In 2007 they represented about 20 percent of the American population. About 40 million of these Gen-Xers are currently in the workforce.

This generation is enjoying the marvelous gifts of its predecessors, the boomers. The Gen-Xers benefited from the most sophisticated network of higher education in history and from almost unlimited access to knowledge. They benefited from countless opportunities in the reformulated work environment that they, and their parents, helped to shape and to reconfigure.

Gen-Xers are the first generation of workers to seamlessly adapt massive technologies in nearly every aspect of their workplace and their lives. They embraced the Internet, cellular telephones, the personal computer, globalization, and the new political and social realities of the end of Soviet communism and the emergence of the European Union, electronic commerce, and an unparalleled era of worldwide progress and prosperity. Gen-Xers also strongly embraced knowledge as the defining component of their generation. In essence, Gen-Xers are what they know. They easily navigate the new knowledge-based economy with its complex technologies, rapid obsolescence, and high-speed knowledge creation and transfer.

THE MILLENNIALS

Millennials are the youngest generation, born after 1980. They are perceived by employers as highly technological. Electronic communication tools are a natural extension of their bodies. They are in constant communication with their peers. They are also perceived as being more confident than the preceding generations. In this sense, the millennials epitomize knowledge workers. They are self-assured, choosy about their employment and their career, and confident in the viability of their knowledge assets. They seem to have very little trust in established organizations and seem to exhibit very little loyalty to their place of employment. They are highly mobile, self-contained within their peer group, and in full command of the technological and knowledge revolutions in which they exist with comfort and confidence.

TRANSGENERATIONAL TRENDS

Figure 7.7, showing the intersection of the four generations described above, offers a unique perspective on the current workplace (Oblinger 2003). Knowledge is the one dimension that ties all these interactive generations. Each generation passed its knowledge to the next, and with each new generation the perception of knowledge as a key asset in the economy, in life, and in individual careers has dramatically increased to the point where knowledge has become the criterion for admission to the elite of the respective group (Howe and Strauss 2000).

The shaded area in Figure 7.7 is the intersection of all four generations. This area is the reality in many organizations. The interface produces a healthy exchange because it has the power synthesizing four different perspectives into a uniquely strong combination of approaches to knowledge. This is not only an exchange of experience, skills, and aptitudes, but also a transgenerational sharing of attitudes and the appreciation of each other's strengths. Millennial knowledge workers learn that their elders do possess technological skills and understand the latest knowledge tools, whereas Gen-Xers and boomers learn to appreciate and to manage the new terminologies and the work and communication habits of the newer generation.

LEARNING OUTCOMES

- What is the nature of human capital and how does it constitute an intellectual asset in the contemporary enterprise?
- What are knowledge workers and in what ways are they unique?
- How do knowledge workers contribute to the creation of value in the organization?
- What are the barriers to the transfer, exchange, and sharing of knowledge and how can managers attempt to overcome them?

Figure 7.7 **Intersection of the Trans-Generational Composition of the Knowledge-Based Workplace**

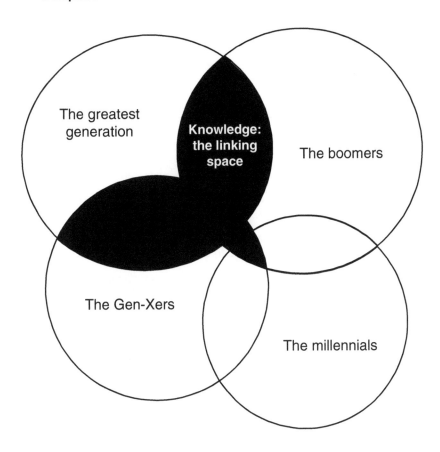

DISCUSSION QUESTIONS

1. Why is managing knowledge workers different from and more difficult than managing other workers?
2. What are the main contributions of knowledge workers to value in the contemporary enterprise?
3. What is the future of knowledge workers and of the role that they play in the organization's competitive position?

8 Designing Knowledge Management Systems

KEY LEARNING OUTCOMES

You will know you have mastered the material in this chapter when you can define and explain the following:

1. Knowledge management systems.
2. What we know about the design of knowledge management systems.
3. Features, dimensions, and architectures of successful design of knowledge management systems.

In this chapter we describe the unique organizational artifact that we call the knowledge management system (KMS). We focus on the design of this type of system and the various aspects of its architecture in the enterprise. The purpose of this chapter is to enable the reader to gain important insights into how organizations compile and manipulate the knowledge they possess into workable knowledge systems (Rubenstein and Geisler 2003).

A KMS is an artifact or mechanism that an organization creates to make the flow of work more efficient, so as to contribute to the competitiveness of the enterprise in the marketplace and to its success and survival (Backer 1991; Quinn 1999). In order to understand how these systems operate and what factors impinge upon their success or failure, readers must first understand how these systems are classified, designed, and implemented. This chapter therefore provides a road map into the design of the KMS and what makes it an asset for the organization. The chapter also explains how and why these knowledge systems are structured and operate within the contemporary enterprise from the perspective of several design modes and architectures (Gibbons et al. 1994; Hayek 1945; Nonaka 1994).

The chapter is therefore structured to focus upon the parameters and their role in the making of the KMS. It starts by examining the nature and purpose of these systems and ends with the key aspects and dimensions of their composition in the organization.

HOW THE KNOWLEDGE MANAGEMENT SYSTEM DIFFERS FROM OTHER SYSTEMS

In the early days of the pursuit of knowledge management (KM) as a separate discipline, knowledge systems were generally equated with management information systems (MIS). But as the study of KM progressed and its role in the enterprise became clearer and more focused, the differences between KMS and MIS became much better delineated (Nerkar and Paruchuri 2005; Van de Ven and Johnson 2006).

The KMS is a unique organizational mechanism in which managers collect, store, manipulate, extract, and utilize knowledge about managerial and related processes, events, methods, techniques, outcomes, and the state of the organization, as well as that of its external environment, the marketplace, and the industry in which it operates. The KMS is a repository of what organizational members know and are willing and able to share with other members. Such knowledge is different from information not only because it is actionable at all levels (including the whole enterprise), but also because it is held by the members, embedded in their minds, and only available for general use via the knowledge system. In this regard, Figure 8.1 shows selected differences between the characteristics of the KMS and other enterprise-wide systems.

The figure shows some aspects of the KMS as a repository of *what workers know* and how they can *apply* such knowledge for solving problems and meeting the competition. Conversely, other systems are limited in the scope of what they measure and what they offer to managers. *Technology systems*, for example, provide information about technological capabilities and equipment or instruments that operate within the enterprise. These systems measure the performance of the technologies, their features and use, and the standards or benchmarks of their operation. In hospitals, for example, technology systems encompass readings on magnetic resonance imaging (MRI) equipment. Specifically, these systems measure the power and the capacity of the MRI, the number of patients it can scan per time unit, the benefits of these scans to patient care, and the cost-effectiveness of operating such a technology (Lu et al. 2007; Rich 1991).

Information systems include, but are not limited to, accounting, personnel, sales, and environmental information that the enterprise routinely collects and stores. Governmental laws and regulations require some of these types of information. For example, companies (and, to an extent, not-for-profit organizations) are required to collect and maintain information about their workers and their benefits, accounting of sales and revenues, and similar categories of information for the purpose of taxation and other government needs. Other types of information, such as specific data on competition, vendors, and customers, are collected and manipulated by these enterprises for use as inputs in decision making and organizational policies.

Organizational systems focus primarily on the collection and use of information on the various functions of the enterprise, such as manufacturing, marketing, human resources, and legal and regulatory news and developments. This system provides

Figure 8.1   **Some Differences Between KMS and Other Systems in the Organization**

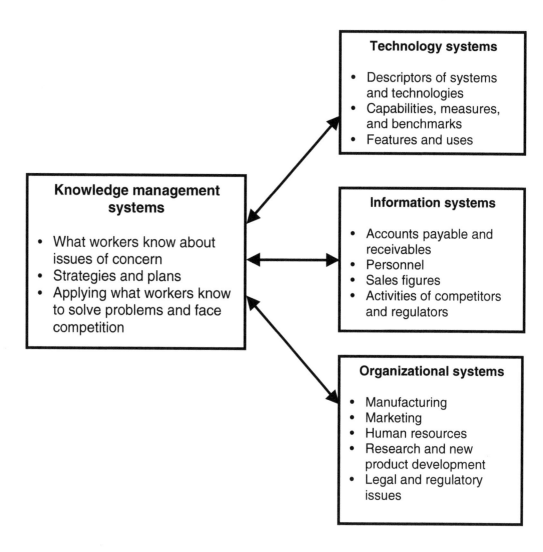

managers with a tapestry of what is happening in virtually all aspects of the life of the enterprise.

Yet, although these systems produce information that is useful as inputs for decision making and other managerial actions, they differ from knowledge systems in that they provide snapshots of particular situations, events, or activities. They provide descriptions of selected aspects of reality that are deemed important to managers—independently of the users of these systems.

In contrast, the KMS are a reflection of the people who possess this knowledge. The KMS is closely linked to the organizational members who generate and ultimately use such knowledge. The KMS does not exist independently of the people who engender its content—namely, the knowledge deposited in the system.

Dimensions and Attributes of the Knowledge Management System

Having described what the KMS is *not* and how it differs from other systems in the organization, in this section we explain what the KMS *is* and what dimensions and attributes can be used to describe it.

As a new discipline struggling for an identity, KM evoked a characteristically rich literature with a variety of definitions and taxonomies of the KMS. Hibbard (1998) complained quite early in the development of KM that the literature was "inundated" with vendors, promises of successful KMS applications, and the labeling of "everything that moves" as KM.

Dalkir (2005), in one of the first textbooks on KM, describes four major classifications for the codification of knowledge: (1) cognitive or concept map, (2) decision tree, (3) manual knowledge, and (4) automated knowledge. Although Dalkir describes various features of each taxonomy (a taxonomy is an orderly classification according to the presumed relationship among the items being classified), the main ingredients of these approaches are the *methods* or *forms* by which knowledge is codified. For example, a cognitive map can be a node in a graph as well as relationships among key concepts. Similarly, a decision tree is a "flowchart type of representation or a decision process" (101).

Classification by Structure, Purpose, and Function

Geisler (2006) proposes a hierarchical classification or taxonomy of knowledge based on three criteria: *structure, purpose,* and *function.* The primary category is structure, which describes how the KMS is designed (form) and what it contains (content). The second category is purpose (what the system is designed for), and the third is function (the entity that receives the impacts and benefits of the KMS). Figure 8.2 shows this hierarchical model.

Geisler (2006) argues that the KMS should be designed and considered in light of its structure, what purpose it seems to serve, and the recipients of its benefits and impacts. This would allow the organization to assess its KMS from design to utilization and subsequent impacts (Fuller 2002; Liebowitz et al. 2007).

Classification by Functions and Processes

A different classification of a KMS is based on the functions and processes in the organization. The intersection of these two dimensions provides a view from the enterprise's perspective of what the KMS contains and the areas of the organization that it covers as a repository of knowledge (Geisler 2007; Rubenstein and Schwartzel 1992).

Figure 8.3 depicts such a classification. The figure shows the cells in which the intersections of function and process contain knowledge specific to the intersection. Additionally, the figure shows the progression from what members of the organization know to what they deposit in the KMS as codified knowledge (Euker 2007; Roberts 2000; Styhre 2003).

Figure 8.2   **A Proposed Taxonomy of KMS**

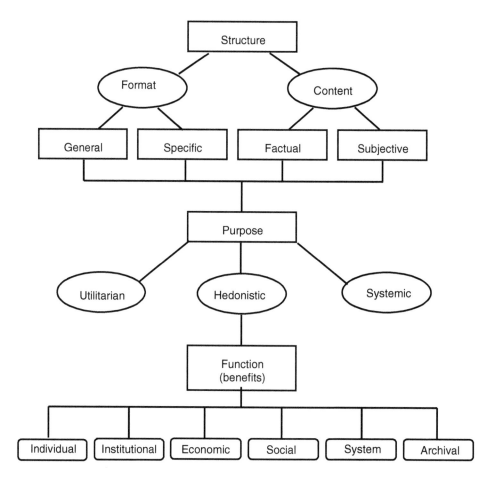

The matrix of functions and processes and the resulting cells that depict the individual design features guide the design of the KMS according to the model in Figure 8.3. For example, the cell in which *technology* and *marketing* intersect in the matrix refers to codified or explicit knowledge deposited by either the technology or research and technology (R&D) members of the enterprise or the members in the sales and marketing units. When accessed by users of the KMS, this cell provides knowledge about the following topics: (1) how technology is used in sales and marketing (e.g., promotion techniques, the use of high-technology media such as the Internet) and (2) how new products and innovations are sold and marketed.

The literature on KMS has raised some issues regarding the transformation of tacit to explicit knowledge within the KMS. Roberts (2000), for example, questions the role of information and telecommunication technologies in the transfer and sharing of knowledge. These technologies, she argues, seem to favor codified knowledge; hence some of the tacit knowledge deposited in the system may be lost. This concern will

Figure 8.3 **Classification of KMS by Dimensions of Function and Process**

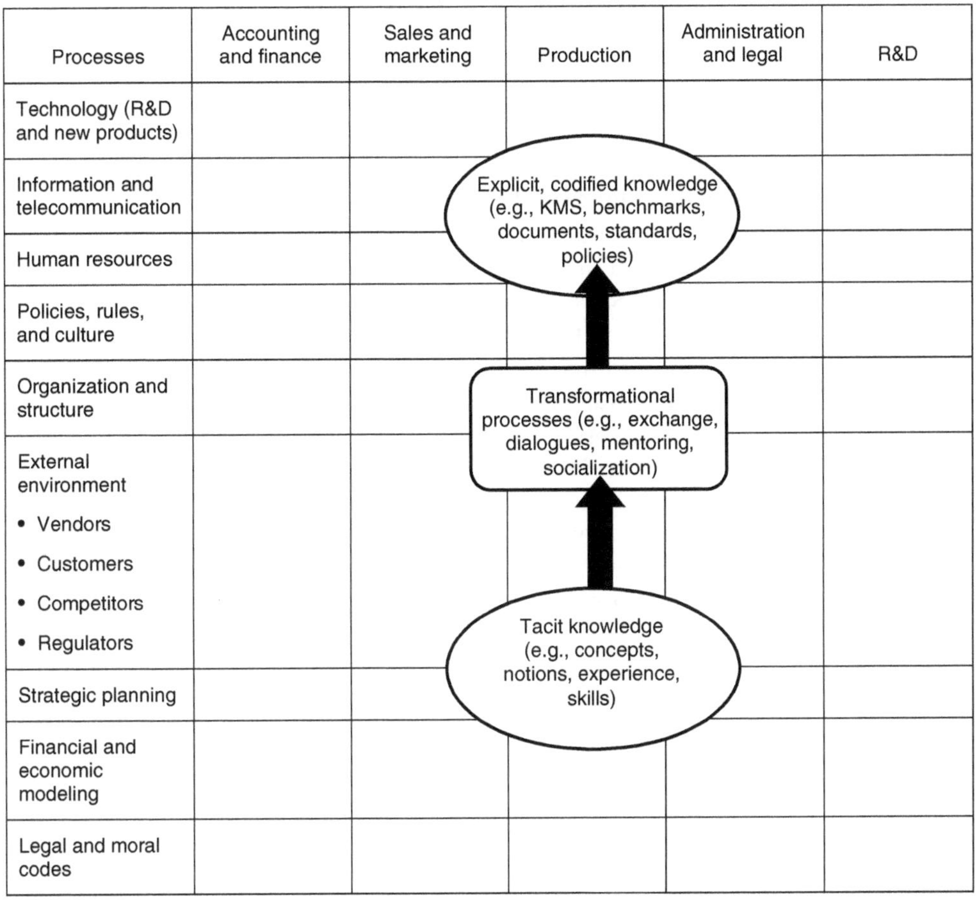
Processes
Accounting and finance
Sales and marketing
Production
Administration and legal
R&D
Technology (R&D and new products)
Information and telecommunication
Human resources
Policies, rules, and culture
Organization and structure
External environment
• Vendors
• Customers
• Competitors
• Regulators
Strategic planning
Financial and economic modeling
Legal and moral codes
Explicit, codified knowledge (e.g., KMS, benchmarks, documents, standards, policies)
Transformational processes (e.g., exchange, dialogues, mentoring, socialization)
Tacit knowledge (e.g., concepts, notions, experience, skills)

be further discussed in Chapter 10 when we describe the utilization of KM systems. Here suffice it to address the issues of the classification of the KMS and the specific terms of knowledge that a KMS will encompass.

ADVANTAGES AND LIMITATIONS

There are several advantages to the "function–process" perspective of the KMS. First, this model provides a framework for the design of a KMS, based on the reduction of what its content should be to the specific cells of the intersection of processes and functions. This allows the designer of the KMS to have a glimpse into the topical knowledge that should be codified into the KMS.

Second, this model encompasses almost all aspects of the life of the enterprise. The model is broad enough to include functional areas and key processes, including the activities of senior managers, such as strategic planning and monitoring the external environment of the organization. This focus on top management will subsequently increase the possibility that this upper level of the organization will be supportive of the KMS.

The key limitation of this model is that it emphasizes the structural features of the organization (functions and processes) while neglecting the elements in the taxonomy proposed in Figure 8.2, such as purpose and the level at which the KMS will operate in the organization. Perhaps a more viable design framework would be one that encompasses elements from both models (Anand et al. 2007).

In this regard, several writers have offered strong opinions on the nature of the knowledge content of the KMS. These opinions contribute to a more precise description of what the KMS should and can contain. Hilsop (2002), for example, argues that focusing overmuch on the technological or objectivist approaches to KM systems may lead to a system that primarily contains "expert" knowledge that conforms to the current cultural standards, beliefs, and attitudes in the organization—meaning a highly restricted and biased knowledge system.

Boland and Tenkasi (1995, 309) advance the notion that the integration of knowledge from different quarters of the organization is "a problem of perspective taking in which the unique thought worlds of different communities of knowing are made visible and accessible to others." This means that when different and unique stocks of knowledge are brought together in a matrix of the KMS (such as depicted in Figure 8.3), the integration of such distinct knowledge bases will be very difficult due to terminology, disciplinary characteristics of uniqueness, and different motivations of those who deposit this knowledge in the KMS.

Design Features of a Knowledge Management System

We propose ten features of the design of a KMS. We recognize, however, that the characterization of a KMS has to contend with two seemingly contradictory views. One is the belief of Polanyi (1966) that all knowledge is tacit; hence its transfer to others is exceedingly difficult. The second is the widely heralded, more recent view that there are ways and means in the organization to share and exchange knowledge (Nonaka 1994).

The design of a KMS will therefore be an exercise in compromising and an effort to account for the difficulties embedded in making the mechanisms for exchange of tacit knowledge an organizational reality (Faniel and Majchrak 2007). The ten features are listed below. They provide a comprehensive view of the issues that a KMS should address and the aspects of its operation that must be emphasized in light of the difficulties and barriers we mentioned earlier in this chapter.

1. *Purpose:* This feature refers to the reason why the KMS is put together. Geisler (2006) proposes three purposes: utilitarian, hedonistic, and systemic. *Utilitarian* is the goal of a KMS designed to achieve objectives such as performance, strategic competitiveness, and organizational efficiencies. *Hedonistic* is the purpose of a KMS designed to gain knowledge simply for the pleasure of its

pursuit, in response to managerial need to gain more knowledge. The third purpose is *systemic*, in which managers gain knowledge to enhance their position and their functioning within the enterprise.

There is a general agreement in the KM literature that the KMS has the purpose of assisting managers to accomplish their organizational tasks. Dawson (2000, 320), for example, defines a KMS as designed to "enhance and increase the value of the generation, sharing, and application of knowledge." In the case of education, Tschannen-Moran and Nestor-Baker (2004, 1484) argue that KMS and the exchange of tacit knowledge provide education workers with "emotional support and intellectual challenge." Similarly, Mauritsen and Flagstad (2004) propose a set of objectives for KM that they define as management challenges in the process of organizational learning. Among these are support in hiring and retaining employees, gaining insight into customers' behavior, improving quality assurance, and creating corporate value.

We can conclude that the goals or purposes of a KMS mirror the challenges that managers face in their strategic and operational tasks. This matching of what managers want from the KMS is reflected in Figure 8.4 (see page 128), in which all the features are shown in light of what the stakeholders of the KMS desire from the system.

2. *Stakeholders:* Who are the audiences or stakeholders for the KMS? In order for the design of the system to be viable, managers must clearly enumerate the constituents of the system and understand what they desire from the system (Geisler 2007; Howells 1996). These individuals or groups have vested interests in the KMS and are able to influence its design and its implementation. Rubenstein and Geisler (2003) identified five categories of stakeholders they call "key players":

   a. *Management champions:* These are managers who support the KMS, contribute to its design, and are willing to commit resources to operate the system and to use it in their executive activities. The KMS must account for their needs, wishes, and challenges, such as how to do their job well; how to learn about customers, suppliers, competitors, and regulators; and how to gain knowledge about internal process and strategic directions.

   b. *Information technology (IT) and KM technical people:* These are IT people already working in the organization. They have some control and some say about the technical aspects of the new KMS. These IT people may be supportive of the KMS or have a strong bias against it, particularly if it is designed to be operated by new experts to the exclusion of the existing IT or MIS functions (Burnett et al. 2004).

   c. *Other managers and functional people:* These are the potential users of the KMS. Like every new system, the KMS represents change in the organization (Chan and Garrick 2003). It is therefore important to incorporate the desires, biases, and concerns of these numerous and powerful users, thus encouraging their support. The idea is to make them allies of the KMS as early as possible.

    d. *Individual and group users:* In addition to the managers and functional people who will form the core of the users or customers of the KMS, there are other users both inside and outside the organization. Among these are corporate directors, vendors, customers, and regulators. These internal and external users have "wish lists" that should be considered at the design stage of the KMS.

    e. *Information specialists, experts, and other intelligent systems:* The KMS is not designed to operate in a vacuum. There are other already existing systems in the enterprise, as well as a host of experts and specialists in databases and information systems. They will have wishes and requirements for collaboration, connectivity, and mutual exchange agreements. They should be consulted during the design stage of the KMS and their expertise somehow integrated into the system.

3. *Structure:* This feature refers to the size of the system, its format, and the technology it contains. The designers should consider the following questions: How big should the KMS be? How much knowledge should it contain? How much and in what form should it collect and absorb the knowledge? What technology (hardware and software) should the system contain? Edwards et al. (2005), for example, report the use of general information technology tools in the design of KM systems, instead of specific tools designed for a KMS, in seven of ten organizations they studied. Structure is crucial to the design of a KMS, which employs specific technologies and other attributes rather than recycling existing concepts and tools.

4. *Locus in the organization:* This feature refers to where the KMS will reside in the organization. Who will assume ownership of the system? Which unit and manager will assume responsibility for hosting the large volume of knowledge that the system will potentially accumulate and store? The location of the KMS is of prime importance to its operation and potential success. Issues of culture and politics may play a role in deciding where to house the KMS and with whom, but this decision must be made during the early stages of the design and planning of the KMS.

5. *Context of the KMS:* This feature addresses the cultural and organizational environment in which the KMS will operate within the enterprise (Liebowitz et al. 2000). The designers of the KMS must understand and account for the norms, rules, procedures, traditions, and modes of behavior that are the essential components of the culture in the organization. At the very least, the KMS will have to exist within this cultural framework; at best, if the KMS turns out to be an agent of change, there should be an understanding of what it is that is being changed.

6. *Content:* What will the KMS contain? What are the categories of knowledge that will be deposited in the KMS? What level of codification will be needed to accommodate the tacit knowledge that organizational members will share with the system? How will such knowledge be structured within the KMS?

7. *Operation:* As a system, how will the input and output operations of the KMS perform? What will be the features of the entry and absorption of knowledge into the KMS? How will knowledge be extracted from the KMS? How will users be able to contact the system to interact with it and to download whatever knowledge they need?

8. *Connectivity*: How will the KMS be connected to other systems, databases, and information systems in the organization? How will the KMS navigate the technological and content issues of linkages to other systems?

9. *Incentives:* This design feature of the KMS concerns the "basket of incentives" that the enterprise needs to prepare and offer to potential users of the KMS. Because of the embedded difficulties in sharing tacit knowledge and in having members of the enterprise interact with the KMS, the organization must offer solid incentives to its members. These incentives may be, for instance, financial, organizational, and social; they should be based on good understanding of the needs, concerns, and predilections of the potential users of the KMS.

10. *Evaluation:* The final feature refers to how the system will be evaluated. We discuss this topic in more detail in Part III of this book, where we address the following issues of the design of a KMS: What are the criteria for evaluation of the KMS? How will these criteria be used? How will they be combined to form indexes? What measures will be used in the evaluation of the KMS? Who will evaluate the KMS and for what purposes? (Burnett et al. 2004)

Matching Design Features to What Stakeholders Want

Stakeholders, particularly managers in the enterprises, want the KMS to deliver to them concrete and useful benefits. Figure 8.4 shows the intersection between the ten design features and what managers, acting as stakeholders of the KMS, desire to have the KMS deliver to them.

The question that Figure 8.4 raises is this: Can the KMS be designed so that its features will match what stakeholders want from a KMS? The stakeholders desire a knowledge system that will support their activities, enhance their skills and position, and contribute to the growth and effectiveness of their organization. By any measure this is a tall order (Rubenstein and Geisler 2003).

Stakeholders have high expectations of the KMS in part because the designers and supporters of the KMS in the enterprise usually promise—or overpromise—extensive advantages that the system can deliver. Figure 8.5 depicts some of these promises.

In Figure 8.5 we list some of the outcomes and benefits that the KMS can realistically deliver. They are, in effect, restricted to a system that is somewhat different from existing information systems, but can hardly deliver all its current promises.

There are several reasons for this gap between what the KMS promises and what it can realistically deliver. One reason is the need to "sell" the system to a variety of constituencies in the organization. In order to obtain wide-range support, the designers of the KMS appeal to different stakeholders and promise to each group some benefit that would match their expectations.

Figure 8.4   **Design Features of KMS and What Stakeholders Want/Expect From It**

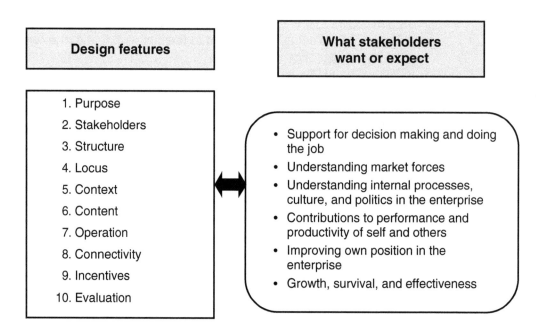

A second reason for the gap is the reliance on external vendors who create KMS. These vendors market their systems and their capabilities by focusing on salable features of a seemingly unique and outstanding solution to the organization's knowledge-sharing problems. The result is a set of promises that may not correspond to the real capabilities of the system.

A third reason is the fact that the field of KM is quite new, and there is limited experience with KM systems and their performance. What we do have are many failures and a few lackluster successes. The paucity of success data tends to motivate vendors, supporters, and designers of KM systems to overemphasize their system's possibilities, potential performance, and benefits to the adopting organization.

In summary, the designers of the KMS must consider the potential and the realistic capabilities of the system as they attempt to match the system with the needs and expectations of potential users and other constituents. Overpromising, however noble and reasonable the motivation to do so, will lead to loss of confidence in KM in general and loss of support by key constituents.

Attributes of a Knowledge Management System

The design of an effective KMS will generate a system that not only satisfies the needs and expectations of its stakeholders, but also possesses certain attributes that will contribute to its resiliency, attractiveness, and success. Figure 8.6 shows these attributes and their implications for the organization.

Figure 8.5 **Design Features of KMS and What It Promises**

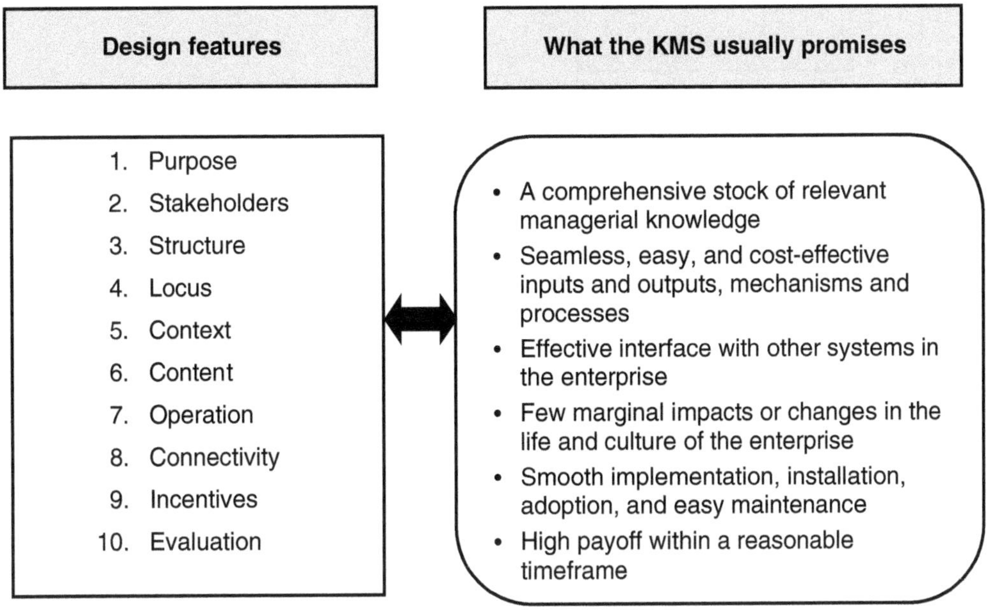

Design features	What the KMS usually promises
1. Purpose 2. Stakeholders 3. Structure 4. Locus 5. Context 6. Content 7. Operation 8. Connectivity 9. Incentives 10. Evaluation	• A comprehensive stock of relevant managerial knowledge • Seamless, easy, and cost-effective inputs and outputs, mechanisms and processes • Effective interface with other systems in the enterprise • Few marginal impacts or changes in the life and culture of the enterprise • Smooth implementation, installation, adoption, and easy maintenance • High payoff within a reasonable timeframe

The attributes of a successful KMS are similar to those of any interactive system in the enterprise. These attributes can be grouped into three categories. The first category is *usage*: the KMS should be user-friendly, accessible, reliable, and interactive. The second category is the *organizational need* for cost-effectiveness. The third category is the *technical* abilities of the system: the KMS should be easily expandable and modifiable, with the capacity for screening and verification.

If a KMS possesses these attributes, there are several implications for the enterprise. The system will be attractive to stakeholders who can then justify the expense and effort devoted to its design and implementation. These attributes may also lead to perceived value from the KMS and increase support from senior management. It is crucial that the organization's members do *not* see the KMS as just another information system or database dreamed up by management. The perception that the KMS is "just another information system" may turn out to be devastating to the future of the KMS. This perception will cause members to limit their use of the system and avoid contributing what they know to it.

A successful KMS is similar to a successful library. For users to appreciate its services and maintain a continuous record of usage, the library must be accessible, cost-effective, relevant, and willing to change so as to meet the needs of its users. In the case of a KMS, we are designing a system that is largely new to the organization. Hence the attributes of a potentially successful system must be clear to users, energize support from stakeholders, and promote a perception within the entire organization that the KMS is a useful, relevant, and different system that deserves a chance.

Figure 8.6   **Attributes of a KMS**

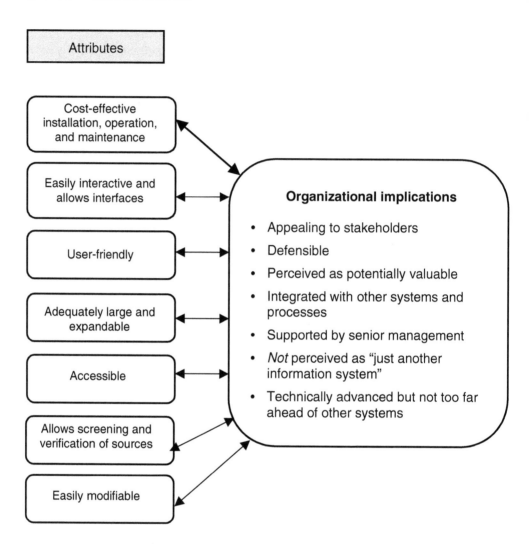

THE COMPLEXITY OF KNOWLEDGE MANAGEMENT SYSTEMS

The design of a KMS must address the issues we have discussed in this chapter. The lessons we can draw from the literature and our own experience with organizations and their KM systems are discussed below. These lessons apply equally to business and nonprofit organizations, including government and international entities.

Designing a KMS means engaging multiple variables in the complex environment of the organization's structure and processes. The complexity of the knowledge environment extends beyond that of the traditional MIS. It includes all that members of the enterprise know and whatever knowledge they are able to share and codify. This framework involves the entire organization and affects every individual in it, so that the set of stakeholders is as large as the organization itself. This complexity makes the design of the KMS a true challenge.

The design of a KMS obviously has to consider the technological aspect of the design, requiring attention to issues of performance, connectivity, and utilization by potential users. However, a consensus seems to emerge among writers on knowledge management that although technology is a key variable in the design of the KMS, it should not be the only variable considered. By giving technology undue attention in the design of the KMS, organizations lose sight of the other crucial variables that impinge upon the success of the system. Such organizational, human, and economic variables play a major role in the design and later in the implementation and utilization of the KMS. The KMS with a high probability of success requires a design that involves several stakeholders and addresses the combination of factors we have discussed in this chapter. To overemphasize one factor at the expense of the others would inevitably lead to failure when the time comes to implement the system.

Designers and supporters of a KMS tend to be overzealous, promising their constituencies a variety of exaggerated features and benefits from the system. As we have shown in this chapter, there are limits to what a KMS can realistically deliver. As an agent of organizational change, the KMS should be marketed with a realistic set of expectations and with the participation of potential users and those in the enterprise who will be impacted by the system.

LEARNING OUTCOMES

- The KMS differs from other information systems because it addresses a combination of issues in technology, organization, human behavior, and economics and because a variety of stakeholders have an interest in its design and implementation.
- The design of the KMS involves the performance aspects of the system as well as the needs and expectations of its potential users and other constituencies who may be impacted by it.

DISCUSSSION QUESTIONS

1. What are the desired features of a KMS?
2. How is the KMS different from other MIS already in existence in organizations?
3. What are the key factors that designers of KMS should address?

Implementing Knowledge Management Systems

9

KEY LEARNING OUTCOMES

You will know you have mastered the material in this chapter when you can define and explain the following:

1. The models of implementation and adoption of knowledge management systems.
2. The barriers and facilitators to successful implementation.
3. What we know about successes and failures of knowledge management systems implementation.

This chapter addresses the topics of implementation, adoption, and adaptation of the knowledge management system (KMS). The chapter is divided into three parts. The first describes the various systems involved in implementing a KMS. The second part of the chapter discusses various models of the implementation of the KMS in the organization. The third part discusses the barriers and facilitators that affect the enterprise-wide implementation of the KMS.

This chapter is based on the research and consulting experience of the authors of this book, as well as research and studies by others. We offer a theoretical framework for the implementation process, complemented by cases and illustrations from actual organizations that have implemented a KMS. The chapter also offers some insights into how to install and implement a KMS so as to increase the probability of its successful adoption by the enterprise (Saviotti 1998; Singh 2005).

THE FOUR SYSTEMS WITHIN THE KNOWLEDGE MANAGEMENT SYSTEM

The implementation and installation of a KMS is not a single event. Rather, it includes four interdependent systems of installation—technological, environmental, organiza-

Figure 9.1   **Dimensions of the Implementation of KMS**

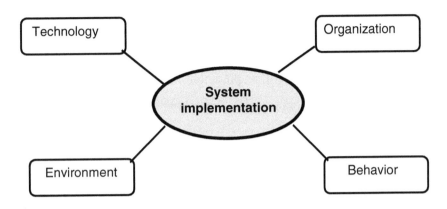

tional, and behavioral—which, combined, form the enterprise-wide implementation of a complex technological system such as the KMS. These four dimensions, each with its own procedures and timelines (Hansen et al. 2005; Wadhwa and Kotha 2006), are shown in Figure 9.1.

TECHNOLOGICAL SYSTEM

Installing and adopting a complex technological system entails several features. First, there is the installation of the hardware and accompanying software. In the case of a KMS, this step involves the selection of the technological system and the applications that will allow for the smooth operation of massive inputs, outputs, and manipulation of knowledge. In addition, this system needs to be totally interactive. Users must be able to interface with the system in a manner that is technologically reliable and user-friendly (Den Hertog and Huizenga 2000; Finnegan and Willcocks 2007; Rubenstein and Geisler 2003).

A second feature is the capability of the technology to connect with other systems in a way that will allow for reliable transfer and sharing of massive volumes of knowledge. The requirement for connectivity is a crucial and highly complex demand that is imposed on the technology (Rao 2004; Reiter 2001). The fact that the KMS is an enterprise-wide system means that it needs to connect to almost all the functional and operational systems that exist in the organization. Since knowledge can be deposited from credible sources anywhere in the organization, the comprehensive reach and appeal of the KMS effectively depend on its ability to connect seamlessly to virtually all other systems (Jennex 2007a; Maier 2007). Ryan and Prybutok (2001), for example, identify three key technologies for use with knowledge management (KM): (1) intranets—for capturing and distributing knowledge; (2) groupware—to allow organizational members to better interact with the KMS; and (3) knowledge or data warehouses.

However crucial the technological features of the implementation of KMS, over-reliance on the technology has been found to be a recipe for failure. The enterprise must align the technological capabilities and attributes of the KMS with the other aspects of implementation: environment, organization, and behavior. If the enterprise fails to do so, the implementation of even an outstanding technological system will produce merely a technological showcase, devoid of the effective performance of a *knowledge* system. In fact, Dijkstra (2001), describing knowledge systems for legal practice, found that the behavioral and social features of the implementation process proved to be as powerful as predictors, or perhaps even more so, than technological features alone.

ENVIRONMENTAL SYSTEM

The implementation of the KMS as an environmental subsystem is predicated upon the relationship of the organization with its external environment. In "hyperturbulent" environments where the pace and magnitude of change may be overwhelming, organizations find themselves in dire need of an inflow of current knowledge in order to maintain a reasonable level of competitiveness (Jennex 2007b; Miller et al. 2007; Pfeffer and Sutton 2000).

This knowledge ecosystem provides a synergy for what management may perceive as circumstances of continual crises that emanate from the external environment of the enterprise. Suppliers, customers, and competitors may force a quick pace of innovations and changes in structures, outputs, and performance. Rapid deployment of knowledge flow into the KMS becomes a necessity, not a luxury (Thorpe et al. 2005; Tsoukas and Mylonopoulos 2004).

A key ingredient in this environmental subsystem is the adoption of a KMS that has the necessary attributes of flexibility to accommodate the rapid deployment of environmental inputs in crisis mode. This requirement goes well beyond design to the actual implementation. The KMS must be connected with systems that monitor the environment and absorb inputs of knowledge from its sources (Taylor and Greve 2006).

ORGANIZATIONAL OR INSTITUTIONAL SYSTEM

This is the aspect of implementation that is usually discussed by scholars and consultants. The "fit" with organizational structures and processes and with parallel systems is often the key variable in the process of implementation. The question is how to install the KMS in a manner that complements existing institutional arrangements without undue conflicts.

The literature identifies two methods by which the implementation of a KMS will be, as much as possible, consonant with existing structures and processes in the enterprise. They are training and the sociotechnical perspective.

Training

Training is a crucial element of the implementation of any technical system, and it is particularly relevant to the KMS (Santhanam et al. 2007). As the system is being installed, both its operators and its potential users must receive training corresponding to the stages and items being implemented. These workers will learn how to enter knowledge into the system and how to locate and extract knowledge from it, thus gaining a thorough understanding of its features. Receiving this instruction during implementation allows operators and users to participate in the implementation while the process is still unfolding. The enterprise cannot wait until the KMS is fully installed before initiating the training program.

Sociotechnical Perspective

The enterprise must make an effort to coordinate the implementation of the KMS—as a technological system—with the social implications for individuals and groups engaged in its installation and future operation. This means that upon installation of the KMS, the enterprise must consider the possible impacts on the social fabric of teams who depend on knowledge that is both deposited in the KMS and extracted from it (Lobas and Jackson 2007; Zhu and Davidson 2007).

For example, a research group within the enterprise maintains a cohesive structure due to a process of sharing of knowledge among its members. Such sharing creates a sense of interdependency and gives the team members a strong feeling of belonging and participation. When a KMS is installed, much of such shared knowledge will now be available upon request, possibly diminishing the cohesive operation of the team (McIntyre-Mills and van Gigoh 2006; Nielsen 2005).

BEHAVIORAL SYSTEM

The key behavioral aspect of implementing KMS is the process of *change management* (Schlindwein and Ison 2004). As we already emphasized, the installation and adoption of the KMS is a major organizational change. Its implementation generates substantial changes in the way work is defined and accomplished, in how teams operate, and in how power is distributed within the enterprise (Gottschalk 2006).

The impact of the KMS on the way knowledge workers conduct their affairs in the organization is made manifest by changes in the cohesion of the teams and groups in which knowledge workers operate. For example, one such change would be the possible weakening of the interfaces and cooperative ties that are the attributes of sociotechnical systems we discussed above. People rely on each other for knowledge about their task, the organization, and their environment (Cunha and Maropoulos 2007). Such interdependency fosters cohesion and a coherent sense of team presence and collaboration.

When a KMS is installed, knowledge can now be obtained from the system rather than through the complex networking effort within the team or work group. This facilitates the performance of the individual at the expense of the pervasive interdependency that existed prior to the KMS (Handzic 2007; Hitchins 2008).

The implementation of technology systems will not be effective unless accompanied by a program of change management. By and large, organizations install the technological system—the hardware, the software, and the linkages to other units and

Table 9.1

Five Models of Implementation of KMS

Models	Attributes
Multiple-core model	Implement simultaneously across multiple core activities Emphasize enterprise-wide nature of the implementation
Piggy-backing model	Implement, at least initially, as add-on to existing IT/IS systems
Exploitation-exploration model	Implement portions of KMS that exploit-explore and push-pull
Stage-process model	Implement following a rigorous and systematic series of stages
Hybrid process-performance model	Implement by carefully monitoring the performance and outcomes from each segment or part of the KMS being installed, if possible in real time

systems in the enterprise (Hitchins 2008)—but fail to complement it with the management program that would address the problems of change and the impacts of the system they installed on the behavior of employees. This is an extremely shortsighted approach to the implementation of such a complex technology systems as the KMS (McInerney and Day 2007; O'Dell 2000).

FIVE MODELS OF IMPLEMENTATION

There are five specific approaches to the implementation of a KMS in the enterprise. The five models are shown in Table 9.1.

THE MULTIPLE-CORE MODEL

The multiple-core model is based on the reliance of the implementation on the total enterprise as the framework in which the KMS is being installed. Thus, implementation is undertaken across multiple core activities—all done simultaneously. This means that the KMS will be installed across core functions, such as marketing, finance, accounting, management information system (MIS), manufacturing, and new product development. In all of the core units, functions, or activities, the KMS will be installed as one overarching system. The procedures for inputs and outputs (deposits and withdrawals) from the system will be the same for all the core units.

There are two reasons for implementing the KMS simultaneously across the enterprise. The first is to achieve an implementation process that is assertive and enterprise-wide. Members of the organization will perceive this action as a fait accompli, showing that senior management is indeed determined to implement the KMS throughout the organization.

The second reason is to ascertain, as early as possible, any problems with the KMS, which may be the result of differences in disciplinary knowledge or distinctions among the various units, departments, or projects (Eppler 2006; Putnik and Cunha 2007). When implemented across diverse departments, the KMS is tested as it deals with a variety of people and units depositing their own types of knowledge and contacting the KMS with requests for their brand of knowledge in terms of the content, form of reporting, frequency of requests, and purpose of the knowledge being extracted from the system.

Rubenstein and Geisler (2003, 101) argue for a more staggered approach. They believe that a piecemeal introduction of the KMS in a functional operating unit would prove a better way to implement the KMS, since such a piecemeal approach "provides an opportunity to back off and reappraise it if the KM approach does not fly immediately." However the enterprise chooses to implement its KMS, such a "test first, then apply overall" tactic has its advantages, anchored in caution and the ability to retry in case of failure. The multiple-core model makes it more difficult to reappraise or retry the implementation of the KMS, once it fails upon installation. Conversely, implementing the system across the enterprise sends a resounding message to all stakeholders that senior management is serious about KM and that the KMS is indeed a necessary reality (Todling et al. 2006).

THE PIGGY-BACKING MODEL

The piggy-backing model of the implementation of the KMS calls for a tentative and less energetic approach than the multiple-core model. It entails, at least initially, the installation of the KMS as an add-on to an existing information system. The idea is to "piggy-back" on the current MIS in the organization, particularly with regard to its hardware and linkages to other systems in the enterprise.

In this model, the KMS becomes at first another feature of the information system in the organization. This is a more cautious approach than the testing of the system in a single unit or function (as advocated by Rubenstein and Geisler). Rather, the implementation of the KMS relies on the established experience and success of the existing information system.

The main advantage of this model is the reduction of risk associated with the KMS, although the piggy-backing on the MIS effectively diminishes the unique appearance of the KMS as a stand-alone and different entity. The model does allow for a more secure installation, since it is on top of a system with prior experience, a system that has already been battle-tested (Komninos 2000; Wang et al. 2006).

THE EXPLOITATION-EXPLORATION MODEL

This model is based on the framework suggested by March (1991) to describe the drivers of organizational learning. The framework addresses the conflict between the need or desire to *exploit* existing resources and the need or desire to *explore* new avenues and new approaches. When applied to the implementation of KMS, this model considers the tension between exploiting the existing systems (such as the MIS) and the exploration of new challenges in the installation of a new and complex technology system (Vanhaverbeke and Gisling 2007).

Figure 9.2   **Illustrative Stages in the Process of Implementation of KMS**

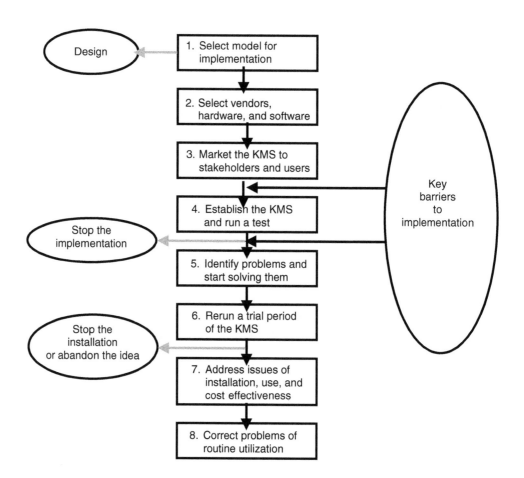

The model of exploitation-exploration may be fused with the previously discussed multiple-core and piggy-backing models. In this combination, the implementation of the KMS is conducted across the enterprise, while exploring new avenues and challenges in the installation of the system. When the KMS is implemented as a test within a single unit or as an add-on to an existing system, it will be exploiting the current resources of the organization.

THE STAGE-PROCESS MODEL

This model is predicated on the idea that a complex technology system, such as a KMS, must be installed in stages, as sequential milestones in the process of implementation (Kodama 2007; Rubenstein and Geisler 2003). In Figure 9.2 we provide illustrative stages of this formalized process of implementation of the

KMS. Implementation is thus viewed as a stage process, starting with the selection of the model to be applied and moving down the stages to the installation and test-run of the system. Among the stages are at least five instances or milestones where implementers reserve the option to stop the process while they assess the feasibility of its continuation.

Throughout the process there are key barriers to the implementation. They are discussed in the next section in this chapter. The barriers may act on the feasibility of the implementation process itself, not necessarily on the further utilization downstream of the stage process.

The Hybrid Process-Performance Model

This model espouses the addition of performance monitoring and testing at each of the stages in the process of implementation. As shown in Figure 9.2 at stages 4 and 6, the hybrid model calls for assessment of performance at *each* of the stages. This means that the option exists to abort the implementation of the KMS at each of the stages. It would seem, therefore, that this model adds a burden to the process of implementation, whereby the implementers have to pause at each stage and assess the feasibility of continuing with the installation.

The model is viable when the implementers accept the existence of credible measures and standards of performance at each stage of the implementation. This is different from the *audit* of the KMS, in which the enterprise evaluates the utilization of the system. Here we are merely concerned with the performance of the *implementation* process itself, rather than the performance of the ongoing KMS (Harryson 2007; Surinach et al. 2007).

In summary, the five models described in this section represent ways and means to implement a KMS in the organization. From a strategy perspective, planning the KMS and its appreciation as a crucial asset to the enterprise are widely accepted as true representations of reality. However, "the devil is in the implementation." In the final analysis, the success or failure of the KMS largely depends on the successful implementation and adoption of the system.

Is there a particular model that would increase the probability of a successful implementation? Experience with KMS installations in commercial and not-for-profit organizations has not yet provided a definite answer (Harryson 2007). In many cases the model selected was a combination of two or more of the five models depicted above. The reasons for selecting a given model vary according to the type of organization, its culture, and the preferences of its managers.

Barriers and Facilitators in Implementation

Table 9.2 shows some barriers and facilitators in the implementation of a KMS. The factors impinging upon implementation of a KMS in the organization are similar to those that generally affect "the implementation of any large-scale and enterprise-wide technology system" (Rubenstein 1989). There are three categories of barriers and three of facilitators.

Table 9.2

Barriers and Facilitators in the Implementation of KMS

Barriers	Facilitators
Choice of a wrong technology system	Support by senior and middle managers
Lack of adequate planning	Attributes of the KMS itself
Choice of a wrong model	Motivation and sophistication of the people who implement the system
Poor execution of the implementation process	Good marketing program to sell the KMS
Reliance on vendors who fail to follow up	

Barriers

The barriers are *technological*, *organizational*, and *human*. The technological barriers include the choice of a system (hardware and software) that is not easily implementable. These are systems that require complex setting-up procedures and high costs or that require the cooperation of too many existing units or systems in the organization, thus making it difficult to obtain acceptance and collaboration across the enterprise.

Another strong technological barrier is the tendency of many vendors of KM systems to simply "throw the system over the wall." This means that vendors will sell the system and make the initial effort to install it within the enterprise. But many vendors stop short of guiding the implementers in the organization through all the stages of the installation of the KMS, thus failing to resolve many problems that might arise during implementation (Rubenstein and Geisler 2003).

In reality, some problems that arise during the implementation process cannot be adequately foreseen, but we already have enough experience to be able to predict several major problems, such as those described above. The shortcomings in the vendor's commitment to full implementation may force the organization to employ secondary vendors whose task is to integrate the various components of the KMS provided by the primary vendor and to assist with the implementation process.

Organizational barriers include the poor choice of an implementation model and the lack of adequate planning of the implementation effort. The latter barrier is common in a variety of corporate settings, where the rush to implement a KMS overshadows the need to plan its implementation carefully. The rush to install a working system is due, among other factors, to management's failure to understand the complexities of a KMS and the need for thoughtful planning of the implementation project.

The human barriers are primarily manifested in a poor execution of the implementation process. This is largely due to the tasks being performed by members of the organization who lack adequate training and the experience needed to install a complex system such as the KMS. The implementation becomes fraught with problems of acceptance, collaboration, technical performance, and breakdowns in the initial connectivity—all issues that few implementers know how to resolve (Todling et al. 2006).

FACILITATORS

There are three categories of facilitators: managerial, systemic, and behavioral. The *managerial* facilitation includes the support provided by senior and middle management for the implementation of the KMS. The *systemic* facilitators are the characteristics of the KMS—as a system—that help to implement it with as few problems as possible (Santhanam et al. 2007). These factors are not necessarily the opposite of some of the barriers we listed in the previous section. This means that the absence of a barrier is not necessarily a facilitator, and the presence of a facilitating factor does not necessarily reduce the impact of a barrier to implementation.

This comes together in the behavioral category. Members of the organization who are motivated, highly trained, and sophisticated enough to understand the value of a KMS will have positive attitudes toward the implementation of the system. They will become a forceful factor in the facilitation of the implementation process.

MARKETING THE KNOWLEDGE MANAGEMENT SYSTEM

The literature on KM provides several descriptions of how to market the KMS. Rubenstein and Geisler (2003, 98), for example, argue that "new systems like KM have to be sold across the organization and to other outside stakeholders, if the system is going to be accepted and effective." Marketing the KMS is a key part of the implementation effort. It is also the link between the implementation process and the utilization of the KMS, following its successful installation.

The question is therefore not whether the enterprise should market the KMS, but how to market the system in an effective manner. Figure 9.3 shows some illustrative steps or activities in the effort to market the KMS. This figure benefited from the work of Rubenstein and Geisler (2003), Ryan and Prybutok (2001), and Troilo (2007).

The marketing effort consists essentially of four activities. The first is the articulation of the benefits that would accrue to all who participate in the KMS. These benefits must be related to the goals and aspirations of the various constituencies and, above all, linked to the overall strategy and needs of the enterprise. This will create good will with senior management.

The second activity in the marketing campaign for the KMS is to create a basket of incentives for people and units who agree to participate in the implementation of the KMS, as well as in its routine operation later. Members of the organization need a strong reminder of the rewards they might get from participating in the KMS, but also need a strong set of incentives to jump-start their participation.

Working with "champions" within the enterprise is the third crucial marketing activity. This is similar to working with those who shape and influence the opinions of the people to whom the enterprise is selling the KMS. Champions are partners in the implementation process. They hold key positions and enjoy the respect of their fellow workers and managers. For example, a large financial institution had implemented its KMS by working very closely with the director of information technology. The director served as a champion for the KMS, almost to the point of taking personal

Figure 9.3 **Illustrate Steps in the Marketing of KMS**

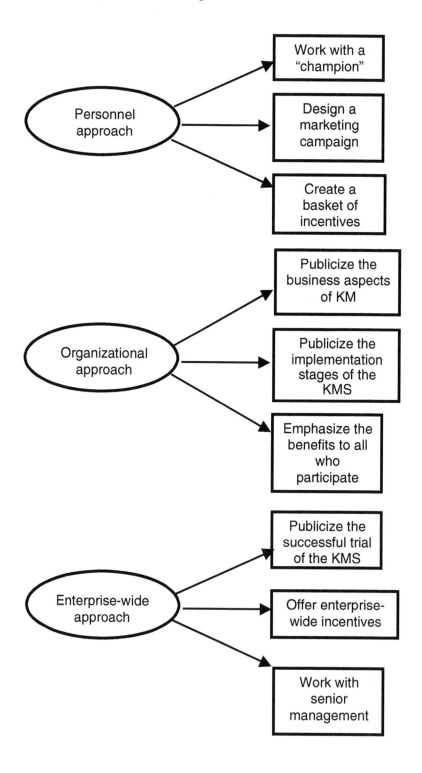

ownership of the system. He publicized the KMS among his subordinates and his contacts outside the organization, declaring it a "winning proposition."

Finally, the marketing effort should focus on acceptance or "buy-in" from as many people and units as possible in the organization. This activity is equated with "counting votes" in an aggressive attempt to pass a motion or a resolution by persuading potential voters to make up their minds in favor of the proposal—the KMS.

MARKETING TO EXTERNAL STAKEHOLDERS

As difficult as the effort to market the KMS inside the enterprise may be, it is not enough. There is also the need to sell the system to external stakeholders, including customers, suppliers, and regulators. Selling to these entities is done by the interactions of members of the organization with their contacts outside the enterprise (Rubenstein and Geisler 2003). The interactions need to emphasize the soon-to-be-installed KMS, its many advantages, and the need to connect with the systems in the external organizations.

The selling of the KMS to the external parties also employs the criteria and arguments used to sell the system inside the organization. The procedures and the potential benefits need to be the focus of the marketing effort.

For example, in a case of a consulting company, the implementation of the KMS was marketed to the customers of the enterprise by asking all the employees to connect with their own contacts in the organizations in which they consulted. Each consultant prepared a list of these contacts, and an aggressive selling campaign was devised to publicize the KMS to this list. In addition to the potential rewards for customers who would use the system, the marketing campaign provided detailed procedures on how to access the system from outside the company and the incentives offered to external users—such as access to sundry reports that the consulting company produced that were not included in the original consulting agreement with the customer. Another incentive was the offering of a guided test run for the client.

In summary, marketing the KMS is a key feature in the implementation process. It is hardly enough to install the system and then hope that users will flock to it or even that they will participate in its implementation. An aggressive marketing effort is required to bring the system to their attention and to establish clearly and forcefully that participation on their part is not only desirable but also a positive experience with built-in rewards.

THE ESSENTIALS OF KNOWLEDGE MANAGMENT SYSTEM IMPLEMENTATION

In Table 9.3 we summarize the lessons learned from the experience of many organizations: What are the dos and the don'ts in KMS implementation? The list in Table 9.3 is not exhaustive. Rather, it gives the key lessons of what has been shown to work and what does not.

The essentials include the steps we discussed in this chapter. Implementation requires a great deal of groundwork to attract and maintain support for the installation of the KMS. Conversely, when implementing the system, managers should avoid the

Table 9.3

The Essentials of KMS Implementation

What to do	Assumptions to avoid
Carefully plan the implementation process	Do not assume that "If you build a KMS, they will come"
Select an adequate implementation model	
Select vendors that provide comprehensive support	Do not rely on the vendor for implementation and the solving of problems
Market the KMS to internal and external entities	Do not underestimate the need to gain support throughout the enterprise for the KMS
Create a basket of incentives	
Work closely with champions of the KMS and with senior management	Do not assume that the implementation of the KMS will be straightforward
	Do not assume that the KMS is just another information system: It definitely is *not*

assumption that the KMS is just another technological or information system. The KMS is an extremely complex enterprise-wide system. It requires a specialized approach, a broad strategic perspective, aggressive marketing, and a carefully designed process for its installation.

LEARNING OUTCOMES

- The implementation of a KMS is a complex process that requires planning, marketing, and widespread support and cooperation across the enterprise.
- Implementers cannot assume that vendors will fulfill their promises or that the KMS is "just another technology or information system."
- A good implementation process for a KMS depends on an enterprise-wide effort of various stakeholders. The KMS has to be implemented with their cooperation and acceptance rather than imposed by executive fiat.

DISCUSSION QUESTIONS

1. What are the barriers to implementation of a KMS?
2. What are the facilitators of the implementation of a KMS?
3. Why is marketing the KMS (internally *and* externally) so important, and what are the steps in the marketing effort?

Using Knowledge Management
Systems

10

Processes, Barriers, and Facilitators

KEY LEARNING OUTCOMES

*You will know you have mastered the material in this chapter
when you can define and explain the following:*

1. Understanding the processes of the utilization
   of knowledge management systems.
2. The barriers to the use and maintenance
   of knowledge management systems.
3. The facilitators to the use and maintenance
   of knowledge management systems.

This chapter addresses the use and maintenance of the knowledge management system (KMS). This topic covers the routine use of the system, the processes involved in its usage, and the factors that inhibit or facilitate the operation of the KMS. This chapter differs from Chapter 9, which dealt with implementation of the KMS, in that it describes the next phase in the life of the KMS: the use of the system by its customers (Mingers 2006; Uzzi and Gillespie 2002).

We define the phase of utilization as the period in the life of the KMS after it has been implemented in the organization and when it becomes ready to be routinely operated. This means that "customers" or users are now able to deposit their knowledge into the KMS and to search the system and extract the knowledge they need (Cassiman 2006; Jashapara 2004).

This chapter also describes the barriers and the facilitators in the utilization of the KMS. As a complex system used throughout the enterprise, the KMS must endure a variety of barriers to its operation. In this chapter we list these factors and offer some relevant examples from organizations that attempted to address the impacts of these and similar factors.

UTILIZATION OF KNOWLEDGE MANAGEMENT SYSTEM: THE PROCESS AND ITS CHARACTERISTICS

An organization installs a KMS based on the underlying assumption that there are users who have needs for knowledge and who will use the system once it is installed and operational (Matusik 2002; Nielsen 2005). But who are these potential users, what are their distinctive attributes and preferences, and how will they interact with the KMS?

THE POTENTIAL USERS

Rubenstein and Geisler (2003) have identified several distinct categories of users. First there are the individual managers with distinctive knowledge-seeking styles and preferences. These differences are due to differences in background, professional training and preferences, and the function these individuals perform in the organization. The tenure and experience of individual managers with other information systems (positive or negative) will also shape their mode of utilization and knowledge-seeking behavior.

Second, there are groups of managers operating within distinct organizational units such as departments, divisions, or projects. They search and procure knowledge relevant to their unit, in many instances as a group or unit-centered activity.

From the perspective of the KMS, all the managers in the organization are potential users. Although they vary by individual attributes and how they use the system, they nevertheless represent the population of users. In addition, managers from organizations outside the focal enterprise in which the KMS is operating may also be potential users. These include managers in client organizations, regulatory agencies, and enterprises with whom the focal organization has ties of cooperation and joint activities or interests.

TYPES OF KNOWLEDGE-SEEKING USERS

In Figure 10.1 we list four types of knowledge users (organizational members) who interact with the KMS.

One such group is *squirrels*. They tend to hoard the system for whatever knowledge it contains and can offer them (Rubenstein and Geisler 2003; Thierauf and Hoctor 2006). These hoarders of knowledge tend to store away whatever they collect, using a variety of formats. They keep such knowledge in their heads, in their computers and other electronic devices, on paper, and in any other venue that allows them to record and store any and all scraps of knowledge.

Another type of user is the *selective*. Selectives search for knowledge that they absolutely need for a very specific task. They target their search very carefully to whatever they deem indisputably essential. Selectives are concerned with the effort, cost, and energy they expend in their search and subsequent collection and use of the knowledge. They are also less likely to forgive any malfunction of the system or to tolerate any excess of cost or effort in pursuing their search.

Figure 10.1 **Users' Knowledge-Seeking Styles**

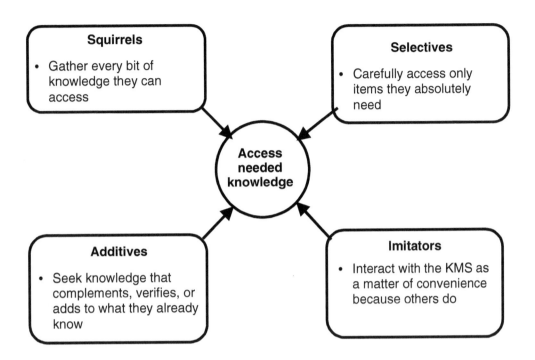

A third group of users search for *additives*, which are items of knowledge they pursue to complement what they already have attained. For example, a manager who receives a report on certain market conditions in the industry may search for additional knowledge on how selected direct competitors of the company performed under similar conditions (Gopalakrishnan and Bierly 2006).

Finally, there are those we may label *imitators*. Their search for knowledge is predicated on imitative behavior that "goes along" with what others are doing. They procure knowledge and interact with the system not necessarily because they need the knowledge but because "it's the thing to do."

This classification of knowledge-seeking styles is important for understanding how the system is used. A distribution of different types of knowledge users in the enterprise allows managers to map the motives behind the search behavior exhibited by users. For example, if a large group of users exhibits selectivity behavior, the KMS may be then adjusted to provide more specific and better-targeted portfolios of knowledge for these users. This classification can also influence the standards and policies that encourage members of the organization to deposit their knowledge in the system. We now turn our attention to this aspect of the utilization of the KMS.

DEPOSITING KNOWLEDGE IN THE KNOWLEDGE MANAGEMENT SYSTEM

Figure 10.2 shows the four approaches to the procedure for depositing knowledge into the KMS. These approaches refer to the kind of knowledge that members of the organization would deposit or share with the system. The first is the *generalist*, in which the member deposits a variety of knowledge items. In this mode a manager would routinely deposit trip reports, analyses of strategic market trends, and thoughts and observations about the enterprise. The sharing is done without a specific aim or need.

Another approach is the *specialized* mode, in which a manager shares with the KMS only knowledge related to a specific segment of what the manager does in the enterprise. For example, a manager in the research and development (R&D) department will share technical reports of the progress of a project, but not any other knowledge about the project, its antecedents, or the manager's thoughts about the technical or commercial probabilities of success.

A third approach is the *reply* to specific requests for knowledge. The KMS administrator may, from time to time, send out requests for a particular item of knowledge. For example: "What do we know about other companies in the business of our main competitor?" or "What are the factors that make our competitors so successful?"

The fourth approach is *automatic* transfer of knowledge that is found in the organization's records, reports, and other systems. The KMS scours the records in search of any knowledge they contain, however scholium this may be, by using methods such as key words and data mining (Davenport and Harris 2007; Leibowitz 2005; Poston and Speier 2005).

The modes of depositing knowledge are crucial to understanding how potential contributors and users interact with the KMS. Based on such understanding, the enterprise in which the KMS operates may structure its policies, procedures, and standards for interaction and depositing knowledge so as to accommodate the manner in which managers feel comfortable in sharing what they know. Incentives may be offered to those managers who focus on specialized knowledge to encourage them to share with the KMS other types of knowledge, perhaps on a more routine basis (Gaveth 2005; Maula 2006).

We should emphasize at this juncture that there is a substantial effort on the part of managers to deposit knowledge into the KMS and to search and extract knowledge from the system. This makes it very important to ensure that the system is commensurate with the habits of the managers in the organization in their effort to interact with the system (Smith et al. 2006).

WHAT IS THE CONTENT OF THE KNOWLEDGE MANAGEMENT SYSTEM?

In discussing the utilization of the KMS, the question that comes to mind is: "What is the knowledge that is being transacted, and in what form is it being deposited, searched, and extracted?" As we explained in previous chapters in this book, the knowledge in the KMS can appear in various modes. The codified form of nuggets of knowledge appears as propositions, statements, and similar ways people normally

Figure 10.2 **Selected Approaches to Depositing Knowledge in the KMS**

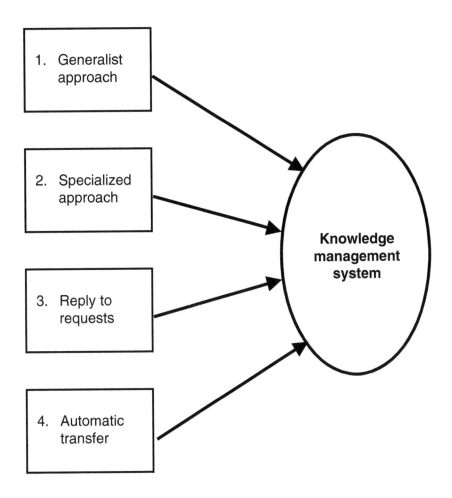

use to express what they know (Rubenstein and Geisler 2003). These linguistic or mathematical representations of knowledge describe ideas, thoughts, events, procedures, processes, standards, and solutions to specific problems (formulas, algorithms, and decision trees).

Once in these formats, knowledge becomes a tangible commodity for the user who searches the KMS and extracts the nuggets that seem to fit the search criteria. The content of the KMS is made of a variety of nuggets, some classified and organized according to a given system, others simply collected and stored under a more comprehensive categorization. Rubenstein and Geisler (2003, 19), for example, list some illustrative engines and "intelligent machines" available for transacting with the KMS in the commercial markets. Examples include "disaster backup," "hopes and dreams," "predicting evolution and progress in a discipline," and "options generation."

In some KMS the nuggets may be classified by organizational events, organiza-

Figure 10.3 **Characteristics of Utilization of KMS**

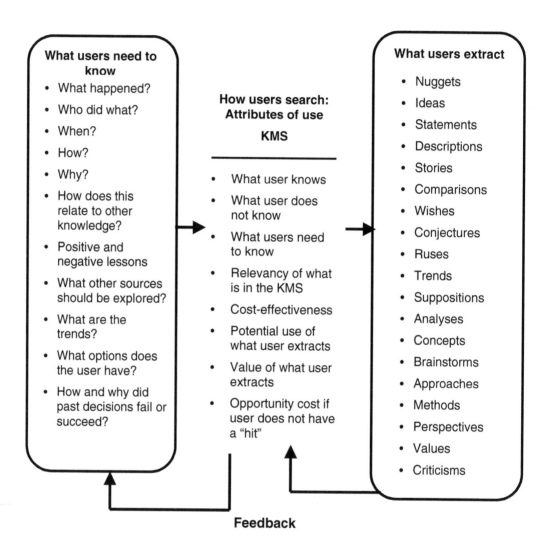

tional structure (for example, marketing or production), customers, regulators and regulations, and strategies of the enterprise. These categories are then integrated and coexplored according to the nature of the search parameters (Leibowitz 2006; Poston and Speier 2005).

Figure 10.3 depicts the types of knowledge that managers would likely be searching, according to what they require (needs) and the general search parameters they would apply in their quest for knowledge stored in the KMS. This figure shows a basic multistep and multiple-content process in the utilization of the KMS.

What Users Know and Do Not Know

What users need to know is a derivative of what they already know and what they believe they do *not* know and therefore need to acquire. At a press conference in 2002, former U.S. Secretary of Defense Donald Rumsfeld elaborated on this very point:

> Reports that say that something hasn't happened are always interesting to me, because as we know, there are known unknowns; there are things we know we know. We also know there are known unknowns; that is to say we know there are some things we do not know. But there are also unknown unknowns—the ones we don't know we don't know. So when we . . . pull all the information together, and we then say, well, that's basically what we see as the situation, that is really only the known knowns and the known unknowns. It sounds like a riddle. It isn't a riddle. It is a very serious, important matter. . . . Simply because you do not have evidence that something exists does not mean that you have evidence that it doesn't exist. And yet, almost always, when we make our threat assessments, when we look at the world, we end up basing it on the first two pieces of that puzzle, rather than all three. (Rumsfeld 2002)

Although this statement by Secretary Rumsfeld was later criticized, even ridiculed, it is a very accurate description of the types of knowledge that users collect and store in the KMS. It also expresses the parameters that managers employ in their searches of the KMS. Basically, Rumsfeld argued the following position:

1. There are items of knowledge that we know.
2. There are items of knowledge that we know (or recognize or concede) that we do not know.
3. There are items of knowledge that we do not know that we do not know. In other words, there is knowledge that we may need or find useful, yet we do not, at present, know that it exists.
4. We tend to make decisions on critical issues, such as threat assessments, that are based on what we currently know and on what we currently know that we lack, but not on that knowledge (which may be substantial) that we do not know that we do not know (the unknown unknowns).

The implications of these statements are crucial to the search parameters used in the KMS. Managers would obviously be concerned about knowledge that they know that they do not know. But what about the knowledge that is there in the system but that the manager does not know is there, somewhere? For example, the managers of a company developing a new product are very interested in the research and development of a competitor. The managers know the kind of R&D the competitor is undertaking, and they may even know that the competitor is secretly engaged in some R&D projects. However, the threats to the company's competitive position in the marketplace are those projects undertaken by the competitor on which there is absolutely no knowledge whatsoever (the "unknown unknowns"). In the old saying, "It's what you don't know that should scare you."

How can managers cross this uneven playing field where perhaps they know only

Table 10.1

Evidence-Based Management: Support and Criticism

Support for EBM	Criticism of EBM
EBM aids in rational decision making.	There is a wide gap between research and practice.
Managerial decisions are grounded in research findings.	Organizational politics often supersede the power of empirical evidence.
EBM helps to attain organizational goals.	EBM is focused on academic research outcomes, not on other types of knowledge.
EBM helps managers focus on their own organization rather than copy "best practices" of others.	Management is not a profession, so it is not required to be updated.
Simple ideas applied through EBM may have powerful influence on organizations.	Managers seem to do well with intuition as a mode of decision making.
Science, research, and evidence provide a solid anchor for cooperation between academia and practice.	

a fraction of what they need to know? (Muller-Merbach 2006; Perrott 2007). As we show in Figure 10.3, definitions of *how* managers search the KMS should be fine-tuned to look for what they do not know, including the possibility of needed items of knowledge that are *currently* beyond the scope of what they consider relevant or needed (Tordoir 1995).

Evidence-Based Management

In recent years there emerged an intensified discussion in the management literature of the concept of evidence-based management (EBM). This concept is amply used and widely accepted in health care delivery, as "evidence-based medicine" (Cascio 2007; Shortell 2006). According to a widely used definition, EBM "deceives principles from research evidence and translates them into practice that solves organizational problems" (Rousseau 2006, 256).

The concept of EBM and its role in organizational and managerial practice have been elevated to the point where Denise Rousseau made it the topic of her 2006 address as president of the Academy of Management. Arguing for wide use of this approach, she has suggested that EBM "promises more consistent attainment of organizational goals, including those affecting employees, stockholders, and the public in general" (Rousseau 2006, 256–257).

However, not all management writers share the optimism about the promise of EBM that Rousseau and other scholars have vigorously articulated. Several voices criticize the core assumptions of EBM as well as its applicability in managerial realities (Arndt and Bigelow 2007; Lawler 2007; Learmonth and Harding 2006). In Table 10.1 we show the supporting and opposing arguments for the theory and use of EBM.

Supporters of EBM argue that managers can indeed apply findings from the research literature to make better decisions and to improve their organizations. Pfeffer and Sutton (2007a), for example, suggest that a simple idea such as the need for hospital personnel to wash their hands frequently became a powerful instrument that, when applied by hospital administrators, helped to control infections within hospitals. Also in the field of health care delivery, Shortell (2006) proposes several mechanisms for health administrators to improve their decision-making procedures by anchoring them in management research in their own industry and in other sectors. Rousseau and McCarthy (2007) have extended the advantages of EBM to show how this perspective can be used to educate current and future managers.

Criticism of Evidence-Based Management

As Table 10.1 shows, critics of EBM have raised five key arguments in their doubts about the potential uses and advantages of this approach. The first is the wide gap that exists between academic research and the sources that practicing managers prefer to consult and to use in their decision-making procedures. Lawler (2007, 1033) suggests that "even where research results are known and have clear implications for practice, they may not impact practice because they run counter to what practitioners prefer to do or believe is right." Similarly, Cohen (2007)—comparing practitioner publications with research journals—concludes that the former are more relevant to what practitioners need, while the latter produce esoteric outcomes of little use or interest to practitioners. Cascio (2007, 1010) goes further when he cites a comment by a business manager: "Have you ever tried to read a research study or academic journal? They're overwritten, irrelevant, convoluted, and have poor sentence structure." This sentiment is also expressed by Rynes et al. (2007).

The second criticism is that EBM is focused on research results, rather than on a broader range of knowledge sources (Learmonth 2006; Ray and Stewart 2007). Although some authors advocate a variety of sources for practitioners (Pfeffer and Sutton 2006a, 2007), the discussion in the management literature on EBM has focused almost exclusively on the advantages to be derived from scientific research for the practice of management. This emphasis leaves out of the discussion such knowledge sources as experience, organizational records, and tacit knowledge of members of the enterprise (McKenna et al. 2006).

The third item in the critique of EBM is that managers are not professionals and hence not required to keep themselves updated nor tested on the latest findings and "best-available evidence" (Rynes et al. 2007). Arndt and Bigelow (2007, 1) suggest that EBM "emulates evidence-based medicine and is presented as a new and exemplary decision-making process for managers that is expected to eliminate over-use, under-use, and misuse of management practices." However, the authors concede that "in contrast to medicine, there are no practice guidelines or systematic reviews of the effectiveness of treatments for managers." Unlike lawyers or physicians, managers do not need certification nor do they undergo periodic testing. Although managers are urged to consult the research literature for their own edification, they are not obligated to do so. Hence, if they have any doubts about the relevance of the literature to their immediate needs, they will decide against consulting the evidence or incorporating it into their decision processes.

The fourth criticism is the argument that there is no unified front or agreement among academics on what constitutes "best evidence." Learmonth and Harding (2006) suggest that political considerations may affect the categorization of what is evidence and what is relevant, thus establishing hierarchies of evidence that are far from being truly objective.

Finally, there is a belief among managers that intuition as a mode for making decisions is "good enough" and that resorting to EBM though consultation with and reliance upon research findings will not improve the effectiveness of these managerial decisions (Dane and Pratt 2007; Nichols 2006). Sadler-Smith (2007, 52) argues that intuition can be effective in making good decisions when the manager has adequate expertise and experience; conversely, when managers overly focus their effort on analyzing evidence they collected from the scientific literature, they may face the risk of "paralysis by analysis." So, in some instances, intuition, "gut feelings," and "hunches" may be a good mode of decision making for managers, thus dispensing with the highly rational analysis that is based on "best available evidence" (Noordink and Ashkanasy 2003, 140).

IMPLICATIONS FOR KNOWLEDGE MANAGEMENT

The discussion in the management literature of EBM is still in its infancy. But scholars are starting to envision a more concise and applicable procedure for the stratification of EBM for managerial decision making and for the training and education of managers (Jensen and Szulanski 2007; Noordink and Ashkanasy 2003). When such a formalized approach is widely implemented, at least two critical questions will have to be answered: (1) How will managers access the knowledge they need to effectively manage within the domain of EBM? and (2) How will the KMS accommodate such a requirement, with what kinds of protocols and with what type of knowledge regime?

Geisler (2008) has explored these questions. He suggests that there currently exists a disconnect in the literature between the design and implementation of the KMS and the movement toward a more viable adoption of the EBM approach. As we describe in this book, the parameters in the design and utilization of the KMS are focused on the needs and preferences of managers. These needs are not yet specified coherently in terms of the variables of EBM (Engelbrecht 2007; Rubenstein and Geisler 2003).

Clearly, the design, implementation, and utilization of the KMS in the organization must be strongly linked to the requirements of EBM. The KMS must be able to include findings, conclusions, and lessons from the scientific literature. Even when studies are not conclusive and the paradigms of management scholarship are in stages of growth, with much uncertainty and internal division (Sadler-Smith 2007; Williams and Doessel 2007), the KMS must be able to serve as a depository for *all* this knowledge base at the discretion of potential searches by managers.

CHARACTERISTICS OF KNOWLEDGE MANAGEMENT SYSTEM UTILIZATION

The actual utilization of the KMS will be subjected to two main factors: (1) the attributes of the system, and (2) the behavior and perceptions of users. Figure 10.4 illustrates these two categories.

Figure 10.4 **Factors Influencing the Utilization of KMS**

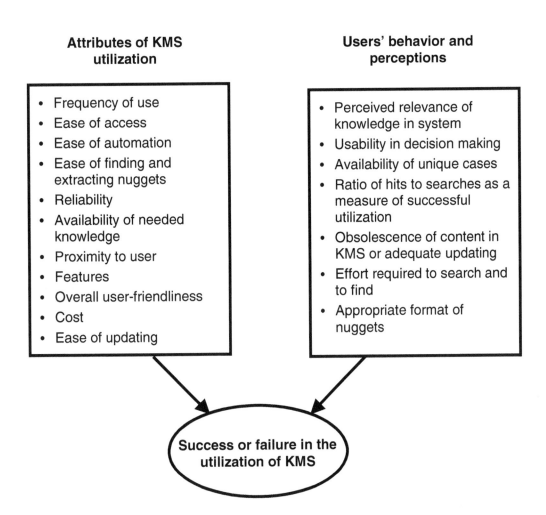

Like any technology system, and especially a system of information or knowledge technology, the KMS must satisfy not only the technical and economic needs of users, but also their perception of what constitutes a "useful" system (Garfield 2006; Rubenstein and Geisler 2003). The KMS provides users with a *service*; hence it must include the attributes of reliability, recoverability, supportability, and flexibility.

Managers in the organization will utilize the KMS if they believe that it has value and provides them with the relevant knowledge that they can easily apply to their daily tasks of making decisions and managing the enterprise. If the KMS is expensive, sluggish, slow, unreliable, not user-friendly, or contains knowledge they do not deem to be relevant, managers will avoid using the system either to deposit their knowledge into it or extract knowledge they need.

We recognize that users will vary in their requirements, patterns of search and

Figure 10.5 **Relationship Between Effort Expended in Operation and Utilization of KMS and Managerial Resistance to the System**

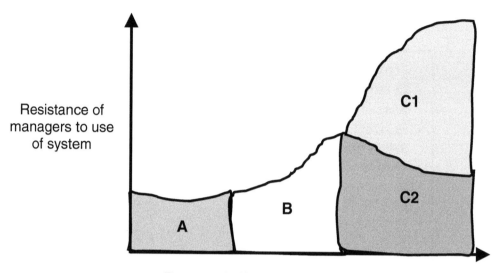

A = Zone of Initial Resistance to New Technology/System
B = Zone of Gradual Increase in Resistance as Managers "Test" the System
C1 = Zone of Second Burst of Resistance After the Systems Utility Is Not Proven to Users
C2 = Zone of Reduction in Resistance if the KMS Is Perceive as Useful to Users

utilization, and their preferences and tolerance for the working of the system. Benchmarks and standards of utility will be established once the system is in operation, but there are already some parameters of the desired performance of such systems that we know from other information technology systems that do provide minimally acceptable service to users (Jensen and Szulanski 2007).

Barriers and Facilitators in Utilization of Knowledge Management Systems

What are the factors that impinge upon the use of the KMS? Why would managers in the organization decide not to share what they know and not to search the KMS for the knowledge they need? This phenomenon reflects the resistance that managers might exhibit to the operation and utilization of the KMS in their organization. In Figure 10.5 we show the relationship between the degree of effort in establishing, maintaining, and using of the KMS by managers and the level of their subsequent resistance to the system.

In Figure 10.5 we see that once the system is in operation and the level of utilization increases, resistance may be reignited (zone C1) if the users perceive the system

Table 10.2

Barriers and Facilitators in the Utilization of the KMS

Category	Illustrative barriers	Illustrative facilitators
Psychological or human factors	Fear of change and new technologies Reluctance to express doubts about system Lack of motivation and psychological rewards	Ego-driven desire to accept challenges of KMS Previous positive experience with IT systems
Economic or financial factors	Lack of cost-effectiveness Less expensive alternative modes of obtaining knowledge	Cost-effectiveness Users' perception that *not* using the system is an expensive choice
Organizational factors	Previous negative experience Lack of adequate organizational rewards Existence of alternative means to gain knowledge Fear of losing power	Good marketing effort Supportive culture Anecdotal support for successful use Adequate system of rewards and incentives
Technological factors	The system is new, unfamiliar, too complex The system is not connected to the enterprise	Adequate training for users Anecdotal experience of a technically "good" system

to be of little value. If, however, users find the system useful, the level of resistance may decline (zone C2).

What then are the factors that influence the degree of utilization, and are they different for the four possible zones of resistance depicted in Figure 10.5? The barriers and facilitators to the utilization of the KMS may be classified into four major categories: (1) psychological or human factors; (2) economic or financial factors; (3) organizational factors; and (4) technological factors. In Table 10.2 we list examples of barriers and facilitators in all four categories.

Lee (2006), for example, describes the use of a KMS in a South Korean company. The Korean managers restricted their use of the KMS, but did not openly express their criticism of the system because it would have been seen as disrespectful to the company. Even items of knowledge perceived to be of little use remained in the KMS and "gained the aura of authority" (368).

Cullison (2006) lists seven barriers to the utilization of KMS. The first is what he calls "tall poppy." Managers are reluctant to interact with the KMS because they do not want to stand out by revealing what they know or what they need. The second barrier is the "shrinking violet" type of managers who are reluctant to use the KMS because they convince themselves (and others) that they have little to offer or that their department or task is unique, so they are unable to share what they know. The third is the barrier that Cullison calls "on the web," whereby managers contend that all useful or needed knowledge has already been codified and exists somewhere in some database, such as the Internet. However, as Zhang (2007) explains, the increasing volume of content in such repositories as the Internet makes it much more difficult to access and to extract the needed items of knowledge.

Cullison next describes the barrier of the "community of practice everything." This phenomenon refers to the emergence of communities or groups of people who share their knowledge within the group but tend to withhold it from those outside. The "not invented here" barrier is well known in research and technology organizations. It refers to managers believing that they and their unit are unique to the extent that they have little to learn from anyone else. The sixth barrier is what Collins calls "ignorance is bliss." Managers become so entrenched in their ways that they tend to reject external knowledge. They have come to believe that they are doing their job well and thus have no need for an infusion of new knowledge. Finally, Cullison describes the barrier of "Tom Tom," which refers to the tendency of managers, particularly men, who reject any help lest it appear as a sign of weakness. They strive for what they believe to be self-sufficiency.

In describing their experience in Hong Kong, Chan et al. (2006) list culture and technology attributes of the KMS as key categories of barriers to use. They suggest that cultural imperatives in Hong Kong favor interpersonal exchange of knowledge and discourage the use of an intermediary in the form of a technology-based system.

Lin and Kwok (2006), describing the use of a KMS at Hewlett-Packard in China, also view cultural imperatives as main drivers of success or failure. For example, they argue that "hoarding rather than sharing knowledge is the predominant social norm in China. One's expertise is supposed to distinguish one from others and it will only be valuable when the expertise is hoarded to the original knowledge owner" (22).

BARRIERS TO UTILIZATION AND ZONES OF RESISTANCE

When we compare the various barriers to utilization of the KMS with the zones of resistance shown in Figure 10.5, it seems that psychological and cultural barriers operate most rigorously in zone A, where the initial resistance takes place because it is embedded in the users and their set of beliefs, norms of behavior, and values. As the KMS is put to use and managers gain experience of its utility, the other categories of barriers (economic, organizational, and technological) would emerge as the main drivers of resistance and underutilization of the KMS.

The organization in which the KMS is implemented and put into operation can learn from this comparison. In summary, the barriers embedded in the user will be the first to impinge upon use of the system, before an adequate mass of experience about its utilization is accumulated. Therefore, any strategies to improve utilization and attenuate users' resistance must first account for the factors of psychology and culture.

LEARNING OUTCOMES

- The utilization of the KMS is subjected to a set of psychological, financial, organizational, and technical barriers and facilitators.

- EBM, albeit at its initial step of academic development, may become a driving force in determining the type of utilization of the KMS.
- The knowledge-seeking styles of potential users are paramount in understanding the mechanisms by which managers utilize the KMS.

DISCUSSION QUESTIONS

1. How do different types of knowledge-seeking users impact the utilization of the KMS?
2. What are the main barriers and facilitators in the utilization of the KMS?
3. Why is the KMS underutilized in countries where cultural norms favor strong personal relations?

PART III

METRICS AND IMPACTS OF KNOWLEDGE MANAGEMENT AND KNOWLEDGE MANAGEMENT SYSTEMS

In Part III of this book we discuss the measurement of knowledge and knowledge management. This part is a novel feature of this textbook. The four chapters in this part of the book introduce notions, processes, and metrics of what constitutes knowledge and knowledge management systems.

The topic of metrics discussed in this part offer the reader a coherent perspective of how to measure and evaluate the knowledge flow and the knowledge systems in organizations. In the current knowledge economy it is necessary to have criteria and measures of the benefits from knowledge systems and the tools to measure such benefits. In this part the reader is exposed not only to the models and theory of what constitutes knowledge, but to actual criteria and metrics. This exposure greatly facilitates the further analyses of the cases included in this book.

This part of the book provides a comprehensive description and analysis of the metrics of knowledge and knowledge systems. The reader will thus be able to evaluate the performance of the knowledge systems in his or her organization. Such abilities represent an important element of competitive advantage that this part of the book offers its readers.

Measuring the Impacts, Value, and Benefits of Knowledge Management

```
╭───────────────────────────────────────────────────╮
        KEY LEARNING OUTCOMES

  You will know you have mastered the material in this chapter
       when you can define and explain the following:

     1. The nature of epistemetrics.
     2. The impacts and the benefits of knowledge
        management.
     3. The value of knowledge management.
╰───────────────────────────────────────────────────╯
```

In this chapter we address the topic of the metrics and measurement of knowledge management (KM). We explore the literature that has attempted to answer such questions as these: What are the impacts of KM? What are the benefits that constituents derive from KM? How can enterprises measure these impacts and benefits? Can enterprises define and measure the value derived from KM?

We provide the reader with an extensive review of the relevant literature, supplemented by our own model and system of metrics. The chapter starts with a discussion of the nature of epistemetrics, a notion coined by Rescher (1989, 2005). We expand the concept and also focus it to concentrate on the measurement of KM and knowledge management systems (KMS). After describing the relevant literature on measuring the impacts and benefits of KM, we discuss the value of KM and the rationale and methods for its evaluation. In all these topics we survey the literature and complement the survey with our own contributions to the state of the art (Geisler 2000).

THE NATURE OF EPISTEMETRICS

Epistemetrics (the metrics of knowledge) is a conceptual space that consists of the measurement of the attributes of knowledge, including its origins, processes, flow, and assessment of its value to users. Epistemetrics is a subfield of the study of knowledge and knowledge systems. It contains three complementary topics: (1) what is measured, (2) how it is measured, and (3) why it is measured. Nicholas Rescher's original conception of epistemetrics is derived from his prolific work in the philosophy of knowledge (Rescher 1989, 2005). The key to his definition of epistemetrics is his focus on the role that methodology plays in the scientific method. He argues for an enhanced epistemological role for the methods used to link scientific conjectures with experiential data. Unlike the notion of epistemetrics that we employ here as the "metrics of knowledge," Rescher's notion of epistemetrics is not about the measurement of knowledge. Rather, it concerns such topics as Kant's conception of knowledge, Spencer's law of cognitive development, and the limits of knowledge.

How people measure knowledge is strongly related to *what* they measure. Epistemetrics is a new perspective on knowledge and KM. It attempts to address the most poignant criticisms of the nascent field of KM and some of the reserved, perhaps timid, explorations of the legitimacy of this new field of study (Fong and Chu 2006; Geisler 2008a; Styhre 2003).

EPISTEMETRICS: WHAT PEOPLE KNOW

Knowledge is shared and externalized in many forms, including nonverbal modes, symbols, and signs. A preferred mode is the use of language in the form of statements or intellectual "nuggets," such as "If x, then y." This mode is preferred by humans for long-term exchange because it offers varied forms of usage and is much more conducive to measurement than symbols and nonverbal communication. As writing and methods of documentation arose, this mode of knowledge sharing became a superior form of extending the sharing of knowledge to posterity. It also added accuracy and attributes such as transportability and accountability, which were far superior to the traditional oral histories and narratives (Sunstein 2006).

These nuggets are transcriptions of *what* people know in a form suitable for exchanging with others. They are different and more complex than merely "meaning" assigned to data (as information is often defined) or just data capable of being communicated (Geisler 2000; Rubenstein and Geisler 2003).

The measurement of knowledge starts with the transcribed form shared as intellectual nuggets. These statements and propositions describe the knowledge being shared. Once in the public domain, they may be entered into a formal framework where they can be stored, edited, preserved, and diffused. The resulting formal structure where such manipulations occur is the core of KM.

What managers know is therefore the content of knowledge that they share and that they collect and maintain in organizational systems. What they know is also the knowledge that they exchange and diffuse through personal contacts, without necessarily resorting to formally established knowledge systems (Bapuji and Crossan 2005; Holsapple and Jones 2005). As we described in earlier chapters, what managers know are the nuggets of their cognition, skills, experience, and insights that they accumulate within their organizations and their jobs.

EPISTEMETRICS: HOW PEOPLE MEASURE

Organizations measure knowledge transfer, sharing, and diffusion by focusing on individuals, groups, and units, and the mechanisms they use to transfer and to diffuse knowledge. Organizations measure the flow of knowledge by concentrating on the formal and informal means of knowledge flow and diffusion. In this context, the KMS is a key, but not the only, means of sharing and transferring knowledge.

We remind the reader that in this chapter we address the topic of measuring the impacts and benefits of KM as a field of inquiry. This is a broad view of how KM contributes to the organization and to society at large. In the next chapter we will provide a more focused and precise review of the outcomes and impacts of the KMS (Guyer 2008).

EPISTEMETRICS: WHY PEOPLE MEASURE

Enterprises measure KM because they are interested in the impacts and benefits that this activity produces in the organization. As enterprises become increasingly dependent on knowledge as an engine of the economy and as a very powerful driver of social change, it becomes necessary to be able to evaluate the impacts of this area of human endeavor (Parisi and Henderson 2001).

In Figure 11.1 we show a conceptual scheme of the reasons for measuring KM. The first reason involves the purpose of the activity. Geisler (2006) has identified three purposes for KM. The *utilitarian* purpose is defined as the need to achieve basic objectives such as the survival, competitiveness, and performance of the organization, its units, and its individual members. Enterprises measure the impacts of KM by how they contribute to the accomplishment of these goals.

The second purpose is *hedonistic*, which is defined as measuring the means by which KM contributes to the pleasure managers derive from attaining knowledge. This means that managers, as human beings, have to satisfy their quest for knowledge. They search for knowledge *per se* as the ultimate goal, rather than as the means to a higher objective. Managers pursue knowledge not only to accomplish their tasks, but also for self-improvement and self-actualization.

The third purpose is *systemic*, the need to add knowledge to the pool of what individuals, units, and the organization itself know and what they need to know. In time, this purpose may assume a life of its own, so that the systems (such as the KMS) will require a continuous supply of knowledge in the form of a bureaucratic process. Initially at least, the purpose is to collect and store managerial knowledge in a system that is available and accessible to stakeholders (Poston and Speier 2005; Van Buren 1999).

A second reason why enterprises measure the impacts of KM is the existence of beneficiaries. These are the individuals and entities that *directly* benefit from KM. They include the members of the enterprise and the stakeholders, such as customers, suppliers, directors, and regulators. Each of these groups imposes its set of requirements and desires for knowledge. It behooves the organization and its managers to generate and to provide the stakeholders with the knowledge they require.

Figure 11.1 **Conceptual Scheme of Why We Measure KM**

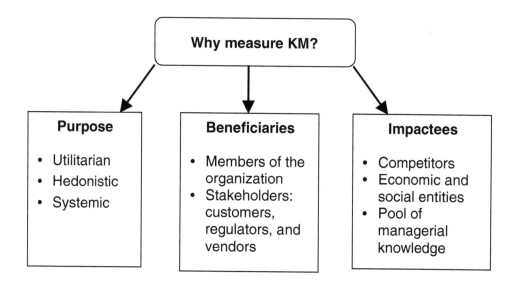

The third reason to measure is the set of other impactees, as shown in Figure 11.1 These include the competing organizations, the economic and social entities in the external environment of the focal enterprise, and the pool of managerial knowledge in the industry and in general. When the organization generates knowledge, it may impact other entities in the external environment of the organization, including those entities that have no direct contact with the organization or are not part of its network (Shin 2004).

People also measure the outcomes and the impacts of KM with the purpose of extending their understanding of how KM influences the social and economic aspects of contemporary life. The emergence and growth of the knowledge economy and the knowledge society, and the continuing empowerment of knowledge workers require an assessment of how knowledge is managed and how it impacts individuals and organizations (Geisler 2008a; Manchester 2006).

IMPACTS AND BENEFITS OF KNOWLEDGE MANAGEMENT

Geisler (2008b, 216) states, "Every nugget of knowledge is relevant and useful. There is no knowledge that can be described as immaterial, irrelevant, unnecessary, or without potential use." KM is the empirical venue through which enterprises are able to assess the value, impacts, and benefits of knowledge (Bassi and McMurrer 2005).

KM has been defined in many ways and via many perspectives—as we have documented earlier in this book. But the convergence of *knowledge* and *management* allows us to broadly define this activity in human affairs as follows: The set, or mix, of concepts, theories, methods, techniques, strategies, and structures by which individuals and organizations acquire, store, manipulate, transact, and utilize knowledge, and the

Table 11.1

The Eight Principles of Value of KM: Categories and Examples of Benefits

Category of benefits	Examples of benefits
1. Impacts on the individual	Improved literacy Improved competence Higher sense of accomplishment and empowerment
2. Impacts on the institution (project, team, enterprise)	Improved efficiency of operations Improved decision making Added prestige and credibility
3. Impacts on the economy and economic and business organizations	Improved productivity Cost savings Improved innovation Higher market share
4. Impacts on society and social organizations	Improved compliance and safety Improved health care, energy, transport, and other social services
5. Impacts on the disciplines of science and technology (S&T)	Refining and verifying existing knowledge in S&T Adding to the pool of S&T
6. Impacts on the system of knowledge management	Higher rate of knowledge dissemination Value-added to users
7. Impacts on the strategy of organizations, their growth and competitiveness	Contributions to growth, survival, and competitiveness Contributions to the art and science of strategic management
8. Impacts on the future	Better forecasts and planning Improved preemptive abilities

ways, means, and processes by which they evaluate its impacts and contributions. This definition is a combination of some salient perspectives common to the KM literature (Dalkir 2005). We reintroduce this broad definition here to establish the boundaries of this discussion of the impacts and benefits of KM. So, based on this definition, as knowledge is transacted by individuals and their organizations, this activity is viewed as KM, and a key component of this activity is the assessment of impacts, benefits, and values *derived from the knowledge being transacted* (Boisot et al. 2008).

EIGHT CATEGORIES OF BENEFITS DERIVED FROM KNOWLEDGE MANAGEMENT

Geisler (2008a, 218) advances a list of five categories of perceived and actual benefits that may accrue to users and beneficiaries of KM. These are individual, organizational, economic, social, and system benefits. We enhanced this list to a model of eight categories of benefits. They are shown in Table 11.1. The table depicts what we consider the eight principles of value, as operationalized by the categories of benefits and the examples for each category.

The eight principles cover the range of possible impacts of KM. These include benefits both to *individuals* and to their *institutions*. People and organizations utilize KM to enhance their capabilities, their efficiency, and the effectiveness of processes and methods they use to conduct their affairs and to perform their tasks (Hansen et al. 2005; Zuber-Skerritt 2005).

Economic benefits are those that can be assessed in economic or financial terms. They include improvements in productivity, use of time, and savings of costs of operations and resources (Strassman 1999). The economic impacts also include improvements in market share, rates of innovation and ideas generated, and a reduction in the effects of barriers to trade and economic growth. In the latter example, the more enterprises know about trade, economic exchange, and potential trading partners, the less likely they will be to oppose trade. Added knowledge allows for the recognition of trade alternatives and for the appreciation of the economic benefits from such trade relations.

Social entities benefit from KM by improvements in social services such as health care delivery, transportation, environmental protection, energy utilization, and military defense. KM also contributes to the effectiveness and operational efficiency of governmental entities. Added knowledge about what the population needs, its constituencies, and its makeup allows government agencies to plan and provide better services.

The impacts of KM on the scientific and technological disciplines (S&T) take two key forms: refining of existing knowledge and adding to the current pool of knowledge. In the first instance, KM contributes to the verification, retesting, and reconceptualization of existing knowledge in the sciences, technology, managerial disciplines, and all other areas of human endeavor where knowledge is of paramount importance (Boisot 1998; Scarbrough 2008).

KM impacts on the *system* by which it is shared and diffused will be described in Chapter 12. Here we list some examples of how KM influences the KM system itself. For example, KM may contribute to a higher rate of knowledge dissemination. As the amount and quality of knowledge increase within the system thanks to KM, so will the rate of diffusion and dissemination (Garrity and Sanders 1998). Furthermore, KM will also contribute to the value-added to users of the system. In essence, we are proposing that a successful management of knowledge will be beneficial to the system of delivery of knowledge itself.

The benefits of KM to *strategic management* in organizations are manifested in two major formats. The first is the contributions that KM provides to the growth, survival, and market competitiveness of the organization. Second, KM may also contribute to the art and science of strategic management. The more managers know about how their organization behaves in its market and environment, the more they are able to engender strategic planning and the more apt they become in strategic thinking (Lee and Lai 2007; Rezgui 2007).

The eighth principle of value refers to the impacts of KM on the *future*. As managers add to the human pool of knowledge and manage such knowledge with acuity and discernment, they become better able to forecast and plan for the future, thereby improving their preemptive capabilities. With the contributions from KM they improve their ability to gaze into the uncertainty of the future.

The knowledge accrued in recent years in the field of genomics, for example, has sharply reduced the unknown health risks confronting the human body. Science is able to predict with a comfortable degree of accuracy the body's predisposition to certain maladies and the potential onset of these illnesses. People can now take preemptive actions, such as a precautionary mastectomy when there is a strong prediction that a woman will contract breast cancer in the future. The more people know about nature and human life and their evolution over time, the more people can reduce the uncertainty about the future and, in some measure, prepare for such eventualities.

LESSONS FROM RESEARCH AND DEVELOPMENT MANAGEMENT

We have now identified the potential impacts and benefits of KM on various entities and beneficiaries. A key question remains to be answered: how do the outcomes from KM create benefits to their recipients? We have already stipulated that KM is an activity conducted by individuals and organizations constituting the transaction in knowledge and its management. How then will such activity produce the benefits we listed in Table 11.1? What are the mechanisms and the processes by which KM produces outputs, which then are transformed into benefits for the various recipients of these outputs?

In many ways, KM is similar to the management of research and development (R&D) or S&T. In both cases, there is an activity conducted by individuals and organizations. This activity entails the transaction in outcomes that are, to varying degrees, intangible. The activity also entails the transformation of these intangibles into outputs that can be diffused to other recipients and incorporated into other activities, hence providing the desired benefits (Geisler 2001; Rubenstein and Geisler 2003).

For over half a century, studies on the management of R&D have provided models of the ways in which the outputs from R&D affect organizations in the economy and society. In exploring this phenomenon, Rubenstein (1989) and Geisler (2000) opted for the process-outputs model, which provides visualization of the progression of the outputs from R&D as they are incorporated by social and economic entities downstream, thus making their contributions and benefiting these entities (Geisler 2001). The outputs from R&D are divided into four categories: (1) immediate, (2) intermediate, (3) preultimate, and (4) ultimate.

Building upon this process-outputs model, we have adapted it to the process or mechanism by which KM contributes to the recipients of its outputs. Figure 11.2 shows the dimensions or basic assumptions of this model.

The two key components of the model are the outputs from KM (classified into four stages) and the stages of transformation and diffusion of these outputs within the recipient organization. This means that it is not sufficient for the outputs from KM to be received by the recipient entities. There is also a need for these outputs to be transformed *within* these entities so that the entities can make use of the outputs and extract benefits from them.

In this model we define *outputs* as the outcomes generated by KM. These include the operational components of knowledge that we discussed in earlier chapters of this book, such as ideas, theories, techniques, models, statements of fact, concepts, notions, and frameworks representing reality, cognition, and emotions or sentiments of the producers of knowledge. The outputs also include the properties and behavior of the physical and biological worlds, such as the freezing temperature of water, the fractures in composite materials that propagate at a certain pace under a given regime, explanations of the diversity of life on Earth, and the behavior of black holes in distant galaxies.

Figure 11.2 **Basic Assumptions of the Process-Outputs Model of KM Contributions**

1. There are four identifiable stages in the process by which KM contributes to recipients of its outputs.
2. The outputs from KM flow through these stages.
3. There are distinct outputs at each stage that can be identified, measured, and compared across stages.
4. Each stage indicates a portal to processes or transformation and diffusion activities that can be identified, measured, and compared.
5. There are economic and social entities that are recipients of the outputs from KM, and such outputs may provide benefits to these entities. These benefits can be measured and they lend themselves to comparisons.

THE PROCESS-OUTPUTS MODEL OF KNOWLEDGE MANAGEMENT EVALUATION

We selected the process-outputs model to assess the benefits and contributions of KM because the phenomenon of the impacts of KM on recipients of its outputs is very complex. It involves a process with several stages and a variety of participating actors (Kleist et al. 2004; Liu, Olfman, and Ryan 2005). Some authors in the area of R&D management have simply attempted to consider the relationship between some attribute or measure of R&D (such as investments in R&D, patents, or publications) and measures of success or performance of the enterprise (such as sales, revenues, profits, market share, or stock prices). By applying these covariation techniques, researchers have ignored the complexities of the processes by which outputs from an activity such as R&D indeed impact ultimate outcomes of an organization. These researchers also have ignored the effects of many variables (besides R&D) that have a legitimate and powerful impact upon the success and performance of the enterprise. Examples include marketing and business strategies, implementation of strategic choices, and the complexities of new product development, design, engineering, and management of innovation (Geisler 2001).

In Figure 11.3 we show the stages of the process-outputs model of KM and the clusters of factors that act as intervening variables in the flow depicted in the model. We modified the original model of R&D evaluation to depict the assessment of KM.

The first group of outputs, the *immediate* outputs of KM, are the direct, intangible products of KM, including ideas, concepts, models, and emotions. Many of these outputs cannot be expressed very well or fully shared with others. Some are subjective interpretations of reality, while others are reflections and speculations.

We again remind the reader that this chapter deals with KM as a human endeavor, not the systems or mechanisms by which knowledge is diffused, transferred, and shared. This is not a trivial distinction. The outputs from KM are produced by KM transactions irrespective of the mechanisms by which they are transacted or the specific recipients who transact through such systems or mechanisms. In terms of R&D, this would be comparable to identifying outputs from research without specifically linking them to the laboratories that produce them or to the mechanisms by which they are transferred downstream.

Figure 11.3 **The Process-Outputs Model of KM Impacts**

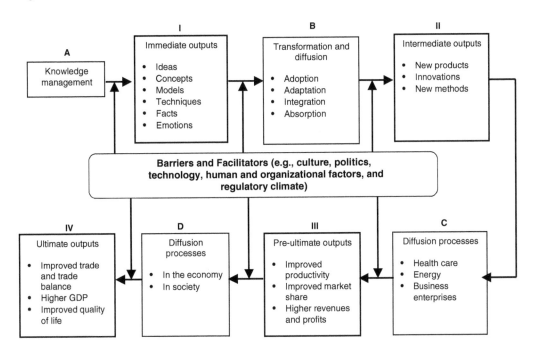

The immediate outputs from KM may be subjected to a series of transformations and diffusion processes. The outputs may be transferred by those who generate them to social and economic recipients—individuals and organizations (Geisler 2007b). These recipients would then adopt, implement, adapt, and absorb such knowledge, thus integrating these immediate outputs into their own activities. The outputs from these recipients are now classified as *intermediate* outputs. Examples include new products and processes, innovations, new production or marketing methods, advances in strategic planning and management, and improved managerial practices.

In a mode similar to the assessment of outputs from R&D, the *preultimate* outputs from KM are the outcomes from the economic and social entities in which KM had some impacts. The *ultimate* outputs, as shown in Figure 11.3, are the outcomes of the overall economy and society, once the outcomes from the economic and social entities have been absorbed and utilized.

The process works in the following way. Outputs from KM are classified into four distinct categories from immediate to ultimate. By themselves, the immediate outputs from KM (e.g., ideas, models, and techniques) do not impinge upon other people and organizations downstream of the knowledge continuum. Rather, as shown in Figure 11.3, they are absorbed along the way by social and economic entities, such as business and government enterprises, and are transformed by them into different types of outputs (intermediate and penultimate). These, in turn, now impact broader economic and social activities, goals, and outcomes (such as balance of trade, quality of life, and health status of the population).

OTHER APPROACHES TO KNOWLEDGE MANAGEMENT EVALUATION

The poet John Milton (1608–1674) wrote, "Where there is much desire to learn, there of necessity will be much arguing, many opinions, for opinions in good men is but knowledge in the making." The field of the exploration of KM outcomes and their consequences is certainly such a territory, where a fertile exchange of ideas and models has led to a variety of approaches discussed in the literature (Carlaw et al. 2006; Hudson 2006; Powell and Snellman 2004).

There are two major categories of variables or indicators in the effort to measure and assess the outcomes, success, and value of KM. The first is the set of factors determined to be critical to the success of KM. These are also considered drivers of the KM activity. The second is the set of outcomes or outputs from KM. We provide below some examples from each category.

CRITICAL SUCCESS FACTORS

There are certain goals or activities that the enterprise must achieve in order to be successful in its marketplace. Alazmi and Zairi (2003, 200), for example, define critical success factors (CSFs) for KM as factors that "are aimed at creating a KM environment that provides the company with some sustainable competitive advantage through the continued creation of knowledge, maintenance of current knowledge resources, and creating an environment in which the KM function can survive and grow." They list more than thirty basic factors, combined into nine driving forces: (1) training, (2) sharing, (3) cultural factors, (4) transferring knowledge, (5) top management support, (6) technology infrastructure, (7) creating new knowledge, (8) knowledge strategy, and (9) knowledge infrastructure.

Hariharan (2005, 19) proposes four basic categories for drivers of KM: (1) leadership, people, and culture; (2) relevance to business; (3) KM processes and technology; and (4) measuring KM. The latter is defined as measuring "the 'outcome' or 'lagging' measure of KM. Capture the impact of each replication on a critical business measure."

Ju et al. (2006) identify four KM value-chain activities: (1) knowledge creation, (2) knowledge storage, (3) knowledge distribution, and (4) knowledge application. Similarly, Ward and Abell (2001) studied forty-four pharmaceutical companies and empirically identified seven drivers for KM success in this industry:

1. Clear leadership and vision
2. A strategic fit of KM with organizational goals
3. Resources for KM identified and acknowledged and their business value demonstrated
4. Effective selection of KM projects
5. Organizational development to support KM activities
6. Marketing of KM initiatives and the involvement of all staff
7. An infrastructure that enables creation, sharing, and reuse of knowledge

Anantatmula and Kanungo (2007) have summarized the literature and extracted thirteen KM drivers or "enablers" of KM success:

1. Strategic focus
2. Effective leadership
3. Support of km by top management
4. Favorable culture
5. Measurement of results
6. Adequate technology infrastructure
7. Standard km processes
8. Involvement of top management with km implementation
9. Adequate content quality
10. Collaboration with and among users
11. Formalization
12. Communication effectiveness
13. Budgetary support

Grossman (2006) provides a summary of KM assessment approaches. He lists such methods as the balanced scorecard, intangible assets monitor, and intellectual capital index. Grossman concludes that although there are many technologies and perspectives available, there is a lack of consensus on which is best suited to adequately assess KM.

Other writers also discuss the various approaches to measuring intangible assets such as knowledge and the impacts of these assets on organizations (Anand et al. 2007; Geisler 1999; Hepler, 2006). There seems to have emerged an agreement among KM researchers that the assessment of KM should consist of metrics that are quantitative *and* qualitative, and that these metrics should include measures of technology, processes, cultural variables, managerial behavior, organizational dimensions, business functions, and the knowledge process itself (Anantatmula 2005; Geisler 2007b; Wong 2005).

MEASURES OF OUTCOMES AND VALUE

Unlike the case of drivers of KM and its critical success factors, there is less emphasis in the literature on outcomes from KM and the impacts they generate on recipients of KM. Most writers tend to link KM to the traditionally used metrics of financial and economic activities in the enterprise, particularly in business firms (Anantatmula 2007). These firms seem to extend the application of the common frameworks for assessing information technology (IT) to the case of KM. Liebowitz and Suen (2000) have correctly identified the problems inherent in using financial and accounting measures. They argue that these metrics leave unmeasured the unique attributes of KM and the impacts KM produces besides its financial contributions.

Table 11.2

The Four I's: Clusters of Metrics of Value Derived From KM

Clusters	Illustrative metrics
Infrastructure	Communication tools
	People skills and development
	Management support
Innovation	New products and services
	Lessons learned
	New ideas, concepts, and methods
Institutional growth and survival	Enhanced productivity
	Sales and revenues
	Comparative strategic advantages
Interorganizational cooperation	Enhanced networks
	Collaborative efforts with others

ADVANTAGES OF THE PROCESS-OUTCOMES MODEL

From the summary description of the literature we provided in this chapter, a pattern emerges in which writers identify a large number of KM metrics and factors, but do not show nor provide mechanisms to explain how these factors act to create value from KM. The critical success factors indicate how KM should be managed so that it will be a successful endeavor. The metrics of KM, as they pertain to financial and other aspects of the organization, simply offer a limited perspective of those variables that should be targeted by evaluators when assessing the value created by KM.

The resulting possibility seems to be to devise a framework by which we can "open the box" and follow the development of the outputs from KM as they are absorbed by downstream social and economic entities. This framework offers the following key advantages:

1. It allows for the introduction of various categories of metrics, financial as well as social and organizational.
2. It allows for tracking the process by which value is generated by KM to downstream entities.
3. It allows for a framework that can easily be tailored to the needs of each particular generator of knowledge.
4. It allows for an in-depth look at how value from KM is created and by whom.

SUMMARY FRAMEWORK: THE FOUR-I'S MODEL

A summary review of this chapter reveals the clustering of metrics of KM into four major categories. These clusters represent the metrics aimed at measuring the value obtained from KM. Table 11.2 shows these cluster categories, with examples of selected metrics for each category.

Figure 11.4 **The Four Eyes Model and Valuation of KM**

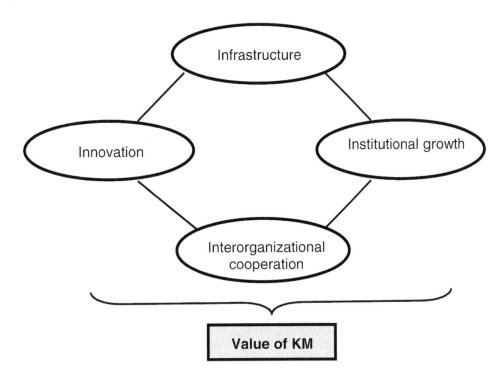

In order for any assessment of KM to successfully target the key elements of KM outcomes, the four "I's" depicted in Table 11.2 must be considered. These clusters define the basic elements of *value* created by KM. They also summarize many of the diverse approaches to KM assessment. Figure 11.4 shows the linking of the four-I's model to the purpose of valuation of KM.

INFRASTRUCTURE

Any assessment of the outcomes of KM and the value that KM generates must consider the elements of the infrastructure of KM. These include the driving factors that contribute to the successful application of KM in organizations. They also include outcomes of an *internal* nature to the organization. For example, by having a KM activity in the organization, members may acquire new skills, and management attitudes may change in favor of knowledge transactions. These outcomes of KM are internalized by people and groups within the organization itself (Geisler 2007b; Parisi and Henderson 2001).

INNOVATION

Perhaps the cluster of outcomes that owes most to the traditions of R&D evaluation, the outcomes in the innovation category include new products and services, ideas, lessons, and other outputs we earlier categorized in Figure 11.3 as the "immediate outputs" from KM. The contributions of KM to the state of innovation of an organization are crucial to the value accrued from KM. Based on the consensus in the literature, innovations are key to the growth, success, and competitiveness of the enterprise in the contemporary economy. If an enterprise can show that KM contributes to innovations, such a link will clearly enhance the role of KM in contributing value to the organization (Geisler 1999; Hepler 2006; Wong 2005).

Recognizing the value of KM in the enhancement of innovation does not necessarily also provide the means and modes by which such contributions indeed occur in the organization. KM contributes to innovations via ideas, concepts, lessons, and the like. However, the enterprise needs to examine the process by which such conversion would occur. This can be done by applying our process-outcomes model, carefully analyzing the integration of the immediate outputs from KM into the organization's processes, including R&D, and then monitoring how these outputs are transformed by the organization into new products, new services, and other innovations (Geisler 2000).

INSTITUTIONAL GROWTH AND SURVIVAL

This is a cluster of the contributions that KM makes to the growth and survival of the enterprise by enhancing productivity, revenues, and profits and by providing the organization with competitive advantages. This cluster includes the contributions of KM to the *strategic* management of the organization.

In some fashion this cluster is similar to the traditional models in which IT is portrayed as contributing to the enterprise's activities and goals (Compton 2004; Delone and McLean 2003). In the business enterprise these contributions are essential to the success and survival of the firm. By linking IT to such variables as productivity and revenues, evaluators of IT have been able to argue for its value to the enterprise. The same holds for KM.

INTERORGANIZATIONAL COOPERATION

In the knowledge-based economy and in a world in which globalization and outsourcing are strong determinants of success, it is imperative to assess KM also in terms of its contributions to interorganizational relations. The more the organization is able to initiate and maintain such cooperative efforts with other institutions, the more the organization will sustain its growth and competitive position in the marketplace. The more, therefore, KM can contribute to this web of relationships and cooperative effort, the more KM will be delivering value to the organization.

KNOWLEDGE MANAGEMENT, PERFORMANCE, AND PRODUCTIVITY

In several contexts above we have discussed the link between KM and the productivity and performance of organizations. This relationship is very similar to the link between IT and economic entities. In the thirty years since the massive proliferation of IT (also described as information and communication technology [ICT]) by and large the studies of the relationship between investments in IT and productivity have shown zero or little impact. Many researchers named this phenomenon the "productivity paradox" (Pilat 2004).

THE PRODUCTIVITY PARADOX

The key problem is that the correlations between investments in IT and statistics of labor productivity—even with lagged analyses—have been puny, to the extent that they could not show the contributions of IT to gains in the productivity of human resources.

In recent years some scholars have attempted to explain the paradox. Three possible reasons have been offered. One reason suggests that labor productivity statistics have underestimated the impacts of IT on the services sector. A second reason is the sampling techniques used in studies of IT productivity, and a third reason is the long time lag required for IT to have an impact on such a complex economic phenomenon as labor productivity.

However, one reason why the relationship has proven to be less strong than expected is the practice of researchers to statistically link two distinct occurrences without properly investigating their relationship. This means that a covariation analysis, in which researchers statistically connect two events that happen to vary simultaneously or even with some time lag taken into account, declares that the events are correlated, perhaps even in content or purpose.

KNOWLEDGE MANAGEMENT AND PRODUCTIVITY

The relationship between KM and productivity is heading in the same direction as that between IT and productivity. Researchers in the area of IT and its impacts have suggested that such impacts occur at the firm level, driven also by other factors such as skills of the workforce, innovation, and organizational change (Pilat 2004).

These factors are well represented in our four-I's model shown in Table 11.2. The contributions of KM to productivity of the workforce are contingent upon the effects of other factors, working in conjunction with KM, so that workers can be in a better position to access, utilize, and exploit knowledge in their enterprise. These other factors include managerial, cultural, and organizational variables.

KNOWLEDGE MANAGEMENT AND ORGANIZATIONAL PERFORMANCE

A different question concerns the link between KM and organizational performance. Does KM contribute to enhancements in the performance of organizations where KM is utilized? Two issues seem to emerge in the literature. The first is the definition of what constitutes organizational performance that can be measured in relation to the impacts from KM. Most writers who explore this issue of organizational performance tend to agree that this notion requires multiple indicators for its measurement (Rogers and Wright 1998).

Figure 11.5 **KM and Organizational Performance**

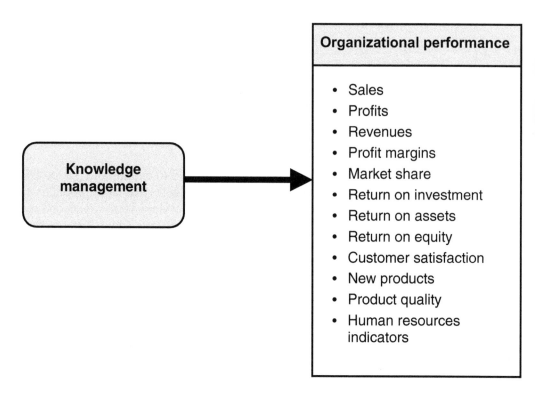

What are these indicators? In early research, Lieberson and O'Connor (1972), for example, measured performance by means of sales, earnings, and profit margins. Thomas (1988) measured the performance of retail companies in the United Kingdom in terms of sales, profits, and profit margins. Youndt and Snell (2004) measured performance with the notions of return on assets (RoA) and return on equity (RoE). Anantatmula (2007) measured performance as customer satisfaction and business growth. Figure 11.5 lists some of the commonly used categories of indicators that authors have used to measure organizational performance.

Several authors have criticized the focus on economic, financial, and accounting measures of organizational performance. Summarizing these comments, Rogers and Wright (1998) conclude that economic metrics of performance have been the dominant measures in the organizational and strategic management studies that linked various organizational dimensions (such as leadership, technology, and strategy formulation) with the performance of the enterprise (Youndt and Snell 2004).

As we show in Figure 11.5, there is room for other, nonfinancial measures of performance. These include process or operational metrics (such as product and service quality) and behavioral and managerial attributes, such as the characteristics of the workshop. The latter can be illustrated by rates of attrition and absenteeism, workers' satisfaction, and individual and group productivity.

Figure 11.6 **KM and Organizational Performance: The Alternative Relationship**

The second issue that emerges in the study of the relationship between KM and organizational performance is the direction of the relationship. In Figure 11.5 we show the direction from KM to organizational performance. KM is hypothesized to impact the various measures of performance: financial, behavioral, and organizational. There may be, however, alternative hypotheses, as shown in Figure 11.6. In this figure the measures of organizational performance also impact KM. As the performance of the enterprise improves, KM will change, becoming sensitive to the variability in the attributes of the performance of the organization.

This phenomenon is analogous to Phillips and Freedman's well-known study of the relationship between satisfaction and motivation (1984). For some time researchers hypothesized that employees who show high satisfaction are also likely to be highly motivated. Curry et al. (1986) conclude, however, that the alternative ordering might also be true—that employees who are motivated also will enjoy a high level of satisfaction. Curry et al. argued that the casual ordering of the variables had important implications for the theory and the practice of the relationship between satisfaction and motivation in organizations. This rationale also applies to the relationship between KM and organizational performance. The question remains: who influences whom? It seems that the relationship may be bidirectional and that both alternative links shown in Figures 11.5 and 11.6 may indeed be valid.

CREATING VALUE WITH KNOWLEDGE MANAGEMENT

The issue of measuring value created by KM has two key facets to it. The first is the definition of value; the second is the possible ways to measure and to extract such value from KM. Figure 11.7 shows illustrative types of value from KM: (1) value embedded in the KM activity itself and the organization that hosts it, and (2) value external to the organization, created by KM and diffused to other entities and enterprises outside the focal KM organization.

EMBEDDED VALUE

The value from KM embedded in the activity of KM itself is composed of impacts and benefits to the focal organization in which KM resides and is practiced (Spender and Grant 1997). The key value items are improvements in operations, processes, efficiency, and cost. These impacts also were listed within the four-I's model shown in Table 11.2.

The value from KM embedded in the organization is relatively easier to measure than the value accrued from KM to entities external to the focal organization. The main problem in measuring such embedded value remains the extraction of value and its isolation from other (non-KM) impacts on the organization. For example, improvements in operations and efficiency may be due to several factors, not necessarily driven by outputs from KM. This problem is also found in the measurement of the embedded benefits from R&D on the organization.

In the literature on R&D management there have been attempts to isolate the impacts of R&D from other factors, primarily in terms of measuring surrogate effects (Geisler 2000; Rubenstein 1989). Similar methodological difficulties in isolating the KM impacts will undoubtedly continue to plague the effort to measure the embedded value from KM.

EXTERNAL VALUE

External value is the value accrued from KM to entities external to the focal organization. They include innovation, economic and financial impacts, and the broader contributions of KM to the economy and society at large. Such value is difficult to measure. The best methodological approach described in this chapter entails opening up the process by examining the flow of KM outputs via the various stages of their

Figure 11.7 **Illustrations of Embedded and External Value From KM**

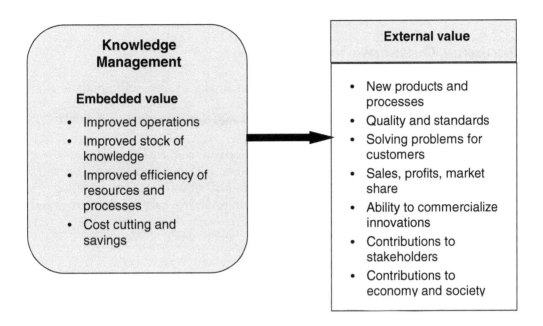

diffusion downstream. In each stage the enterprise is thus able to identify specific items of value created (Small and Sage 2006).

In summary, the measurement of outcomes and value from KM has benefited from similar models applied in the metrics of R&D. The issue of sharing tacit knowledge continues to be a major deterrent to the measurement of outcomes from KM. When individuals share the tacit knowledge they possess, the value of such knowledge is diminished (Boisot 1998). We have addressed this issue throughout this book. However, when this issue is explored across many individuals and their organizations, the knowledge that is being shared and the knowledge that remains in the possession of individuals seem to generate outcomes and value that lend themselves to measurement. Individuals who have knowledge perform better in their tasks so, as this phenomenon multiplies, value is created in organizations (Groff and Jones 2003).

LEARNING OUTCOMES

- Epistemetrics is the intellectual space in which we measure what KM *is, how* its outcomes are measured, and *why* we measure it.
- There are eight categories of benefits from KM: (1) impacts on the individual, (2) impacts on the institution, (3) impacts on economic enterprises, (4) impacts on social organizations, (5) impacts on the disciplines of science and technology, (6) impacts on the system of KM, (7) impacts on strategy, and (8) impacts on the future of humankind.

- The four-I's model of value derived from KM is based on the following key clusters of measures: (1) infrastructure, (2) innovation, (3) institutional growth and survival, and (4) interorganizational relationships and cooperation.

DISCUSSION QUESTIONS

1. Why is the process-outcomes model of measuring outputs from KM more useful than similar models?
2. What is the four-I's model of measuring value from KM? What are the pros and cons of this model?
3. How are impacts and value derived from KM measured?
4. What is the relationship between KM and organizational performance?
5. How is the "productivity paradox" of information technology related to the case of measuring outputs from KM? What are the similarities and differences between the two cases?

12 Metrics of Outputs, Benefits, and Value of Knowledge Management Systems

KEY LEARNING OUTCOMES

You will know you have mastered the material in this chapter when you can define and explain the following:

1. Measuring outcomes from knowledge management systems.
2. Models of value from knowledge management systems: What we learn from management information systems.
3. Structured and unstructured forms of knowledge management systems.

In this chapter we focus on the metrics of the knowledge management system (KMS). Whereas in the previous chapter we addressed the metrics and value of knowledge management (KM) as an activity in the broad sense of what constitutes knowledge, here we focus on the knowledge *system* itself. We address the mechanisms by which knowledge is transacted in organizations and the instruments that are used in the sharing, diffusion, and transfer of knowledge.

In this chapter we also concentrate on the evaluation of KMS and how enterprises can measure the outcomes and value derived from the use of these systems—for the enterprise itself and for all the stakeholders of the enterprise (Hall and Paradice 2005; Shin 2004). We consider the contributions from similar topics, such as the evaluation of information systems and information technology in organizations. There is much to be learned from the principles and methodology of evaluating information systems. These principles and methods can then be reconceptualized and adapted to the evaluation of KMS in organizations (Carlucci et al. 2004).

We also describe in this chapter the state of the literature on information systems evaluation, the lessons we can draw from this literature, and potential applications to the evaluation of the KMS. Chapters 11 and 12, taken together, offer a comprehensive view of the assessment of KM as an activity and of the KMS as a system or mechanism by which knowledge is transacted. By distinguishing between the metrics of KM evaluation and the assessment of KM systems, we thus address both perspectives of what constitutes knowledge and its valuation in the organization (Christakis and Bausch 2006; Small and Sage 2006).

THE DELONE AND MCLEAN MODEL FOR THE EVALUATION OF MANAGEMENT INFORMATION SYSTEMS

There is an extensive literature on the evaluation of management information systems (MIS). This literature extends over five decades, beginning with the initial implementation of computers and information systems in work organizations (Gray and Durcikova 2005; Verworn 2006). In general, the literature accomplished two objectives. First, it identified a variety of dimensions or categories of success of information systems and, in particular, the success of MIS. Second, the literature explored several models used in the evaluation of such systems.

Delone and McLean proposed one of the salient models in 1992. Searching for the "dependent variable" of the success of MIS, they surveyed the literature and identified several measures of MIS success, effectiveness, and contributions to the organization. Figure 12.1 summarizes their findings. The figure shows six major categories of success measures for MIS: (1) system quality, (2) information quality, (3) information use, (4) user satisfaction, (5) individual impacts, and (6) organizational impacts.

Delone and McLean also identified many studies of MIS success that employed multiple categories of measures. In essence, there are three main groups of measures: (1) those that assess *quality*, (2) those that assess *use* and *satisfaction* with use, and (3) those that assess *outputs* and their *impacts* on individual users and on the organization. Basically, these groups evaluate MIS in terms of (1) how good the system and its content are (quality), (2) how well it has been used, and (3) what the *impacts* on users are.

Delone and McLean then proposed a model of the assessment of MIS success that employs these three groups of measures. They suggested that the quality measures affect the nature of the use of MIS and the satisfaction of users with the system. Next, they proposed that the use of the MIS affects individual inputs that in turn affect organizational impacts. The authors also argued that the number of measures used overall, and in each category, should be substantially reduced to allow better comparisons among the many studies that evaluate MIS and utilize many different measures.

A decade later, the authors surveyed the use of their model (Delone and McLean 2003). They updated their model by adding the categories of service quality and intention to use. They also combined the individual and the organizational impacts into one category, net benefits, which includes such measures as cost savings, expanded markets, incremental additional sales, reduced search costs, and time savings.

As we envision a model for the evaluation of KMS, we have taken advantage of the almost two decades of studies assessing MIS. We identified four general lessons from the MIS experience. They are shown in Table 12.1. The first three lessons suggest that the MIS model is based on several categories and on multiple measures within

Figure 12.1 **Success Measures of MIS in the Survey of the Literature**

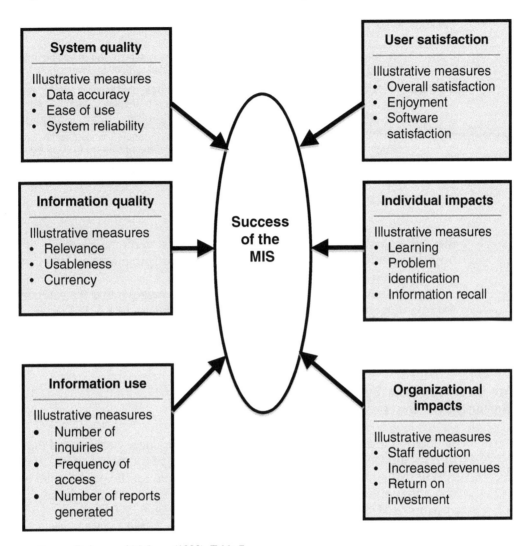

System quality

Illustrative measures
- Data accuracy
- Ease of use
- System reliability

User satisfaction

Illustrative measures
- Overall satisfaction
- Enjoyment
- Software satisfaction

Information quality

Illustrative measures
- Relevance
- Usableness
- Currency

Success of the MIS

Individual impacts

Illustrative measures
- Learning
- Problem identification
- Information recall

Information use

Illustrative measures
- Number of inquiries
- Frequency of access
- Number of reports generated

Organizational impacts

Illustrative measures
- Staff reduction
- Increased revenues
- Return on investment

Source: Delone and McLean (1992), Table 7.

each category. However, the model fails to include a system of weights or preferences of the categories and their measures. Such weights are needed not only to create, if necessary, indexes and macromeasures by bringing the categories together, but also to join the various individual measures within each category (Geisler 2000).

For example, the category of system quality includes several measures such as reliability and accuracy of the data. But what is quality, and how can an enterprise merge these measures into a "macroindicator," an index of what quality is, thereby focusing on a single quantity? Additionally, if the enterprise is planning on change or improvement in a category (such as quality), how can managers introduce a change

Table 12.1

Lessons to Be Learned From Evaluation and Metrics of the MIS Experience

Lesson 1: The MIS model is similar to models that evaluate research and development (R&D), utilizing several categories of varied metrics. (Geisler 2000; Seddon 1997)

Lesson 2: The MIS model utilizes a large number of measures, but does not offer a system to index or to combine these metrics into a macromeasure of the key categories, such as quality and use.

Lesson 3: The MIS model does not contain a framework to measure the relative importance of categories and metrics (weights); all categories of metrics seem to have equal value.

Lesson 4: The MIS model contains generic categories that can easily be applied to the evaluation of the KMS. Quality, use, and outcomes or impacts are also key to the assessment of the KMS.

that will be cost-effective? That is, do they focus on *all* the measures as targets for improvement or only on a few? If so, which few are preferable and have more weight within the category?

The fourth lesson has a more positive tone. It suggests that the categories used in the MIS model are generic and thus easily adaptable to the KMS. The success of both the KMS and MIS depend on attributes such as quality, aspects of use, and benefits derived from the system. Hence, the model, with some modifications, is applicable to the effort to assess KMS.

THE LITERATURE ON EVALUATION OF KNOWLEDGE MANAGEMENT SYSTEMS

In addition to lessons gained from the MIS experience, we surveyed the KM literature for models of the evaluation of KMS. Twelve journals devoted specifically to KM or that publish research on KM were surveyed for the period 1990 to 2007. We concentrated on models designed to evaluate KMS rather than variants of information systems or MIS (Hammer et al. 2004; Nidumolu et al. 2001).

The results of our survey were puny. The academic field of KM is in its infancy, and empirical studies are still few. Even fewer are empirical studies that employ evaluation of the success of a KMS. There are some theoretical perspectives explaining why KM systems should succeed or fail, but we did not identify a coherent, workable model aimed at evaluating their success (Carrillo and Gaimon 2004; Davenport et al. 2002; Lapre and van Wassenhove 2001). The survey showed a disjointed array of measures used to evaluate KM systems. The categories and their various measures were used, at best, empirically for specific instances of KMS implementation, without a solid theoretical background or unifying framework (Heisekanen and Hearn 2004; Newell et al. 2003; Wing and Chua 2005). Table 12.2 provides a snapshot of the findings from our research.

A critical analysis of the metrics used in the literature suggests that the evaluation of a KMS largely rests on two perspectives: the evaluation of the *system* itself, and

Table 12.2

Categories/Dimensions and Measures of the Evaluation of KMS in the Literature

Categories/dimensions	Illustrative measures
Knowledge demand in reuse	Cognitive style of individuals (Cappelin 2003; McGrath and Parkes 2007)
Behavior of communities of practice	Operations Roles and responsibilities Subgroup structure and organization (Stein 2005)
Quality of the system and its contents	Relevance Access (Kulkarni, Ravindran, and Freeze 2006; Wu and Wang 2006)
Organizational features	Reward system Goal setting (Kulkarni, Ravindran, and Freeze 2006)
Rate of diffusion	Culture Top management support Benefits to individuals (Quaddus and Xu 2005)
Reformulated MIS model	Quality, benefits, satisfaction, and systems use (Wu and Wang 2006)

Source: Survey conducted by Mansari Sharda, Stuart School of Business, Illinois Institute of Technology.

the evaluation of its outputs, *benefits*, and impacts. The first set of metrics—the KMS itself—is more prolific and has wider use by authors. Kulkarni et al. (2006) advocate using a mix of the quality of the system and organizational measures, such as goals set by the enterprise for the KMS and the reward system offered to users, as success factors. Stein (2005) focuses on the communities of practice as the mechanisms by which KMS develop and are utilized. Stein considers the practices and structural variables of communities of practice as factors that impinge on the success of knowledge diffusion in organizations.

The second perspective, the incorporation of benefits and impacts in measuring the success of the KMS, is not as frequently practiced by KM authors. Quaddus and Xu (2005) list benefits to individuals as one of four key variables that impact the diffusion of KMS and can be used as measures of its success. The other variables are culture, executive support, and the dream of having a KMS in the organization. Wu and Wang (2006) adapt a slightly reconfigured version of the Delone and McLean model.

There are, perhaps, three main reasons for the lack of original models that focus on outcomes, benefits, and impacts of the KMS. First, there has not been a sufficient array of KMS successes and failures that could or should have been studied and evaluated. The field of KM research, as we have argued throughout this book, is very much in its infancy.

Second, and as a consequence of the first reason, the scholars who have studied the few cases of KM systems in business and government organizations were not necessarily compelled to generate new models, since they could rely on proven models used by information scientists to analyze and evaluate MIS (Frydman and Goldberg 2007).

Third, because KM has only recently begun to distance itself from information systems science, much of the theoretical work and the design of an evaluation framework had to rely on the previous work by information scientists. This was a normal course of events, since the more established discipline (MIS) possessed research tools that could be adapted to the emerging structures and need of the new discipline (KMS).

Given the limited experience of KMS in practice, there are also fewer cases that lend themselves to a thorough analysis of outputs, benefits, and impacts on the constituencies and, in particular, the customers of the KMS. Murphy and Jennex (2006) illustrate a case in which a natural disaster (Hurricane Katrina and its aftermath) provided the opportunity to study the effectiveness of a knowledge system. Even in this case, the authors did not resort to the design and utilization of an evaluation framework specifically aimed at assessing KMS success. The study by Cooper et al. (2005) of KM at the Jet Propulsion Laboratory is another example of the phenomenon.

TOWARD A MODEL OF KNOWLEDGE MANAGEMENT SYSTEM EVALUATION

There is a clear need for a model aimed at the evaluation of the KMS. As the field of KM emerges from under the academic tutelage of information systems research and assumes the attributes of a separate discipline, it requires assessment tools designed for its own use. These tools may borrow from other disciplines, but should address the unique needs and characteristics of KM (Butler and Murphy 2007; Kincaid 1996).

In Figure 12.2 we propose such a model. This framework for the evaluation of a KMS emphasizes the outputs generated by the system and their impacts on the constituents of the system and the organization (Cabreva et al. 2006; Kleist et al. 2004).

SYSTEM ATTRIBUTES

In the search for the value that the KMS generates in and for the enterprise, the model starts with the attributes of the system itself. These attributes include the measures of use of the system, such as ease and frequency of use, the economics (cost), the degree to which the system is accessible to users, and the system's flexibility, which refers to the degree to which the KMS can adapt to the changing needs, objectives, and requirements of the enterprise. In Part IV of this book we offer two cases that address the issue of flexibility and adaptability of the KMS (JetBlue and Siemens).

CONTENT ATTRIBUTES

A related set of attributes refers to the knowledge content of the KMS. How relevant, useful, and current is the knowledge that the KMS contains? Can it be seamlessly extracted and adapted to the knowledge base of the user? How much of the knowledge in a given area or discipline does the content of the KMS cover? When a user searches for an item of knowledge, there should be an acceptable probability that the item of knowledge indeed exists in the KMS (Chen and Chen 2005; Wei et al. 2002).

The content attributes offer a glimpse into the characteristics of the knowledge in

Figure 12.2 **Toward a Model of KMS Evaluation: Metrics of Success**

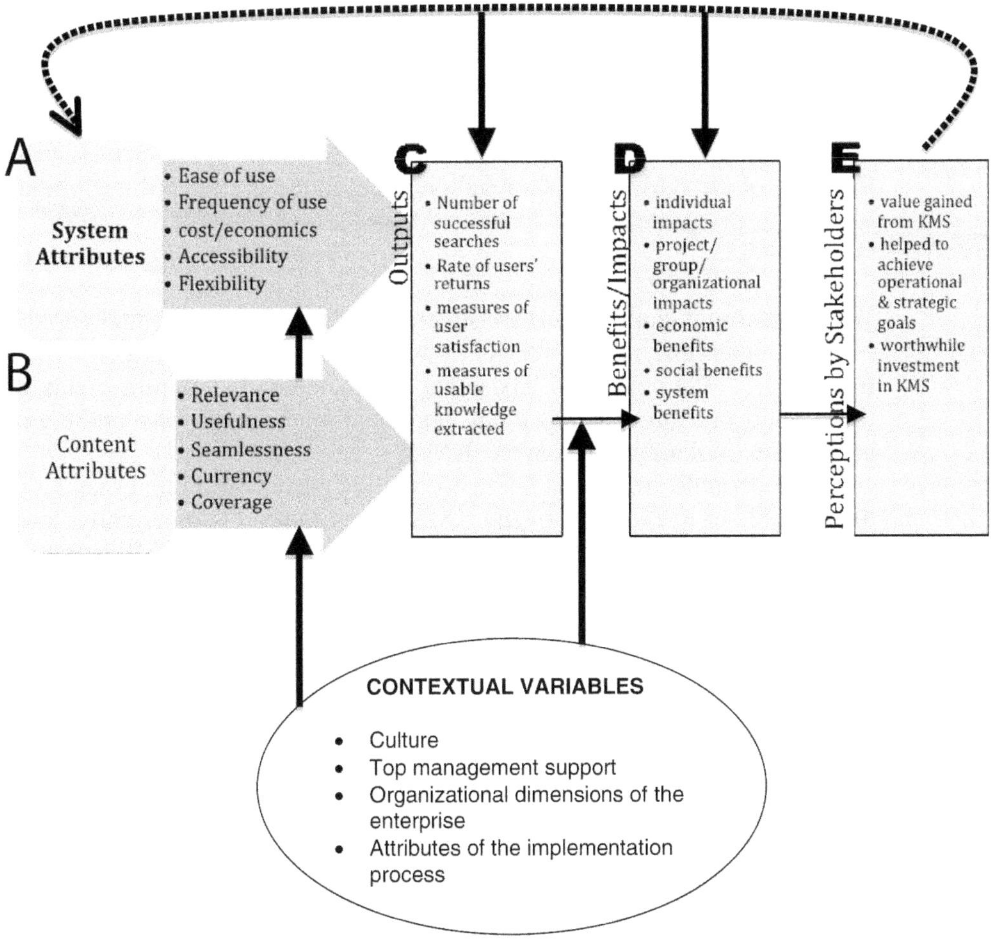

the KMS. The content attributes combined with the system attributes describe the degree to which the KMS is usable and applicable to the needs of the users and the enterprise that houses the KMS (Vinsonhaler and Vinsonhaler 1995). This system (and its contents) will generate outputs when members of the organization utilize it.

OUTPUTS FROM THE KNOWLEDGE MANAGEMENT SYSTEM

There are two categories of outputs. The first is a technical measure, focused on the use of the system. This category includes the number of successful searches completed by users per time period (e.g., weekly, monthly, yearly). Included also is the rate at which users return to search the system. Users who are frustrated by an unsuccessful first try at a search for knowledge will not return, and the pool of users will diminish.

The second category is a perceptual measure of the users' satisfaction with the KMS and how much usable knowledge they have extracted from the KMS in a given period of time. The latter measure is a confirmation or rejection of selected attributes of the system's content. The KMS must generate outputs that entail usable knowledge. Thus, metrics of outputs in this category would focus on measuring the amount of usable knowledge extracted by users of the system.

Combined with the measures of satisfaction, the metrics of outputs describe the immediate or proximal outcomes from the KMS (Geisler 2000; Poston and Speier 2008). These are the outputs generated by the system and transferred to recipients, both the users of the KMS and other stakeholders in the organization (Skok et al. 2001).

CONTEXTUAL VARIABLES

Within the organization there are several contextual or situational variables with the power to intervene in the process by which outputs are generated by the KMS and transferred to the recipients. These variables include the culture of the organization, the support of senior management, organizational dimensions, and the relative success of the implementation of the KMS.

These variables represent a situation in the organization that may be favorable or unfavorable to the success of the KMS. The situation is essentially "given," in that few changes, if any, can be made to the variables once the KMS is in operation. But the contextual variables may offer a plausible alternative explanation of why the KMS is a success or failure (Guo and Sheffield 2008; Rezgui 2007).

BENEFITS AND IMPACTS

There are five categories of the impacts of the KMS on recipients or beneficiaries of the system. The first is the individual benefits. People in the organization may benefit from the outputs of KMS by being able to successfully extract usable knowledge from the system. By receiving and adapting this knowledge, the individuals increase their stock of knowledge and improve their abilities and their particular skills and competencies (Geisler 2007).

A second category is a more complex group of impacts: the benefits accrued to work groups and to the entire organization. Examples of these impacts are improved efficiency of operations, harmonized standards, improvements in the decision-making process, and reduction in levels of resistance to change by members of the organization (Hansen et al. 2005).

A third category includes economic and financial benefits to recipients of the outputs from KMS. Illustrative metrics include, but are not restricted to, the following: improvements in competitiveness and level of productivity in the organization, savings in cost and time, and higher rates of growth and market share (Adams and Lamont 2003).

A fourth category is the social impacts and benefits to recipients of the outputs. These are metrics of the improved capabilities of recipients (individuals, work teams, and organizations) to meet the requirements of regulatory compliance, safety and health standards, and the quality of their products and services (Anantatmula 2007; Mu-Jung et al. 2007). The metrics in this category also measure the impacts on various social or public goods, such as contributions to environmental protection, energy savings, and health care delivery. For example, individuals in the organization may extract knowledge from the KMS about the behavior of compounds in the environment. This knowledge would allow them to improve the disposal of the compounds, hence to improve their compliance with environmental protection. In this example, the important step (as shown in Figure 12.2) is the ability of recipients to absorb and to adapt the extracted knowledge into their processes (Geisler 2007).

Finally, there are benefits to the KMS itself. By having knowledge items extracted from it and used by recipients, the KMS receives justification of its system and content attributes. The reputation of the KMS will thus be enhanced in the organization. The more knowledge that users successfully extract and utilize from the KMS, and the more benefits they receive from such knowledge, the more willing they will be to continue using the KMS, to support its enhancement, and to invest in its growth and expansion.

PERCEPTIONS OF STAKEHOLDERS

Having impacts of various kinds on individuals, groups, and organizations is not sufficient to evoke a positive or negative reaction from recipients of the outputs from KMS. As we show in Figure 12.2, there is also a stage in this process in which stakeholders who are recipients of KMS outputs evaluate these outputs and the benefits derived from them (Heisekanen and Hearn 2004; Poston and Speier 2008).

Stakeholders perceive the system's value by assessing whether the knowledge extracted from the KMS contributes to achieving operational and strategic goals and whether the KMS is a worthwhile investment. They also perceive the value they receive in broad terms, assessing in general whether any, some, or much value was gained from the KMS.

EXPECTED VALUE FROM KNOWLEDGE MANAGEMENT SYSTEM

The expected value perceived by stakeholders, as we show in Figure 12.2, will be the combined computation of the sum of the probabilities that recipients will absorb outputs, and that these outputs will then generate benefits to the recipients, and that recipients will perceive these as providing value to them (Geisler 2007). The first equation will be:

$$P_v = \sum_{i=1}^{3} P_a \times P_b \times P_c,$$

where

P_v = probability of value created and perceived by recipients;

P_a = probability that outputs will be generated from KMS use (*cluster C in Figure 12.2*);

P_b = probability that outputs will be absorbed, adopted, and implemented by recipients and will generate impacts and benefits (*cluster D in Figure 12.2*);

P_c = probability that the benefits from the outputs will be perceived by recipients as having generated value for the recipients (*cluster E in Figure 12.2*).

This equation measures the probabilities along the process by which outputs from KMS are transformed and implemented by recipients, all the way to the possible creation of value.

The second equation focuses on the weights or importance of the value created as these are perceived by the stakeholders who receive and process the said outputs from KMS (Geisler 2007).

$$EV = \sum_{i=1}^{n} P_n \times \text{Im},$$

where

EV = expected value;

N = stages of transformation and diffusion;

P_n = probabilities that outputs and benefits will be realized (from equation 1);

Im = importance, preferences, or weights that stakeholders who benefit from the outputs assign to each type of value.

In a scenario where, for example, the recipient attaches high importance to strategic goals but the knowledge received from the KMS provided value only to the operational goals, the recipient may not perceive high value received from the KMS. Thus, the expected value from the KMS depends on both the actual diffusion and transformation of outputs from the KMS, and the preferences that stakeholders have for different types or categories of value they hope to gain from the KMS.

LESSONS AND SUMMARY

A key lesson from the proposed model of KMS evaluation shown in Figure 12.2 is the sheer complexity of this process. The flow of codified knowledge from the KMS to the users and the potential benefits that may be accrued from such knowledge are dependent on a variety of factors. Some of these factors, such as rate of use of the KMS, are within the control of users. Other factors, such as contextual variables and the preferences of stakeholders, are a given, so that the actual benefits—as perceived by stakeholders—are contingent upon these perceptions.

Ever since technological advances in the tools of information management in the late 1980s and early 1990s, KM has emerged from the combination of the Internet, intranets, massive databases, data warehouses, and their management. From these instruments and the new realities in organizations about information management, there appeared more structural frameworks of knowledge such as communities of practice, reviews, knowledge centers (e.g., knowledge cafés), social networks and exchange, and professional instruments of diffusion and sharing of knowledge (Gray and Durcikova 2005).

With the converging of technologies and social tools of knowledge exchange, organizations have developed structured repositories that we call KMS. This development leads to a second lesson. We find a continuous tension, if not an actual rift, between a structured, centralized KMS managed and controlled by the enterprise and the much more diffused and decentralized agglomeration of systems used by organizational members and stakeholders to exchange and share knowledge.

Figure 12.3 **Forms of KMS: Centralized Versus Diversified Frameworks**

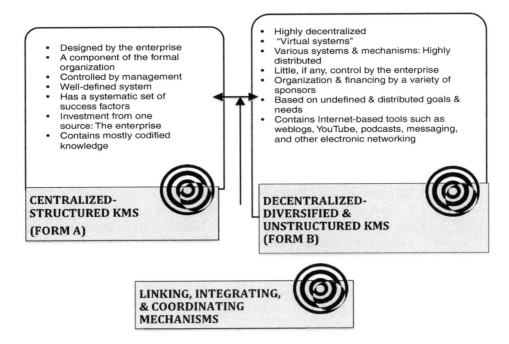

Figure 12.3 shows these two different frameworks of the KMS in the organization. It is very difficult to frame and adequately evaluate the decentralized KMS. As a highly diffused set of systems by which people exchange knowledge, this form of KMS has undefined goals and relies on a large variety of tools, such as those based on the Internet and other electronic means of communication and exchange of knowledge.

In the structured KMS, access and extraction of knowledge are controlled by the enterprise. The decentralized and nonstructured KMS is a social phenomenon, so that control over access, content, and extraction of knowledge are relatively "free for all." The two forms of KMS sometimes influence each other. For example, members of the enterprise who share knowledge via the unstructured mechanisms may find it unnecessary or redundant to deposit such knowledge into the structured, centralized KMS.

The third lesson, drawn from Figure 12.3, is the next challenge to organizations. As centralized KM systems proliferate and the need to evaluate them increases, organizations will have to create mechanisms that will link, integrate, and coordinate the two forms of knowledge exchange. Form A (structured) lends itself more readily to evaluation, as shown in Figure 12.3. Form B (unstructured) is so distributed among several modes and ways of interface and exchange that traditional methods of assessment and evaluation are insufficient and inadequate.

As we increasingly ponder whether KM and the corporate KMS are on the decline, we should consider the existence of the two forms of KMS, rather than solely the structured form within the enterprise. Perhaps the main reason that the formal KMS in many organizations lacks the luster of an ever-growing phenomenon of knowledge sharing is because some or much of the knowledge exchanged among stakeholders (including members of the enterprise) is carried out by means of the unstructured form of knowledge exchange.

Organizations should also consider linking or integrating mechanisms to assess the impacts of knowledge exchanged in the unstructured KMS. Examples of such mechanisms are monitoring, periodic debriefing of members and stakeholders, and surveys of the knowledge exchanged in the system and the impacts of such exchanges.

LEARNING OUTCOMES

- Measures of outputs from KMS are similar to those used by MIS evaluators.
- A model of KMS evaluation should contain the flow of outputs from KMS as they are absorbed and implemented by impacted individuals and organizations and as these impacts are perceived by the stakeholders as having generated benefits and value to the stakeholders.
- There are two distinct forms of KMS: structured and unstructured. The evaluation of KMS in the organization must address and assess both forms of KMS.

DISCUSSION QUESTIONS

1. How do the success factors for KMS differ from those of MIS?
2. What lessons can be learned from MIS research?
3. How do the two forms of KMS differ, and what are the mechanisms for integration of these two forms?

The Knowledge Management Audit 13

KEY LEARNING OUTCOMES

You will know you have mastered the material in this chapter when you can define and explain the following:

1. The nature of audit of knowledge management.
2. Process and outcomes of the audit of knowledge management systems.
3. Issues in the audit of knowledge management.

This chapter addresses the audit of knowledge management (KM) and the knowledge management system (KMS) in the enterprise. We distinguish between the traditional roles of organizational or system audits and the audit of the KM phenomenon, including the KMS. We identify the key components of the audit and the possible outcomes and uses of such an audit.

Normally, the audit is a unique intervention, albeit of a repetitive and periodic nature. The audit is an activity aimed at the identification and measurement of specific variables, attributes, achievements, and factors of success or failure (Messier 1997). This is different from the evaluation activity, which is usually an integral, ongoing component of management and control processes in the organization (Rubenstein and Geisler 2003).

THE NATURE OF THE AUDIT OF KNOWLEDGE MANAGEMENT

In Figure 13.1 we show the components of the audit of KM. This is a combination of several types of audit, including the variables that the audit looks to measure, the outcomes from the audit, and the corrective actions that may result from the audit (Lusiguan et al. 2005; Tong 2005; Wright et al. 2004).

Figure 13.1 **The Nature of Audit of KM**

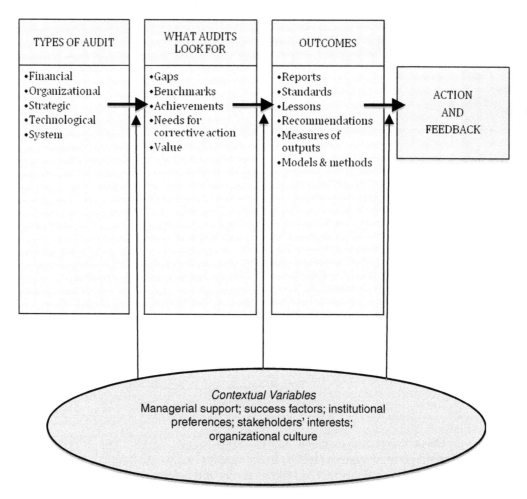

There are five types of possible audits of KM. The first is a financial or accounting assessment (Dalkir 2005). This audit addresses the costs of the activity being audited, its monetary and fiscal performance, and other aspects of the economics of the activity. The second type, the organizational audit, addresses issues of human resources, such as the utilization of personnel, and the work design, operations, and performance of the organization and its constituent unit. The third type, the strategic audit, reviews the goals of the organization and its relation to its environment. This type of audit focuses on the degree to which the objectives of the organization have been met and the compliance of the organization with regulatory demands. The fourth type of audit is the technological audit. This is an examination of the state of technology of the organization: how it fares with its stock of technology.

Finally, the fifth type of audit reviews how the KMS is operating and how successful and cost-effective it has been. This type of audit reviews the composition and performance of the system itself, in addition to the previous types that focused on the activity or process of KM (Allary and Holsapple 2002).

WHAT THE AUDIT EXAMINES

The audit of a KMS looks at a variety of topics for its review. The audit looks for gaps between what the organization was supposed to do or accomplish and what actually happened. If, for example, the financial goals included a certain return on investment (RoI), the audit will examine the gap between the planned and the actual levels of the RoI of the KM activity or the KMS (Skyrme 2001).

The audit will look for benchmarks and standards of specific activities or performance levels and whether such benchmarks had been achieved. When there are no benchmarks or standards, the audit will point to the need for corrective action. The audit also looks for the value that KM may have generated for stakeholders, and any gaps between whatever value was promised or planned and the measurable value actually created (Sullivan 2000).

OUTCOMES FROM THE AUDIT

The audit generates reports, standards, lessons, recommendations, models, metrics, and methods (Geisler 2000). Normally, the outcomes from the audit will be a mix of the above forms of outputs. These products of the audit of KM contain the "knowledge about knowledge" in reference to a specific period (such as a fiscal year) and a specific unit (such as the organization, a department within it, or the KMS). These outcomes then lead to recommendations for any corrective action that is needed, and this action serves as feedback to the organization for future planning.

THE CLIENTS AND IMPACTEES OF THE KNOWLEDGE MANAGEMENT AUDIT

The KM audit is a concentrated effort to review and assess how the KM activity and KMS are structured, how they operate, and how successful they may be for a given time period. But who are the clients for the audit? Who requests the audit and funds its execution?

The audit of KM is usually requested and funded by the management of the enterprise. Managers will initiate an audit for various reasons—for example, to satisfy regulatory requirements or the legal or fiduciary responsibilities of management or corporate directors. Other reasons for an audit are the strategic need to learn about the performance of the organization in its competitive market or to review KM as an activity in the enterprise that needs to be examined in the same manner as other units and activities are periodically reviewed.

The impactees of the KM audit are the units and entities that are being reviewed and other stakeholders of the organization who transact with it or have links to it and its units. Any corrective actions resulting from the audit will affect these entities. For example, if an audit of the KMS recommends increasing its rate of utilization in order to reduce the costs per search, those units that use the KMS are going to be impacted by the recommendation. They will have to improve the selling of the system to the potential users or reduce the cost of operating the system.

AUDITING THE UNSTRUCTURED KNOWLEDGE MANAGEMENT SYSTEM

Applying an audit to the unstructured form of the KMS is a difficult task. In order to have a viable audit, the enterprise needs to have in place the following stock of concepts or notions. First, mangers need a workable definition of what constitutes measurable knowledge: What is it that is being audited? Second, managers need a workable set of performance benchmarks against which the audit will assess any gaps and levels of achievement. Third, managers need a workable definition of the ownership of KM and the KMS in the enterprise, as well as the people and units responsible for KM and in charge of the KMS, so that they may execute any corrective action recommended by the audit. Finally, managers need, for each type of audit shown in Figure 13.1, workable definitions of what constitutes value and how any recommended corrective actions will improve the KM process in the organization.

The emphasis on organizational responsibilities ("who is in charge") is essential in the quest to make the audit of KM a useful tool of assessment and improvement. The enterprise is now in a position to assign responsibilities and tasks that are recommended by the auditors.

Once these pieces are in place, the enterprise can address the problems caused by the diversified and unstructured nature of its KM. At this juncture, however, most of the items listed above, such as the workable definitions and measures of what knowledge is, are still in their infancy. By and large, organizations lack adequate definitions and measures of knowledge, its management, its organizational focus, and the value derived from it. This means that currently an audit of KM and the KMS will be limited to the types of audit where benchmarks already exist and definitions of what is measured are already part of the lexicon of organizational activities and processes. Most enterprises, therefore, are a long way from being able to conduct audits of KM as they conduct audits of such activities as manufacturing, research and development (R&D), or even information systems.

LEARNING OUTCOMES

- There are five types of audits of KM: financial, organizational, strategic, technological, and focused on the KMS.
- The audit of KM depends on the existence in the organization of workable definitions of knowledge, its organizational locus, the benchmarks of its performance, and the operational definitions of the value that the enterprise may derive from it.

DISCUSSION QUESTIONS

1. What are the outcomes from a KM audit?
2. What is the role that contextual variables play in the implementation of a KM audit?
3. Give at least two examples of strategic audits of a knowledge-based company.

What the Future Holds

14

KEY LEARNING OUTCOMES

You will know you have mastered the material in this chapter when you can define and explain the following:

1. What we know, do not know, and need to know about knowledge management.
2. Where we are leading: Future scenarios.

In the fall of 2007 we interviewed the chief technology officer of a major electronics company. As the conversation focused on knowledge management (KM), the executive expressed himself in a very assertive tenor: "Knowledge management is as good as dead! We have a system in the company, but I don't see much of a future for this kind of thing." When we asked the reason for his strong opinion, he said, "It simply did not deliver. Too many promises, too little value."

This sentiment echoes throughout both industry and government organizations. There is a running theme among many managers that KM is just another failed technological or information system. Some managers compare the current KM in their organization with other systems that were hastily introduced to effect a technological solution to a very complex problem. These managers are also distrustful of vendors of various KMS and their components, complaining that there has been too much hype and too few results.

Other managers are more confident in the potential of KM and are willing, as one executive aptly suggested, "to give it the benefit . . . and give it more time to prove itself." Our limited studies and the state of the literature are not sufficient to ascertain how big each camp is and how influential its opinions. What emerges from this difference in views about the future of KM is a set of three possible scenarios: pessimistic, optimistic, and realistic. Table 14.1 shows these scenarios.

Table 14.1

Future Scenarios of KM: Three Perspectives of Managers

Scenario	Assumptions	Worldview	Possible future steps
Pessimistic	KM is a failure. Our problems are not knowledge problems. Too many promises were unkept.	Information or technology systems are not the panacea for solving problems.	Eliminate the KMS. Decrease the importance of KM. Divert resources to other systems.
Optimistic	KM is still in its infancy. Limited experience is insufficient to draw lessons from. There is a bright future for KM.	When properly implemented, technology systems can generate value.	Enhance the KMS. Investigate how the KMS impacts the organization. Allocate resources to improve the KMS.
Realistic	Need more data on the assessment of KM. KM is not just a system but also a change process. KM is a complex process.	One can draw conclusions only when armed with sufficient experiential results.	Conduct more studies of KM and the KMS. Withhold opinion until there are concrete lessons. Wait and see.

THE PESSIMISTIC SCENARIO

The pessimistic perspective entails several assumptions held by some managers. They assume that KM is a failure and that problems in their organizations are not knowledge-based. These managers also have a worldview that information or technology systems are not a panacea to solve problems. These managers have little confidence in technology systems, although not to the point of suffering from technophobia. Rather, they need to be persuaded that the system they install will indeed produce the results that vendors and their own experts have promised them. Nonetheless, as in the case of KM, they will adopt a system if there are promises of performance and value. When such promises do not materialize within a given time, these managers perceive that their fears and distrust have indeed been realized.

Based on this perspective, it is safe to forecast some future steps that these managers might take with respect to their KM activities. They will probably decrease or eliminate the current version of their KMS and divert the freed resources (people and finances) to other systems in the organization. In the case of the electronics company we interviewed in 2007, the action taken by the chief technology officer was aimed at reducing the size of the firm's KMS, arresting its growth, and diminishing its importance in the organization.

THE OPTIMISTIC SCENARIO

This scenario is based on optimistic assumptions held by managers. Primarily, these managers assume that KM is still in its infancy; hence it is not feasible or advisable to draw lessons from the experiences of organizations with their KMS. These managers also assume that KM has a bright future. The worldview of these managers is predicated upon their belief that technology does provide answers and solutions to crucial and complex organizational problems, but that technological systems must be properly and adequately implemented and adopted (Ackerman et al. 2002; Malhan 2008; Mutch 2008; Scarbrough 2008).

It stands to reason that the managers with an optimistic outlook on KM will act to enhance its presence in the enterprise. They will allocate resources for the improvement of KM and for enhancing its role and prestige in the organization (Huseman and Goodman 2007).

THE REALISTIC SCENARIO

The realistic perspective assumes that there is more complexity to the implementation of a KMS than organizations normally consider and that KM is a change process rather than simply another managerial system. Managers who subscribe to this perspective believe that conclusions about KM are possible only after the enterprise obtains results from experiments. Hence, the current state of research does not provide a sufficient pool of knowledge that would allow adequate evaluation of KM in organizations (Burnett et al. 2004; Jennex 2007; Nerkar and Paruchuri 2005).

These managers will tend to adopt a strategy of "wait and see" before they commit themselves and their organizations to further investments in KM. They may, in the future and in light of further knowledge, adopt one of the two other perspectives: optimistic or pessimistic (Land 2008).

The propensity of managers to adopt one of these perspectives is contingent upon several factors. It is first dependent on the manager's own view of the world. Is this view, in general, optimistic, pessimistic, or realistic? Managers tend to project their own view of the world to the perspective of KM.

Another factor is the manager's experience, both quantitative (years in managerial positions) and qualitative (exposure to challenges and to interesting assignments). Experience tends to energize the manager's view of change and new systems, but may also obfuscate the propensity for change and for risk taking (Liebowitz 2009; Sidhu 2008).

A third factor is the level and type of education and training of these managers. The higher the levels of their education, skills, and training, the more they might be willing to accept change and to positively approach the evaluation of a new KMS in their organizations (Ericsson and Smith 1991; Ericsson et al. 2006; Wallace 2007).

The fourth factor is the growth of the KM discipline and the KM industry. As the discipline matures and industrial companies continue to perfect their KM products and systems, managers may become more interested in the growing area of KM and see it as a more promising endeavor.

In his popular book *The Lucifer Principle*, Howard Bloom (1995) compares the human brain to a neural network and the human belief system to the operation of such a network. He suggests that when an idea, event, or ideology is received in the brain, people accept or reject it according to how it fits with their network or system

Figure 14.1 **What KM Already Has Achieved**

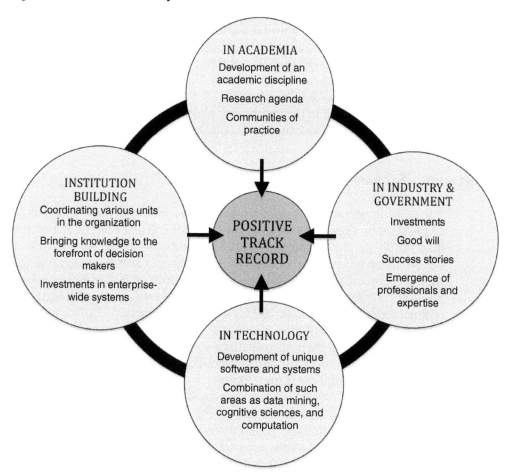

of beliefs. In this vein, the operation and success of a KMS will be viewed in light of the manager's view of the world and the place or importance that KM as a change phenomenon occupies in the manager's "neural network."

WHAT KNOWLEDGE MANAGEMENT ALREADY HAS ACHIEVED

Having reviewed the literature and the empirical evidence about KM, we can now summarize the achievements of the KM effort at the time we composed this book. These achievements are shown in Figure 14.1.

ACADEMIC ACHIEVEMENTS

There are four areas in which KM has made considerable strides since the mid-1990s. One area, as depicted in Figure 14.1, is in the academic pursuit of KM as a discipline.

Researchers have begun to explore various topics in KM. There is a growing body of knowledge that distinguishes KM from information systems and focuses on research questions that are unique to KM. For example, research on KM explores the nature of knowledge and KM (Jensen et al. 2007; McAdam 2008; Skillicorn 2008; Yolles 2008), and the flow and transfer of knowledge in organizational frameworks (Brown 2007; Gray 2008; Liebowitz 2009; Nerkar and Paruchuri 2005).

Another accomplishment in the academic category has been the gradual proliferation of scholarly journals dedicated to KM. Examples include *Journal of Knowledge Management* and *Knowledge and Process Management.* In addition, between 1995 and 2005, numerous conferences targeted the exploration of KM, and several scholarly organizations have established KM as an area of inquiry as well as accepting papers in KM for presentation at their periodic meetings. These organizations include the Academy of Management, INFORMS (Institute for Operations Research and the Management Sciences), and the Institute of Electrical and Electronic Engineers. This academic surge of interest in KM will clearly continue on its own power in the foreseeable future (Nonaka et al. 2000; Osterich and Frey 2000).

TECHNOLOGY ACHIEVEMENTS

The effort in the area of KM has produced a host of academic and commercial software programs and systems. Several hundred vendors have emerged since 1995, creating and selling systems for KM, data mining, data discovery, and similar purposes. Many organizations in the private and public sectors have already purchased and implemented such systems (Melvor et al. 1997; Wiig 1997).

The progress of KM has also generated a combination of disciplinary methods and systems. Many of the technologies that make up the commercial and academic systems have benefited from developments in a diversity of disciplines, such as cognitive sciences, computation, software compilation, and data mining and analysis. In a way, this evolution of KM is similar to that of management in the early 1900s, when the new discipline began to explore and absorb methods, techniques, and approaches from a variety of disciplines in economics, social research, psychology, history, and engineering.

INDUSTRY AND GOVERNMENT

KM has already made some strides in government and industrial implementations. In addition to the many companies that work in the KM area and produce software and systems, government and industrial entities have made considerable investments in KM and related activities. The federal government in the United States and central governments in other countries have invested heavily in the design and implementation of KMS, driven by reasons of security and efficiency in administration (Skillicorn 2008).

Industrial companies have also joined the trend. Large companies have made investments in KMS, albeit—as we have already mentioned—with mixed results. However, some systems in government and industry have begun to yield some promise (Liebowitz 2009), generating good will and adding to the perception of KM as a positive development.

There are success stories of KM implementation in government and industry (Brown 2007; Scarbrough 2008). There is also the emergence of a community of experts skilled in handling the problems, advances, and challenges of KM (Sidhu 2008).

INSTITUTION BUILDING

The fourth area in which KM has made considerable progress is institution building. This notion refers to the impact of the establishment of KM and KMS in the organization. As the KMS is designed and put into place, the enterprise makes an effort to coordinate various units within the umbrella of KM. Coordination tends to produce collaborative ties, mechanisms, and efforts that are beneficial to the growth of the organization.

The establishment of a KMS also contributes to bringing knowledge that has hitherto been diversified across the organization to a central repository where it is put at the disposal of decision makers. This feat alone helps the organization improve its use of existing knowledge and other resources, again contributing to building the institutional framework.

In summary, KM has achieved a presence in organizational life. Although many KMS have either failed or have not achieved their expected level of performance, KM is, nonetheless, a growing resource in organizations. Investments are continually being made in KM in various forms and by a growing number of organizations that are recognizing the power embedded in what their members know (Bloom 1995). So the track record of KM is positive, and the trend is for KM to continue accumulating accomplishments.

CHALLENGES FOR KNOWLEDGE MANAGEMENT

Despite its successes, KM faces several major challenges in the near future, challenges that encompass the issues that are still woven into the path of growth of this new disciplinary area of academic inquiry and its applications in government and industrial organizations. The challenges vary by their focus—involving KM's organizational or structural nature, human attributes, or institutional culture—and severity. Severity refers to the degree to which individuals and organizations may find it difficult to overcome the challenges and to arrive at constructive and useful solutions (Guyer 2008).

CHALLENGES IN KNOWLEDGE MANAGEMENT SCHOLARSHIP

Since KM is in its infancy, there are several challenges to the development of a strong academic field of KM research. The first of these challenges is the basic difficulty of defining knowledge and KM. The inherent conflict between knowledge as a tacit dimension and the need to share and diffuse it continues to be a pressing issue of intellectual importance and a key ingredient in any plan for advancement in the scholarly pursuit of KM.

Another challenge for KM scholarship is the need to distance KM from information systems, concepts, and research. As the theoretical and operational definitions of KM start to emerge, there is also an urgent and compelling need to channel these definitions away from information systems research and to differentiate KM from information systems and management information systems.

The creation of paradigms of research in KM and the emergence of a KM community of science are major challenges in KM scholarship. There is a clear need to generate research directions and methods specifically tailored to KM. Also, the development of KM scholarship must be accompanied by the development of a dedicated community of scientists engaged in KM research.

CHALLENGES IN KNOWLEDGE MANAGEMENT APPLICATIONS

How do we overcome the existing barriers to the successful and progressive application of KM in organizations? The challenges may be classified in two groups. One set of challenges relates to the organizational issues of evaluation and integration of KM. Evaluation includes developing acceptable metrics of performance for KM and showing measurable results. Integration includes the connectivity of KM with other systems in the organization and the consolidation of KM practices with the rest of the enterprise. These are not easy challenges to tackle. There are powerful barriers in the organization, culture, and operations of enterprises that make it difficult for relatively new systems to perform and to succeed.

As an increasing number of organizations apply KM in their operations, the challenges also include the need to better define and gain acceptance for KM as a crucial asset within the enterprise. The literature is quite prolific in its discussions of the "knowledge society" and the "knowledge economy," but these scenarios are not enough to create lasting prestige for KM as a critical asset for the organization. Much more is needed at the level of the enterprise to gain acceptance and to improve the prestige of KM *within* the organization that applies it as an internal system.

PUBLIC PERCEPTION OF KNOWLEDGE MANAGEMENT

Perhaps the most salient challenge is derived from the experience of KM scholarship and applications: the resultant public perception of KM. Public awareness of the achievements of KM is still fuzzy and still being formed.

First, the status and position of KM must be established. Where does KM—as an academic discipline and an area of application—belong within the structure and operations of the organization? KM should be viewed not as an addendum to information systems, but as a stand-alone area of importance in the structuring and assessment of the organization.

Second, there has to be substantial improvement in the public perception of KM as a strategic asset that contributes to the competitive position of the enterprise, hence as an indispensable asset. Clearly, this improvement in public perception is closely linked to the ability to evaluate KM with metrics that are acceptable to the enterprise.

Third, KM must be viewed as a worthy activity, in whatever assessment termi-

Figure 14.2 **Challenges for KM**

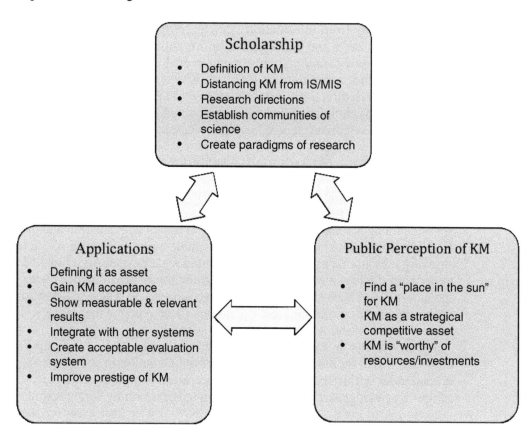

nology one prefers to use. Once so perceived, KM will be a serious contender for organizational investments.

The road to improved public perception is difficult but not impossible. There is already a positive track record on which to build. Once some of the challenges in Figure 14.2 are met, public perception will start to improve.

RESEARCH AGENDA FOR KNOWLEDGE MANAGEMENT

We propose a research agenda for KM. This agenda may be known as the 3-D Research Agenda for KM. It is shown in Figure 14.3.

The research agenda covers three categories: (1) *definition* of knowledge and KM so they can be thoroughly studied as a distinct phenomenon; (2) *differentiation* of knowledge and KM from information systems; and (3) *diffusion* of knowledge, including the investigation of KM systems in organizations: how they operate, how they work in conjunction with other systems, and how they are evaluated.

Figure 14.3 **The 3-D Research Agenda for KM: Illustrative Research Questions**

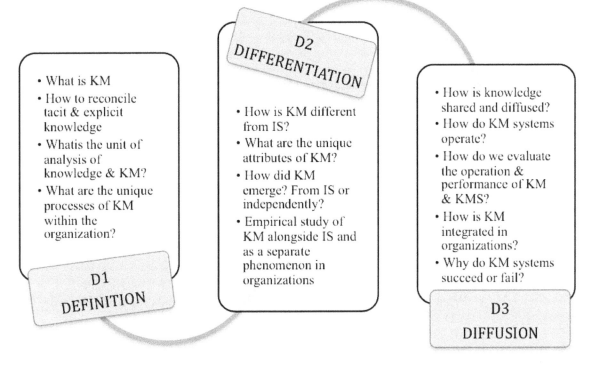

This research agenda contains all the fundamental questions that KM needs to address. We clustered them in three major groups, but these questions would help researchers conduct incisive inquiry into virtually every aspect of the KM experience in organizations.

WHERE WE GO FROM HERE

What is the future of KM? We believe that the gap between the rhetoric about the knowledge society and the initial experience with KM will soon be closed. We are concluding this textbook with a strong sentiment of optimism that there is a bright future for KM. The knowledge-driven society and its corollary knowledge economy are here to stay, and they will continue to expand, becoming the key driving force in the foreseeable future. This trend seems to be irreversible. It has already manifested itself in the developed world, particularly in North America and Western Europe, as well as Australia, Singapore, and Japan. Knowledge is now the key economic resource of the twenty-first century, and KM is the critical architecture and mode of organization and administration of this resource.

We are now entrusted with the objective of ensuring that the knowledge resource will be well managed. This requires the incorporation of KM evaluation into university curricula as well as in secondary education. The challenge of the twenty-first century is not only to generate and apply knowledge in the pursuit of solutions to economic, social, and human problems, but also to understand and continuously improve the management of this precious, versatile, and ever-expanding gift possessed by the human race.

LEARNING OUTCOMES

- There are three future scenarios of the evaluation of KM: pessimistic, optimistic, and realistic.
- We believe that the knowledge society and knowledge economy are the irreversible trends of the twenty-first century. Hence, KM is a crucial component of a well-managed economy in the foreseeable future.
- KM has already achieved important, durable outcomes in academia, industry, and government in the areas of technology and institution building.
- The challenges for KM are in the development of a viable, relevant research agenda and research methodology and in the betterment of the actual and perceived roles of KM in society and the economy.

DISCUSSION QUESTIONS

1. What are the elements of a proposed research agenda for KM? Describe the 3-D agenda proposed in this book.
2. In your opinion, what is the future of KM? Are you pessimistic, optimistic, or realistic about its future?
3. Give two or three examples of KM accomplishments in each of these fields: industry, government, and institution building.
4. Do you consider yourself a knowledge worker? Why? Please elaborate your answer.

PART IV

CASES

Case 1

A Five-Stage Model for Implementing Electronic Patient Records

Electronic patient record (EPR) systems are currently being implemented in many health care organizations on both sides of the Atlantic. These systems, through their ability to integrate several functions and provide seamless access to information, are expected to enable value-driven, patient-centric health care delivery. At a time when health care is under tremendous pressure globally, EPR appears to be the panacea. However, EPR implementation has major organizational and cultural implications that, to date, have not always been addressed and thus play a major role in the less than optimal results currently being experienced after EPR implementation. To address this issue, we discuss the need to incorporate the penta-stage model that we developed by analyzing various EPR implementations in health care settings in both the United Kingdom and the United States.

THE CULTURAL COMPONENT

The difficulty in refining to a single definition of culture is exacerbated since more than 150 different definitions of the term *culture* have been suggested (Kroeber and Kluckhohn 1952). The plethora of definitions can be readily explained by the fact that the entire concept of culture has been extrapolated from the area of anthropology, where there is no consensus of meaning (Smircich 1983).

Perhaps the most frequently cited definition of culture is that of Geert Hofstede (1994a), who suggests that culture is the collective programming of the human mind that distinguishes the members of one human group from those of another. In very basic terms, organizational culture can be described as an attitude that governs the way things are done in that organization, a definition closely aping Bower's (1966) concept of culture as the way things are done around here. Hofstede (1994b) further states that people carry patterns of thinking and feeling that stay with them throughout their life. Acquired and learned during childhood, when the person is most open to learning, assimilation, and dissemination of information, these patterns gradually become entrenched within the persona. Hofstede suggests that all countries possess a factor called management, its meaning changing from one country to another. In order to understand its processes and problems, historical and cultural insights into

211

local phenomena are taken into account. Hofstede's various contributions explain the effects of culture on decision making, executive award systems, and training regimens, respectively.

CONCEPTUALIZING CULTURE

Examples of indexes (Harrison 1972) that can combine to form the basis of an organization's culture include reports, letters, memos, e-mails, health and safety regulations, and rule books. Some examples of protocols of a more verbalized nature are forms of addresses, repeated stories and myths, in-jokes, rumors, and speculation. Factors such as dress requirements and de rigueur career paths can also contribute to an organization's culture.

It is this same organizational culture that defines behavior, motivates individuals, and affects the way that the organization processes information. The prevalent patterns of behavior that form an organization's culture are generally less explicit than formal rules and procedures. Nevertheless, these patterns can be a powerful influence on the way that employees and managers approach commercial objectives, be they client care or profit maximization. Additionally, cultures can have either a positive (helping productivity) or negative (hindering productivity) effect. Increasing importance has been attached to improving or, in some cases, creating an organization's culture. Organizational culture is influenced by the sociotechnical systems of the organization, which are, in turn, influenced by the common beliefs, attitudes, and values of its members. The procedures adopted by management create the work environment for the other members.

If managers have been members of the organization for some time, they themselves can be a product of the culture. Hence their strategies and procedures have, almost inevitably, been conditioned by the culture. Given that culture is both an input and an output, it is likely that this attitude is both self-perpetuating and highly resistant to change. Changing, or creating from scratch, an organization's culture is far from easy as culture seems to protect itself from any external attempts to alter its familiar state. Once established, cultures—and those persons operating within its familiar confines—are reluctant to change. Once practices and attitudes are learned and firmly established, new methods are treated with suspicion and resistance to change sets in. Organizational culture can be idealized in the form of two models (McAuley 1994):

- corporate culture (in which managerial control is emphasized)
- ensemble culture (in which organizational members' autonomy is preserved)

These two stylized cultures have been used to demonstrate the relationship among the managerial process, organizational culture, and competence. Competence in this context refers to the aptitude and proficiency of organizational members. Competence can be used in the same manner as an index in order to measure the acceptance or rejection of activities or behavior of an organizational member. In this manner, competence can indicate the cultural bearing of the organization.

In a corporate culture, the emphasis of competence is on the extent and flexibility of control (McAuley 1994). Culture is viewed as a control subsystem and a determinant that can be controlled and managed by managers deemed to be competent. In the organization's culture, management of precepts and variables (including culture itself) is through a variety of control mechanisms. Managerial structures and controls are present in the organization's interests that have been referred to as the Competency Movement. Ensemble cultures occur when managerial expertise (the art or practice of management) is on a level with other skills and knowledge brought into the organization by other members.

CULTURAL CHANGE IN GENERAL PRACTICES

Organizations attempt to change their culture in order to bring about a strategic change; there is continued debate as to whether culture change is overtly intentional or an unavoidable side effect of management's attempts to introduce new working practices (Williams et al. 1993). When planning organizational change, managers need to be acutely aware of the link between organizational culture and organizational goals.

Established researchers in the field of culture have offered many models of cultural change, with no framework gaining clear dominance. The reason for this is primarily that these researchers are using different basal definitions for culture. By extension, changing culture according to one researcher's model may seem significantly easier than using another researcher's framework.

A review of the literature (Bali et al. 1999) demonstrates very clearly the different cultural bases that established researchers have used. Although we could argue that none of them may be inherently wrong, how do we know which one is right? Is one better than another? Or is the ideal cultural change model a skillful blend of the most pertinent tools and techniques from the existing range? The review has shown that organizational culture change involves four common precepts: an initial crisis, strong leadership, the importance of success (and relating this importance across the organization), and the importance of supporting change.

EXPERIENCES FROM THE UNITED KINGDOM

A particularly interesting area in which to study the impact of culture on information technology (IT) implementation is in health care. Health care is a complex industry affected by many factors, including the payment system (private or public) and the microenvironment. EPRs are widely used across the United States and the United Kingdom. For instance, about 60 percent of primary care physicians now use EPRs in the United Kingdom, while 31 percent of hospital emergency rooms in the United States have fully implemented EPRs (Haller et al. 2007). These systems are being hailed as panaceas for facilitating the delivery of cost-effective, quality health care. And yet, too often, the results have often been disappointing. In fact, in the United States it is noted that medical errors increased significantly after the increase in EPR implementation (Institute of Medicine 2001; Porter and Teisberg 2007). We believe that a disregard for the organizational culture at the time of the implementation is one reason why many EPRs are performing suboptimally. To analyze this situation in more depth, we constructed a qualitative study that examined EPR implementation in both United States and United Kingdom health care settings.

Specifically, data was collected from three medical practices in the United Kingdom's Midlands region. To preserve anonymity, the practices will be referred to as Surgery-A, Surgery-B, and Surgery-C:

1. Surgery-A employs two full-time doctors, one practice manager, two nurses, and six part-time administration staff. The practice cares for 5,000 people.
2. Surgery-B employs two full-time doctors, one practice manager, one nurse, and eight administration staff (four full-time and four part-time). The surgery cares for 5,000 people.
3. Surgery-C employs two full-time doctors, one practice manager, one nurse, and one full-time administrator. The practice cares for 700 people.

All the practices are run according to regional and national health care administration guidelines.

In a similar fashion, data was collected from three health care practices in the United States:

1. Specialty Docs is a closed staff multispecialty physician group practice that has been in operation since 1946 and was purchased by a large health system in 1989. The practice itself has three ambulatory care sites and four single-specialty offices. Its primary care specialties include obstetrics and gynecology, pediatrics, and internal medicine. Out of a total of 110 physicians, 56 are primary care physicians (PCPs).
2. Independent Docs is an independent practice association, a group of physicians who have formed a medical group so they appear as one legal entity, which is advantageous when contracting with various managed care organizations. It consists of 140 nationally qualified PCPs.
3. Faculty Docs is a typical faculty practice. Each of the medical specialties (e.g., medicine, pediatrics, obstetrics and gynecology, cardiovascular, and surgery) in this faculty practice established itself as a unit chiefly as a vehicle to manage financial and administrative issues. This process began in the late 1960s and was driven by the economic climate of the time. By the mid-1980s, twenty-three of these different groups, which make up the faculty practice as it is today, had formed. This group practice has a strong affiliation with both the health system and the local university's school of medicine. In fact, the head of each department is also on the faculty at the school of medicine.

Hence, although all three practices in the United States were located in the Midwest region, they had quite distinct cultures and microenvironments. All three practices were in the process of implementing EPRs at the time data was being collected.

Case Figure 1.1 **Penta-State Model**

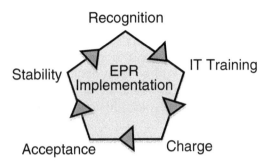

KEY ISSUES

Using qualitative-based techniques, such as ethnographic observations and structured and semistructured interviews with key personnel, we identified several issues that are directly relevant to EPR implementation issues in health care organizations. In applying these techniques, we subscribed to the recommendation for performing systematic and careful thematic analysis on the data that were gathered in order to facilitate the understanding of significant themes and pertinent issues (Boyatzis 1998; Kavale 1996). From this thematic analysis we were able to identify critical states in the EPR implementation requiring appropriate action so that the inputs for the consequent stage would be correct and the end result would be successful. We conceptualize these issues in the model we call the penta-stage model (Case Figure 1.1) for successful EPR implementation.

STAGE 1: RECOGNITION

This initial stage represents an analysis of the current state and serves to identify previous and current organizational and human resource problems. Health care organizations face tremendous external and internal pressures. Established research (Lundberg 1985) has confirmed that many organizations are likely to face a range of external pressures. These pressures, with relevance to EPR implementation, may include such tasks as the replacement of legacy systems, redesign of key processes pertaining to capturing and storing patient data, and the subsequent access and reuse of these data as well as ensuring that the system will comply with all regulations, such as HIPAA (Health Information Portability and Accountability Act) in the United States. These pressures may cause the organization to change the way its internal processes and procedures are carried out. Established culture-change authors (Lewin 1952; Lundberg 1985; Schein 1990) agree that these changes almost always face resistance from staff within the organization. In some sense, the recognition stage corresponds to the unfreeze state in the Lewin-Schein model (Schein 1996).

STAGE 2: INFORMATION TECHNOLOGY TRAINING AND EDUCATION

An initial feasibility study can be used as a basis for identifying key areas of the organization where attitude, belief, and value changes are necessary to fully implement the system. The feasibility study facilitates identification of the level and extent of IT and EPR training and education required. This training and education is an IT preparatory stage that will be built upon with the constructs within Stage 3. In too many instances in our case data, we noted that physicians did not know how to use the EPR system effectively, leading to wasted time and less than satisfactory consultation with the patient. For example, some patients noted that the PCP would "focus on the screen and not listen to me," while the physician complained that "the new system takes too much of my time away from treating patients, my number one role, to doing secretarial work like typing."

STAGE 3: CULTURAL AND ORGANIZATIONAL CHANGE

Initial indications suggest that this third stage consists of six steps. The prospect of IT-driven change can be daunting for many health care employees. They question whether the impending change will adversely affect their established working routines or significantly reduce their role in the organization. They may display fear, stress, and a tendency to be objectionable, argumentative, or skeptical regarding the impending change program. This skepticism can manifest itself in the form of questioning the merits of change—"What is the benefit of this system?"

The initial stages of our research show these six change steps: (1) IT pilot schemes, which will show demonstrable benefits of the system; (2) communication, which will serve to alleviate much of the confusion and fear; (3) education, which enables more effective use of the system; (4) facilitation, which enables real-time troubleshooting when and as problems arise; (5) mentoring, which fosters a cohesive team environment important in health care delivery; and (6) dissemination of both information and knowledge so that relevant information reaches everyone and all users of the system can access the pertinent information and germane knowledge they require. Having carried out cultural and organizational change steps in Stage 3, the organization can then move to the next stage. Before doing so, however, the effects of the six steps should be appraised and evaluated. If the effects of change have not been sufficient or if instigated changes have not been established, this may be indicative of an ineffective change program. Deficiencies of the organization or of the culture-organization change process should be noted and the process should return to Stage 2 (IT training and education). Especially for large, complex health care organizations, it may, in fact, be necessary to cycle through Stages 2 and 3 for a few iterations.

STAGE 4: ACCEPTANCE

If the analysis and evaluation phase (part of Stage 3) does not identify any inadequacies, the model moves to Stage 4 (acceptance). This stage is reached when cultural and structural change methods have been successfully deployed within the health care organization. Once again we can see (and should expect) a logical mapping in the Lewin and Schein model's stage of refreeze. In essence, the new future state has been reached.

STAGE 5: STABILITY

Having reached the acceptance stage and reentering the cultural barrier, if necessary, to resolve any difficulties, the model should take an evolutionary route to the stability stage. The route to this stage should be supported by continued mentoring and facilitation—elements already displayed and conveyed by the change manager. Although near the end of the process, the transition between Stage 4 and Stage 5 should not be executed complacently. Only when full stability has been achieved should the change manager be sure that the work is complete.

CLOSING THE LOOP

Having achieved the objective of attaining a new culture (a culture that has successfully accommodated an EPR system and has made appropriate changes to organizational structure), the health care organization may need to go through the five stages again at a future time. Health care operations are conducted in a dynamic environment that continuously experiences exogenous changes; thus it is not unusual to have to cycle through the stages of the penta-stage model again after such an exogenous change. The strength of this model is that it can be repeated easily after any change while providing a systematic, thorough approach for effecting a successful outcome.

IMPLICATIONS AND DIRECTIONS

In the twenty-first century, implementations of enterprise-wide systems (such as EPRs) in health care organizations are going to become more prevalent globally. Our study demonstrates that, regardless of the health care system (NHS in the United Kingdom or managed care in the United States), it is vital to consider critical microenvironmental issues such as culture when implementing IT in health care organizations.

The management of the different stages of the proposed model is an important determinant of employees' commitment to the organization in a period of change. Therefore, as illustrated in this case, the model's ability to represent and portray change relating to the different areas offers a way of highlighting particular facets that will affect employees' commitment to the organization. Health care managers can use this information as the basis for IT strategic planning that seeks to influence the level of commitment felt by those who live and work with the change. The model emphasizes the impact of the approaches adopted by an organization upon the employees' reactions and the organization's need to both develop a strategy to rebuild employees' commitment and monitor the impact of this strategy over time. The model therefore avoids prescription for the management of change. The elicitation of these perceptions of change provides both a focus for specifically designed organizational action and a message that the concerns of health care professionals are acting directly upon the management of the change process. This latter aspect should, by itself, positively influence employees' perceptions and maintain their commitment to the organization.

FUTURE DIRECTIONS FOR RESEARCH

Future research should focus on two interrelated themes. The first relates to the effectiveness of EPR implementation models, relative to other assisted means of technology transfer in health care organizations. In particular, this research needs to highlight qualitatively significant issues in a meaningful way. The second relates to further development of the conceptual framework. Our study set out to address the important issue of culture. In the 1990s, Edgar Schein (1996) wrote an article about how culture is missing or given too little consideration in many studies pertaining to IT implementation. In the health care literature that discusses IT implementation, culture considerations are almost nonexistent so there is clearly much work to do in developing this model further and examining its usefulness with other IT implementations apart from EPRs in health care settings.

The development of the conceptual model reported in this case uses three small general practices in the United Kingdom and three practices in the Midwest of the United States. While the different areas that the model seeks to represent have considerable face validity, further work is needed to establish the validity of the framework's constructs in different sized organizations both in different locations in the two respective countries as well as in other countries. Thus, at present, it can be said that these constructs appear to offer a means to gauge and represent cultural shifts across areas in which organizations can act to encourage their employees' commitment.

CONCLUSIONS

Culture change is often necessary when implementing EPR programs in health care organizations. The anticipated benefits of EPR systems must be offset by the operational and procedural changes necessary to both initially receive and successfully accommodate the new technology. This case has established that there are cultural and organizational aspects of implementing such a system in health care organizations. The paper lays the foundations for an innovative implementation framework that managers and practitioners could use to implement EPR systems in their organizations.

Qualitative-based research (such as ethnography, case studies, and action research) may reveal pertinent data that traditional quantitative research overlooks. Discussion regarding strategic approaches is vital so that key personnel at the organization are actively involved in any implementation or change process. Organizational and cultural changes can be a key inhibitor or facilitator to successful implementation. However, attempting to change an organization's culture is far from easy. The change process is riddled with a variety of challenging barriers that must be overcome in order to change the culture. Recognizing and acknowledging the existence and complexity of these difficulties is central to the change process because, without this recognition, cultural and structural change will meet with failure, as will the anticipated benefits of the EPR implementation.

DISCUSSION QUESTIONS

1. What aspects of knowledge management are shown in this case study?
2. Describe how the health care organizations in this case are trying to become "smart organizations."
3. Are there any cultural or organizational issues that need to be considered for effective knowledge management in such health care organizations?
4. Critique the penta-stage model presented in the case—what are its strengths and weaknesses?

NOTE

This case was prepared by Rajeev Bali of Coventry University in the United Kingdom and Nilmini Wickramasinghe of the Illinois Institute of Technology in Chicago. It is intended as an illustration of a scenario in knowledge management and as a basis for classroom discussion. It is not intended to illustrate or to recommend effective or ineffective handling of a management decision or situation.

Case 2

Intellectual Capital in the Public Sector

An Assessment of City Councils' Web Pages

The information society has allowed for a generalized application of information and communication technologies (ICT), transforming the way people relate to each other, work, and manage organizations. At the same time, due to increasing economic globalization, markets have become progressively more competitive and unstable and are in constant change.

Given these challenges in today's economies, intangible factors have become increasingly important for developing competitive advantages in organizations and territories. Nowadays, intangible assets, such as knowledge, information, employees' creativity and skills, product and service trademarks, customer satisfaction, marketing, and quality, constitute the main production factors of organizations, altering their respective value.

This transition from an economy based on tangible goods to an economy based on intangible assets, the so-called knowledge-based economy, has given rise to new areas of research, such as the study of intellectual capital. Intellectual capital consists of the set of intangible assets capable of generating value for an organization (Edvinsson 2003).

Although some models have been developed that are directly applicable to private organizations, this does not mean that the concept of intellectual capital cannot be applied to public organizations. This concept is also applicable to geographic and territorial entities. Cities and regions, faced with increased competition in attracting new companies, are responding to the challenge by fielding new technologies and transforming their areas into knowledge territories. A knowledge territory is defined as a concentration of assets and economic activities based on knowledge, institutional environments that stimulate innovation, and modern technological infrastructures that are suitable for the interconnection of individuals, organizations, and local or regional areas (Serrano et al. 2005).

This case intends to demonstrate the importance of intellectual capital for public sector organizations, specifically for local state administrations. Thus, it consists of an assessment of intellectual capital through analyzing the Web pages of local state administrative institutions by applying an intellectual capital model to the public sector. The most appropriate model for the present study is the Queiroz model (Queiroz

2003), which makes it possible to demonstrate how the new ICTs can be used to incorporate intellectual capital indicators into the public sector.

INTELLECTUAL CAPITAL

The first studies in intellectual capital management resulting in scientific papers and studies with practical applications mainly in business were carried out by Brooking (1996), Sveiby (1997), Edvinsson and Malone (1997), and Stewart (1998).

The intellectual capital of organizations is usually classified as human capital, structural capital, and relational capital. Human capital includes the knowledge, qualifications, collective capacities, skills, experiences, creativity, innovation capability, motivation, and professional training of the employees of the organization. Structural capital includes organizational processes and procedures, hardware, software, databases, organizational structure, trademarks, patents, and intellectual property rights. Relational capital includes the value of the company's relationships with clients, suppliers, investors, and distribution channels.

Most of the models developed for measuring intellectual capital are business-related—for example, the Balanced Scorecard (Kaplan and Norton 1996); the Technology Broker (Brooking 1996); the Skandia Navigator (Edvinsson and Malone 1997); and the Intangible Assets Monitor (Sveiby 1997). These models present problems when applied directly to the public sector or territories because they center the definition of intellectual capital on the difference between the market value of a company and its book value, a method that is difficult to apply to the public sector. Because of this difficulty, some authors, including Bossi et al. (2001) and Queiroz (2003), have developed models explicitly for the assessment of intellectual capital in the public sector. Other authors have developed models for assessing intellectual capital at the territorial level, with examples of national, regional, or local applications in order to establish their contribution to productivity and development of the region in question. For example, the Intellectual Capital Monitor (Andriessen and Stam 2004) was applied by its authors to assess the intellectual capital of the European Union countries, and the Cities' Intellectual Capital Benchmarking System (CICBS) (Marti 2003) was applied to the Spanish city of Mataró.

INTELLECTUAL CAPITAL AND THE ROLE OF LOCAL AUTHORITIES IN DEVELOPMENT

Municipalities often represent one of the main driving forces of their local and regional economy. The responsibilities and capabilities of local authorities are related to satisfying the needs of the local community, with objectives that are related to socioeconomic development, land management, public utilities, basic sanitation, education, culture, environment, and sports. Thus, the local authorities are entities that play a fundamental role in creating a favorable socioeconomic climate, capable of attracting and promoting the creation and development of businesses.

In today's society, which is constantly subject to permanent mutations, it is necessary to manage territory wisely. Authorities need to know how to select regional and local development models that allow a close relationship with citizens and organizations and promote the sharing of knowledge. It is in this context that intellectual capital emerges as an important tool in land management. Identification, assessment, and management of intangible assets are of recognized importance and interest for improving decision making and management processes. Although the concept of intellectual capital has been most often applied to business, the public sector represents a very appropriate area for application of the concepts related to intangible assets, especially because intangibility seems to be more evident in this sector, whether with regard to its objectives (mostly of a social nature, such as national security, justice, health, social protection, and education), resources (above all, human resources and information), and products (mostly services, which are basically intangible).

Today, the rapid and continuous development of ICT has made it possible to modernize state administration and reformulate governance. In this process, e-government emerges as a possibility for greater proximity between the government and the citizens. The Internet is a powerful tool, and state administration can use Web pages for disseminating information, sharing knowledge, and providing services. These Web pages contribute to the process of change by helping the local administration to modernize, rationalize, integrate procedures, decrease bureaucracy in services, improve service to citizens, and promote the development of the region.

Within this context, the management of Web pages becomes extremely important. Therefore, assessment of their contents and usefulness is decisive for their improved management.

INSTRUMENTS FOR ASSESSING THE WEB PAGES OF MUNICIPALITIES IN PORTUGAL

In Portugal, the Action Plan for the Information Society[1] (2003) defines the quality and efficiency of public services as one of the pillars of action in the development of electronic government. For materializing this strategy, the Action Plan establishes a priority measure for evaluation of the Web sites of the public services under direct or indirect state administration in the seventh line of action.

The study carried out in Portugal by Santos et al. (2005)—*Assessment of the Presence of Portuguese City Councils on the Internet in 2003*[2]—is within the scope of the above-mentioned priority measure. Its objective was to assess the maturity of the presence of city councils on the Internet through studying all the municipalities that were on the Internet at the time of the assessment, which was carried out during the third trimester of 2003. The services offered by Portuguese city councils on the Internet were analyzed through online observation of their Web sites.

The proposal for the model that was used is an adaptation of the e-Europe[3] program, which is based on four levels of maturity, with level 4 representing the lowest and level 1 the highest degree of maturity.

The method used was adapted from the *Method for Assessment of the Websites of Direct and Indirect State Administration* and based on the recommendations in *Guidelines for Design of Websites for Direct and Indirect State Administration.*[4] This method involved an exhaustive process of gathering information through content analysis, using the quality of the online services provided by State Administration to citizens and businesses as the main criterion for assessment.

Data collection was done according to a grid with five criteria (content, content update, accessibility, navigability, and ease of use for citizens with special needs). Maturity was assessed using online services as the criteria with eight indicators.

The collected data helped to determine a quality and a maturity index for the Web sites. The quality and maturity indexes were calculated from the average sum of their indicators. Crossing the maturity data with the quality data makes it possible to determine the quality of the respective Web sites for each stage of maturity.

For each level of maturity considered, a qualitative classification was defined, which made it possible to identify the best Web sites—that is, the best applications. They were then divided equally into four groups using the relative classifications of *Good, Satisfactory, Poor,* and *Very Poor.*

The results of the assessment were also screened by the *size of the municipalities* to further refine the analysis at each level of maturity. This step was justified because the size of the municipality has a direct relationship with its financial and technical capacity as well as with the pool of potential users of online services. Thus, this separation makes it possible to minimize the effects of the size of the municipalities on the comparative process, which is reflected in the different amounts of available human and financial resources. Thus, the municipalities were divided into four classes according to the number of voters (Santos et al. 2005):

- A—municipalities with more than 100,001 voters (very big municipalities, on the Portuguese scale)
- B—big municipalities, between 50,001 to 100,000 voters
- C—medium-sized municipalities, between 10,001 to 50,000 voters
- D—small municipalities, up to 10,000 voters

The results of the assessment,[5] carried out in 2003, make it possible to confirm the following (see Case Table 2.1):

- From a total of 308 city councils, the assessment identified 259 with a Web site, which is 84.09 percent of the municipalities. Therefore 15.9 percent of the city councils did not have a Web site.
- The best Portuguese city council applications on the Internet are in the C category, with the city council of Loulé leading the ranking with 389,585 points, followed by the city councils of Palmela and Covilhã (all in the C category).

STATE OF THE ART IN ASSESSMENT OF WEB PAGES WITH EMPHASIS ON INTELLECTUAL CAPITAL

There have been few intellectual capital assessments of the public sector and even fewer analyses of intellectual capital through Web pages, either in private or public organizations.

In this context, Queiroz had an innovative role in applying the model he had devel-

Case Table 2.1

Results of the Study of Santos, Amaral, and Rodrigues, 2005

Level of maturity	Ranking	Total	City halls	Size	Points	General comments
4 (Availability of	1	166/	Évora	C	81.7	8.11% of the Web
information)	2	54%	Seixal	A	75.2	sites are in the Good
2	3		Marinha Grande	C	72.2	category, 47.88% are in
	4		Estarreja	C	70.117	the Satisfactory category,
	5		Manteigas	D	66.867	40.93% are classified as Poor, and 3.09% as Very Poor.
3	1	60/	Porto	A	109.6	2 Web sites are in the Good
(Availability of forms	2	20%	Leiria	B	105.4	Category (2.41%), 2 in
for download)	3		Faro	C	70.4	the Satisfactory category,
	4		Arouca	C	69.3	33.73% in the Poor
	5		Moita	B	50.4	category, and 61.45% are in the Very Poor category.
2	1	33/	Covilhã	C	256.8	33.33% of the Web sites
(Online submission	2	11%	Loulé	C	255.4	are in the Good category,
of forms and	3		Felgueiras	C	255.2	9.09% in the Satisfactory
process status)	4		Águeda	C	250.2	category, 27.27% in the
	5		Chaves	C	250.2	Poor category, and 30.3% are classified as Very Poor.
1 (Online service transactions)		0				

oped for the assessment of intellectual capital in the public sector to the assessment of the Web pages of Spanish municipalities. The main objective of his study was to understand the outline of the information provided by the Spanish municipalities through the Internet in order to identify the intellectual capital elements in them (Queiroz 2003). To do this, an online assessment of the Web pages of the municipalities was carried out. This assessment was based on a set of variables that were assigned according to the characteristics that define the intangible assets in the public sector—that is, it was based on the Queiroz model for assessing intellectual capital.

Another study, realized by Mello et al. (2003) under the direction of Queiroz, also assessed Web pages with the emphasis on intellectual capital—in this case, the intellectual capital of the Web pages of the Brazilian legislative assemblies. In this case also, a set of variables classified according to the above-mentioned model was defined.

METHODOLOGY OF INVESTIGATION: THE QUEIROZ MODEL

The study of the intellectual capital of city councils intends to illuminate the importance of intellectual capital for local state administration through an assessment of Web pages.

City councils are an important tool in creating knowledge territories because they are able to unite educated and uneducated citizens, dynamic and competitive companies, and social and political support structures. In this way, they are involved

Case Figure 2.1 **The Queiroz Model, 2003**

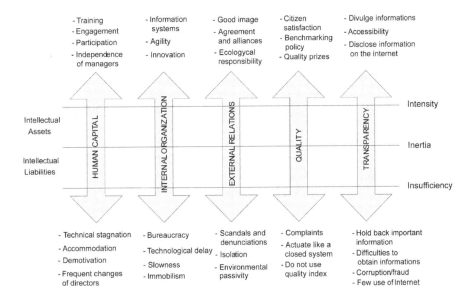

in creating regions of excellence that attract wealth and promote social well being. Web pages, as the portals of a municipality, are, in themselves, an instrument for the development of the region.

Web pages provide information, promote services, and encourage interactive communication and commercial transactions. All these benefits are considered intangible assets that constitute the intellectual capital existent in the Web pages of the city councils, so it is important to apply the intellectual capital models to their assessment, analysis, and management. Therefore, it is necessary to acknowledge a territory-based intellectual capital that has recognized importance and relational viability for urban development and advancement of the region.

In this study, the municipalities' Web pages were the instrument of analysis, constituting, from the intellectual capital point of view, an important tool for the development of the region, in this case cities and municipalities. It is the responsibility of political decision makers, at diverse levels of state administration, to prepare the ground for modern, integrated land management based on high standards of service and quality management where intellectual capital has an increasingly more important role.

The research methodology used the Queiroz model (Queiroz 2003), an intellectual capital model for the public sector with the following elements (see Case Figure 2.1): human resources (human capital), internal processes (structural capital), public relations (relational capital), quality, and transparency.

The model consists of two main parts that call to mind a scale of intellectual capital, with intellectual asset on one side and intellectual liability on the other. Positive attitudes or actions contribute to the increase of intellectual capital, and negative ones can create intellectual liability. This idea of intellectual liability is used because, in addition to highlighting the results of efficient management, situations of inadequate management do exist and should also be shown, whether at the internal or the external level.

The elements of intellectual capital encounter three situations shown by the three dotted lines:

- intensity of intellectual capital, which indicates a condition of excellence
- inertia, which represents conformity or mediocrity
- inadequacy, which represents the situation in which public services do not meet the needs of the population in a satisfactory manner

A scale of –100 to +100 is used, in which zero represents the situation of inertia, the negative numbers represent an inadequate intellectual capital management, and the positive numbers a good management. The maximum application of knowledge management is represented by +100.

The methodology used in the present study was based on the Queiroz model used by Mello et al. (2003) in their study of the assessment of intellectual capital in the Web pages of the Brazilian legislative assemblies.

A questionnaire was prepared to verify the intangible information and services assets in each category of the Queiroz model whose presence in a city council's Web site was considered essential. Variables were defined for each category of intellectual capital included on the questionnaire, which was applied online to the Web pages.

The constant quality element of the Queiroz model was not considered because this element had already been studied by Santos et al. (2005; *Assessment of the Presence of Portuguese City Councils on the Internet in 2003, Through the Qualitative Assessment Grid of the Websites of Direct and Indirect State Administration*).

The practicality of the Web pages was not analyzed; therefore elements such as the structuring of the information, navigability, and aesthetics were not assessed. However, basic navigation aspects necessary for accessing the information under study, such as the existence of a site map and search methods, were considered.

The questionnaire had fifty-six questions. Each question was given a certain weight proportional to its relevance to the asset analyzed in the research:

- 0.00—when there was no information about the asset in question
- 1.00—important
- 2.00—very important
- 2.50—most important

The weight assigned to all fifty-six questions made a total of eighty points, which were distributed in the following manner:

- human capital = 13 points
- structural capital = 13 points
- relational capital = 39 points
- transparency = 15 points

Relational capital is the element of the model with the most points and the most questions because it is the one with the greatest importance or use for citizens in their daily use of the city councils' Web pages, and therefore it is the element with the most assets to be analyzed. The Web page of a municipality is used, above all, to facilitate, stimulate, or otherwise improve the interaction of citizens and other institutions with city councils.

Transparency, with fifteen points, is increasingly fundamental in the modernization of public management. Transparency makes it possible to inform citizens about the government's activity, allowing them greater control over public management.

The score obtained by each city council corresponds to the ratio of the total points obtained divided by the total points possible:

$$N = \frac{(PO \times 100)}{PP},$$

where
N = score;
PO = total points obtained;
PP = total points possible.

SAMPLE

The chosen sample for this study consisted of a set of the twenty-seven city councils with the best applications as revealed in the above-mentioned study of Santos et al. (2005). As studying all the city councils would have greatly increased the scope of our study, it was decided to select those with the highest scores in the above-mentioned study.

The model establishes four levels of maturity and is based on the type of contents that were made available through the Web for citizens and businesses by state administration. Level 4 represents the lowest and level 1 the highest degree of maturity.

The results of the best ten applications were presented for each of these levels, with the exception of the last, level 1, where no city council was found. Since there were three city councils that had the best applications in more than one level, the size of the sample was reduced from a total of thirty city councils to twenty-seven.

RESULTS

The data were collected in February and March 2006, with direct application, through direct observation of the Web pages of the municipalities. The following results, presented in Case Table 2.2 and Case Figure 2.2, were obtained.

The obtained results make it possible to see that Lisbon had the best score and Póvoa do Lanhoso the worst. The average score in IC is 58.02, with 55.56 percent of the city councils (15) having obtained a higher score. The standard deviation was 11.52.

The second column of Case Table 2.3 shows the classification obtained by the same city councils in the study of Santos et al. (2005), which assessed the maturity and quality of the presence of the city councils on the Internet. This table compares the position of the Web pages in the two studies.

Case Figure 2.2 **The Scores of Intellectural Capital of the City Councils' Web Page**

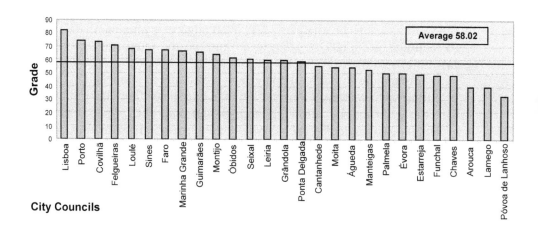

Case Table 2.2

General Ranking of the Intellectual Capital of the City Councils' Web Pages

Ranking	City Hall	Score
1st	Lisbon	81.21
2nd	Porto	74.20
3rd	Covilhã	72.91
4th	Felgueiras	70.47
5th	Loulé	67.85
6th	Sines	67.63
7th	Faro	67.25
8th	Marinha Grande	66.09
9th	Guimarães	65.25
10th	Montijo	63.59
11th	Óbidos	60.92
12th	Seixal	60.47
13th	Leiria	59.50
14th	Grândola	59.25
15th	Ponta Delgada	58.69
16th	Cantanhede	54.91
17th	Moita	54.25
18th	Águeda	53.97
19th	Manteigas	52.38
20th	Palmela	49.72
21st	Évora	49.63
22nd	Estarreja	48.81
23rd	Funchal	48.38
24th	Chaves	47.84
25th	Arouca	39.50
26th	Lamego	39.44
27th	Póvoa de Lanhoso	32.51

In comparing the classifications, there are significant differences that must be pointed out. We can see that, in the Santos et al. (2005) study, Loulé appears in the first place, indicating that it is the city council whose Web page presents the highest degree of maturity and the greatest quality, whereas in the present study Loulé appears in the fifth place in the general ranking of intellectual capital. Lisbon is almost in the reverse situation, as it holds the first place in the intellectual capital ranking and the fourth place in the 2003 study.

The situation of Sines is still more significant, as in this study it is classified in the sixth place and in the above-mentioned study in the twenty-seventh, in the comparative ranking (ninety-sixth in the general ranking). The city councils of Felgueiras, Faro, and Marinha Grande also obtained good scores (4th, 7th, and 8th places, respectively) despite lower classifications in the former study (11th/25th, 16th/35th, and 20th/40th places, respectively).

Conversely, Palmela has a high maturity level, placing it second in the Santos et al. study (2005), while placing twentieth in the intellectual ranking. Similarly, Grândola, Chaves, Águeda, and Cantanhede occupy significant positions in the earlier study (5th/5th, 6th/7th, 7th/8th, and 9th/10th, respectively) but obtained poorer classifications in the present study (14th, 24th, 18th, and 16th, respectively). Covilhã has a balanced classification, occupying the third position in both studies, indicating a high level of maturity and intellectual capital.

Comparison of the results of the two studies shows that a Web site with a high level of maturity and quality does not always indicate the availability of many intellectual capital assets, and, vice versa, a good score in intellectual capital does not mean that the Web site has a high level of maturity and quality.

Case Figure 2.3 **Human Capital Scores**

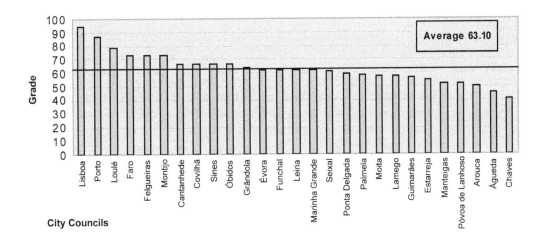

Case Table 2.3

Comparison Between the Santos, Amaral, and Rodrigues (2005) Ranking and the Ranking of the Present Study

City hall	Classification obtained in the Santos, Amaral, and Rodrigues (2005) study	Position according to the analyses[a]	Classification obtained in the present study
Loulé	1st	1st	5th
Palmela	2nd	2nd	20th
Covilhã	3rd	3rd	3rd
Lisbon	4th	4th	1st
Grândola	5th	5th	14th
Chaves	7th	6th	24th
Águeda	8th	7th	18th
Porto	9th	8th	2nd
Cantanhede	10th	9th	16th
Ponta Delgada	24th	10th	15th
Felgueiras	25th	11th	4th
Guimarães	26th	12th	9th
Évora	29th	13th	21st
Lamego	30th	14th	26th
Leiria	34th	15th	13th
Faro	35th	16th	7th
Estarreja	36th	17th	22nd
Arouca	38th	18th	25th
Moita	39th	19th	17th
Marinha Grande	40th	20th	8th
Funchal	41st	21st	23rd
Montijo	42nd	22nd	10th
Manteigas	45th	23rd	19th
Póvoa de Lanhoso	47th	24th	27th
Óbidos	52nd	25th	11th
Seixal	94th	26th	12th
Sines	96th	27th	6th

[a]This column refers to the ordering of the twenty-seven city halls according to the Web page points obtained in the Santos, Amaral, and Rodrigues (2005) study, which was aimed at making a comparative analysis between the two studies.

The study of Santos et al. (2005) was based on four levels of maturity. Case Table 2.4 shows an analysis of these levels that was the basis for selection of our sample. It can be seen that there is no direct relationship between the scores obtained in the two studies—that is, a good score at a specific level of maturity does not always imply a good score in intellectual capital. Through analysis of the average value at each level of maturity, it can be seen that as the level of maturity increases and the relationship between the entity and citizens becomes more coherent, the average intellectual capital score increases. Although there is no direct relationship in comparing the obtained scores in the two studies, the fact that the sample was chosen based on the ten best applications at each level seems to have some influence here. It is noted

Case Table 2.4

Results of Intellectual Capital by Level of Maturity

Level of maturity	City council	Position in Santos, Amaral and Rodrigues (2005)	Position in general IC ranking (2006)	Score in IC	CI average per level of maturity
Level 4	Évora	1st	21st	49.63	53.06
Availability of	Seixal	2nd	12th	60.47	
information	Marinha Grande	3rd	8th	66.09	
	Estarreja	4th	22nd	48.81	
	Manteigas	5th	19th	52.38	
	Póvoa de Lanhoso	6th	27th	32.51	
	Lamego	7th	26th	39.44	
	Sines	8th	6th	67.63	
	Cantanhede	9th	16th	54.91	
	Ponta delgada	9th	15th	58.69	
Level 3	Porto	1st	2nd	74.20	57.22
Availability of forms	Leiria	2nd	13th	59.50	
for download	Faro	3rd	7th	67.25	
	Arouca	4th	25th	39.50	
	Moita	5th	17th	54.25	
	Óbidos	6th	11th	60.92	
	Cantanhede	7th	16th	54.91	
	Funchal	8th	23rd	48.38	
	Montijo	9th	10th	63.59	
	Palmela	10th	20th	49.72	
Level 2	Covilhã	1st	3rd	72.91	62.72
Online submission	Loulé	2nd	5th	67.85	
of forms and	Felgueiras	3rd	4th	70.47	
process status	Águeda	4th	18th	53.97	
	Chaves	4th	24th	47.84	
	Grândola	4th	14th	59.25	
	Guimarães	4th	9th	65.25	
	Lisbon	4th	1st	81.21	
	Palmela	4th	20th	49.72	
	Ponta Delgada	4th	15th	58.69	
Level 1	0				
Online service					
transactions					

Note: In 2003 when this study was carried out, no Web site was found at level 1, the maximum level of maturity considered in the model, which refers to online service transactions.

that the councils with the best rankings in intellectual capital are concentrated at level 2 (Case Table 2.4).

Case Table 2.5 shows the ranking obtained through grouping the intellectual capital scores by the classes used in the Santos et al. (2005) study, according to the number of voters. Santos et al. concluded that the maturity of the Web pages increases with the size of the municipality. Our study shows that the largest municipalities—Lisbon and Porto—are those that have the best intellectual capital scores. However, this situation does not seem to be generalized for the rest of the group, because $r^2 = 0.15$, which

Case Table 2.5

Results of Intellectual Capital According to Number of Voters

Class according to number of voters	City council	Number of voters	Score	Position in general IC ranking
Class A: More than 100,001 voters	Lisbon	566,162	81.21	1st
	Porto	245,797	74.20	2nd
	Guimarães	124,764	65.25	9th
	Seixal	111,842	60.47	12th
Class B: 50,001 to 100,000 voters	Funchal	96,634	48.38	23rd
	Leiria	93,894	59.50	13th
	Moita	56,322	54.25	17th
	Ponta Delgada	50,482	58.69	15th
Class C: 10,001 to 50,000 voters	Covilhã	49,296	72.91	3rd
	Loulé	47,667	67.85	5th
	Faro	47,592	67.25	7th
	Évora	45,462	49.63	21st
	Felgueiras	42,352	70.47	4th
	Chaves	42,223	47.84	24th
	Águeda	40,562	53.97	18th
	Palmela	39,711	49.72	20th
	Montijo	34,238	63.59	10th
	Cantanhede	32,754	54.91	16th
	Marinha Grande	29,698	66.09	8th
	Lamego	25,604	39.44	26th
	Estarreja	22,492	48.81	22nd
	Arouca	20,165	39.50	25th
	Póvoa de Lanhoso	19,273	32.51	27th
	Grândola	12,863	59.25	14th
	Sines	10,922	67.63	6th
Class D: Up to 10,000 voters	Óbidos	9,474	60.92	11th
	Manteigas	3,548	52.38	19th

shows a weak correlation between the number of voters of the city council and the intellectual capital score. Covilhã, Felgueiras, Loulé, and Sines occupy good ranking positions although they are much smaller than Lisbon and Porto.

The analysis of intellectual capital elements is represented in Case Figures 2.3, 2.4, 2.5, and 2.6, where it is possible to see the scores obtained by each Web site and those that are above average in each element.

Case Table 2.6 shows the best and the worst five applications in each intellectual capital element, as well as the general score for intellectual capital. It is also possible to see the average and the percentage of the Web pages with above-average scores. We can see that Lisbon holds the lead in almost all the elements with the exception of the relational capital; Covilhã is the municipality with the greatest number of intangible assets in this category. Póvoa de Lanhoso, almost always, has the worst scores, as do Arouca, Lamego, and Chaves, which seem to have the worst applications in almost all the elements.

Case Figure 2.4 **Structural Capital Scores**

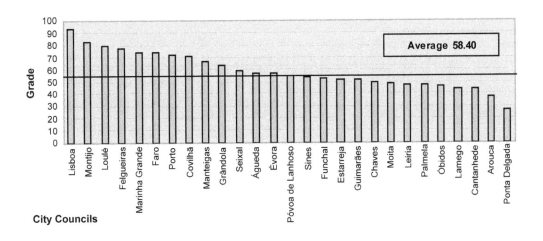

Case Figure 2.5 **Relational Capital Scores**

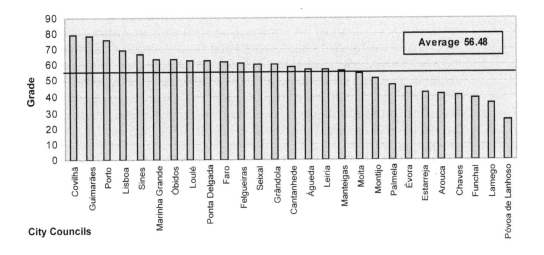

The best average was obtained in human capital, which turned out to be the element with the most positive responses and therefore with the greatest presence in the Web pages. The worst average was obtained in relational capital, which demonstrates that the main function of a Web site as a communication channel is still not being fully used.

Case Figure 2.6 **Transparency Scores**

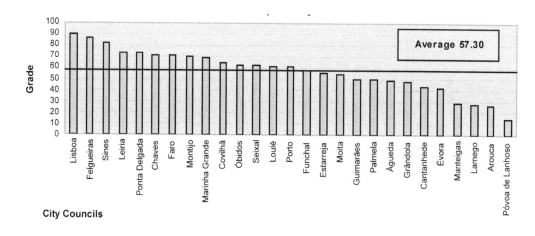

CONCLUSIONS

In today's economies, intellectual capital is of increasing importance in creating competitive advantages for organizations and regions. Cities and districts respond to ever-increasing challenges, competing for assets and economic activities based on knowledge, institutional environments that stimulate innovation, and modern, technological infrastructures that are suitable for interaction of individuals with organizations. Local authorities responding to problems associated with these transformations in the ways the citizens work and live are increasingly dependent on intellectual capital. This constitutes a decisive element for the development of the region.

The local state administrations must take advantage of the potentialities inherent in the use of ICT to provide the best services to citizens through e-government. The Internet is an important tool for state administration, as it makes possible a bidirectional, transparent, direct, and personalized relationship between citizens and institutions. Therefore, it is necessary to have an adequate management of the contents of the Web pages and the services they provide.

Assessment of the city councils' Web pages through the Queiroz model can provide an instrumental analysis of the intellectual capital of a region and can constitute a basis for its appraisal. The results obtained in this study demonstrate that the largest municipalities, Lisbon and Porto, had the best intellectual capital scores, but other, smaller municipalities, such as Covilhã, Felgueiras, Loulé, Sines, Faro, and Marinha Grande, also obtained outstanding scores, which demonstrate these city councils' concern for providing information and services to citizens and businesses. Although 55.56 percent of the city councils obtained a score above

Case Table 2.6

The Best and the Worst Intellectual Capital Applications

	Human	Structural	Relational	Transparency	Intellectual
Best 5	Lisbon	Lisbon	Covilhã	Lisbon	Lisbon
	Porto	Montijo	Guimarães	Felgueiras	Porto
	Loulé	Loulé	Porto	Sines	Covilhã
	Faro	Felgueiras	Lisbon	Leiria	Felgueiras
	Felgueiras	M. Grande	Sines	Pta Delgada	Loulé
	Montijo[a]				
Worst 5	Manteigas	Óbidos	Arouca	Évora	Funchal
	P. Lanhoso	Lamego	Chaves	Manteigas	Chaves
	Arouca	Cantanhede	Funchal	Lamego	Arouca
	Águeda	Arouca	Lamego	Arouca	Lamego
	Chaves	Pta Delgada	P. Lanhoso	P. Lanhoso	P. Lanhoso
Average	63.10	58.40	56.48	57.30	58.02
Comments	40.74% of the Web pages are above this value	40.74% of the Web pages are above this value	62.96% of the Web pages are above this value	55.56% of the Web pages are above this value	55.56% of the Web pages are above this value

[a]There are six Web pages mentioned here because three Web pages—those of Faro, Felgueiras, and Montijo—had the same score and were in fourth place.

the general average for intellectual capital, the worst scores show that there is still work to be done in this field if municipalities want to use ICT to achieve a leading role in the promotion and development of regions and communities of excellence.

DISCUSSION QUESTIONS

1. Why has intellectual capital become especially important for public sector organizations?
2. How do the tools, techniques, and strategies pertaining to knowledge management enable a better understanding of such intangible assets in public sector organizations?
3. How generalizable are the issues and solutions presented here to other public sector organizations?
4. What are the strengths and weaknesses of analyzing Web pages as described in this case study? How do they relate to knowledge management?

NOTES

This case was prepared by Sandra Bailoa of the Polytechnic Institute of Beja, Portugal, and Paulo esende da Silva of the University of Évora, Portugal. It is intended as an illustration of a scenario in knowledge management and as a basis for classroom discussion. It is not intended to illustrate or to recommend effective or ineffective handling of a management decision or situation.

1. Resolution of the Council of Ministers no. 107, June 26, 2003.

2. This study was carried out within the scope of the above-mentioned priority measures and resulted in a request made by the Innovation and Knowledge Mission Unit (UMIC) at the Sociology Research and Study Center of the Higher Institute of Work and Business Sciences (CIES/ISCTE) and at the Information Systems Department of the University of Minho (DSI/UM). It is a follow-up of the objectives of the Resolution of the Council of Ministers no. 22, 2001, which establish mechanisms for systematic assessment of the Web pages of state administration with the aim of determining their compatibility with basic criteria for quality.

3. The e-Europe 2005 Action Plan was launched at the Seville European Council in June 2002 and endorsed by the Council of Ministers in the e-Europe Resolution of January 2003. It aims to develop modern public services and a dynamic environment for e-business through widespread availability of broadband access at competitive prices and a secure information infrastructure (http://europa.eu.int/information_society/eeurope/2005/index_en.htm).

4. These documents can be found on the Web site of the UMIC (www.umic.pcm.gov.pt).

5. Complete results can be seen in Santos et al. (2005).

Case 3

HSprovider

Knowledge-Based Solutions for the Tourism and Travel Industry

INDUSTRY AND BUSINESS CHALLENGE

The tourism and travel (T&T) industry represents a historical success for both e-commerce and e-business and is among the sectors with the most mature implementations of Web-based information and communication technology (ICT). In almost all countries, there exist a number of Web portals helping potential tourists plan their trip and find the most suitable accommodations. Most hotels have their own Web site and allow their guests to make reservations through the Internet. Given the number of paths that a user can follow to reach a hotel (search engines, multiple tourism portals, travel and accommodation sites, etc.), the industry is experiencing a high level of intermediation. This intermediation is creating new business-to-business service opportunities. HSprovider has been able to recognize and leverage one of these new service opportunities.

Web portals allow tourists to make direct, precise comparisons among the levels of service offered by different hotels. This has radically changed the way tourists make their accommodation decisions. For example, they can make queries that select hotels offering given services and then make price versus quality evaluations on a restricted number of options. These aids to their decision process translate into a lower level of loyalty to hotels that they have previously visited, a higher turnover, and an overall greater sensitivity to price.

From the hotel's perspective, being able to set the correct price level becomes more critical. Hotels have to face the usual trade-off between price and sold quantity in terms of the number of guests. They know very well that in the off-season lowering the price can pay off with globally higher returns. Since hotels have high fixed costs, volume plays an important role in determining their financial success.

Yield management represents the discipline that provides the theoretical underpinnings of the managerial decisions related to the price-volume trade-off. Yield management requires sophisticated data analysis tools, including advanced data mining functionalities. The software tools that support yield management can be considered knowledge management systems (KMS), since they provide intelligent learning functionalities that support forecast, simulation, and optimization. Yield management applications collect and analyze a number of data, including a hotel's costs, number of rooms, room services, historical reservation data, event calendars, customer preferences, customer profiles, customer opinions, marketing opportunities, etc. On this basis, they provide the prices that maximize profits based on an estimate of market demand.

Not all this information is internal. Clearly, the behavior of competitors represents an important piece of external information that can dramatically influence the accuracy of yield management decisions. As a straightforward example, if competitors are not lowering their prices, even small discounts can significantly increase volumes. Vice versa, if competitors are applying aggressive discounts, raising volume will be more challenging and applying no discount at all may become an option.

HSprovider has designed a yield management application that is capable of automatically collecting information on competitors from Web sites and industry portals. By means of Web crawlers (see below), HSprovider can simulate the behavior of a potential customer who is making a reservation. In this way, it collects both occupancy and price information on competitors and builds a precise map of local competition. This information is an input to its yield management application, which combines the input with internal information on the hotel's services, customers, and business goals to provide a best price estimate.

According to Carlo Paoloni, HSprovider's CEO, the main business challenge is the Italian market culture:

> The Italian tourism industry is rich and represents an interesting market. However, there is little or no yield management culture. Managers know that the level of service that they offer to their guests is critical to customer retention. Their main focus is on the service vs. cost trade-off. They are aware of the changes brought about by the Internet, but they are slow in moving from a cost to a yield management mentality. While international hotel chains have a revenue manager who is in charge of yield management, most Italian hotels have no revenue manager. More often than we would like, our job is to be yield management evangelists, rather than software providers.

HSPROVIDER: HISTORY AND ECONOMICS

HSprovider was created in 2005 by four cofounders. Three of them are computer scientists, with two having longtime experience in the tourism industry. The fourth cofounder has a background in business administration. Initially, their business idea was to build occupancy forecast models to be integrated into hotels' ERP (Enterprise Resource Planning) software. However, the founders quickly understood that hotels needed a full-fledged application that allowed them to understand the benefits of price optimization. A simulation tool was added to the software solution to enable scenario analyses and support qualitative price analyses.

In 2006, one of HSprovider's customers showed an interest in price optimization functionalities. HSprovider was committed to the development of this new software component for an entire year. Two developers were hired and trained on yield management. The application was released in March 2007 and offered as a Web service to all the company's customers. Success was almost immediate. More than 80 percent of HSprovider customers subscribed to the service by July 2007 and more than thirty new customers were acquired.

At this point, the market penetration strategy of HSprovider was to sell its services to only one customer per each hotel category within the same geographical zone. The main target was usually a four-star hotel. Geographical zones were defined based on the density of hotels and the overall size of the demand. Rome and Milan were the initial targets. By the end of 2006, HSprovider served more than sixty hotels in these cities.

The gross revenue of HSprovider has been linearly increasing since 2005. In 2005 the gross revenue was 100k euros, with a profit and loss (P&L) index of −7k euros due to initial investments. Last year HSprovider recorded revenues of 220k euros, with null P&L index. A set of about 150 hotels constitutes the HSprovider customer base. Customers are spread across Italy, with a strong concentration in art cities such as Rome and Venice.

HSprovider's organizational structure is a two-level hierarchy. The CEO controls the yield and allocation managers. Each manager is responsible for yield management or information allocation for hotels in a given geographical area. Finally, a marketing specialist is responsible for HSprovider promotion among new potential customers.

THE TRAVEL AND TOURISM BUSINESS SCENARIO: ISSUES AND HSPROVIDER'S SOLUTIONS

THE ITALIAN TOURISM INDUSTRY

Representing 9.95 percent of the gross domestic product, the T&T industry is a strategic resource for the Italian economy. As shown in Case Figure 3.1, Italy ranks in the world's top five countries for both the number of yearly foreign visitors and the total revenue generated by international tourists, with both indicators increasing in the last year.

A snapshot of the Italian T&T industry, which gives the flavor of the centrality of the industry to the Italian economy, was given in 2007 by the World Travel and Tourism Council (WTTC), reported in Case Figure 3.2. It is worth noticing that Italian T&T market size ranks eighth in the world, while, although decreasing in the last few years, Italy's global T&T market share is about 4 percent.

The total number of hotels in Italy is 33,500. Only 20 percent of them are owned or managed by a hotel chain. These hotels belong to forty different hotel chains, both national and international. The remaining 80 percent of Italian hotels are independent, usually family owned.

In family-owned hotels, the hotel manager decides the course of action on the basis of experience. The family manager typically considers the quality of rooms, hospitality, and politeness as the basic critical success factors. Only recently, managers have also started to consider the hotel's presence on global distributed systems (GDSs), Internet distributed systems (IDSs), and Web portals as further success factors for their business. Price determination and, more generally, yield management are performed by the manager on the basis of past experience. Family managers tend not to trust external companies or, more important, computer-based systems in making sugges-

Case Figure 3.1 **World Statistics for International Arrivals and the T and T Incomes**

International Tourist Arrivals						International Tourism Receipts						
									US$			Local currencies
Rank		million		Change (%)		Rank		billion		Change (%)		Change (%)
	Series	2005	2006*	05/04	06*/05			2005	2006*	05/04	06*/05	05/04	06*/05
1 France	TF	75.9	79.1	1.0	4.2	1 United States		81.8	85.7	9.7	4.8	9.7	4.8
2 Spain	TF	55.9	58.5	6.6	4.5	2 Spain		48.0	51.1	6.0	6.6	6.0	5.6
3 United States	TF	49.2	51.1	6.8	3.8	3 France		42.3	42.9	3.5	1.5	3.5	0.6
4 China	TF	46.8	49.6	12.1	6.0	4 Italy		35.4	38.1	-0.7	7.7	-0.7	6.7
5 Italy	TF	36.5	41.1	-1.5	12.4	5 China		29.3	33.9	13.8	15.9	13.8	15.9
6 United Kingdom	TF	28.0	30.7	9.2	9.3	6 United Kingdom		30.7	33.7	8.7	9.8	9.5	8.5
7 Germany	TCE	21.5	23.6	6.8	9.6	7 Germany		29.2	32.8	5.4	12.3	5.4	11.3
8 Mexico	TF	21.9	21.4	6.3	-2.6	8 Australia		16.9	17.8	11.0	5.8	6.9	7.3
9 Austria	TCE	20.0	20.3	3.0	1.5	9 Turkey		18.2	16.9	14.2	-7.2	14.2	-7.2
10 Russian Federation	TF	19.9	20.2	0.2	1.3	10 Austria		16.0	16.7	2.8	4.0	2.7	3.1

Source: World Tourism Organization (UNWTO)© (2007).

tions on price strategies. Thus, family managers avoid investing in professional figures such as revenue managers and, in general, make limited investments in ICT. These considerations do not apply to hotel chains, where the point of view of managers is quite different and ICT opportunities tend to be carefully evaluated.

From HSprovider's perspective, the Italian T&T market is therefore very appealing, since it lacks the offer of an outsourced service of global revenue management and, generally, the offer of integrated ICT solutions for family-owned hotels.

As noted before, HSprovider offers its ICT tools both as a product, which can be installed and run by the hotel manager, and as a (Web) service, which can be remotely accessed in a way that is very similar to the application service provider (ASP) access paradigm for ERP systems. For a hotel manager, the choice between the service and the product offered is based on specific context-dependent variables. Generally speaking, most managers prefer the service solution because it does not require a high initial investment or knowledge transfer to hotel employees for the appropriate installation and usage of HSprovider's ICT tools. The product solution is preferred in contexts where the adoption of revenue policies is more mature and/or where both the employees and the hotel manager have some understanding of the potential impact of ICT tools in the T&T industry.

HSPROVIDER'S SERVICE OFFER

HSprovider's ICT tools aim at solving two main problems that consistently affect Italian hotels: automated integration with the extranet of GDSs and Web portals, and automated information retrieval and support for yield management.

Case Figure 3.2 **Overview of the Italian Travel and Tourism Industry**

In association with

Italy
The 2007 Travel & Tourism Economic Research

TOTAL DEMAND

Italy Travel & Tourism is expected to generate EUR204.2 bn (US$272.0 bn) of economic activity (Total Demand) in 2007, growing (nominal terms) to EUR325.5 bn (US$396.0 bn) by 2017. Total Demand is expected to grow by 1.4% in 2007 and by 2.0% per annum, in real terms, between 2008 and 2017. 2007 Total Demand represents 3.9% of world market share.

GROWTH   2007: 1.4%   10Yr: 2.0%

WORLD MARKET SHARE: 3.9%

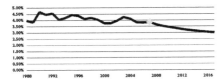

Italy Travel & Tourism market share of worldwide Total Demand is generally decreasing.

WORLD RANKING (176 Countries)

8	ABSOLUTE size
82	RELATIVE contribution to national economy
173	GROWTH forecast

Italy is a very large, middle-tier intensive, and slow growing Travel & Tourism economy.

GDP

	T&T Industry:	T&T Economy:
	4.2%	10.2%

Italy's T&T Industry is expected to contribute 4.2% to Gross Domestic Product (GDP) in 2007 (EUR64.9 bn or US$86.5 bn), rising in nominal terms to EUR93.5 bn or US$113.7 bn (4.2% of total) by 2017. The T&T Economy contribution (percent of total) should rise from 10.2% (EUR156.7 bn or US$208.7 bn) to 10.2% (EUR230.0 bn or US$279.7 bn) in this same period.

Italy Travel & Tourism Industry GDP contribution to Total GDP is generally decreasing, and Travel & Tourism Economy GDP contribution to Total GDP is generally decreasing.

Italy
Travel & Tourism Gross Domestic Product
(% of Total GDP)

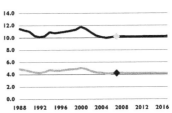

Light Blue Line is T&T Industry GDP; Dark Blue is T&T Economy GDP

JOBS

	T&T Industry:	T&T Economy:
	1,068,166	2,651,702

Italy T&T Economy employment is estimated at 2,652,000 jobs in 2007, 11.5% of total employment, or 1 in every 8.7 jobs. By 2017, this should total 2,825,000 jobs, 12.7% of total employment or 1 in every 7.9 jobs. The 1,068,000 T&T Industry jobs account for 4.6% of total employment in 2007 and are forecast to total 1,118,000 jobs or 5.0% of the total by 2017.

Italy relative Travel & Tourism Industry Employment contribution to Total Employment is generally increasing, and relative Travel & Tourism Economy Employment contribution to Total Employment is generally increasing

Italy
Travel & Tourism Employment
('000s of Jobs)

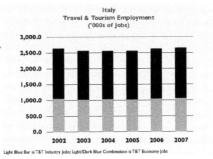

Light Blue Bar is T&T Industry Jobs; Light/Dark Blue Combination is T&T Economy Jobs

Case Figure 3.3 **Overview of HSprovider's Technology Platform**

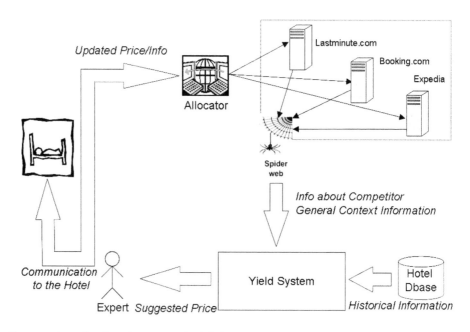

Concerning the first issue, each GDS and IDS has its own extranet. The extranet of such systems is the interface accessible to the external actors (e.g., the hotels) through which they can upload information, such as room availability, applied rates, minimum stay policies, and promotional offers. In principle, a hotel has to upload all this information by interacting in a different way (e.g., manually or with an ad hoc client) with the extranet of each GDS, IDS, or Web portal. The tool proposed by HSprovider to solve this issue is the allocator system (AS), which automatically manages the interaction with the heterogeneous interfaces of GDSs and Web portals, while providing a unique interface for the hotel manager.

On the other hand, the problem of yield management also requires the collection of information about competitors (once again, applied rates, room availability, or promotional offers). Such information is collected and processed by a second tool offered by HSprovider, called the yield management system (YMS). The management and economic underpinnings of yield management and revenue management practices are described in depth in the appendix. As previously discussed, both solutions provided by HSprovider (AS and YMS) can be accessed as a service or purchased as a product. The overview of HSprovider's technology platform is shown in Case Figure 3.3.

The AS tool automatically collects context information about competitors of the customer hotel from the distributed systems (DSs). Such information, together with historical information concerning the customer hotel, is the input of the YMS tool. The price forecast produced by the YMS must be validated by an HSprovider expert. If the forecast is positively validated, it is forwarded to the customer hotel and uploaded into the DSs hosting the hotel by means of the AS tool.

The sections below provide the technological details of the YMS and the AS.

HSPROVIDER'S YIELD MANAGEMENT SYSTEM

For a given hotel, the challenges solved by HSprovider's YMS are the following:

- Determination of the right occupation curve for a given date, that is, the optimal theoretical hotel occupation as per the discussion reported in the appendix
- Determination of the optimal pricing schema for the different price classes in order to optimize the occupation curve

The yield management problem solved by HSprovider's tools can be quite complex (far more complex than the example discussed in the appendix). Yield management in real-world business scenarios must consider a number of different variables, such as a fine-grained classification of the hotel's customer base, the overbooking policies, and the penalties associated with the no-show of a customer. Moreover, predictions made only on the basis of the historical occupation of an individual hotel are not accurate, since they require a global analysis of the market. Since GDSs, IDSs, and Web portals are the primary channels for selling hotel rooms, historical data from these sites on the hotel and on its competitors can significantly improve the quality of the assessment.

The yield management process starts 120 days before the target date. The process is composed of several phases:

- the collection of the inputs for the YMS
- the collection of information for validating the output of the YMS
- the definition of the pricing schema maximizing the occupation curves
- the validation of the pricing schema

The yield management process is based on a knowledge base. This knowledge base is divided in two parts. The first is related to the hotel and stored in a local, permanent database. The second stores information about competitors—that is, highly volatile data that are considered temporary.

There are two classes of *inputs* to the YMS. The first is knowledge about the target hotel, including the following information:

- Historical information concerning the hotel bookings, including the total occupation of the hotel for the same date in previous years, the occupation for different customer segments (e.g., business vs. retail clients), the total number of rooms, and the time distribution of reservations for a specific date with their service characteristics
- Different types of business rules, including the prices applied for different customer segments and the average advance time of reservations

The second class of inputs includes knowledge about the context:

- Information about the number of queries performed on the considered GDSs, IDSs, or Web portals for the considered geographical zone and date

- Information about special events around the target date, such as fairs, shows, or sport events

The knowledge for validating the *output* of the YMS is also divided in two classes. The first includes knowledge about the target hotel—that is, historical information on the price applied by the hotel for the considered date. If the context conditions are very similar to the ones of the previous year, the proposed price should be comparable with the rate applied the year before. When a discrepancy occurs, the hotel manager should carefully analyze the situation.

The second class of outputs includes knowledge about the context:

- Information about the price applied by the competitors and their corresponding available services
- Information about special events, such as fairs, shows, or sport events

Knowledge about the target hotel is usually stored in the hotel's databases. Therefore, this knowledge is very easily retrieved if HSprovider is granted full access to the hotel's databases. Usually, hotels prefer to grant access to HSprovider through their extranet systems without actually delivering the database to HSprovider, since these data are extremely sensitive and also very dynamic (for instance, current reservations for the target date).

The collection of knowledge about the context is usually the most challenging task of HSprovider's YMS. Knowledge about the context has to be collected from sources to which HSprovider does not usually have access. While information about special events, fairs, shows, or sport events might be directly possessed by the target hotel and can be easily shared, HSprovider has to find a way to collect information about the room allocation and prices of competitors.

GDSs, IDSs, and Web portals gain minimum benefits from interacting with T&T service providers like HSprovider. On the one hand, this is due to strategic and privacy reasons. On the other hand, especially in the case of IDSs, granting access to service providers may degrade the performance of their Internet systems as perceived by customers. The performance of the architectural infrastructure of these Web sites, in terms of response time and availability, is already challenged by the high number of daily customers. Therefore, IDSs are not interested in granting access to external service providers that may generate a lot of additional traffic on their network without providing direct economic returns.

The collection of knowledge about the context can follow a *collaborative* or a *transparent* approach. The collaborative approach involves a formal agreement between HSprovider and the GDS, IDS, or Web portal, whereas the transparent approach does not involve any formal agreement. Both approaches raise different technological challenges. In the collaborative approach, HSprovider must minimize the overhead for the GDS, IDS, or Web portal servers, but it gains access to the whole set of required information. The transparent approach consists in simulating the activity of a user on each GDS, IDS, or Web portal through a knowledge engine that collects the necessary information and stores it in a knowledge base.

Collaborative Approach

Key information for the YMS is the number of queries performed on the GDS, IDS, or Web portal for the considered geographical zone and date. This information can be retrieved only if a collaborative approach exists. In fact, the simulation of human interaction on a T&T site only provides information on the queries performed, but it does not provide information on the number of similar queries that have been made by other customers on the same portal.

After the agreement has been signed, information is collected when the servers are less used, typically at night. This data collection usually involves a single automatic interaction (or very few) between HSprovider's system and the interface provided by the IDS server. This approach clearly minimizes the stress on the IDS servers while guaranteeing the required information to HSprovider.

Data are highly sensitive and have to be carefully managed. The quantity and quality of data depend on the agreement, which usually involves a cost for HSprovider. Sometimes, this information is also used to associate the type of queries with specific classes of customers.

Transparent Approach

This is the most interesting approach for collecting context knowledge from a technological standpoint. In this case, HSprovider's YMS can retrieve information on applied prices, promotional offers, available services, and occupation for competitors.

This aim is achieved through a Web crawler, which is able to surf the Web and to perform a very high number of queries on different T&T sites in order to collect the information. The Web crawlers developed by HSprovider are quite different from classic Web crawlers (e.g., Google's crawlers), which need to index a huge number of static pages. The target of the crawler in the T&T industry is data on specific and relatively small domains that are built dynamically—that is, the content of Web pages is built on the basis of the queries made by the system users. Therefore, besides state-of-the-art techniques for collecting data on static pages, HSprovider's crawlers implement specific algorithms for performing various queries on the site and store data to be subsequently processed by the YMS. These algorithms, which are usually proprietary, focus on the simulation of the typical human interaction with a T&T site.

The use of this kind of crawler is not welcomed by Web sites because the crawlers can also be used maliciously to degrade the performance of the Web site or to shut down specific services exported by the site. Web crawlers therefore need to be able to avoid some software traps that can be deployed by Web portals. One of the most famous traps is Internet protocol (IP) address blocking, which blocks connections from an IP address—that is, a machine that is making too many queries in too short a time. In order to overcome this blocking, Web crawlers are implemented to periodically change the IP address of the machine on which they are running and to learn the IP address blocking policies of the different Web sites.

The definition of the right price for maximizing the corresponding occupation curves is performed by the proprietary software system developed by HSprovider. The validation of the proposed price is performed on the basis of both the data stored in the knowledge base and the expertise of HSprovider's operators. While the knowledge base provides several flags and suggestions—for example, it signals a discrepancy between the output price with the price applied the year before—the operators, relying on their expertise, make the final decision on the validation of the proposed price. This is why, when the YMS is bought as a product by a hotel, HSprovider needs to train the employees of the hotel in order to transfer the expertise on the validation of proposed prices.

HSPROVIDER'S ALLOCATOR SYSTEM

The AS is in charge of automatically forwarding the information on applied prices, room availability, and promotional offers from a hotel to a T&T site. This second tool completes the set of services offered to customers by HSprovider (see Case Figure 3.3). This type of software product is more mature than the YMS. It is largely appreciated by the hotel owners because it delivers a direct benefit to the hotel in terms of significant time savings in the interaction with T&T Web sites.

Hotels need to upload information on different sites. The basic idea of HSprovider's AS is to require the hotel to specify this information only once. The AS is then in charge of forwarding the appropriate information to the different sites.

As discussed above, each site has an extranet that, usually, has a proprietary interface. Uploading information through this interface requires human interaction. Thus, building a software system that can automatically manage multiple interactions with different extranets raises several technical challenges. From a technological point of view, the issue of uploading information on software systems with different interfaces is a classical problem called *schema matching*. The data schema of the extranets and the one of the AS can be considered as fixed, so the schema-matching problem can be viewed as static. This assumption reduces the complexity of the AS.

Some site interfaces only allow the direct interaction with a human user. In these cases, the AS must emulate the manual interaction of human users. A specific set of functionalities can translate the information that must be uploaded into a human interaction pattern. These functionalities are very complex from a technological point of view, since they rely on complex models of human interaction.

Other site interfaces can be accessed automatically by other software systems. In this case, the allocator uploads a file containing all the necessary information, usually a well-defined XML file. The problem of producing this file in the right format is again a classic schema-matching problem where both source and destination have fixed schemas.

The incoming file is then parsed by the site that internally validates it and ultimately updates the information about the hotel. This kind of interaction is welcomed both by the AS and also by T&T sites as it reduces update errors. For this reason, the Open Travel Alliance (www.opentravel.org), composed of many important actors in the T&T industry, is developing a communication standard. For the time being, since site interfaces change over time, HSprovider has to face the problem of continuously updating the AS tool.

Several market products support the automated upload of information on Web sites. The next section provides a comparative analysis between the HSprovider's AS product and its competitors.

COMPARATIVE ANALYSIS OF TECHNOLOGICAL SOLUTIONS

HSprovider is not the only solution provider for interoperable applications and yield management in the Italian T&T industry. This section presents a comparative analysis of software solutions and applications for the T&T industry in the Italian market. On the one hand, this analysis aims at describing all the available solutions and providing possible classifications; on the other hand, it aims at positioning HSprovider within the market.

To summarize what has been discussed in the previous sections, HSprovider offers two main applications for knowledge management (KM): the YMS, which identifies the best pricing solution for a specific context, and the AS, which automatically uploads room rates and availabilities on a selection of T&T distribution systems. Case Table 3.1 presents a comparison of HSprovider with six other similar solutions that offer both the functionalities described above. All these solutions are offered by Italian companies, making them directly comparable to HSprovider.

A first classification of these solutions can be made based on the development technology and the platform typology. Whereas a number of solutions are based on proprietary stacks, as HSprovider's is, a rising number of solutions are being developed on open source stacks, basically Apache and Java. Figaro HDT and Leo Web are two brilliant examples of open source-based solutions. With regard to platform typology, solutions are usually available as ASP, stand-alone applications, or terminal applications. Remarkably, Figaro HDT and Nuconga also provide mobile infrastructures.

YMS, which leverage Web-crawling functionalities, are quite homogeneous across the analyzed solutions. First, Web crawlers find and retrieve the public parts of relevant portals. The retrieval of Web portal contents, as has already been mentioned, requires the analysis of dynamic pages. Next, Web mining and parsing techniques are applied to the contents of these portals to identify relevant information. The main difference among the presented solutions can be found in the methodologies adopted for managing and storing these data once they have been identified and retrieved. Fidelio is the only solution that stores all the data related to all the analyses performed. This allows the application to analyze historic data and to provide users with advanced services that take past trends into consideration. In addition, Fidelio also provides advanced statistical functionalities that allow it to define ad hoc Bayesian models to better estimate the trend of the demand for a particular category of lodging in particular periods and areas. These estimations also consider the competitors. The solutions for rate allocations are much more heterogeneous than the ones analyzed for yield management.

Basic-level technologies are based on Web- and screen-scraping technologies to analyze and comprehend the interfaces of IDS portals so that updates can be automatically uploaded. When a new channel (i.e., a new IDS) is acquired in the platform, a manual analysis of the interface of the extranet is required. Similarly, every small

Case Table 3.1

Comparative Analysis of Software Solutions for the Italian T and T Industry

Solution	Link	Development technology	Platform typology	Xml interface	Additional services and features	Standards
HS provider	N.A.	Proprietary	ASP		• Offering on Ebay • Strategic and commercial consultancy • Web marketing	
Figaro HDT	www.figarohdt.com	Open source (Java, Apache)	ASP	Yes	• Mobile • Wi-fi infrastructure	OTA
Hotel Management	www.hotelmanagement.biz	Proprietary	Stand-alone		• Web design • Web marketing and management	
Leo Web	www.leowebrates.com	Open source (Java)	Terminal server	Yes	• Management of Web portals and restaurants	
Fidelio	www.micros-fidelio.it	Proprietary (Microsoft, Delphi, Oracle)	ASP/Stand-alone		• Historic analyses • Integrated suite • Training	
Nuconga	www.nuconga.com	Proprietary (Microsoft)	Stand-alone		• Mobile • Consultancy • Custom designing	OTA Iso 9001: 2000
Hermes Hotel Athena Solutions	www.athenasolutions.it	Proprietary (Microsoft)	n/a	Yes	• Consultancy • Market analysis	

change (e.g., the name of fields in the updating forms) requires human intervention; otherwise the whole mediator application cannot work correctly. This approach is very expensive, as manual interventions are required not only in the setup phase but also for maintenance.

More innovative approaches rely on XML technology for exchanging data. This technology allows mediators to operate on a noncontinuous basis and portals to diminish the computational load on their servers. A lot of portals have not been very cooperative toward automatic service providers up to now exactly because of the huge computational load that this cooperation may lead to. For this reason, the most diffused portals are beginning to provide advanced interfaces for exchanging data through XML and specific Web services. In the near future, it is also very likely that Web services will develop more advanced modalities of interaction. Smaller portals, which are nevertheless very interested in cooperating with allocator companies, often support the exchange of XML files through secure HTTPS protocols. Once the file has been acquired, each portal invokes specific internal routines that read the new data and update the offers stored in the database.

Only some of the analyzed solutions support XML interfaces: Figaro HDT, Leo Web, Nuconga, and Hermes Hotel Athena Solutions. This functionality is a source of competitive advantage as it makes interactions with portals easier and more efficient.

Another significant dimension of comparison is the availability of additional services. These services range from training and customized designing to marketing and strategic consultancy. HSprovider offers a particularly complete suite of additional services, including preparing and selling specific holiday packages on eBay.

Only two of the analyzed solutions, Figaro HDT and Nuconga, comply with acknowledged international standards.

To sum up, the panorama of solutions that combine YMSs and ASs is rapidly evolving. Innovation is boosted by means of new and intelligent use of consolidated technologies, such as XML, data warehousing, and data mining. HSprovider is not as advanced as some of its competitors in this respect. However, HSprovider offers premium additional services that are extremely valued and appreciated by the market, making it a successful solution. It must not be forgotten that the users of these solutions are hotel owners and managers who often have low computer literacy. It is therefore essential to provide all-round consultancy and marketing services that leverage new technologies and applications, but that allow customers to reach their business objectives without annoying them with technical and process details.

CONCLUSIONS

The typical scenario for KM initiatives in real-world companies concerns the management of the company's so-called *knowledge assets.* Knowledge assets may refer to the skills and competences of knowledge workers (Voelpel et al. 2005), to the codification of successful organizational routines, or to knowledge of business processes (Garud and Kumaraswamy 2005). Generally, the firm's knowledge assets are *internal;* that is, they are generated by people and formal structures that lie within the boundaries of the firm. Although they work on data generated outside the boundaries of the firm, Customer Relationship Management (CRM) applications that manage knowledge about customers and markets can be assimilated to the classes of KM initiatives previously introduced. For a telecommunication company or a bank, for instance, knowledge about customers and markets constitutes a fundamental asset that must be managed and improved in time in order to sustain competitive advantage. Besides the management of customer-related issues, CRM applications also have a positive impact on complex back-end business processes, such as network infrastructure and workforce management in the telecommunication industry or portfolio management in the financial industry.

HSprovider's KM initiative presents some basic distinctive features with respect to the management of knowledge as an organizational asset (Earl 2001). The knowledge needed by HSprovider is external and generated by the actors of the T&T industry. Moreover, HSprovider does not present complex back-end processes. Knowledge about hotels and tourist behaviors is exploited to provide a high-quality service to customers in the T&T industry.

The HSprovider case shows a typical example in which KM becomes very close to the actual core business of the company. For typical examples of KM initiatives that focus on internal knowledge, such as knowledge networks, content repositories, or knowledge maps, it is not easy to underline a direct (positive) correlation between the amount of resources allocated in the KM initiatives and the benefits for the company. Benefits may be evaluated with a variety of indicators, such as the board's perceived effectiveness, key performance indicators of key business processes, or costs and resource savings. The success of KM on internal knowledge initiatives is usually measured by project-centric metrics—that is, typical variables that evaluates the success of projects—rather than the actual impact of such projects on the firm's efficiency and effectiveness (Davenport et al. 1998). Hence, the success of KM initiatives on internal knowledge is usually measured by variables such as the amount of resources allocated to the project, the number of people and organizational units involved in the project, or other quantitative evaluation of KM usage, such as the extension of the knowledge base or the monthly number of contributions to a knowledge network. Most of the time, demonstrating a correlation between the aforementioned success metrics and the benefits of the KM initiatives for the company is a cumbersome issue.

With respect to the aforementioned scenario, the HSprovider case presents an important difference. At HSprovider, KM of external knowledge about competitors and customers represents the actual core business of the company. Thus, the success of the KM initiatives can be directly tied to strategic dimensions that define the success of the company itself. For instance, the success of the AS is clearly demonstrated by the benefits that the system introduces for the target hotel, such as cost savings in the interaction with DSs. Similarly, for yield management, HSprovider's success is tied to its ability to provide low-cost solutions to family-owned hotels for revenue and yield management.

The HSprovider case also presents several other peculiarities. First, it demonstrates the importance of the industry context in defining the type of KM initiative and its success (Zander and Kogut 1995). As reported above, the Italian T&T industry is extremely fragmented. Moreover, while Web portals do not have specific interest in sharing aggregated knowledge on room allocation and rates, family-owned hotels do not have sufficient resources and technical skills to perform such an aggregation on their own. Therefore, the features of the industry have a strong impact on the success of the knowledge service provisioned by HSprovider. With respect to state-of-the-art solutions adopted by international hotel chains, HSprovider clearly fills a gap in management practices that characterize the fragmented Italian T&T industry. HSprovider's success is driven by technological innovation, but it actually builds on the company's ability to provide a lightweight, off-the-shelf solution for revenue management.

Second, the case underlines how the management of external knowledge about customers and markets requires a large technological effort. While internal knowledge is usually less structured, knowledge about the external environment is created by the aggregated analysis of transactions that take place in the market (Binney 2001). The analysis requires very specialized technological skills, including data mining techniques and artificial intelligence techniques for transactional data analysis.

Finally, we want to stress that service innovation, rather than technological innovation, is the actual driver of the success of HSprovider. Its ability to provide an innovative service to the tourism industry, in fact, allows HSprovider to overcome some limitations of its technological solutions, such as the adoption of proprietary solutions and the lack of interoperable XML-based interfaces in its technological infrastructure.

APPENDIX: THE YIELD MANAGEMENT PROBLEM

The T&T industry clearly demonstrates the five features that make the practice of yield management appropriate for a business environment (Netessine and Shumsky 2002):

1. It is expensive or impossible to store excess resources. (A hotel cannot store tonight's room for use by tomorrow night's customer.)
2. Commitments need to be made when future demand is uncertain. (A hotel must set aside rooms for business customers, protecting them from low-priced leisure travelers, before knowing how many business customers will arrive.)
3. The firm can differentiate among customer segments and each segment has a different demand curve. (Purchase restrictions and refundability requirements help to segment the market between leisure and business customers. The latter are more indifferent to the price.)
4. The same unit of capacity can be used to deliver many different products or services. (Rooms are essentially the same, whether used by business or leisure travelers.)
5. Producers are profit-oriented and have broad freedom of action.

Yield management is the problem of determining the price of the resource for the different customer segments in order to maximize revenues derived from its occupation. Generally, this is achieved by evaluating the demand curves for each customer segment and determining prices by creating barriers between market segments. In the T&T industry, for instance, a Saturday-night stay may be required to receive a discounted room on Monday, because most business travelers prefer to go home on the weekend, while leisure customers are more likely to accept, or may even prefer,

Case Figure 3.4 **The Occupation Curves for a Date T**

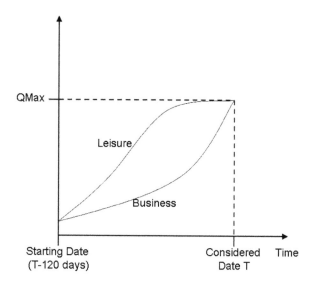

a weekend stay. Again, since leisure customers are more price-sensitive, the hotel wishes to sell as many rooms to business customers at a higher price as possible while keeping room utilization high.

The yield management problem can be resolved by applying the expected marginal seat revenue (EMSR) technique, originally developed for the airline industry (Belobaba 1989).

The yield management problem faced by HSprovider in the T&T industry is usually more complicated than the one in the airline industry. The price of hotel rooms can be quite variable—that is, the number of customer segments is very high and the price associated with each segment can be varied by a hotel in time. Therefore, price represents the actual driver used for maximizing the room occupation on any given date. Moreover, price determination is also influenced by the *context* information around a given date, such as the occurrence of fairs or special offers made by competitors.

For each hotel and for each customer segment, HSprovider defines an occupation curve that refers to the 120 days before the day for which the curve is intended. The shape of the curves depends on the category of the hotel, the city where the hotel is located, and the aforementioned contextual information. Two typical curves for a generic date are reported in Case Figure 3.4.

Generally, customers in the T&T industry are segmented on the basis of their motivation to travel shows. For the same date T, the two curves show, respectively, the customers traveling for business and for leisure. Customers' motivation to travel is hard-to-find information for HSprovider. Therefore, HSprovider usually defines a single curve for each hotel destination and each date, biasing its shape on the basis of the hotel's customer classification and on the study of actual occupation curves in previous years. For instance, the curve for business customers usually increases

Case Figure 3.5 **Gap Between Theoretical and Actual Occupation Curves**

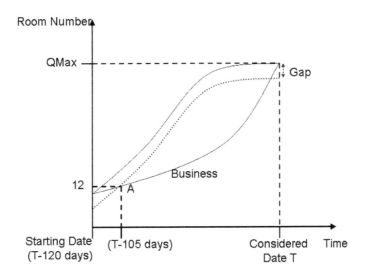

steadily in the two or three days before the target date, whereas the curve for leisure customers increases long before the target date, and it tends to remain flat in the days just before the target date.

The occupation curve assessment could be performed daily, but, since the process is very time-consuming, it is usually performed in specific booking windows. These windows are larger in the beginning and tend to reduce as the target date approaches. The booking windows considered by HSprovider in its forecasts are the following:

- $t = 120$ days before the date
- $120 < t < 90$ days before the date
- $90 < t < 60$ days before the date
- $60 < t < 30$ days before the date
- $30 < t < 15$ days before the date
- $15 < t < 7$ days before the date
- $7 < t < 2$ days before the date
- the last day before the date

Let us consider the occupation curves for one hotel and for two customer segments, e.g., business and leisure customers (see Case Figure 3.5). The theoretical curves (straight lines) have to be validated by the actual data. If actual data on bookings (dotted line) does not follow the theoretical curve, then price is used as a lever for biasing the actual curve in order for it to fit the forecasted theoretical occupation curve.

Let us suppose to be 105 days before the considered date T (T–105). Actual data report that the number of booked rooms for date T is 12 (point A). If we are considering a business destination or a date on which the hotel customers are typically traveling for business, then actual data are in line with the forecast. If we are considering a leisure destination or a date on which customers are typically traveling for leisure, then there is a gap between the actual and the theoretical occupation curve. As reported in Case Figure 3.5, such a gap might be propagated until date T if the hotel does not take corrective actions on price. In this specific case, the hotel should lower the price of rooms in order to increase the number of bookings and get to the theoretical forecast. It is worth noticing that corrective actions are also useful when the actual bookings exceed the forecasts of the theoretical occupation curve. In this case, the price of the rooms can be increased while maintaining the occupation rate in line with the theoretical forecasts.

DISCUSSION QUESTIONS

1. What are the main differences between the HSprovider case and other cases that involve IT applications such as knowledge networks or corporate repositories?
2. Describe the main aspects of the competitive advantage created by HSprovider through its KM initiative.
3. Provide a description of the services offered by HSprovider in the T&T industry. What is the knowledge required for such services?
4. What are the IT tools used by HSprovider in its KM initiative? How do these tools differ from the ones adopted by competitors in the Italian T&T industry?
5. What are the sources of the knowledge base built by HSprovider?
6. What is the difference between the collaborative and transparent approaches for the interaction with the DSs?
7. Why does the information about the number of queries performed on GDSs have to be collected through a collaborative approach?

ACKNOWLEDGMENT

This work has been partially supported by the Italian FIRB Project No. 2003/2186.

NOTE

This case was prepared by Eugénio Capra, Marco Comuzzi, Chiara Francalanci, and Stefano Modafferi, all from the Politécnico di Milano in Milan, Italy. It is intended as an illustration of a scenario in KM and as a basis for classroom discussion. It is not intended to illustrate or to recommend effective or ineffective handling of a management decision or situation.

Case 4

Fraud and Knowledge Management at Société Générale

On January 24, 2008, Société Générale, the second largest bank in France, announced that it had uncovered a massive fraudulent scheme of the magnitude of $7.14 billion. The CEO of the bank, Daniel Bouton, said that the fraud, discovered the previous weekend, had been perpetrated by a single individual, Jerome Kerviel, a trader, soon to be described by the press as a "rogue trader." Kerviel had joined the bank in 2000 and his salary at the time of this news was less than $145,000 a year. Apologizing to customers and shareholders, the CEO offered his resignation and the foregoing of his salary for six months.

This massive fraud occurred at the time when Société Générale, like other large banks in the United States and Europe, was suffering from the aftermath of the subprime crisis of 2007. This crisis began in the United States when millions of customers purchased homes with loans based on variable interest rates or with subprime mortgages offered by the banking industry without proper verification that the borrower could repay the loan. When interest rates began to climb, many borrowers could not meet the monthly obligations and defaulted on the loans, thus creating a massive loss for the banks.

Upon learning of the massive fraud and loss at Société Générale, the Paris stock exchange suspended transactions of the bank's shares that same day. These shares had already lost almost half their value in the last six months of 2007 due to the subprime crisis. When trading was resumed later in the day, shares of Société Générale lost over 4 percent, trading at 75 euros.

SOCIÉTÉ GÉNÉRALE

Société Générale had a market capitalization of 36 billion euros and 123,000 employees. Its areas of business included mergers and acquisitions, brokerage, derivatives, cross-asset research, asset management, and retail and private banking. Société Générale operated in three geographical areas: Europe, the Mediterranean basin, and in Africa and the former French colonies and territories. In retail and financial services, the bank had more than 22 million customers worldwide.

At the time of the fraud, the bank's knowledge management system (KMS) con-

Case Table 4.1

The Timeline of the Kerviel Fraud

2000	Jerome Kerviel, 23 years of age, is hired by Société Générale in the office that monitors trade.
2005	Kerviel is promoted to the arbitrage trading office.
2006	Kerviel starts making fraudulent transactions by building a virtual company within the Bank.
January 18, 2008	A routine audit raised a red flag when a compliance officer called Mr. Jean-Pierre Mustier, the head of investment banking at Société Générale, and told him that a counterparty to a futures trade knew absolutely nothing about the supposed transaction. Mustier launched an emergency in-house investigation.
January 19, 2008	Kervier is asked to explain the discrepancies. He then admits other fictitious trades.
January 20, 2008	The bank realizes the degree of the fraud and its exposure to the loss. The CEO, Daniel Bouton, notified the Central Bank of France.
January 21, 2008	Societe Generale began unwinding its positions in the market; many are closed or hedged.
January 24, 2008	The bank announces the loss to the public.
January 26, 2008	Jerome Kerviel is arrested by the French authorities, charged with forgery, breach of trust, and fraud—with a possible sentence, if convicted, of seven years imprisonment.

sisted of two complementary systems. The first was the PeopleSoft 8 human resources system. This was an integrated management tool, focused on the human resources database and global payroll. In October 2001 the bank had merged the different applications into a unified system. The second system was the TIBCO integration technology. It involved retail banking, asset management, private banking, and investments. These two systems, PeopleSoft 8 and TIBCO, consisted of information systems that provided standard, basic integration of banking transactions.

Although the bank had many control systems in place, Kerviel, who held a degree in marketing operations from the University of Lyon, was able to breach *five* different levels of controls. He had intimate and extensive knowledge of control systems in different parts of the bank. Professor Michael Gorham of the Stuart Business School at the Illinois Institute of Technology suggested that there should be systems in place that would constitute a wall between the back office in charge of controls on trading and the traders themselves. Such an impenetrable wall would help to prevent this type of fraud.

HOW KERVIEL PERPETRATED THE FRAUD

On January 27, three days after its initial announcement, Société Générale published an explanatory note about what it called "exceptional fraud." The bank concluded that Jerome Kerviel had falsified documents, swiped computer access codes, and bet over 50 billion euros of future contracts in three equity indexes in the European market.

The bank also explained that risks to its arbitrage activities existed and therefore it had "put in place a large number of controls designed to monitor the risks involved: control of operations and control of market risks linked to the changes in the prices of portfolios of financial instruments." The bank continued: "The exceptional fraud which we have suffered consisted of avoiding these controls or making them inoperable: the trader inserted fictitious operations into portfolio B in order to give the impression that this portfolio genuinely offset portfolio A which he had purchased, when this was not the case. These fictitious operations were registered in Société Générale systems but did not actually correspond to any economic reality."

Some financial experts, particularly in the United States, have questioned the bank's explanation of the rogue trader's abilities. A common theme in their criticism was that this fraud demonstrated a breakdown in the bank's basic controls of its operations. There was also a sentiment that this event was the result of both organizational failures and human incompetence at Société Générale.

The bank, however, offered a more detailed listing of the methods used by Jerome Kerviel:

"In practice, the trader combined several fraudulent methods to avoid the controls in place:

- Firstly, he ensured that the characteristics of the fictitious operations limited the chance of a control: for example, he chose very specific operations with no cash movements or margin call and which did not require immediate confirmation;
- He misappropriated the integration technology (IT) access codes belonging to operators in order to cancel certain operations;
- He falsified documents allowing him to justify the entry of fictitious operations;
- He ensured that the fictitious operations involved a different financial instrument to the one he had just cancelled in order to increase his chances of not being controlled."

The bank had a pretax profit in 2007 of 5.5 billion euros, so Bouton insisted that Société Générale was indeed able to withstand and absorb this massive loss and to overcome the crisis. The bank also announced on January 24 that it would write off 2 billion euros of its exposure to the American mortgage crisis. Some financial experts have expressed their concern that the bank is mixing losses from the fraud and those from exposure to the U.S. housing market.

THE CASE OF THE BARINGS BANK FRAUD

The fraudulent trading by Kerviel at Société Générale reminded many people of the famous trading scandal a decade earlier at Barings Bank. In 1995, Nick Leeson, Barings's general manager of futures trading in Singapore, lost $1.38 billion trading Asian future markets. His rogue trading wiped out the bank's cash reserves. The pride of British banking, which had been in business for over two centuries and counted the royal family among its prominent customers, collapsed.

How did Leeson do it? He had arrived at the Singapore office of Barings in 1992. His job was to manage traders, not to perform trades, but he nevertheless passed the exam needed to become a trader and started doing two things. First, he traded futures and options for customers of the bank, and second, he started to arbitrage price differences between the Japanese Nikkei futures traded on the Simex (Singapore Exchange) and the Osaka Exchange. Leeson traded via an unused Barings error account (number 88888). By 1994 the account had losses of over 200 million pounds. On February 23, 1995, when the losses he caused reached a staggering 827 million pounds sterling, Leeson escaped to Malaysia.

Barings Bank collapsed and was purchased by ING Bank of the Netherlands (for the symbolic price of one pound sterling). In 2001 ING Bank made Barings one of its divisions in Europe, with the name of Baring Asset Management (BAM). In 2005 ING Bank sold BAM to Massachusetts Mutual, and the financial services part of BAM was sold to the American Northern Trust.

Barings Bank never learned about Leeson's losses until it was too late. The bank's management in London continually infused cash into Leeson's accounts to make margin payments for fictitious trades and customers. Two reasons were given at the time why the bank failed to discover and to act on the losses. The first was that in 1994 Barings implemented a rudimentary risk management program, with controls established in London, Tokyo, and Hong Kong—though not in Singapore. Second, Leeson was a true confidence man. He filed false reports that senior managers of Barings accepted at face value, since no one wanted to "look silly" and raise questions about a successful trading manager in Singapore who was presumably making money for the bank.

Leeson was tried and convicted of fraud. He spent six years in a Singapore prison and was released in July 1999. A movie was made about his life and the fraud he perpetrated at Barings Bank.

DISCUSSION QUESTIONS

1. What were the similarities and differences between the Leeson affair and the Kerviel fraud?
2. Could a knowledge management system (KMS) have helped to avert the Kerviel fraud? Could it have helped to uncover it early on or perhaps halfway? How?
3. What are the differences and similarities between a KMS and risk management programs? Can or should they be integrated in a banking environment?
4. How would you incorporate Gorham's recommendation for the impenetrable wall to separate traders from the main office—and an effective KMS?
5. Despite the lessons learned from the Leeson affair and the risk management controls established in the banking industry, Kerviel was able to commit his new fraud. Could such a fraud happen again? Why or why not?
6. Some financial experts argue that banks and investment firms hire traders to trade, and trade involves risk, and often there are losses, so we should accept these losses as "the nature of the beast." These experts also note that neither Leeson nor Kerviel personally profited from their trades. Do you agree? Why or why not?

NOTE

This case was prepared by Elie Geisler and graduate student Manjari Sharda at the Illinois Institute of Technology in Chicago. It is intended as an illustration of a scenario in knowledge management and as a basis for classroom discussion. It is not intended to illustrate or to recommend effective or ineffective handling of a management decision or situation.

Case 5

JetBlue

The Nightmare on Valentine's Day

JetBlue Airways is an American airline owned by JetBlue Airways Corporation. It provides passenger air transportation services in North America. The company is headquartered in the Forest Hills area of New York City (famous for its tennis tournaments). The home hub of the company is Kennedy International Airport in New York City. JetBlue is a nonunion company.

Founded in 1999, the airline operated in 2007 about 500 daily flights to fifty cities in twenty-one states, Puerto Rico, Mexico, and some destinations in the Caribbean Islands. JetBlue operated a fleet of ninety-eight AirBus A320s and twenty-three Embraer-190s.

In 2002 JetBlue acquired Live TV for $41 million in case and $39 million in retirement of Live TV's debt. The airline's planes were thus equipped with thirty-six channels of live DirectTV satellite TV programming at every seat, and movies were shown free of charge on flights outside the United States. The in-flight entertainment became a true trademark of the airline's advertised outstanding regard for customer service and satisfaction. JetBlue emphasized its customer service by advertising that it encourages passengers to use the call button on their TV set and to ask for on-board service.

In 2004 the airline added flights from New York's LaGuardia Airport and in 2005 from Liberty International Airport in Newark, New Jersey. Thus, JetBlue was now flying from all three major airports in the New York area (see Case Figure 5.1).

THE BEGINNING AND THE EARLY YEARS

JetBlue was founded as a low-cost airline. Although it followed in the footsteps of other such attempts that were unsuccessful (e.g., People's Express), JetBlue copied many of the attributes that animated the success of another low-cost company, Southwest Airlines. JetBlue was founded by CEO David Neeleman, who, together with fellow executives of the new airline, was a former employee of Southwest Airlines (Case Figure 5.1). Neeleman's approach was to offer a low-cost airline with exceptional service and the added benefit of superior in-flight entertainment.

After the terrorist attacks of September 11, 2001, the young airline JetBlue was

Case Figure 5.1 **Senior Executives of JetBlue in 2007**

David Neeleman
Founder & Chief Executive Officer
Salary: $200,000

Dave Barger
President Schiff Operating Officer
Salary: $200,000

John Owen
Executive Vice President of Supply Chain
& Information Technology
Salary: $200,000

one of the very few airlines showing a profit. The airline went public in 2002 and since that time accumulated over $2 billion in market capitalization. However, when jet fuel prices soared after 2005, JetBlue, like other carriers, showed a decline in profits, even with higher revenues. The company had operational problems with its Brazilian-made Embraer aircraft. The company also experienced pressures from organized labor to unionize. In 2006 the International Association of Machinists took the airline to the National Mediation Board but lost the case to unionize the carrier (see Case Table 5.1).

When in early 2006 JetBlue reported its first loss since going public four years earlier, Neeleman, President David Barge, and CEO John Owen publicized their return to profitability plan. The plan entailed cutting costs, selling some aircraft, and even removing some seats from the planes to make them lighter and more comfortable for the passengers (Case Table 5.2).

Valentine's Day 2007

It was Wednesday, February 14, 2007, when the nightmare began. A snow and ice storm had covered the Eastern Seaboard of the United States. The ice storm was particularly unforgiving in the New York area. At John F. Kennedy International Airport, most

Case Table 5.1

JetBlue in Its Competitive Environment in the Industry (as of December 3, 2006)

	JBLU	AMR	LUV	UA	Industry
Market cap	2.12 B	7.89 B	11.98 B	4.33 B	839.37 M
Employees	8,393	86,600	32,664	53,000	3.85 K
Quarterly rev growth (yoy)	41.90%	4.40%	14.50%	4.60%	25.90%
Revenue (ttm)	2.36 B	22.56 B	9.09 B	19.34 B	1.68 B
Gross margin (ttm)	30.94%	27.47%	64.13%	36.11%	3.57%
EBITDA (ttm)	290.00 M	2.44 B	1.53 B	1.30 B	165.21 M
Operational margins (ttm)	4.87%	4.70%	10.28%	2.13%	7.89%
Net income (ttm)	−1.00 M	231.00 M	499.00 M	22.88 B	28.99 M
EPS (ttm)	−0.006	0.977	0.606	206.671	0.61
P/E (ttm)	N/A	33.65	25.08	0.19	16.80

Note: AMR = American Airlines; LUV = Southwest Airlines; UA = United Airlines; Industry = Regional Airlines.

major airlines canceled their flights. United Airlines canceled more than 200 flights and American Airlines soon followed. JetBlue was the exception.

Due to problems with deicing the wings and the loss of priorities in the line of departure, JetBlue kept a plane destined for Cancun, Mexico, in readiness on the tarmac at Kennedy Airport for over nine hours. Nine other JetBlue airplanes also were paralyzed on the tarmac. The airline kept the passengers—soon without food, water, or the use of sanitary facilities—on board, refusing to return the aircraft to the gates and allow the passengers to deplane. JetBlue managers at the airport communicated with the New York Port Authority (the agency in charge of the airport) only at 3 P.M. on that eventful Valentine's Day, when the passengers had been already stranded for almost eight hours. The Port Authority then provided buses to unload the passengers and by 6 P.M. all had deplaned and been brought back to the terminals.

This unfortunate event received immediate and immense media attention. The reaction of the press was multifaceted. There was talk in the days that followed of a "passenger bill of rights." The Internet blogs were abuzz with stories about the suffering of the stranded passengers. On February 19, Jeff Bailey wrote in the *New York Times* about JetBlue's failure to accommodate its stranded customers: "JetBlue's CEO is mortified after fliers are stranded. . . . David Neeleman said . . . his company's management was not strong enough. And he said that the current crisis . . . was the result of a shoestring communications system that left pilots and flight attendants in the dark, and an undersize reservation system." In the interview, Neeleman also said, "We had so many people in the company who wanted to help who weren't trained to help. . . . We had an emergency control center full of people who did not know what to do. I had flight attendants sitting in hotel rooms for three days who couldn't get a hold of us. I had pilots e-mailing me saying: 'I'm available, what do I do.'"[1]

Other airlines also had a history of keeping passengers stranded on board due to weather. Three months earlier, American Airlines flight 1348 had been stranded on the tarmac in Austin, Texas, for nine hours (the captain finally disobeyed his orders and brought the airplane back to the gate). Similar incidents had occurred at United

Table 5.2

The Variations of JetBlue's Stock Before and After February 14, 2007

Date	Open	High	Low	Close	Volume	Adj Close
Mar-2-07	12.16	12.41	11.90	11.91	6,973,000	11.91
Mar-1-07	12.12	12.442	12.00	12.21	6,633,700	12.21
Feb-29-07	12.39	12.47	12.12	12.31	7,308,600	12.31
Feb-27-07	12.58	12.65	12.07	12.29	9,767,400	12.29
Feb-26-07	13.00	13.00	12.63	12.75	9,714,400	12.75
Feb-23-07	13.14	13.20	12.93	13.08	6,713,100	13.08
Feb-22-07	13.30	13.35	12.99	13.16	10,674,500	13.16
Feb-21-07	13.30	13.56	13.10	13.19	26,329,000	13.19
Feb-20-07	12.57	12.99	12.51	12.90	30,940,700	12.90
Feb-16-07	13.82	13.84	13.50	13.56	5,226,400	13.56
Feb-15-07	13.67	14.02	13.50	13.85	10,592,700	13.85
Feb-14-07	12.98	13.23	12.82	13.23	5,200,400	13.23
Feb-13-07	13.15	13.21	12.89	12.99	3,399,100	12.99
Feb-12-07	13.09	13.25	12.95	13.13	5,240,600	13.13
Feb-9-07	13.32	13.40	12.82	12.92	6,476,900	12.92
Feb-8-07	13.42	13.58	13.19	13.30	4,520,300	13.30
Feb-7-07	13.63	13.68	13.29	13.42	6,377,800	13.42
Feb-6-07	13.45	13.78	13.33	13.69	5,139,800	13.69
Feb-5-07	13.75	13.75	13.36	13.57	3,035,300	13.57
Feb-2-07	13.75	13.94	13.56	13.65	3,846,400	13.65

Airlines and Continental Airlines. But JetBlue had ten aircraft stranded on the tarmac at one airport at the same time, and the nightmare occurred when public awareness, heightened by these other incidents, had reached a tipping point from understanding to outrage. The impact on JetBlue was devastating. Long considered the darling airline with superior customer service, JetBlue suddenly became the airline that kept hundreds of passengers captive aboard their airplanes without the minimum means of subsistence: food, water, and sanitary facilities.

EXPLANATIONS, APOLOGY, AND MARKET REACTION

The company (now referred to by the media as "Jet Blew-it") offered several explanations for the debacle.

1. JetBlue had a policy of making every flight, however late and in any weather.
2. Weather forecasts were not clear, and the airline's operations people believed that the planes would be able to take off soon.
3. There was a breakdown in communication between the operations people and flight crews, not only in New York, but also throughout the country.
4. JetBlue lacked agreements with other airlines that could honor JetBlue tickets and accommodate JetBlue passengers. Unable to direct their passengers to other airlines when the passengers deplaned back at the terminal, JetBlue ground personnel booked them on flights already or soon to be canceled.

> This exacerbated an already tense situation and further angered the frustrated JetBlue customers.
> 5. The airline's reservation system was "undersized," hence unable to cope with such a massive breakdown in the entire corporate system.

Between February 14 and 18, 2007, JetBlue canceled almost one-fourth (23 percent) of its flights, including all its flights with the Embraer 190 aircraft. The company's stock plunged by almost 30 percent from its January level.

It was time to act, and fast. The founder and CEO, David Neeleman, appeared on several media shows and offered a public apology. He said he felt "humiliated and mortified" at the events that unfolded on Valentine's Day and the subsequent near-paralysis of his airline. He promised drastic changes and his own version of a passenger bill of rights. He also promised compensation to JetBlue's stranded passengers totaling almost $30 million.

The market reacted with caution. As shown in Case Table 5.2, the stock lost ground. On February 15, the day after the debacle, 10.5 million JetBlue shares were traded, and several days later, on the February 20 and 21, over 57 million shares changed hands. Yet Neeleman's massive media campaign and his profound apology made a good impression on the flying public and on Wall Street. JetBlue was rising from the ashes and there was a sense of forgiveness from customers and investors. Yet this forgiveness and understanding apparently did not extend to the CEO, despite his apology. On May 10, the JetBlue board of directors removed David Neeleman as chief executive, offering him instead the title of nonexecutive chair. He was replaced by David Barge, the president of the company.

Following this change in management, JetBlue shares went up by 45 percent. The country's number eight airline was recuperating three months after the nightmare on February 14—by, among other changes, sacrificing its founder, chief, executive, and the person who had assumed full responsibility for the debacle. At the time of his demotion, David Neeleman owned about 6 percent of the company's shares, valued at $112 million.

CONCLUSIONS

Why do such mishaps happen? In the case of JetBlue, perhaps the answer has two dimensions: (1) a combination of actual conditions and events on the ground, and (2) organizational breakdowns and the failure of the company's information system, plus the lack of a knowledge management system (KMS).

The combination of conditions includes duty-time limits for pilots, stormy weather, and the rules and regulations imposed by the Federal Aviation Administration and the airport authorities. Duty-time limits imposed on pilots deter pilots from returning to the gate. If the aircraft sits on the tarmac, the pilot has a limit of sixteen hours of flying time—whereas when the aircraft returns to the gate, the starting time would push over the eight-hour limit in the controls of the aircraft. The flight is terminated and the pilot has whatever is left of the sixteen hours to restart in the new flight code.

The other set of factors includes organizational and policy implications of JetBlue's own procedures and philosophy. The company's policy was to maintain a flight schedule under any weather conditions. This policy broke down in the crisis when ice and snow hit the city. Afterward, the company changed its policy. A month later, on March 16, 2007, JetBlue canceled 215 flights departing or arriving at New York's main airports—about one-third of the company's flights—due to severe weather on the Eastern Seaboard.

In the crisis of February 2007 there was a breakdown in the operations of the company's information and communication systems. Flight crews were stranded all over its hubs and destinations, unable to communicate with its center of operations and unable to arrive for duty. The company's lack of a KMS had put it in a crisis mode without the ability to learn and apply the lessons of other airlines in past similar situations. These lessons were not learned nor absorbed into JetBlue's policies, procedures, and operations.

Like other airlines, JetBlue had the usual management information system (MIS). This system comprised its reservations system, fuel and crew assignments, and other managerial functions such as billing, accounts payable, and market research. The company did not, at the time, possess a KMS of the kind currently advocated in the knowledge management literature. The breakdown of JetBlue's operations and communication network was also the failure of its MIS to perform under conditions of crisis, albeit quite predictable. If the company had possessed a workable KMS, could it have avoided the breakdown and its negative repercussions? Would a KMS be superior to the traditional MIS in a crisis mode?

DISCUSSION QUESTIONS

1. Why was JetBlue unable to learn from the experience of other airlines in similar crisis situations?
2. How could a KMS have assisted the company in its planning?
3. How could a KMS have helped to solve the issues of crew assignments?
4. What effect did the hub system of this airline (as well as other airlines) have on the breakdown in operations? Could a KMS have assisted in avoiding the breakdown? How?
5. Were the airline and its MIS ready for such a crisis, albeit a predictable event? How can a KMS help an airline in a crisis?
6. How could the company improve its KMS (e.g., input the experience of other companies and their own flight crews; share the knowledge across the company, its managers, and its flight crews)? Give two or three examples.

NOTES

This case was prepared by Elie Geisler and graduate student Manjari Sharda at the Illinois Institute of Technology in Chicago. It is intended as an illustration of a scenario in knowledge management and as a basis for classroom discussion. It is not intended to illustrate or to recommend effective or ineffective handling of a management decision or situation.

1. *New York Times*, February 19, 2007.

Case 6

The Implementation of a Billing and Patient Management System in an Independent Practice Association

The Role of Actor-Network Theory

To date, unlike other industry sectors, health care has been slow to embrace information and communication technology (ICT) (Wickramasinghe and Schaffer 2006). This is perplexing, since at the same time medical and biomedical science have made revolutionary advances by embracing technology (Wickramasinghe et al. 2007). However, given the tremendous pressures now facing health care organizations, we can evidence more and more instances of implementation of billing practice management systems and/or electronic patient record systems. As is well documented in the information systems literature (Simon 1997; Zuboff 1988), it is not sufficient to simply implement an ICT system in order to realize its full potential; rather, careful analysis of as-is processes and information flows and even business process reengineering (Davenport 1994) are necessary in conjunction with any such implementation if the benefits of the system are to be realized. To do this requires the adoption of appropriate frameworks and analysis tools and techniques. Actor-network theory (ANT) is proffered as such a technique, and we illustrate its power with a case study detailing the implementation of a billing practice management system in an independent practice association (IPA) in Chicago.

PURPOSE OF THE INDEPENDENT PRACTICE ASSOCIATION

Health care, to a large extent, has been shaped by the economic, governmental, and cultural norms, perspectives, and structures of the country. Managed care is not only one of the most recent influences in the United States, but is now the dominant influence in health care delivery. It is aimed at creating value for money competition in an attempt to combat "an extremely wasteful and inefficient system that has been bathed in cost-increasing incentives for over 50 years" (Enthoven 1993, 40).

The intended result of these changes and the move toward a managed care environment is to provide adequate, quality health care and yet minimize, or at least reduce, costs. However, managed care is not a homogeneous system: rather, several forms of managed care coverage exist, differing primarily in the choice or lack of choice of

266

hospital and/or provider offered to the patient. The three predominant forms include the health maintenance organization (HMO), the preferred provider organization (PPO), and the point-of-service plan (POS). The major distinctions between these vehicles are connected with how they contract with the enrolled physicians and whether or not patients can be reimbursed for covered services from any provider (Kongstvedt 1993; Wolper 1995).

In such a competitive health care context, individual physicians find themselves at a huge disadvantage when trying to enter into contracts with large and powerful insurance companies. In order to address this limitation, many physicians started to group together as IPAs. An IPA brings a group of physicians together as one voice purely for the purpose of negotiating contracts with insurance companies. In all other respects, and most especially in the delivery of health care services from a medical standpoint, the physicians in the association are independent (Kongstvedt 1993; Wolper 1995).

BACKGROUND OF CASE STUDY

Dr. Martinez started his medical practice in June 2006 in Lombard, Illinois, a western suburb of Chicago. Dr. Martinez had worked in another practice before starting his own. He has two physicians working with him and intends to hire additional doctors over time. Currently, there is a single, part-time office manager or administrative assistant, Bea, coordinating all the administrative and nonclinical activities. These activities fall into three general categories: maintaining patient records, scheduling appointments with patients and physicians, and medical billing. The practice, which can be classified as an IPA, does not use any electronic-based system for these functions, which are done by hand using a paper-based system. Since the practice is small, this manner of running the business, although paper-intensive, is doable, and the office manager manages to keep the three functions working.

Recently, Dr. Martinez purchased an electronic office-based management system called Office Helper and is in the process of converting over to it. The office manager is responsible for coordinating the conversion. The process is going very slowly, because as a part-time employee, Bea is able to work on the conversion only when not engaged with other activities. She is currently entering customer records into the patient record portion of the new tool.

The following account documents the current and future state of the practice, utilizing Actor Network Theory (ANT) to facilitate the analysis of a health care informatics scenario. This case is being coordinated from the perspective of the Healthcare Value Proposition of Access, Quality, and Value as presented from the perspective of the patient, provider, and payer. There is a small regulator component, HIPAA (Health Information Portability and Accountability Act), but it has a relatively minor position throughout the case.

Dr. Martinez was looking for a fully integrated system that would closely connect the patient medical records, scheduling, and medical billing applications. "We basically wanted three applications that would function as one product," he said. An integrated package enables the seamless sharing of patient information across all three applications. The three applications in Officer Helper—Practice Partner Patient Records, Appointment Scheduler, and Medical Billing—all use a single database, so information entered in one application is immediately available in the other two. For example, when a patient is registered in Medical Billing, the patient information is instantly accessible in Appointment Scheduler and Patient Records. "This shared patient information has two major benefits," explains Bea. "First, it reduces redundant data entry, saving us a lot of time. Secondly, it eliminates errors and inconsistencies from having to enter patient information twice."

CURRENT OPERATION

Bea does all the administrative work for each of the doctors. This includes logging in patients, passing out paperwork, sending paper bills, checking up on bills, making appointments for the patients, and updating the doctors' personal digital assistants (PDAs). New patients choose the practice using the Internet or the yellow pages or are referred by friends or other doctors. Bea asks new patients to fill out forms that will gather all the pertinent information necessary to begin a relationship with the practice:

1. Name and address
2. Insurance carrier
3. Family background
4. Medical condition
5. Medical history
6. Payment information; the practice accepts only Blue Cross Blue Shield (BCBS) or cash

The office manager keeps these records and enters them into her filing system.

Bea keeps the appointment records and notifies the doctors of their appointments by updating their PDAs with the scheduling program that she uses. She also secures the records after each patient visit. She enters the billing codes provided by the doctors on each visit in order to create a bill. She does this by hand. Once she establishes the billing rate, she bills either the patient or the insurance company after the visit. She gives clients a paper bill if they need one to submit to their own insurance company after repayment. The medical practice does not have a patient payment plan except on a case-by-case basis, and Bea does all the tracking for these cases.

Once bills are submitted to BCBS, it is the office manager's responsibility to follow up on payments. When they are received, she enters them in the patient's billing record, indicating that the bill has been paid. At times she receives only a partial payment, which requires more paper tracking. At other times, bills are returned due to incorrect or incomplete information. Then she must recreate the billing trail, often referring back to the doctors for clarification. She is not able to keep an aggressive accounts receivable record because of the paper-intensive nature of the activity.

Bea is concerned that as the practice grows she will not be able to keep up with the workflow and billing requirements using her current methods. She foresees the possibility of making serious errors and getting behind in the billing and tracking process. She also is concerned with the safety and privacy of her paper records. They are only as secure as the locks on the office doors.

Fundamentally, the paper flow in Dr. Martinez's office is an extremely linear process with each piece of the billing document sourced from a different file; there is no connection between them. From the perspective of knowledge management (KM), the process of capturing, storing, manipulating, and transmitting information is extremely inefficient.

The capturing of information is tedious and time-consuming. The office manager must create a paper trail for each item. She enters certain patient information; the patient enters information; the clinical practitioner enters information—all into at least four different paper files. The likelihood of incorrect or missing information is great. There are no checks and balances at the time of information capture to alert the system about incorrect or missing information.

The storing of information is done in a paper file environment with a well-established filing system. Although the system is well organized, the safety and availability of the files are inadequate. The multiple filing systems take up a large amount of room, and the process of retrieving, opening and closing, replacing, and duplicating files is very time-consuming. The system also leads to errors as files may be misplaced or lost. These files are not stored in such a way as to protect them from damaging conditions such as flooding, fire, or theft. This may be one of the greatest areas of concern in a HIPAA environment, since the files are only as secure as the locks on the doors.

This information is manipulated only by creating more paper records in order to keep track of patient visits, clinical information, billing information, scheduling dates, and reports to monitoring agencies. There is a clear lack of opportunity to create any sort of business or clinical report that might be beneficial from a business intelligence perspective. A serious concern is the billing information required to receive payment from the paying organization. Bea must transcribe by hand the information on the billing form that she retrieves from the multiples sources of information described above. There is a great chance of error under these circumstances, and, as the caseloads and billing paperwork increase, the chance of error increases as well.

Mail and fax are the only means of transmitting information in the current environment. The drawbacks of time and chance of error become obvious with these methods. In addition, Bea and the doctors can merely assume that the "right" person or "right" department received the information and acted on it in a timely manner. It is very difficult to determine when information was received and who is responsible for acting on it.

In the current state of the practice, the value proposition is based on paper files and reports, entering information by hand, storage and retrieval of paper files, and mail and fax for recovering payments. There are certainly more cost-effective, accurate ways to perform these tasks, as will be described below. The quality of the actual clinical services that a patient receives should not change regardless of the vehicle selected for addressing the administrative activities of running a practice.

SUMMARY

With such an enormous amount of work involved in the maintenance of patient records and the fact that there is only one person responsible for the bookkeeping and expense tracking, this practice needed to come up with an easily maintainable solution. Easily maintainable systems are not necessarily easily installable systems. However, our focus is on easy maintenance. Before we proceed further, let us summarize the steps explained earlier.

1. Patient registration and appointment: The patient schedules an appointment by phone, fax, mail, or in person.
2. Appointment reminder to physicians: The office manager updates the appointment calendar and reminds the physicians of their patients' appointments on a daily basis.
3. Medical history and insurance information: If the patient's medical history is not already available in the IPA's records, that information has to be entered before the patient meets with the physician.
4. Medical prescriptions: The physician prescribes the medications with the billing code.
5. Billing: The office manager prepares the billing information based on the billing code and insurance information provided.
6. Claims: Medical claims are sent to the respective insurance companies.
7. Accounting operations: The office manager tracks the payments received (full or partial) and sends reminders to the providers who have not paid in full.

ASSOCIATED ACTORS

As inferred from the above operations, the key actors include patient, physician, phone, fax machine, mail carrier, referring physician, office manager, and insurance company (BCBS). To date the office manager has been more or less the focal actor as she has the most authority and control over the other actors as far as the IPA is concerned.

ADVANTAGES OF THIS PRACTICE

Because the practice is relatively small, this tedious but simple administrative approach has a number of advantages. Primarily, the practice does not operate on a full-time basis. It is operative only on a few weekdays (and/or weekends), allowing the impression that managing such a small audience of patients is a simple and manageable task.

Second, the practice currently accepts payments only in cash or through BCBS. Since there is only one insurance payer, the office manager could logically keep track of the payments received and also send payment reminders.

Third, since the task does not involve any computer operations and is completely paper-intensive, it probably incurs fewer costs.

Finally, because there is currently a single point-of-care (the office manager), patients and physicians have effective assistance in fixing any problems. The office manager does not need to possess any complex computer skills, just general office management skills. She easily communicates to the patients and physicians in a simple and understandable manner.

DISADVANTAGES OF THIS PRACTICE

Although the practice is small, with just three physicians and a single office manager, Dr. Martinez started this practice with a hope that it would grow into a bigger practice. Today, it is one of the fastest-growing IPAs in the Lombard area. Due to the excellent quality of treatment that patients get for an affordable price, more and more patients are coming to this IPA for treatment. An increasing number of referring physicians will probably be recommending more patients to Dr. Martinez. With this growth potential, there are numerous disadvantages associated with the existing approach.

Primarily, the increasing number of patients will require more file storage space. Since the existing system is paper-intensive, each new patient will be associated with new sets of paper and folders.

As the number of patients increases, the practice might consider accepting payments from other insurance providers, not just BCBS. This would result in more bookkeeping and increase the possibility of making errors.

The increased number of patients and insurance providers would also increase the time taken for processing a single patient and thus may reduce the number of patients examined per day.

Data entered may often be redundant and thus may result in a chaotic situation with reference to insurance claims of patients' responses or any other people-centric queries.

Finally, sending claims manually through the regular mail is a very slow process that may involve considerable delay. Electronic claim submissions may ease this process and speed up the processing time.

PRACTICE MANAGEMENT TOOLS

With all these disadvantages and the high likelihood that the practice will expand, Dr. Martinez now demands a system that reduces this paperwork and manual maintenance and cancels redundant data. Such a system should also be scalable and adaptable to the dynamic changes involved in the practice. This requires the use of the practice management tools that have found wide applications in today's software-driven operations. In the discussion that follows, we shall examine this practice management system (PMS) and its relevance to the current IPA.

HELPER SOFTWARE

The PMS used here is called Helper Software. Helper Software is based on the concept of databases. The data are stored in the database and, on user queries, retrieved. To be precise, the data are populated into what are called libraries. The underlying premise in this PMS is that data should first be entered before they are retrieved.

1. Libraries: The libraries can be physician library, provider library, facilities library, procedures library, or even insurance companies library. The libraries include the type of treatment, type of medication, duration of appointments, and other information.
2. Face sheets: The information about patients is stored in the form of face sheets, which include patient information, insurance information to be mapped, and the billing setup.
3. Transactions: The accounting information about each payment (and payment tracking), adjustment, and encounters is stored as transactions in the same way as patient information is stored in a face sheet.
4. Billing: The billing ledger is used to manage and bill the patient and/or the insurance provider. The bills can be printed at this stage or even be rebilled, depending on the receipt of the payments.

The module described above is mainly concerned with the registration, medical history, treatment codes, and billing phases discussed earlier. This method considerably automates the data flow and reduces the need for the office manager to backtrack for various sources of information.

SecureConnect

Electronic claims processing is handled by another module called SecureConnect, which is plugged into Helper Software. In order to adhere to HIPAA regulations, SecureConnect can be password protected, so that any access to it is restricted by a password. The status and history of the claims can easily be tracked through the billing ledger. This method of electronic filing saves a lot of transit time in processing and results in more efficient handling of patient claims. Rejected claims also can be verified quickly and immediately rectified.

Therapist Traveler

Another module, Therapist Traveler, handles the third vital task of sending appointment-confirmation reminders to the physicians. Until now, Bea has been manually sending the information to the physicians' PDAs. Using Therapist Traveler, physicians can access the insurance, patient, medication, and referring physician info on their PDA. Physicians can update, delete, or add new data on Therapist Traveler through the PDA. However, in order for these changes to be reflected on the Helper Software, the PDA needs to be synchronized with the Helper system every time such changes happen. For ease of use, physicians might consider synchronizing them once every day.

This not only eliminates the manual effort involved in sending reminders of ap-

Case Table 6.1

Mapping of Case Study With the Stages in ANT

Stage	Case study
Inscription	From Helper Software
Translation	New and augmented roles have resulted after initial implementation of Helper Software.
Problematization	Problem to be resolved is that of ensuring the Helper Software enables value driven, patient-centric healthcare delivery.
Interessement	Roles are currently being re-negotiated with the implementation of the Helper Software.
Enrollment	Roles are slowly becoming accepted as familiarization with Helper Software occurs.
Mobilization of allies	This stage has yet to occur.
Framing	This stage has yet to occur.

Note: This case was prepared by Nilmini Wickramasinghe and her graduate student at the Illinois Institute of Technology, Chicago. It is intended as an illustration of a scenario in KM and as a basis for classroom discussion. It is not intended to illustrate or to recommend effective or ineffective handling of a management decision or situation.

We are indebted to the two students, Ray Arias and Srinath Tumu, who helped us to gather the data.

pointments and so on, but also avoids the redundant entry of data. Data entered on the Therapist Traveler are immediately available in the Helper Software after a HotSynch.

Summary of Case Analysis

Having carefully observed the disadvantages of the existing practice and the potential of the new PMS that is about to be put in use, we find that the PMS has a considerable number of advantages. However, these benefits are not quantifiable and cannot be immediately weighed using the normal return on investment (ROI) or techniques.

Also, this PMS is restricted by the linear approach. Any phase that needs to be used in a later phase should first be entered in a prior phase. This procedure might not be very scalable for large organizations. However, for small and midsize practices, this does not pose a danger or negative effect. In the current practice, Dr. Martinez wants an application that will closely integrate the electronic medical records, scheduling, and medical billing applications. The office manager is concerned that as the practice grows she will not be able to keep up with the workflow and billing requirements using her current methods. She also is concerned with the HIPAA regulations. Clearly the underlying PMS satisfies all these goals.

CONCLUSIONS

It is indeed possible to map the current state of the IPA implementation onto the stages of actor-network theory (Case Table 6.1). Presently, the IPA is at stages 2 and 3, negotiating the newly augmented roles given the implementation of the Helper Software and working toward the complete acceptance of these roles. Mobilization and framing will only occur once stages 2 and 3 are complete. It becomes possible from such an analysis to provide feedback to Dr. Martinez so that he can take corrective actions and attain the best possible scenario at the framing stage. What might Dr. Martinez do when presented with such an analysis?

DISCUSSION QUESTIONS

1. Draw the process and information flows.
2. What would the actor network look like for this IPA?
3. How might the ANT analysis in Case Table 6.1 help Dr. Martinez to make modifications to the design?
4. Outline the role for KM that would be particularly useful for this IPA.

Case 7

Siemens

Continuous Innovation of a Knowledge Management System

Siemens AG is Europe's largest conglomerate. With its headquarters located in Berlin and Munich, Germany, the company has six major business segments: Information and Communications, Automation and Control, Power (plants and equipment), Transportation, Medical, and Lighting. Siemens employs more than 450,000 people in 190 countries. More than 50,000 scientists and engineers work in its research and development (R&D) facilities, with a budget in 2006 of over 5 billion euros. Reported sales were approximately 87 billion euros in 2006. Siemens AG is listed on the Frankfurt Stock Exchange and has been listed on the New York Stock Exchange since 2001.

Werner von Siemens founded the company in 1847 as a result of his invention of a telegraph that was distinctly different from those using Morse code. By 1870 the company had systems in the United Kingdom, Russia, and India. Throughout its growth, the company has always been at the forefront of providing technologies and equipment of quality and importance.

Siemens has a decentralized matrix structure that is largely a result of the numerous acquisitions throughout its history. This structure has been particularly helpful in facilitating entrepreneurial responsibility and fostering close development ties with customers. It also has enabled interdivisional cooperation and systematic sharing of best practices.

The company's largest business segment is Information and Communications. This segment has three groups: Siemens Business Services (SBS), which offers single-source information technology solutions and services; Information and Communication Mobile (ICM), which covers all mobile communications and applications; and Information and Communication Networks (ICN), which develops, manufactures, and sells public communication systems. In 2003, ICN's sales were over 7 billion euros but the ebit (electronic business information technology) had a deficit of 366 million euros. This was the result of the difficulties generally experienced by the telecommunications industry at that time.

In 2003–2004, Siemens ICN decided it would be a solution provider for other global networks. In order for this strategy to be successful, ICN needed to establish an appropriate knowledge management system (KMS). Vice President Janina Kugel headed the team that was put together to establish and support the knowledge-sharing initiatives and the implementation of the community-based KMS, ShareNet.

KNOWLEDGE MANAGEMENT SYSTEM AT SIEMENS

ShareNet was a global knowledge-sharing network that was developed initially for the sales and marketing functions of the company. During the late 1990s, the market was in tremendous flux, and Siemens realized it was vital to predict and then provide its customers with flexible bundles of services and products. To achieve this goal, managers had to have the appropriate knowledge available so they could rapidly extract relevant and pertinent information to provide customers with what they wanted when they wanted it. Moreover, the KMS had to be able to capture both explicit knowledge, such as structured knowledge objects in the form of project descriptions, functional and technical solutions, customers, competitors, and markets, as well as tacit knowledge in the form of newsgroups, discussion forums, and chats.

The first key step in the development of ShareNet was the definition and prototyping stage, which lasted from August 1998 to March 1999. During this time, the project team was established and the conceptual definitions and refinements developed so that the technical prototyping could take place. The commitment was to increase value to the customer by creating and reapplying leading-edge solutions. Benefits were to include the reduction of costs by avoiding expensive mistakes or reinvention of the wheel, using or reusing technical and functional components that had already been developed, and shortening project delivery times thanks to enhanced throughput and better utilization of solutions. It was also envisaged that quality would improve, as reusable modules would be continuously enhanced. Four critical elements of the KMS were to be (1) the sales value creation process, a series of the important sales activities and decisions where knowledge should be used; (2) the ShareNet content, which was to consist of best practices and lessons learned; (3) the ShareNet community, which was to help people connect to experts easily; and (4) the ShareNet systems, which consisted of technical systems to ensure low effort, speedy searching, and publishing of content as well as managerial systems to encourage the critical steps of knowledge management (KM), namely, capture, storage, use, and dissemination.

From April to July 1999, the next stage—setup and pilot—took place. Pilots were necessary not only to test the capabilities of the technical and managerial systems but also, and perhaps more important, to get buy-in from headquarters and local companies. It was important that all managers were committed to KM, and while no formal change management strategy was implemented in conjunction with the development of the system, various methods were used as and when they were deemed necessary to keep the level of commitment at an appropriate state. One challenge at this stage was avoiding scope creep while making sure that the ultimate system would be appropriate to meet all user needs. The aim was for users to develop their own personal networks so that they felt involved and connected with the project without getting a system that was too large and too complex.

The next key stage of the project was the global rollout. This started in July 1999 and lasted until February 2000. It was anticipated that at the end of this period the system would be up and running in thirty countries. To reach such a target required the design and development of several incentive programs as well as a significant emphasis on training. In fiscal year 2000 Siemens earned over 70 million euros from global knowledge exchange by ShareNet.

After the global rollout phase was complete, stage 4 operations, expansion, and development started. This phase lasted until November 2001. The major objective was to continuously expand ShareNet throughout ICN and to simultaneously and continuously refine its technical specifications. By December 2001, the fifth phase of the project was in progress, namely, shifting to a multicommunity concept. Specifically, CEO Peter von Pierer believed that ShareNet should be a Siemens-wide system rather than an ICN system. He believed that a Siemens-wide system would facilitate the development, and the support thereafter, of various communities of practice as well as ensure best practices throughout the corporation. To realize this objective, it was necessary to develop a new technical platform.

By September 2002, the ShareNet operating team had modified the knowledge-sharing incentives. This was deemed appropriate since implementation had now been successfully established and it was becoming more apparent that emphasis should be placed on supporting R&D with less emphasis on the marketing aspect of the KMS.

CONCLUSIONS

The 2003 business environment was looking increasingly stark, primarily due to the collapse of the telecommunications sector in 2001, and certain to get even more difficult before it got better. Cutting costs through decentralization and simultaneously keeping R&D high was the company's main challenge. Kugel was certain that the tools, techniques, and technologies of ShareNet would play an integral role in the solution, but she was still unsure about the best way to extend and expand ShareNet to incorporate R&D. She was well aware that over time, as employees were being laid off, the incentive to share knowledge was decreasing dramatically. In fact, both the number of pages viewed and the number of page additions were less than half what they were in 2001. In such a climate, she was gravely concerned that extending the KMS to incorporate R&D might be an injudicious strategy that would actually foster the negative KM culture that was apparently developing. And yet what else could she do?

DISCUSSION QUESTIONS

1. Outline an appropriate way forward for Siemens. How should Ms. Kugel proceed?
2. Do all KM systems have a finite lifetime or are they systems that grow and evolve in an organization as it changes and adapts? Use ShareNet as an example in your answer.
3. How should Siemens encourage a knowledge-sharing culture in a time of economic contraction and layoffs?
4. Is KM only a solution in times of economic challenge? Explain with ShareNet as an example.

NOTE

This case was prepared by Nilmini Wickramasinghe and her graduate students at the Illinois Institute of Technology in Chicago. It is intended as an illustration of a scenario in knowledge management and as a basis for classroom discussion. It is not intended to illustrate or to recommend effective or ineffective handling of a management decision or situation.

Case 8

Reconfiguring the National Health Service in the New Millennium

Information and communication technology (ICT) has revolutionized numerous business practices and operations. One of the last fiefdoms yet to fully experience the magnitude of change that ICT intervention can bestow is health care. However, this state is soon to be short-lived, especially in the case of the United Kingdom's National Health Service (NHS).

Currently, the NHS is undergoing a significant reconfiguration. The implementation of various ICTs is an attempt to make the organization more in keeping with a knowledge economy. Specifically, the vision for the future includes secure access to up-to-date, accurate information about diagnosis, treatment, and care for all those involved in the care of a patient; easier access for patients to their own health and care information; more choice and control for patients over their own health and care; a health service designed around the patient; and a more modern, efficient NHS.

Many challenges arise concerning what is appropriate (or not) for a public sector organization as it grapples with the effort to incorporate modern management techniques as well as the tools, technologies, and strategies of the current knowledge economy.

BACKGROUND

The United Kingdom, unlike the United States, has a public health care system that consists of four large, independent subsystems—namely, the NHS, NHS Scotland, NHS Wales, and Health and Social Care in Northern Ireland. These systems have developed separately due to different legislation, management, practices, and distinct government influences.

Most of England's health care services are provided by the NHS under the National Health Service Act of 1946, which was established when the then Labor government decided that, especially in a time of peace, it should be possible to provide health care services in addition to other social benefits to the citizens of the country. Even today, the creation of the NHS is considered the best achievement by the Labor Party in its whole history. In the United Kingdom today, parallel private health care insurance exists, but only a small percentage of the population presently subscribes to private

Case Table 8.1

Bodies That Make Up the NHS

Administrative:	
Strategic Health Authorities	These oversee all NHS operations.
Special Health Authorities	National Institutes of Health and Clinical Excellence
	NHS direct
	NHS business services authority and NHS pension scheme
	NHS professionals special health authority
Direct Healthcare Providers:	
NHS Trusts	Primary care trusts
	Hospital trusts
	Ambulance trusts
	Foundation trusts
	Care trusts
	Mental health service trusts
NHS Programs:	
Connecting for Health	NHS' ICT program
Organizations associated with NHS	NHS Confederation
Department of Health Bodies	Various executive agencies of the Department of Health
Non-departmental Bodies	Non-departmental public bodies including: Healthcare Commission, Council for Healthcare Regulatory Excellence
Health Care	General Medical Council
	Nursing and Midwifery Council
	General Dental Council
	British Medical Association
	Royal College of Nursing
	Royal Pharmaceutical Society of Great Britain
	Royal College of Surgeons of England

health insurance. The estimated cost of running the NHS is over £100 billion for 2007–2008. This cost is covered through general taxation.

The world's largest health service and one of the world's largest employers after the Chinese army and Indian railway, the NHS is a complex organization consisting of many units and subunits working together in a coordinated fashion to deliver health care services to any patient at any time across the United Kingdom. It is useful to think of the various units and subunits of the NHS as the various bodies of the NHS. Case Table 8.1 depicts not only the maze of administrative layers but also the complex and unique organizational structure of the NHS. This complexity has a significant impact on how and what information and/or knowledge is created and generated, stored and captured, used and reused and disseminated. In such a complex system, a sound and solid organizational memory is of great importance. Case Figure 8.1 provides an overview of the structure of the NHS in England.

Another unique feature of the NHS that tends to differentiate it from other national health care systems in Europe and in other countries such as Australia is that it not only pays directly for health care services, but also it employs the doctors and nurses who provide these services.

Case Figure 8.1 **Structure of the NHS in England**

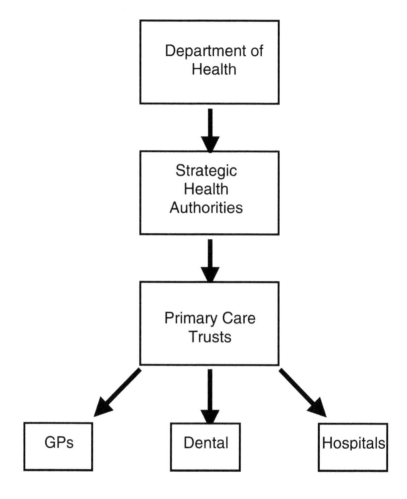

CHANGES IN THE NATIONAL HEALTH SERVICE

The value proposition of any health care system is to provide the best possible access, quality, and value to all its patients (Wickramasinghe and Schaffer 2006). In order to embrace technology effectively and efficiently and move into the knowledge management (KM) abyss, the NHS has embarked on some rather large-scale changes and reconfigurations. The goal is to use ICT to create a patient-led NHS in which there is faster and more convenient access to care through increases in capacity and changes in the way the system works.

Since 2000, the NHS has built up capacity and made some early reforms necessary to improve services, reduce waiting times, and dramatically decrease mortality rates. Clinical governance standards and new arrangements for ensuring patient safety have been introduced. However, these improvements are seen as only the first small step, for the grander ambition is to deliver a truly professional change to the whole system, offering more choice; providing personalized, patient-centric care; and truly empowering people to improve their health. The key slogan that encapsulates this new dawn for the NHS is creating a "patient-led NHS" in which patients have all the supports required for their health care needs.

Naturally, to support such a grand ambition, a key enabler is information technology. Many new ICT practices and systems have been identified and rolled out across the NHS.

THE NATIONAL HEALTH SERVICE IMPROVEMENT PLAN

In June 2004, the NHS Improvement Plan: Putting People at the Heart of Public Services set out the ways in which the NHS needs to change in order to realize its goal of patient-led health care. The plan identified learning and leadership as particularly important since changes made to a complex system can create much uncertainty. The changes required in the NHS by the shift from a centrally directed system to a patient-led system would clearly increase uncertainty. Hence, it is essential to develop robust systems for providing feedback, learning lessons, and adapting the approach while maintaining its overall direction. Specifically, the feedback and learning need to be service-wide and involve patients, staff, and partner organizations. They need to be undertaken locally while brought together nationally. To accomplish this goal, the NHS established the National Leadership for Health and Social Care to play a key role in taking the work forward, collecting feedback, and shaping the way change is implemented.

As stated by the NHS chief executive, Sir Nigel Crisp, on March 17, 2005, "The past five years have been about building capacity and capability. The next will be about improving quality, making sure that we give the very best value for money, and use the new capacity and capability to build a truly patient-led service."[1]

THE ESSENTIALS OF THE PLAN

The commissioning of a patient-led NHS requires the following four key deliverables to be realized:

1. Better engagement with local clinicians in the design of services
2. Fast, universal rollout of practice-based commissioning
3. Developing primary care trusts (PCTs) to support practice-based commissioning and taking on the responsibility for performance management through contracts with all providers, including those in the independent sector
4. Reviewing the functions of strategic health authorities (SHAs) to support commissioning and contract management

Without these specific changes it will not be possible to create a patient-led NHS. Case Table 8.2 highlights key aspects and stages of the program. The first stage focuses on getting the right configuration, while the second stage focuses on enhancing the ability of practices to do their new or enhanced jobs. Case Table 8.3 highlights the roles and responsibilities, and, finally, Case Table 8.4 provides the anticipated timetable.

Case Table 8.2

The Program

Strategic health authorities will be responsible for coordinating the exercise locally.

Proposals will be addressed according to the following criteria:
Secure high-quality safe services
Improve health and reduce inequalities
Improve the engagement of GPs and rollout of practice-based commissioning with demonstrable
practice support
Improve public involvement
Improve commissioning and effective use of resources
Manage financial balance risk
Improve coordination with social services through greater congruence of PCT and local
government boundaries
Deliver at lest 15 percent reduction in management and administrative costs

Reconfiguration of PCTs to have a clear relationship with local authority social services boundaries.

Securing services from a range of providers not just directly through PCT.

SHAs should:
Actively seek new and innovative ways to improve new services with a range of providers
Assess what services should move away from direct PCT provision and at what pace
Where PCTs continue to manage services, separate decision making on commissioning and on
provision in order to enhance contestability

Different service models will be explored in the White Paper.

Reconfigured SHAs will move toward alignment with government office boundaries and SHAs must
deliver a significant reduction in management and administrative costs through their configuration
proposals.

SHAs proposals should consist of the following (due October 2005):
Future organizational configurations
Proposed changes to PCT
A plan for roll-out of practice-based commissioning
A business continuity plan
Evidence of views and contributions of all the relevant parties they have consulted

The department will then test the proposals with the aim that each SHA by the end of November
2005 may proceed to consultation and then implementation.

Statutory consultation will be completed no later than March 2006.

This stage is about identifying the development support that organizations will need to be successful
in the future.

Focus on internal capability and capacity of SHAs to discharge new functions and most especially
leadership ability.

PCTs and SHAs across the country will undergo an independent diagnostic and benchmarking
assessment.

Case Table 8.3

Roles and Responsibilities

Practice Base Commissioning (PBC)
The government is committed to Practice Based Commissioning as a way of devoting power to local doctors and users to improve patient care as well as aligning local clinics and financial responsibilities.
Under PBC, GP practices will take on responsibility from their PCTs for commissioning services that meet the needs and demands of their local population including:
Designing improved patient pathways
Working in partnership with PCTs to create community based services
Responsibility for a budget delegated from the PCT
Managing the budget effectively
Under PBC, GPs will not be responsible for managing contracts.

Primary Care Trusts (PCT)
PCTs will ensure access and choice to a range of high quality health services.
As custodians, the PCTs are charged with ensuring correct prioritization and value for money.
Functions include:
Improving the health of the community
Securing the provision of safe, high quality services
Contact management
Engaging with local people and other local services
Acting as a provider of services only when it is not possible to have separate providers of service
Emergency planning
The need for PCTs to be involved in contract negotiation will be reduced.
PCTs will be accountable to their local communities and the Secretary of State through Strategic Health Authorities.

Strategic Health Authorities (SHAs)
SHAs will focus on:
Performance managing the NHS local public health function
Ensuring successful delivery
Ensuring robust and integrated emergency planning
Taking their NHS trusts to foundation status
SHAs will be accountable to the Secretary of State through the NHS Chief Executive.

NHS Foundation Trusts (FTs)
FTs will have the following functions:
Deliver service agreements with PCTs on a contractual basis
Work with PCTs, PBCs, and clinical networks in the redesign of services to ensure they are patient centered and integrated across the continuum of care
Work with PCTs and other partners to contribute to health improvement
Provide an environment conducive for training, development, and research

NHS Trusts (Trusts)
All trusts should become FTs by April 2008.
To facilitate this endeavor, the Monitor, the Department, and SHAs will lead a development program to help trusts identify areas that must be addressed in order to become FTs.
The diagnostic process covers:
Financial health and delivery track record of trusts
Leadership and governance
Risk assessment of local health economy covering PCTs and SHAs
The development of interventions identified as needed as a result of this process will be coordinated by the SHA in conjunction with the Monitor and the Department.
Other providers: Alongside the program for trusts there will be greater use of other providers.

Ambulance Trusts
Complete review of the ambulance system and ambulance trusts also will move to Foundation Status.

Case Table 8.4

Time Table

Commissioning functions
 August—mid-October 2005: SHAs to review and reconfigure plans.
 October 2005: Commissioning development support program launched.
 March 2006: All statutory consultation completed and first wave of enhanced PBC.
 October 2006: All reconfigurations undertaken.
 December 2006: PCTs have universal coverage in place.
 April 2007: SHA reconfiguration complete.
 December 2008: Changes in PCT service provisions complete.

Trusts
 Mid-September 2005: Monitor and SHAs to publish diagnostics for NHS trusts.
 January–June 2006: SHAs conduct trust diagnostic process.
 July 2006: SHAs to report back on NHS trusts review.

Ambulance
 September–November 2005: Formal consultation to elicit patient and public views.
 December 2005: Ministerial decision and announcement.
 April 2006: Implementation begins.
 March 2007: Implementation complete and all trusts in place and fully operational.

INSTITUTIONAL MEMORY

Although the NHS plan is indeed ambitious, it has been criticized for not leveraging one of its critical resources—namely, its institutional memory. Clearly, over the last sixty years, the largest health care service organization in the world has generated much knowledge in many forms. The fear is that in the reconfiguration of PCTs, SHAs, and other bodies partaking in the NHS, much of this vital knowledge may evaporate. Moreover, little effort is being placed into developing synergies and bringing together high-level experience and skill. Indeed, this fear raises a larger issue—in general, how should public sector organizations realign themselves in today's knowledge economy?

CONCLUSIONS

The NHS Improvement Plan: Putting People at the Heart of Public Services—that is, developing a patient-led NHS—sets a clear agenda for reconfiguring the NHS between July 2000 and 2008. Such a complex, large-scale reconfiguration has required and still requires significant investment. The expectations of improved access, quality, and value and a more patient-centric focus are indeed laudable goals. However, the big question is whether these goals can be realized and why the tools, techniques, and technologies of KM have not played a bigger role. Only time will show the true success of this immense, ambitious project, but time is beginning to run out for the NHS as the 2008 clock ticks on.

DISCUSSION QUESTIONS

1. Where is the KM the current plans?
2. How can the current plans be enhanced with more effective implementation of the tools, techniques, and tactics of KM?
3. In general, how should public sector organizations realign themselves in today's knowledge economy?
4. What improvements in access, quality, and value can be expected in the new design?

NOTES

This case was prepared by Nilmini Wickramasinghe and her graduate students at the Illinois Institute of Technology in Chicago. It is intended as an illustration of a scenario in knowledge management and as a basis for classroom discussion. It is not intended to illustrate or to recommend effective or ineffective handling of a management decision or situation.

1. NHS News bulletin.

References

CHAPTER 1

Allen, T. 1984. *Managing the Flow of Technology: Technology Transfer and the Dissemination of Technological Information Within the R&D Organization.* Boston: MIT Press.

Bacon, C.J., and B. Fitzgerald. 2001. "A Systemic Framework for the Field of Information Systems." *Database for Advances in Information Systems* 32 (2): 46–67.

Becker, G. 1993. *Human Capital.* 3rd ed. Chicago: University of Chicago Press.

Carrillo, F. 1998. "Managing Knowledge-Based Value Systems." *Journal of Knowledge Management* 1 (4): 280–286.

Clegg, S. 1999. "Globalizing the Intelligent Organization: Learning Organizations, Smart Workers, (Not So) Clever Countries and the Sociological Imagination." *Management Learning* 30 (3): 259–280.

Croasdell, D.C. 2001. "IT's Role in Organizational Memory and Learning." *Information Systems Management* 18 (1): 8–11.

Davenport, T., and L. Prusak. 1998. *Working Knowledge: How Organizations Manage What They Know.* Cambridge, MA: Harvard Business School Press.

Davis, S., and J. Botkin. 1994. "The Coming of Knowledge-Based Business." *Harvard Business Review* (September–October): 165–170.

Drucker, P. 1988. The Coming of the New Organization." *Harvard Business Review* (January–February): 45–53.

———. 1999. *Management Challenges for the 21st Century.* New York: HarperBusiness.

Duffy, J. 2000. "The KM Technology Infrastructure." *Information Management Journal* 34 (2): 62–66.

———. 2001. "The Tools and Technologies Needed for Knowledge Management." *Information Management Journal* 35 (1): 64–67.

Ellerman, D.P. 1999. "Global Institutions: Transforming International Development Agencies Into Learning Organizations." *Academy of Management Executive* 13 (1): 25–35.

Ellinger, A., K. Watkins, and R. Bostrom. 1999. "Managers as Facilitators of Learning in Learning Organizations." *Human Resource Development Quarterly* 10 (2): 105–125.

Grandstrand, O. 2000. "The Shift Towards Intellectual Capitalism—The Role of Infocom Technologies." *Review Policy* 29 (9): 1061–1080.

Gupta, J., S. Sharma, and J. Hsu. 2004. "An Overview of Knowledge Management." In *Creating Knowledge Based Organizations,* ed. J. Gupta and S. Sharma, 1–28. Hershey, PA: Idea Group.

Hansen, M., and B. Oetinger. 2001. "Introducing T-Shaped Managers: Knowledge Management's Next Generation." *Harvard Business Review* 79 (3): 106–116.

Holt, G., P. Love, and H. Li. 2000. "The Learning Organization: Toward a Paradigm for Mutually

Beneficial Strategic Construction Alliances." *International Journal of Project Management* 18 (6): 415–421.

Ives, W., B. Torrey, and C. Gordon. 1998. "Knowledge Management: An Emerging Discipline with a Long History." *Journal of Knowledge Management* 1 (4): 269–274.

Lee, J., Sr. 2000. "Knowledge Management: The Intellectual Revolution." *IIE Solutions* 32 (10): 34–37.

Leonard-Barton, D. 1995. *Wellsprings of Knowledge: Building and Sustaining Sources of Innovation.* Boston: Harvard Business School Press.

Lesser, E., D. Mundel, and C. Wiecha. 2000. "Managing Customer Knowledge." *Journal of Business Strategy* 21 (6): 35–37.

Levine, L. 2001. "Integrating Knowledge and Processes in a Learning Organization." *Information Systems Management* 18 (1): 21–33.

Lipnack, J., and J. Stamps. 2000. *Virtual Teams: People Working Across Boundaries with Technology.* New York: Wiley.

Mahe, S., and C. Rieu. 1998. "A Pull Approach to Knowledge Management." Paper presented at the Proceedings of the Second International Conference on Practical Aspects of Knowledge Management, Basel, Switzerland, October 29–30.

Malhotra, Y., ed. 2000. *Knowledge Management and Virtual Organizations.* Hershey, PA: Idea Group.

———, ed. 2001. *Knowledge Management and Business Model Innovation.* Hershey, PA: Idea Group.

Moore, K. 2000. "The E-volving Organization." *Ivey Business Journal* 65 (2): 25–28.

Nonaka, I. 1991. "The Knowledge-Creating Company." *Harvard Business Review* (November–December): 96–107.

———. 1995. *The Knowledge-Creating Company.* New York: Oxford University Press.

Nonaka, I., and H. Takeuchi. 1995. *The Knowledge-Creating Company: How Japanese Companies Create the Dynamics of Innovation.* New York: Oxford University Press.

O'Dell, C. 1996. "A Current Review of Knowledge Management Best Practice." Paper presented at the Knowledge Management 96 Conference, London, December.

Onge, A. 2001. "Knowledge Management and Warehousing." *Modern Materials Handling* 56 (3): 33.

Orlikowski, W., and S. Barley. 2001. "Technology and Institutions: What Can Research on Information Technology and Research on Organizations Learn from Each Other?" *MIS Quarterly* 25 (2): 145–165.

Orlikowski, W., and J. Hoffman. 1997. "An Improvisational Model for Change Management: The Case of Groupware Technologies." *Sloan Management Review* 38: 11–21.

Phillips, T., and M. Vollmer. 2000. "Knowledge Management in the Current Marketplace." *Oil & Gas Journal* 98 (39): 4–5.

Popper, M., and R. Lipshitz. 2000. "Organizational Learning: Mechanisms, Culture, and Feasibility." *Management Learning* 31 (2): 181–196.

Roberts, J. 2000. "From Know-How to Show-How? Questioning the Role of Information and Communication Technologies in Knowledge Transfer." *Technology Analysis & Strategic Management* 12 (4): 429–443.

Rogers, E. 2003. *Diffusion of Innovation.* 5th ed. New York: Free Press.

Rubenstein, A., and E. Geisler. 2003. *Installing and Managing Workable Knowledge Management Systems.* Westport, CT: Praeger.

Sharma, S., and J. Gupta. 2001. "Managing Business-Consumer Interactions in the E-World." In *Knowledge and Information Technology Management in the 21st Century Organizations: Human and Social Perspectives*, ed. A. Gunasekaran, O. Khalil, and M. Rahman Syed, 192–213. Hershey, PA: Idea Group.

Sharma, S., J. Gupta, and N. Wickramasinghe. 2004. "Information Technology Assessment for Knowledge Management." In *Creating Knowledge-Based Organizations*, ed. J. Gupta and S. Sharma, 29–44. Hershey, PA: Idea Group.

Silver, C. 2000. "Where Technology and Knowledge Meet." *Journal of Business Strategy* 21 (6): 28–33.

Simon, N. 1999. "The Learning Organization." *Competitive Intelligence Magazine* 2 (2): 40–42.

Skyrme, D. 1991. "Knowledge Networking." *Intelligent Enterprise* 1 (9/10): 9–15.

Skyrme, D., and D. Amidon. 1997. *Creating the Knowledge-Based Business.* London: Business Intelligence.

Stewart, T. 1997. *Intellectual Capital: The New Wealth of Organizations.* New York: Currency/Doubleday.

Stratigos, A. 2001. "Knowledge Management Meets Future Information Users." *Online* 25 (1): 65–67.

Thorne, K., and M. Smith. 2000. "Competitive Advantage in World-Class Organizations." *Management Accounting* 78 (3): 22–26.

Wickramasinghe, N., S. Sharma, and J. Gupta. 2004. "From Data to Decisions: Knowledge Discovery Solutions for Intelligent Enterprises." In *Intelligent Enterprises of the 21st Century,* ed. J. Gupta and S. Sharma, 234–245. Hershey, PA: Idea Group.

CHAPTER 2

Alavi, M., and D. Leidner. 2001. "Knowledge Management and Knowledge Management Systems: Conceptual Foundations and Research Issues." *MLS Quarterly* 25 (1): 107–136.

Anand, N., H. Gardner, and T. Morris. 2007. "Knowledge-Based Innovation: Emergence and Embedding of New Practice Areas in Management Consulting Firms." *Academy of Management Journal* 50 (2): 406–428.

Argyris, C. 2004. *Reasons and Rationalizations: The Limits to Organizational Knowledge.* New York: Oxford University Press.

Baskerville, R., and A. Dulipovici. 2006. "The Theoretical Foundations of Knowledge Management." *Knowledge Management Research & Practice* 4 (2): 81–105.

Chesbrough, H. 2006. *Open Business Models: How to Thrive in the New Innovation Landscape.* Cambridge, MA: Harvard Business School Press.

Choo, C. 1998. *The Knowledge Organization: How Organizations Use Information to Construct Meaning, Create Knowledge, and Make Decisions.* New York: Oxford University Press.

Collins, J. 2001. *Built to Last: Why Some Companies Make the Leap and Others Don't.* New York: HarperCollins.

Dalkir, K. 2005. *Knowledge Management in Theory and Practice.* New York: Elsevier.

Davenport, T., and L. Prusak. 1998. *Working Knowledge: How Organizations Manage What They Know.* Cambridge, MA: Harvard Business School Press.

Dessler, G. 2003. *Management: Principles and Practices for Tomorrow's Leaders.* 3rd ed. Englewood Cliffs, NJ: Prentice-Hall.

Foray, D. 2004. *Economics of Knowledge.* Cambridge, MA: MIT Press.

Geisler, E. 1997. *Managing the Aftermath of Radical Corporate Change: Reengineering, Restructuring, and Reinvention.* Westport, CT: Quorum Books.

———. 1999. "Harnessing the Value of Experience in the Knowledge-Driven Firm." *Business Horizons* 42 (3): 18–26.

———. 2005. "The Measurement of Scientific Activity: Research Directions in Linking Philosophy of Science and Metrics of Science and Technology Outputs." *Scientometrics* 62 (2): 269–284.

———. 2006. "A Taxonomy and Proposed Codification of Knowledge and Knowledge Systems in Organizations." *Knowledge and Process Management* 13 (4): 285–296.

———. 2007. *Knowledge and Knowledge Systems: Learning from the Wonders of the Mind.* Hershey, PA: Idea Group.

Hammer, M., and J. Champy. 1993. *Reengineering the Corporation: A Manifesto for Business Revolution.* New York: HarperBusiness.

Kaplan, R., and D. Norton. 1996. *The Balanced Scorecard: Translating Strategy into Action.* Cambridge, MA: Harvard Business School Press.

Laudon, K., and J. Laudon. 1999. *Essentials of Management Information Systems.* 3rd ed. Upper Saddle River, NJ: Prentice-Hall.

Michelli, J. 2006. *The Starbucks Experience: 5 Principles for Turning Ordinary into Extraordinary.* New York: McGraw-Hill.

Nonaka, I., and H. Takeuchi. 1995. *The Knowledge-Creating Company: How Japanese Companies Create the Dynamics of Innovation.* New York: Oxford University Press.

Patmayakuni, R., A. Rai, and A. Tiwana. 2007. "Systems Development Process Improvement: A Knowledge Integration Perspective." *IEEE Transactions on Engineering Management* 54 (2): 286–300.

Polanyi, M. 1966. *The Tacit Dimension.* London: Routledge & Kegan.

Prusak, L., ed. 1997. *Knowledge in Organizations.* Boston: Butterworth-Heinemann.

Schwartz, D. 2006. *Encyclopedia of Knowledge Management.* Hershey, PA: Idea Group.

Senge, P. 1990. *The Fifth Discipline: The Art and Practice of the Learning Organization.* New York: Doubleday.

Smith, H., J. McKeen, and S. Singh. 2006. "Making Knowledge Work: Five Principles for Action-Oriented Knowledge Management." *Knowledge Management Research & Practice* 4 (2): 116–124.

Tallman, S., and A. Phene. 2007. "Leveraging Knowledge Across Geographic Boundaries." *Organization Science* 18 (2): 252–260.

Tordoir, P. 1995. *The Professional Knowledge Economy.* Dordrecht, Netherlands: Kluwer Academic.

Von Krogh, G., K. Ichijo, and I. Nonaka. 2000. *Enabling Knowledge Creation: How to Unlock the Mystery of Tacit Knowledge and Release the Power of Innovation.* New York: Oxford University Press.

Weick, K. 2001. *Making Sense of the Organization.* Malden, MA: Basil Blackwell.

White, D. 2002. *Knowledge Mapping and Management.* Hershey, PA: Idea Group.

Wiig, K. 1993. *Knowledge Management Foundations: Thinking About Thinking. How People and Organizations Create, Represent, and Use Knowledge.* Arlington, TX: Schema Press.

Wilson, T. 2002. "The Nonsense of Knowledge Management." *Information Research* 8 (1): Paper No. 144.

CHAPTER 3

Abramson, B. 1998. "Translating Nations: Actor-Network Theory in/and Canada." *Canadian Review of Sociology and Anthropology* 35 (1): 1–19.

Adriaans, P., and D. Zantinge. 1996. *Data Mining.* New York: Addison-Wesley.

Alavi, M., and D. Leidner. 2001. "Review: Knowledge Management and Knowledge Management Systems: Conceptual Foundations and Research Issues." *MIS Quarterly* 25 (1): 107–136.

Bijker, W.E., T.P. Hughes, and T.J. Pinch, eds. 1987. *The Social Construction of Technological Systems: New Directions in the Sociology and History of Technology.* Cambridge, MA: MIT Press.

Boland, R., and R. Tenkasi. 1995. "Perspective Making and Perspective Taking in Communities of Knowledge." *Organization Science* 6: 350–372.

Boudreau, J., and P. Ramstad. 2007. *The New Science of Human Capital.* Boston: Harvard Business School Press.

Callon, M., and B. Latour. 1981. "Unscrewing the Big Leviathan: How Actors Macro-Structure Reality and How Sociologies Help Them to Do So." In *Advances in Social Theory and Methodology: Towards an Integration of Micro- and Macro-Sociologies,* ed. A.V. Cicourel and K. Knorr-Cetina, 277–303. London: Routledge & Kegan.

Callon, M, and J. Law. 1986. "Some Elements of a Sociology of Translation: Domestication of the Scallops and the Fishermen of St Brieuc Bay." In *Power, Action and Belief: A New Sociology of Knowledge?* 196–229. London: Routledge & Kegan.

Callon, M., J. Law, and A. Rip. 1986. "The Sociology of an Actor-Network: The Case of the Electric Vehicle." In *Mapping the Dynamics of Science and Technology*, 19–34. London: Macmillan.

Campbell, D. 1974. "Evolutionary Epistemology." In *The Philosophy of Karl Popper*, ed. P. Schilpp, 412–463. LaSalle, IL: Open Court.

Chagani, F. 1998. "Postmodernism: Rearranging the Furniture of the Universe." *Irreverence* 1 (3): 1–3.

Chomsky, N. 2006. *Language and Mind*. 3rd ed. New York: Cambridge University Press.

Choo, C. 2005. *The Knowledge Organization: How Organizations Use Information to Construct Meaning, Create Knowledge, and Make Decisions*. New York: Oxford University Press.

Collins, H.M., S. Yearley, and A. Pickering. 1992. "Epistemological Chicken." In *Science as Practice and Culture*, 301–326. Chicago: Chicago University Press.

Dalkir, K. 2005. *Knowledge Management in Theory and Practice*. Burlington, MA: Butterworth-Heinemann.

Davenport, T., and L. Prusak. 1998. *Working Knowledge: How Organizations Manage What They Know*. Cambridge, MA: Harvard Business School Press.

Geisler, E. 2001. "Good-Bye Dodo Bird: Why Social Knowledge Is Cumulative, Expansive, and Non-evolutionary." *Journal of Management Inquiry* 10 (1): 5–15.

———. 2006. "A Taxonomy and Proposed Codification of Knowledge and Knowledge Systems in Organizations." *Knowledge and Process Management* 13 (1): 1–12.

———. 2007a. *Knowledge and Knowledge Systems: Learning from the Wonders of the Mind*. Hershey, PA: Idea Group.

———. 2007b. "Knowledge, Information, and Knowledge Systems: Explaining the Conceptual Confusion." In *Knowledge-Based Enterprise: Theories and Fundamentals*, ed. N. Wickramasinghe and D. von Lubitz, 346–356. Hershey, PA: Idea Group.

———. 2007c. "A Typology of Knowledge Management Transactions: Strategic Groups and Role Behavior in Organizations." *Journal of Knowledge Management* 11 (1): 1–14.

Humphrey, N. 1992. *A History of the Mind*. New York: Springer.

———. 1993. *We Have Never Been Modern*. Cambridge, MA: Harvard University Press.

———. 1996. "On Actor-Network Theory—a Few Clarifications." *Soziale Welt* 47 (4): 367, 369–381.

———. 2003. "Why Has Critique Run Out of Steam? From Matters of Fact to Matters of Concern." *Critical Inquiry* 30 (2): 225.

Latour, B. 2005. *Reassembling the Social: An Introduction to Actor-Network Theory*. Oxford, UK: Oxford University Press.

Latour, B., and B. Elliott. 1988. "The Prince for Machines as Well as for Machinations." In *Technology and Social Process*, 20–43. Edinburgh: Edinburgh University Press.

Latour, B., and J. Law. 1991. "Technology Is Society Made Durable." In *A Sociology of Monsters: Essays on Power, Technology and Domination*, 103–131. London: Routledge.

Law, J. 1992. "Notes on the Theory of the Actor-Network: Ordering, Strategy and Heterogeneity." *Systems Practice* 5 (4): 379–393.

Law, J., W.E. Bijker, T.P. Hughes, and T.J. Pinch. 1987. "Technology and Heterogeneous Engineering: The Case of Portuguese Expansion." In *The Social Construction of Technological Systems: New Directions in the Sociology and History of Technology*, 111–134. Cambridge, MA: MIT Press.

Law, J., and M. Callon. 1988. "Engineering and Sociology in a Military Aircraft Project: A Network Analysis of Technological Change." *Social Problems* 35 (3): 284–297.

Law, J., and E. Hassard, eds. 1999. *Actor-Network Theory and After*. Oxford, UK: Blackwell and Sociological Review.

Lynn-Fink, J., and P. Bourne. August 2007. "Reinventing Scholarly Communication for the Electronic Age." www.ctwatch.org.

Massey, A., M. Montoya-Weiss, and T. O'Driscoll. 2002. "Knowledge Management in Pursuit of Performance: Insights from Nortel Networks." *MIS Quarterly* 26 (3): 269–289.

Newell, S., M. Robertson, H. Scarbrough, and J. Swan. 2002. *Managing Knowledge Work.* New York: Palgrave.

Nonaka, I. 1994. "A Dynamic Theory of Organizational Knowledge Creation." *Organizational Science* 5: 14–37.

Nonaka, I., and T. Nishiguchi. 2001. *Knowledge Emergence.* Oxford, UK: Oxford University Press.

Nonaka, I., and H. Takeuchi. 1995. *The Knowledge-Creating Company: How Japanese Companies Create the Dynamics of Innovation.* New York: Oxford University Press.

Orlikowski, W. 1992. "The Duality of Technology: Rethinking the Concept of Technology in Organizations." *Organization Science* 3 (3): 398–427.

Polanyi, M. 1966. *The Tacit Dimension.* Gloucester, MA: Peter Smith.

Popper, K. 1972. *Objective Knowledge: An Evolutionary Approach.* Oxford, UK: Clarendon Press.

Radnitzky, G., ed. 1987. *Evolutionary Epistemology, Rationality, and the Sociology of Knowledge.* La Salle, IL: Open Court.

Rubenstein, A., and E. Geisler. 2003. *Installing and Managing Workable Knowledge Management Systems.* Westport, CT: Praeger.

Schultze, U., and D. Leidner. 2002. "Studying Knowledge Management in Information Systems Research: Discourses and Theoretical Assumptions." *MIS Quarterly* 26 (3): 212–242.

Singleton, V., and M. Michael. 1993. "Actor-Networks and Ambivalence: General Practitioners in the UK Cervical Screening Programme." *Social Studies of Science* 23: 227–264.

Stankovsky, M. 2005. *Creating the Discipline of Knowledge Management: The Latest in University Research.* New York: Butterworth-Heinemann.

Tatnall, A., S. Clarke, E. Coakes, M.G. Hunter, and A. Wenn. 2003. "Actor-Network Theory as a Socio-Technical Approach to Information Systems Research." In *Socio-Technical and Human Cognition Elements of Information Systems*, 266–283. Hershey, PA: Information Science.

Tatnall, A., and A. Gilding. 1999. "Actor-Network Theory and Information Systems Research." 10th Australasian Conference on Information Systems (ACIS). Wellington, Victoria: University of Wellington.

Ter Hark, M. 2004. *Popper, Otto Selz and the Rise of Evolutionary Epistemology.* Cambridge, UK: Cambridge University Press.

Walsham, G. 1997. "Actor-Network Theory and IS Research: Current Status and Future Prospects." *Proceedings of the IFIP TC8 WG 8.2 International Conference on Information Systems and Qualitative Research.* Philadelphia: IFIP.

Weick, K. 2001. *Making Sense of the Organization.* Malden, MA: Basil Blackwell.

Weinberger, D. 2007. *Everything Is Miscellaneous: The Power of the New Digital Disorder.* New York: Times Books.

Wickramasinghe, N. 2006. "Knowledge Creation: A Meta-Framework." *International Journal of Innovation and Learning* 3 (3): 326–347.

Wiig, K. 1993. *Knowledge Management Foundations: Thinking About Thinking. How People and Organizations Create, Represent, and Use Knowledge.* Arlington, TX: Schema Press.

———. 2004. *People-Focused Knowledge Management: How Effective Decision Making Leads to Corporate Success.* London, UK: Butterworth-Heinemann.

Wilbanks, J. August 2007. "Cyberinfrastructure for Knowledge Sharing." www.ctwatch.org.

Wuketitis, F., ed. 1983. *Concepts and Approaches in Evolutionary Epistemology: Towards an Evolutionary Theory of Knowledge.* New York: Springer.

Zuboff, S. 1989. *In the Age of the Smart Machine: The Future of Work and Power.* New York: Basic Books.

CHAPTER 4

Aunger, R. 2000. *Darwinizing Culture: The Status of Memetics as a Science.* New York: Oxford University Press.

———. 2002. *The Electric Meme: A New Theory of How We Think.* New York: Free Press.

Blackmore, S., and R. Dawkins. 1999. *The Meme Machine.* Oxford, UK: Oxford University Press.

Brodie, R. 1996. *Virus of the Mind: The New Science of the Meme.* Seattle, WA: Integral Press.

Dawkins, R. 1978. *The Selfish Gene.* Oxford, UK: Oxford University Press.

Distin, K. 2004. *The Selfish Meme: A Critical Reassessment.* New York: Cambridge University Press.

Edmonds, B. 2002. "Three Challenges to the Survival of Memetics." *Journal of Memetics* 6 (2).

Frappaolo, C. 2006. *Knowledge Management.* Oxford, UK: Capstone.

Frydman, R., and M. Goldberg. 2007. *Imperfect Knowledge Economics: Exchange Rates and Risk.* Princeton, NJ: Princeton University Press.

Geisler, E. 2006. "A Taxonomy and Proposed Codification of Knowledge and Knowledge Systems in Organizations." *Knowledge and Process Management* 13 (4): 285–296.

———. 2007. *Knowledge and Knowledge Systems: Learning from the Wonders of the Mind.* Hershey, PA: Idea Group.

Ichijo, K., and I. Nonaka. 2006. *Knowledge Creation and Management: New Challenges for Managers.* New York: Oxford University Press.

Lynch, A. 1998. *Thought Contagion: When Ideas Act Like Viruses.* New York: Basic Books.

Rubenstein, A., and E. Geisler. 2003. *Installing and Managing Workable Knowledge Management Systems.* Westport, CT: Praeger.

Thompson, R., and S. Madigan. 2007. *Memory: The Key to Consciousness.* Princeton, NJ: Princeton University Press.

Tulving, E., and D. Schachter. 1990. "Primary and Human Memory Systems." *Science* 247: 301–306.

von Krogh, G., K. Ichijo, and I. Nonaka. 2000. *Enabling Knowledge Creation: How to Unlock the Mystery of Tacit Knowledge and Release the Power of Innovation.* New York: Oxford University Press.

Wilson, E. 1998. *Consilience: The Unity of Knowledge.* New York: Knopf.

CHAPTER 5

Agion, P. 1998. *Endogenous Growth Theory.* Cambridge, MA: MIT Press.

Barro, R., and X. Sala-Martin. 1995. *Economic Growth.* New York: McGraw-Hill.

Baskerville, R., and S. Smithson. 1995. "Information Technology and New Organizational Forms: Choosing Chaos over Panaceas." *European Journal of Information* 4 (2): 66–73.

Bassi, L. 1997. "Harnessing the Power of Intellectual Capital." *Training and Development* 25 (6): 167–187.

Beal, T. 2000. "SMEs and the World Wide Web: Opportunities and Prospects." In *Small and Medium Enterprises in Asia Pacific:* Vol. 3, *Development Prospects,* ed. A.M. Asri, 102–134. Commack, NY: Nova Science.

Benhabib, J., and M.M. Spiegel. 1994. "The Role of Human Capital in Economic Development: Evidence from Aggregate Cross-Country Data." *Journal of Monetary Economics* 34 (2): 143–173.

Blundell, R., R. Griffith, and J. Van Reenen. 1995. "Dynamic Count Data Models of Technological Innovation." *Economic Journal* 105 (429): 333–344.

Braim, S. 1998. "Policy Evolution in the Information Economy: An Assessment of the Victoria 21 Strategy." *Telecommunications Policy* 22 (4–5): 443–452.

Cameron, G. 1996. "Innovation and Economic Growth." In *Our Competitive Future: Building the Knowledge-Driven Economy.* London: Department of Trade and Industry.

Churchman, C. 1971. *The Design of Inquiring Systems: Basic Concepts of Systems and Organizations.* New York: Basic Books.

Diaz, A., and C. Federico. 1970. *Essays on the Economic History of the Argentine Republic.* New Haven: Yale University Press.

Drucker, P. 1999. *Management Challenges for the 21st Century*. New York: HarperBusiness.

Foray, D., and B. Lundvall. 1996. "The Knowledge-Based Economy: From the Economics of Knowledge to the Learning Economy." In *Employment and Growth in the Knowledge-Based Economy*, 11–32. Paris: OECD.

Gagnon, M. 2007. "Capital, Power, and Knowledge According to Thorstein-Veblen: Reinterpreting the Knowledge-Based Economy." *Journal of Economic Issues* 41 (2): 593–598.

International Labor Organization. 2001. *World Employment Report 2001: Life at Work in the Information Economy*. Geneva: ILO.

Johnston, R., and R. Blumentritt. 1998. "Knowledge Moves to Centre Stage." *Science Communication* 20 (1): 99–105.

Kelly, K. 1997. "New Rules for the New Economy." *Wired*, September.

Lundvall, B., and B. Johnson. 1994. "The Learning Economy." *Journal of Industry Studies* 1 (2): 23–42.

Mansell, R., and U. Wehn, eds. 1998. *Knowledge Societies: Information Technology for Sustainable Development*. Oxford, UK: Oxford University Press.

OECD. 1996. The Knowledge Economy, *Science, Technology and Industry Outlook*. Paris: OECD.

Porter, M.E. 1990. *The Competitive Advantage of Nations*. New York: Free Press.

Romer, P. 1990. "Endogenous Technological Change." *Journal of Political Economy* 98 (5): 71–102.

Rubenstein, A., and E. Geisler. 2003. *Installing and Managing Workable Knowledge Management Systems*. Westport, CT: Praeger.

Spath, D., J. Warschat, and J. Kemp, eds. 2007. *Knowledge Synergy: A Practical Guide to Collaborative Knowledge Management*. New York: Springer.

Sugasawa, Y., and L. Shantha. 1999. "Technology and Business Opportunities for Small and Medium Enterprises in Japan: The Role of Research Networks." *International Journal of Technology Management* 18 (3–4): 308–325.

Sveiby, K. 1997. *The New Organizational Wealth: Managing and Measuring Knowledge-Based Assets*. San Francisco: Berrett-Koehler.

Tapscott, D. 1997. *Growing Up Digital: The Rise of the Net Generation*. New York: McGraw-Hill.

Turpin, T., and L. Xielin. 2000. "Balanced Development: The Challenge for Science, Technology and Innovation Policy." In *Contemporary Development and Issues in China's Economic Transition*, ed. C. Harvie, 103–142. Melbourne: Macmillan.

United States Department of Commerce. 1998. *The Emerging Digital Economy*. Washington, DC: Department of Commerce.

Wade, R. 1990. *Governing the Market: Economic Theory and the Role of Government in East Asian Industrialization*. Princeton, NJ: Princeton University Press.

Westland, H. 2006. *Social Capital in the Knowledge Economy: Theory and Empires*. New York: Springer.

CHAPTER 6

Aguayo, R. 2004. *The Metaknowledge Advantage: The Key to Success in the New Economy*. New York: Free Press.

Allen, K. 2003. *Bringing New Technology to Market*. Upper Saddle River, NJ: Prentice-Hall.

Anand, N., H. Gardner, and T. Morris. 2007. "Knowledge-Based Innovation: Emergence and Embedding of New Practice Areas in Management Consulting Firms." *Academy of Management Journal* 50 (2): 406–428.

Andriessen, D. 2003. *Making Sense of Intellectual Capital: Designing a Method for the Valuation of Intangibles*. Burlington, MA: Butterworth-Heinemann.

Bahrami, H., and S. Evans. 2004. *Super-Flexibility for Knowledge Enterprises*. New York: Springer.

Brown, J. 2001. "Knowledge and Organization: A Social-Practice Perspective." *Organization Science* 12 (2): 198–213.

Burgelman, R., C. Christensen, and S. Wheelwright. 2003. *Strategic Management of Technology and Innovation.* 4th ed. New York: McGraw-Hill/Irwin.

Chatzkel, J. 2003. *Knowledge Capital: How Knowledge-Based Enterprises Really Get Built.* New York: Oxford University Press.

Cohen, D. 2006. "What's Your Return on Knowledge?" *Harvard Business Review* 84 (12): 28–29.

Colling, N., and B. Dankbaar. 2003. *Innovation Management in the Knowledge Economy.* London, UK: Imperial College Press.

DeSouza, K., and J. Raider. 2006. "Cutting Corners: CKOs and Knowledge Management." *Business Process Management Journal* 12 (2): 129–134.

Ettlie, J. 2000. *Managing Technological Innovation.* New York: Wiley.

Fuller, S. 2002. *Knowledge Management Foundations.* Burlington, MA: Butterworth-Heinemann.

Geisler, E. 2008. *Knowledge and Knowledge Systems: Learning from the Wonders of the Mind.* Hershey, PA: Idea Group.

Grant, R. 1996. "Towards a Knowledge-Based Theory of the Firm." *Strategic Management Journal* 17 (2): 109–122.

Groff, T., and T. Jones. 2003. *Introduction to Knowledge Management: KM in Business.* Burlington, MA: Butterworth-Heinemann.

Hansen, M., N. Nohria, and T. Tierney. 1999. "What's Your Strategy for Managing Knowledge?" *Harvard Business Review* 77 (2): 106–116.

Harris, P. 2005. *Managing the Knowledge Culture.* Amherst, MA: HRD Press.

Herschel, R., and H. Nemati. 2000. "Chief Knowledge Officer: Critical Success Factors for Knowledge Management." *Information Strategy: The Executive Journal* 16 (4): 16–22.

Hildreth, P., and C. Kimble. 1999. "Knowledge Management: Are We Missing Something?" Paper presented at the Proceedings of the Fourth UKAIS Conference, York, UK, September 1999.

Kaplan, R., and D. Norton. 2004. "Measuring the Strategic Readiness of Intangible Assets." *Harvard Business Review* 82 (2): 52–63.

Kendal, S., and M. Creen. 2006. *An Introduction to Knowledge Engineering.* New York: Springer.

Kerfoot, K. 2002. "The Leader as Chief Knowledge Officer." *Nursing Economics* 20 (1): 40–43.

Ketchen, J., G. Hult, J. David, et al. 2007. "Toward Greater Understanding of Market Orientation and the Resource-Based View." *Strategic Management Journal* 28 (9): 961–964.

King, W. 2007. "Knowledge Management: A Systems Perspective." *International Journal of Business and Systems Research* 1 (1): 5–28.

Lakshman, C. 2005. "Top Executive Knowledge Leadership: Managing Knowledge to Lead Change at General Electric." *Journal of Change Management* 5 (4): 429–446.

Lehr, J., and R. Rice. 2002. "Organizational Measures as a Form of Knowledge Management: A Multitheoretic, Communication-Based Exploration." *Journal of the American Society for Information Science and Technology* 53 (12): 1060–1073.

Leonard, D., and W. Swap. 2005. *Deep Smarts: How to Cultivate and Transfer Enduring Business Wisdom.* Boston: Harvard Business School Press.

Leonard-Barton, D. 1998. *Wellsprings of Knowledge: Building and Sustaining the Sources of Innovation.* Boston: Harvard Business School Press.

Martin, R. 2007. "How Successful Leaders Think." *Harvard Business Review* 85 (6): 60–67.

Narayanan, V. 2001. *Managing Technology and Innovation for Competitive Advantage.* Upper Saddle River, NJ: Prentice-Hall.

Nissen, M. 2006. *Harnessing Knowledge Dynamics: Principled Organizational Knowing and Learning.* Hershey, PA: IGI Global.

Pearce, C., and C. Manz. 2005. "The New Silver Bullets of Leadership: The Importance of Self and Shared Leadership in Knowledge Work." *Organizational Dynamics* 34 (2): 130–140.

Poston, R., and C. Speier. 2005. "Effective Use of Knowledge Management Systems: A Process Model of Content Ratings and Credibility Indicators." *MIS Quarterly* 29 (2): 244–268.

Rubenstein, A. 1989. *Managing Technology in the Decentralized Firm.* New York: Wiley-Interscience.

Rubenstein, A., and Geisler, E. 2003. *Installing and Managing Workable Knowledge Management Systems.* Westport, CT: Praeger.

Schilling, M. 2006. *Strategic Management of Technological Innovation.* 2nd ed. New York: McGraw-Hill.

Schwartz, D. 2006. *Encyclopedia of Knowledge Management.* Hershey, PA: IGI Global.

Southon, G., R. Todd, and M. Seneque. 2002. "Knowledge Management in Three Organizations: An Exploratory Study." *Journal of the American Society for Information Science and Technology* 53 (12): 1047–1059.

Stankovsky, M. 2005. *Creating the Discipline of Knowledge Management: The Latest in University Research.* New York: Butterworth-Heinemann.

Starbuck, W. 1992. "Learning by Knowledge-Intensive Firms." *Journal of Management Studies* 29 (4): 713–740.

Stewart, T. 2003. *The Wealth of Knowledge: Intellectual Capital and the Twenty-First Century Organization.* New York: Currency.

Sutcliffe, K., and K. Weber. 2003. "The High Cost of Accurate Knowledge." *Harvard Business Review* 81 (5): 74–82.

Thamhain, H. 2005. *Management of Technology: Managing Effectively in Technology-Intensive Organizations.* New York: Wiley.

Tissen, R., D. Andriessen, and F. Deprez. 2000. *The Knowledge Dividend: Creating High-Performance Companies Through Value-Based Knowledge Management.* New York: Prentice-Hall.

Tsoukas, H. 1996. "The Firm as a Distributed Knowledge System: A Constructionist Approach." *Strategic Management Journal* 17 (1): 11–25.

Wickramasinghe, N., and D. von Lubitz. 2007. *Knowledge-Based Enterprise: Theories and Fundamentals.* Hershey, PA: Idea Group.

Yeh, Y., and C. Lung-Hung. 2007. "Transforming a Semiconductor Company into a Learning Organization: A Bottom-Up Approach of Knowledge Management Implementation." *International Journal of Technology Management* 39 (112): 219–234.

Zack, M. 2003. "Rethinking the Knowledge-Based Organization." *Sloan Management Review* 44 (4): 67–74.

Chapter 7

Abbott, A. 1988. *The System of Professions: An Essay on the Division of Expert Labor.* Chicago: University of Chicago Press.

Alverson, M. 2004. *Knowledge-Work and Knowledge-Intensive Companies.* Oxford, UK: Oxford University Press.

Amar, A. 2001. *Managing Knowledge Workers.* Westport, CT: Quorum Books.

Angle, H. 1989. "Psychology and Organizational Innovation." In *Research on the Management of Innovation: The Minnesota Studies*, ed. A. Van de Ven, H. Angle, and M.S. Poole, 135–170. New York: Oxford University Press.

Badawy, M. 1982. *Developing Managerial Skills in Engineers and Scientists.* New York: Van Nostrand Reinhold.

Bahrami, H., and S. Evans. 1997. "Human Resource Leadership in Knowledge-Based Entities: Shaping the Context of Work." In *Tomorrow's HR Management*, ed. D. Ulrich, M. Cosey, and G. Lake, 209–216. New York: Wiley.

Barthelme, F., J. Ermine, and C. Rosenthal-Sabroux. 1998. "An Architecture for Knowledge Evolution in Organizations." *European Journal of Operations Research* 109 (2): 414–427.

Boudreau, J., and P. Ramstad. 2007. *Beyond HR: The New Science of Human Capital.* Boston: Harvard Business School Press.

Brokaw, T. 2004. *The Greatest Generation.* New York: Random House.

Bryan, L., and C. Joyce. 2007. *Mobilizing Minds: Creating Wealth from Talent in the 21st Century Organization.* New York: McGraw-Hill.

Cano, C., and P. Cano. 2006. "Human Resources Management and Its Impacts on Innovation Performance in Companies." *International Journal of Technology Management* 35 (1–4): 11–27.

Carayannis, E. 2001. *Strategic Management of Technological Learning.* Boca Raton, FL: CRC Press.

Cohen, W., and D. Levinthal. 1990. "Absorptive Capacity: A New Perspective on Learning and Innovation." *Administrative Science Quarterly* 35 (1): 128–152.

Connell, R., and J. Crawford. 2007. "Mapping the Intellectual Labor Process." *Journal of Sociology* 43 (2): 187–205.

Cortada, J. 1998. *Rise of the Knowledge Worker.* Burlington, MA: Butterworth-Heinemann.

Davenport, T. 2005. *Thinking for a Living: How to Get Better Performance and Results from Knowledge Workers.* Boston: Harvard Business School Press.

Davenport, T., and L. Prusak. 2003. *What's The Big Idea: Creating and Capitalizing on the Best Management Thinking.* Boston: Harvard Business School Press.

Euker, T. 2007. "Understanding the Impact of Tacit Knowledge Loss." *KM Review* 10 (1): 10–13.

Fitz-enz, J. 2000. *The ROI of Human Capital.* New York: American Management Association.

Flamholtz, E. 1985. *Human Resource Accounting.* 2nd ed. San Francisco: Jossey-Bass.

Geisler, E. 2000. *The Metrics of Science and Technology.* Westport, CT: Greenwood Press.

———. 2001. *Creating Value with Science and Technology.* Westport, CT: Greenwood Press.

———. 2007. "A Typology of Knowledge Management Transactions: Strategic Groups and Role Behavior in Organizations." *Journal of Knowledge Management* 11 (1): 84–96.

Gould, E. 2006. "Professor or Knowledge Worker? The Politics of Defining Faculty Work." *Higher Education in Europe* 31 (3): 241–249.

Hamel, G. 2007. *Moving Management On-Line.* Harvard Business On-Line. http://discussionleader. hbsp.com/hamel.

Hildreth, P., and C. Kimble. 2002. The Duality of Knowledge." *Information Research* 8 (1): 1368–1613.

Horibe, F. 1999. *Managing Knowledge Workers: New Skills and Attitudes to Unlock the Intellectual Capital in Your Organization.* New York: Wiley.

Howe, N., and W. Strauss. 2000. *Millennials Rising.* New York: Vintage Books.

Huang, N., C. Wei, and W. Chang. 2007. "Knowledge Management: Modeling the Knowledge Diffusion in Community of Practice." *Kybernetics* 36 (5): 607–621.

Huselid, M., B. Becker, and R. Beatty. 2005. *The Workforce Scorecard: Managing Human Capital to Exercise Strategy.* Boston: Harvard Business School Press.

Jones, S., and D. Schilling. 2000. *Measuring Team Performance.* San Francisco: Jossey-Bass.

Katz, R. 1988. *Managing Professionals in Innovative Organizations.* Cambridge, MA: Ballinger.

———, ed. 2003. *The Human Side of Managing Technological Innovation.* 2nd ed. New York: Oxford University Press.

Leydesdorff, L. 2006. *The Knowledge-Based Economy: Modeled, Measured, Simulated.* New York: Universal.

Lord, R., and P. Farrington. 2006. "Age-Related Differences in the Motivation of Knowledge Workers." *Engineering Management Journal* 18 (3): 20–26.

Mello, J. 2002. *Strategic Human Resource Management.* Cincinnati: Southwestern College.

Miller, D., M. Fern, and L. Cardinal. 2007. "The Use of Knowledge for Technological Innovation within Diversified Firms." *Academy of Management Journal* 50 (2): 308–326.

Nag, R., K. Corley, and D. Gioia. 2007. "The Intersection of Organizational Identity, Knowledge, and Practice: Attempting Strategic Change via Knowledge Grafting." *Academy of Management Journal* 50 (4): 821–848.

Oblinger, D. 2003. "Boomers, Gen-Xers, Millennials: Understanding the New Students." *Educause Review* (July–August): 36–47.

Ong, C., and J. Lai. 2007. "Measuring User Satisfaction with Knowledge Management Systems: Scale Development, Purification, and Initial Test." *Computers in Human Behavior* 23 (3): 1329–1346.

Quinn, J., P. Anderson, and S. Finkelstein. 1997. "Managing Intellect." In *Managing Strategic Innovation and Change*, ed. M. Tushman and P. Anderson, 506–523. New York: Oxford University Press.

Ravn, I. 2004. "Action Knowledge in Intellectual Capital Statements: A Definition, a Design, and a Case." *International Journal of Learning and Intellectual Capital* 1 (1): 61–71.

Roos, J. 1998. *Intellectual Capital.* New York: New York University Press.

Rubenstein, A. 1989. *Managing Technology in the Decentralized Firm.* New York: Wiley.

Scarborough, H. 1999. "Knowledge as Work: Conflicts in the Management of Knowledge Workers." *Technology Analysis & Strategic Management* 11 (1): 5–16.

Senge, P. 1990. *The Fifth Discipline: The Art and Practice of the Learning Organization.* New York: Doubleday.

Sensiper, L. 1998. "The Role of Tacit Knowledge in Group Innovation." *California Management Review* 40 (2): 112–132.

Sveiby, K. 1997. *The New Organizational Wealth: Managing and Measuring Knowledge-Based Assets.* San Francisco: Berret-Koehler.

Tallman, S., and A. Phene. 2007. "Leveraging Knowledge across Geographic Boundaries." *Organization Science* 18 (2): 252–260.

Werr, A., and T. Stjernberg. 2003. "Exploring Management Consulting as Knowledge Systems." *Organization Studies* 24 (4): 881–908.

CHAPTER 8

Anand, N., H. Gardner, and T. Morris. 2007. "Knowledge-Based Innovations: Emergence and Embedding of New Practice Areas in Management Consulting Firms." *Academy of Management Journal* 50 (2): 406–428.

Backer, T. 1991. "Knowledge Utilization: The Third Wave." *Science Communication* 12 (3): 225–240.

Boland, R., and R. Tenkasi. 1995. "Perspective Making and Perspective Taking in Communities of Knowledge." *Organization Science* 6: 350–372.

Burnett, S., L. Illingworth, and L. Webster. 2004. "Knowledge Auditing and Mapping: A Pragmatic Approach." *Knowledge and Process Management* 11 (1): 25–37.

Chan, A., and J. Garrick. 2003. "The Moral Technologies of Knowledge Management." *Information Communication & Society* 6 (3): 291–306.

Dalkir, K. 2005. *Knowledge Management in Theory and Practice.* Burlington, MA: Elsevier Butterworth-Heinemann.

Dawson, R. 2000. "Knowledge Capabilities as the Focus of Organizational Development Strategy." *Journal of Knowledge Management* 4 (4): 320–327.

Edwards, J., D. Shaw, and P. Collier. 2005. "Knowledge Management Systems: Finding a Way with Technology." *Journal of Knowledge Management* 9 (1): 113–125.

Euker, T. 2007. "Understanding the Impact of Tacit Knowledge Loss." *KM Review* 10 (2): 10–13.

Faniel, I., and A. Majchrak. 2007. "Innovating by Accessing Knowledge Across Departments." *Decision Support Systems* 43 (4): 1684–1691.

Fuller, S. 2002. *Knowledge Management Foundations.* Burlington, MA: Butterworth-Heinemann.

Geisler, E. 2006. "A Taxonomy and Proposed Codification of Knowledge and Knowledge Systems in Organizations." *Knowledge and Process Management* 13 (4): 285–296.

———. 2007. "A Typology of Knowledge Management Transactions: Strategic Groups and Role Behavior in Organizations." *Journal of Knowledge Management* 11 (1): 84–96.

Gibbons, M., H. Limoges, S. Nowotny, S. Schwartzman, P. Scott, and M. Trow. 1994. *The New Pro-*

duction of Knowledge: The Dynamics of Science and Research in Contemporary Societies. London, UK: Sage.

Hayek, F. 1945. "The Use of Knowledge in Society." *American Economic Review* 35 (4): 519–532.

Hibbard, J. 1998. "Users' Skepticism Grows as Vendors Push Products." *Information Week*, March 16, 58–62.

Hilsop, D. 2002. "Mission Impossible? Communicating and Sharing Knowledge via Information Technology." *Journal of Information Technology* 17 (2): 165–177.

Howells, J. 1996. "Tacit Knowledge, Innovation, and Technology Transfer." *Technology Analysis & Strategic Management* 8 (2): 91–106.

Leibowitz, J., B. Montano, D. McCaw, J. Buchwalter, and C. Browning. 2000. "The Knowledge Audit." *Knowledge and Process Management* 7 (1): 3–10.

Leibowitz, J., H. Nguyen, D. Carran, and J. Simien. 2007. "Cross-Generational Knowledge Flows in Edge Organizations." *Industrial Management & Data Systems* 107 (8): 1123–1153.

Lu, I., C. Wang, and C. Mao. 2007. "Technology Innovation and Knowledge Management in the High-Tech Industry." *International Journal of Technology Management* 39 (1–2): 3–19.

Mauritsen, J., and K. Flagstad. 2004. "Managing Organizational Learning and Intellectual Capital." *International Journal of Learning and Intellectual Capital* 1 (1): 72–90.

Nerkar, A., and A. Paruchuri. 2005. "Evolution of R&D Capabilities: The Role of Knowledge Networks within a Firm." *Management Science* 51 (5): 771–785.

Nonaka, I. 1994. "A Dynamic Theory of Organizational Knowledge Creation." *Organization Science* 5 (1): 14–37.

Polanyi, M. 1966. *The Tacit Dimension.* London: Routledge.

Quinn, J.B. 1999. "Strategic Outsourcing: Leveraging Knowledge Capabilities." *Sloan Management Review* 40 (4): 9–21.

Rich, R. 1991. "Knowledge (Reaction, Diffusion, and Utilization)." *Science Communication* 12 (3): 319–337.

Roberts, J. 2000. "From Know-How to Show-How? Questioning the Role of Information and Communication Technologies in Knowledge Transfer." *Technology Analysis & Strategic Management* 12 (4): 429–443.

Rubenstein, A.H., and E. Geisler. 2003. *Installing and Managing Workable Knowledge Management Systems.* Westport, CT: Praeger.

Rubenstein, A.H., and H. Schwartzel. 1992. *Intelligent Workstations for Professionals.* Berlin: Springer.

Styhre, A. 2003. "Knowledge as a Virtual Asset: Bergson's Notion of Virtuality and Organizational Knowledge." *Culture and Organization* 9 (1): 15–26.

Tschannen-Moran, M., and N. Nestor-Baker. 2004. "The Tacit Knowledge of Productive Scholars in Education." *Teachers College Record* 106 (7): 1484–1511.

Van de Ven, A., and P. Johnson. 2006. "Knowledge for Theory and Practice." *Academy of Management Journal* 31 (4): 802–821.

CHAPTER 9

Cunha, P., and P. Maropoulos, eds. 2007. *Digital Enterprise Technology: Perspectives and Future Challenges.* New York: Springer.

Den Hertog, F., and E. Huizenga. 2000. *The Knowledge Enterprise: Implementation of Intelligent Business Strategies.* Hackensack, NJ: World Scientific.

Dijkstra, J. 2001. "Legal Knowledge-Based Systems: The Blind Leading the Sheep?" *International Review of Law Computers & Technology* 15 (2): 119–128.

Eppler, M. 2006. *Managing Information Quality: Increasing the Value of Information in Knowledge-Intensive Products and Processes.* 2nd ed. New York: Springer.

Finnegan, D., and L. Willcocks. 2007. *Implementing CRM: From Technology to Knowledge.* New York: Wiley.

Gottschalk, P. 2006. *Knowledge Management Systems: Value Shop Creation.* Hershey, PA: IGI Global.

Handzic, M. 2007. *Socio-Technical Knowledge Management: Studies and Initiatives.* Hershey, PA: IGI Global.

Hansen, M., M. Mors, and B. Lovas. 2005. "Knowledge Sharing in Organizations: Multiple Networks, Multiple Phases." *Academy of Management Journal* 48 (5): 776–793.

Harryson, S. 2007. *Know-Who Based Entrepreneurship: From Knowledge Creation to Business Implementation.* Northampton, MA: Edward Elgar.

Hitchins, D. 2008. *Systems Engineering: A 21st Century Systems Methodology.* New York: Wiley.

Jennex, M., ed. 2007a. *Knowledge Management: Concepts, Methodologies, Tools, and Applications.* Hershey, PA: IGI Global.

Jennex, M. 2007b. *Knowledge Management in Modern Organizations.* Hershey, PA: IGI Global.

Kodama, M. 2007. *Knowledge Innovation: Strategic Management as Practice.* Northampton, MA: Edward Elgar.

Komninos, N. 2000. *Intelligent Cities: Innovation, Knowledge Systems, and Digital Spaces.* London: Routledge.

Lobas, J., and P. Jackson, eds. 2007. *Becoming Virtual: Knowledge Management and Transformation of the Distributed Organization.* Heidelberg, Germany: Physica.

Maier, R. 2007. *Knowledge Management Systems: Information and Communication Technologies for Knowledge Management.* 3rd ed. New York: Springer.

March, J. 1991. "Exploration and Exploitation in Organizational Learning." *Organization Science* 2 (2): 71–87.

McInerney, C., and R. Day, eds. 2007. *Rethinking Knowledge Management: From Knowledge Objects to Knowledge Processes.* New York: Springer.

McIntyre-Mills, J., and J. van Gigoh. 2006. *Wisdom, Knowledge, and Management: A Critique and Analysis of Churchman's Systems Approach.* New York: Springer.

Miller, B., P. Bierly, and P. Daly. 2007. "The Knowledge Strategy Orientation Scale: Individual Perceptions of Firm-Level Phenomena." *Journal of Managerial Issues* 19 (3): 414–435.

Nielsen, B. 2005. "Strategic Knowledge Management Review: Tracing the Co-Evolution of Strategic Management and Knowledge Management Perspectives." *Competitiveness Review* 15 (1): 1–13.

O'Dell, C. 2000. *Stages of Implementation: A Guide for Your Journey to Knowledge Management Best Practices.* Washington, DC: American Productivity Center.

Pfeffer, J., and R. Sutton. 2000. *The Knowing-Doing Gap: How Smart Companies Turn Knowledge into Action.* Boston: Harvard Business School Press.

Putnik, G., and M. Cunha, eds. 2007. *Knowledge and Technology Management in Virtual Organizations.* Hershey, PA: IGI Global.

Rao, M. 2004. *Knowledge Management Tools and Techniques: Practitioners and Experts Evaluate KM Solutions.* London: Butterworth-Heinemann.

Reiter, R. 2001. *Knowledge in Action: Logical Foundations for Specifying and Implementing Dynamical Systems.* Boston: MIT Press.

Rubenstein, A. 1989. *Managing Technology in the Decentralized Firm.* New York: Wiley.

Rubenstein, A., and E. Geisler. 2003. *Installing and Managing Workable Knowledge Management Systems.* Westport, CT: Praeger.

Ryan, S., and V. Prybutok. 2001. "Factors Affecting the Adoption of Knowledge Management Technologies: A Discriminative Approach." *Journal of Computer Information Systems* 41 (4): 31–38.

Santhanam, R., L. Seligman, and D. Kang. 2007. "Postimplementation Knowledge Transfers to Users and Information Technology Professionals." *Journal of Management Information Systems* 24 (1): 171–199.

Saviotti, P. 1998. "On the Dynamics of Appropriability of Tacit and Codified Knowledge." *Research Policy* 26 (4): 843–856.

Schlindwein, S., and R. Ison. 2004. "Human Knowing and Perceived Complexity: Implications for Systems Practice." *Emergence* 6 (3): 27–32.

Singh, J. 2005. "Collaboration Networks as Determinants of Knowledge Diffusion Patterns." *Management Science* 51 (5): 756–770.

Surinach, J., R. Moreno, and E. Vaya, eds. 2007. *Knowledge Externalities, Innovation Clusters, and Regional Development.* Northampton, MA: Edward Elgar.

Taylor, A., and H. Greve. 2006. "Superman or the Fantastic Four? Knowledge Combination and Experience in Innovation Teams." *Academy of Management Journal* 49 (4): 723–740.

Thorpe, R., R. Holt, A. MacPherson, and L. Pittaway. 2005. "Using Knowledge within Small and Medium-Sized Firms: A Systematic Review of the Evidence." *International Journal of Management Reviews* 7 (4): 257–281.

Todling, F., P. Lehner, and M. Trippl. 2006. "Innovation in Knowledge Intensive Industries: The Nature and Geography of Knowledge Links." *European Planning Studies* 14 (8): 1035–1058.

Troilo, G. 2007. *Marketing Knowledge Management: Managing Knowledge in Market-Oriented Companies.* New York: Edward Elgar.

Tsoukas, H., and N. Mylonopoulos, eds. 2004. *Organizations as Knowledge Systems: Knowledge, Learning, and Dynamic Capabilities.* New York: Palgrave Macmillan.

Vanhaverbeke, W., and V. Gisling. 2007. "Exploration and Exploitation in Technology-Based Alliance Networks." *Academy of Management Proceedings* 1–6.

Wadhwa, A., and S. Kotha. 2006. "Knowledge Creation Through External Venturing: Evidence from the Telecommunications Equipment Manufacturing Industry." *Academy of Management Journal* 49 (4): 819–835.

Wang, L., L. Jiao, G. Shi, X. Lu, and J. Lu, eds. 2006. *Fuzzy Systems and Knowledge Discovery.* New York: Springer.

Zhu, X., and I. Davidson, eds. 2007. *Knowledge Discovery and Data Mining: Challenges and Realities.* Hershey, PA: IGI Global.

CHAPTER 10

Arndt, M., and B. Bigelow. 2007. "Evidence-Based Management in Healthcare Organizations: A Critique of Its Assumptions." *Academy of Management Proceedings* 1–6.

Cascio, W. 2007. "Evidence-Based Management and the Marketplace for Ideas." *Academy of Management Journal* 50 (5): 1009–1012.

Cassiman, B. 2006. "In Search of Complementarity in Innovation Strategy: Internal R&D and External Knowledge Acquisition." *Management Science* 52 (1): 68–82.

Chan, I., A. Au, and K. Chao. 2006. "Barriers to Knowledge Sharing in Hong-Kong." *KM Review* 9 (2): 8–9.

Cohen, D. 2007. "The Very Separate Worlds of Academic and Practitioner Publications in Human Resource Management: Reasons for the Divide and Concrete Solutions for Bridging the Gap." *Academy of Management Journal* 50 (5): 1013–1019.

Cullison, C. 2006. "Avoiding the Typical Barriers to Effective KM." *KM Review* 9 (4): 16–18.

Dane, E., and M. Pratt. 2007. "Exploring Intuition and Its Role in Managerial Decision Making." *Academy of Management Review* 32 (1): 33–54.

Davenport, T., and J. Harris. 2007. *Competing on Analytics: The New Science of Winning.* Boston: Harvard Business School Press.

Engelbrecht, H. 2007. "The (Un)Happiness of Knowledge and the Knowledge of (Un)Happiness: Happiness Research Ad Policies for Knowledge-Based Economies." *Prometheus* 25 (3): 243–266.

Garfield, S. 2006. "10 Reasons Why People Don't Share Their Knowledge." *KM Review* 9 (2): 10–11.

Gaveth, G. 2005. "Cognition and Hierarchy: Rethinking the Microfoundations of Capabilities Development." *Organization Science* 16 (6): 599–617.

Geisler, E. 2008. "Evidence-Based Management and Knowledge Management: Towards Explanation, Convergence, or Collision Course?" Unpublished manuscript, Stuart School of Business, Illinois Institute of Technology.

Gopalakrishnan, S., and P. Bierly. 2006. "The Impact of Firm Size and Age on Knowledge Strategies During Product Development: A Study of the Drug Delivery Industry." *IEEE Transactions on Engineering Management* 53 (1): 3–16.

Jashapara, A. 2004. *Knowledge Management: An Integrated Approach.* Essex, UK: Pearson Education.

Jensen, R., and G. Szulanski. 2007. "Template Use and the Effectiveness of Knowledge Transfer." *Management Science* 53 (11): 1716–1730.

Lawler, E. 2007. "Why HR Practices Are Not Evidence-Based." *Academy of Management Journal* 50 (5): 1033–1036.

Learmonth, M. 2006. "Is There Such a Thing as 'Evidence-Based Management?' A Commentary on Rousseau's 2005 Presidential Address." *Academy of Management Review* 31 (4): 1089–1093.

Learmonth, M., and N. Harding. 2006. "Evidence-Based Management: The Very Idea." *Public Administration* 84 (2): 245–266.

Lee, O. 2006. "Psychological Barriers to Maintaining Knowledge Management Systems." *Cyberpsychology & Behavior* 9 (3): 367–368.

Leibowitz, J. 2005. "Linking Social Network Analysis with the Analytic Hierarchy Process for Knowledge Mapping in Organizations." *Journal of Knowledge Management* 9 (1): 76–86.

———. 2006. *Strategic Intelligence: Business Intelligence, Competitive Intelligence, and Knowledge Management.* Boca Raton, FL: Auerbach.

Lin, L., and L. Kwok. 2006. "Challenges to KM at Hewlett Packard in China." *KM Review* 9 (1): 20–23.

Matusik, S. 2002. "An Empirical Investigation of Firm Public and Private Knowledge." *Strategic Management Journal* 23 (3): 457–467.

Maula, M. 2006. *Organizations as Learning Systems: Living Composition as an Enabling Infrastructure.* New York: Elsevier Science.

McKenna, B., D. Rooney, and P. Liesch. 2006. "Beyond Knowledge to Wisdom in International Business Strategy." *Prometheus* 24 (3): 283–300.

Mingers, J. 2006. *Realizing Systems Thinking: Knowledge and Action in Management Science.* New York: Springer.

Muller-Merbach, H. 2006. "Heraclitus: Philosophy of Change, a Challenge for Knowledge Management." *Knowledge Management Research & Practice* 4 (2): 170–171.

Nichols, J. 2006. "Balancing Intuition and Reason: Tuning In to Indecision." *Journal of Rehabilitation* 72 (4): 40–48.

Nielsen, B. 2005. "Strategic Knowledge Management Research: Tracing The Co-Evolution of Strategic Management and Knowledge Management Perspectives." *Competitiveness Review* 15 (1): 1–13.

Noordink, P., and A. Ashkanasy. 2003. "Decision Making in a High-Risk Industry: Why Is Intuition Only Effective Some of the Time?" *Australian Journal of Psychology* 55 (Supplement): 139–143.

Perrott, B. 2007. "A Strategic Risk Approach to Knowledge Management." *Business Horizons* 50 (3): 523–533.

Pfeffer, J., and R. Sutton. 2007a. *Hard Facts, Dangerous Half-Truths and Total Nonsense: Profiting from Evidence-Based Management.* Boston: Harvard Business School Press.

———. 2007b. "Evidence-Based Management." *Harvard Business Review* 84 (7–8): 184–185.

Poston, R., and C. Speier. 2005. "Effective Use of Knowledge Management Systems: A Process Model of Content Ratings and Credibility Indicators." *MIS Quarterly* 29 (2): 221–244.

Ray, T., and C. Stewart. 2007. "Can We Make Sense of Knowledge Management's Tangible Rainbow? A Radical Constructionist Alternative." *Prometheus* 25 (2): 161–185.

Rousseau, D., and S. McCarthy. 2007. "Educating Managers from an Evidence-Based Perspective." *Academy of Management Learning & Education* 6 (1): 84–101.

Rousseau, M. 2006. "Is There Such a Thing as 'Evidence-Based Management'?" *Academy of Management Journal* 31 (3): 256–269.

Rubenstein, A., and E. Geisler. 2003. *Installing and Managing Workable Knowledge Management Systems.* Westport, CT: Praeger.

Rumsfeld, D. 2002. Press conference, NATO headquarters, Brussels, June 6. Department of Defense transcript.

Rynes, S., T. Giluk, and K. Brown. 2007. "The Very Separate Worlds of Academic and Practitioner Publications in Human Resource Management: Implications for Evidence-Based Management." *Academy of Management Journal* 50 (5): 987–1008.

Sadler-Smith, E. 2007. "The Twin Imperatives of Intuition and Analysis in Decision-Making." *People Management* 13 (4): 52–53.

Shortell, S. 2006. "Promoting Evidence-Based Management." *Frontiers of Health Services Management* 22 (3): 23–29.

Smith, H., J. McKeen, and S. Singh. 2006. "Making Knowledge Work: Five Principles for Action-Oriented Knowledge Management." *Knowledge Management Research & Practice* 4 (2): 116–124.

Thierauf, R., and J. Hoctor. 2006. *Optimal Knowledge Management: Wisdom Management Systems Concepts and Applications.* Hershey, PA: IGI Global.

Tordoir, P. 1995. *The Professional Knowledge Economy.* Dordrecht, Netherlands: Kluwer Academic.

Uzzi, B., and M. Gillespie. 2002. "Knowledge Spillover in Corporate Finance Networks: Embeddedness and the Firm's Debt Performance." *Strategic Management Journal* 23 (3): 595–618.

Williams, R., and D. Doessel. 2007. "The Role of Knowledge Accumulation in Health and Longevity: The Puzzling Case of Suicide." *Prometheus* 25 (3): 283–303.

Zhang, J. 2007. *Visualization for Information Retrieval.* New York: Springer.

CHAPTER 11

Alazmi, M., and M. Zairi. 2003. "Knowledge Management Critical Success Factors." *Total Quality Management* 14 (2): 199–204.

Anand, N., H. Gardner, and T. Morris. 2007. "Knowledge-Based Innovations: Emergence and Embedding of New Practice Areas in Management Consulting Firms." *Academy of Management Journal* 50 (2): 406–428.

Anantatmula, V. 2005. "Outcomes of Knowledge Management Initiatives." *International Journal of Knowledge Management* 1 (2): 50–67.

———. 2007. "Linking KM Effectiveness Attributes to Organizational Performance." *Journal of Information and Knowledge Management Systems* 37 (2): 133–149.

Anantatmula, V., and S. Kanungo. 2007. "Modeling Enablers for Successful KM Implementation." *Proceedings of the 40th Hawaii International Conference on Systems Science.* Honolulu: HIMSS.

Bapuji, H., and J. Crossan. 2005. "Co-Evolution of Social Capital and Knowledge: An Extension of the Nahapiet and Ghoshal (1988) Framework." *Academy of Management Proceedings*: DD1–DD6.

Bassi, L., and D. McMurrer. 2005. "Learning from Practice: Developing Measurement Systems for Managing in the Knowledge Era." *Organizational Dynamics* 34 (2): 185–196.

Boisot, M. 1998. *Knowledge Assets: Securing Competitive Advantage in the Information Economy.* New York: Oxford University Press.

Boisot, M., I. MacMillan, and K. Han. 2008. *Explorations in Information Space: Knowledge, Actor, and Firms.* New York: Oxford University Press.

Carlaw, K., L. Oxley, P. Walker, D. Thorns, and M. Nuth. 2006. "Beyond the Hype: Intellectual Property and the Knowledge Society/Knowledge Economy." *Journal of Economic Surveys* 20 (4): 633–690.

Compton, J. 2004. "Knowledge Management Plays a Key Role in CRM Success." *CRM Magazine* 8 (11): 15–16.

Curry, J., D. Wakefield, J. Price, and C. Mueller. 1986. "On the Causal Ordering of Job Satisfaction and Organizational Commitment." *Academy of Management Journal* 29 (4): 847–858.

Dalkir, K. 2005. *Knowledge Management in Theory and Practice.* Burlington, MA: Butterworth-Heinemann.

Delone, W., and E. McLean. 2003. "The Delone and McLean Model of Information Systems Success: A Ten-Year Update." *Journal of Management Information Systems* 19 (4): 9–30.

Fong, P., and L. Chu. 2006. "Exploratory Study of Knowledge Sharing in Contracting Companies: A Sociotechnical Perspective." *Journal of Construction Engineering & Management* 132 (9): 928–939.

Garrity, E., and G. Sanders, eds. 1998. *Information Systems Success Measurement.* Hershey, PA: Idea Group.

Geisler, E. 1999. "Harnessing the Value of Experience in the Knowledge-Driven Firm." *Business Horizons* 42 (3): 18–26.

———. 2000. *The Metrics of Science and Technology.* Westport, CT: Greenwood Press.

———. 2001. *Creating Value with Science and Technology.* Westport, CT: Greenwood Press.

———. 2006. "A Taxonomy and Proposed Codification of Knowledge and Knowledge Systems in Organizations." *Knowledge and Process Management* 13 (4): 285–296.

———. 2007a. "A Typology of Knowledge Management Transactions: Strategic Groups and Role Behavior in Organizations." *Journal of Knowledge Management* 11 (1): 1–14.

———. 2007b. "The Metrics of Knowledge: Mechanisms for Preserving the Value of Managerial Knowledge." *Business Horizons* 50 (6): 467–477.

———. 2008a. "Evidence-Based Management and Knowledge Management: Towards Explanation, Convergence, or Collision Course?" Unpublished manuscript, Stuart School of Business, Illinois Institute of Technology.

———. 2008b. *Knowledge and Knowledge Systems: Learning from the Wonders of the Mind.* Hershey, PA: Idea Group.

Groff, T., and T. Jones. 2003. *Introduction to Knowledge Management.* New York: Elsevier Butterworth-Heinemann.

Grossman, M. 2006. "An Overview of Knowledge Management Assessment Approaches." *Journal of American Academy of Business* 8 (2): 242–247.

Guyer, P. 2008. *Knowledge, Reason, and Taste: Kant's Response to Hume.* Princeton, NJ: Princeton University Press.

Hansen, M., M. Mors, and B. Lovas. 2005. "Knowledge Sharing in Organizations: Multiple Networks, Multiple Phases." *Academy of Management Journal* 48 (5): 776–793.

Hariharan, A. 2005. "Critical Success Factors for Knowledge Management." *KM Review* 8 (2): 16–19.

Hepler, B. 2006. "The New Economy of the United States: A New Mode of Production." PhD dissertation, University of Maryland.

Holsapple, C. 1995. "Knowledge Management in Decision-Making and Decision Support." *Knowledge & Policy* 8 (1): 5–23.

Holsapple, C., and K. Jones. 2005. "Exploring Secondary Activities of the Knowledge Chain." *Knowledge and Process Management* 12 (1): 3–31.

Hudson, J. 2006. "Inequality and the Knowledge Economy: Running to Stand Still?" *Social Policy and Society* 5 (2): 207–222.

Ju, T., B. Lin, C. Lin, and H. Kuo. 2006. "TQM Critical Factors and KM Value Chain Activities." *Total Quality Management* 17 (3): 373–393.

Kleist, V., L. Williams, and G. Peace. 2004. "A Performance Evaluation Framework for a Public University Knowledge Management System." *Journal of Computer Information Systems* 44 (3): 9–16.

Lee, C., and S. Lai. 2007. "Performance Measurement Systems for Knowledge Management in High

Technology Industries: A Balanced Scorecard Framework." *International Journal of Technology Management* 39 (112): 158–176.

Leibowitz, J., and C. Sven. 2000. "Developing Knowledge Management Metrics for Measuring Intellectual Capital." *Journal of Intellectual Capital* 1 (1): 57–67.

Lieberson, S., and J. O'Connor. 1972. "Leadership and Organizational Performance: A Study of Large Corporations." *American Sociological Review* 37 (2): 117–130.

Liu, S., L. Olfman, and T. Ryan. 2005. "Knowledge Management System Success: Empirical Assessment of a Theoretical Model." *International Journal of Knowledge Management* 1 (2): 68–87.

Manchester, A. 2006. "Understanding the Value of Knowledge." *KM Review* 9 (4): 2–3.

Parisi, S., and J. Henderson. 2001. "Knowledge Resource Exchange in Strategic Alliances." *IBM Systems Journal* 40 (4): 908–924.

Phillips, J., and S. Freedman. 1984. "Situational Performance Constraints and Task Characteristics: Their Relationship to Motivation and Satisfaction." *Journal of Management* 10 (3): 321–331.

Pilat, D. 2004. "The ICT Productivity Paradox: Insights from Micro-Data." *OECD Economic Studies, 2004* 1: 37–65.

Poston, R., and C. Speier. 2005. "Effective Use of Knowledge Management Systems: A Process Model of Content Ratings and Credibility Indicators." *MIS Quarterly* 29 (2): 221–244.

Powell, W., and K. Snellman. 2004. "The Knowledge Economy." *Annual Review of Sociology* 30 (3): 199–220.

Rescher, N. 1989. *Cognitive Economy: The Economic Dimensions of the Theory of Knowledge.* Pittsburgh: University of Pittsburgh Press.

———. 2005. *Epistemetrics.* New York: Cambridge University Press.

Rezgui, Y. 2007. "Knowledge Systems and Value Creation." *Industrial Management & Data Systems* 107 (2): 166–182.

Rogers, E., and P. Wright. 1998. "Measuring Organizational Performance in Strategic Human Resource Management: Problems, Prospects, and Performance Information Markets." *Human Resource Management Review* 8 (3): 311–339.

Rubenstein, A. 1989. *Managing Technology in the Decentralized Firm.* New York: Wiley.

Rubenstein, A., and E. Geisler. 2003. *Installing and Managing Workable Knowledge Management Systems.* Westport, CT: Praeger.

Scarbrough, H. 2008. *The Evolution of Business Knowledge.* New York: Oxford University Press.

Shin, M. 2004. "A Framework for Evaluating Economics of Knowledge Management Systems." *Information & Management* 42 (1): 179–196.

Small, C., and A. Sage. 2006. "Knowledge Management and Knowledge Sharing: A Review." *Information Knowledge Systems Management* 5 (3): 153–169.

Spender, J., and R. Grant. 1997. "Knowledge and the Firm: Overview." *Strategic Management Journal* 17 (1): 5–9.

Strassman, P. 1999. "Knowledge Metrics-Ticker-Tape Parade." www.Strassman.com/Pubs/Km/1999–11.php.

Styhre, A. 2003. "Knowledge as a Virtual Asset: Bergson's Notion of Virtuality and Organizational Knowledge." *Culture and Organizations* 9 (1): 15–26.

Sunstein, C. 2006. *Infotopia: How Many Minds Produce Knowledge.* New York: Oxford University Press.

Thomas, A. 1988. "Does Leadership Make a Difference to Organizational Performance?" *Administrative Science Quarterly* 33 (3): 388–400.

Van Buren, M. 1999. "A Yardstick for Knowledge Management." *Training & Development* 53 (5): 71–79.

Ward, S., and A. Abell. 2001. "How Knowledge Management Is Impacting the Pharmaceutical Sector." *Knowledge Management Review* 4 (1): 11–12.

Wong, K. 2005. "Critical Success Factors for Implementing Knowledge Management in Small and Medium Enterprises." *Industrial Management & Data Systems* 105 (3): 261–279.

Youndt, M., and S. Snell. 2004. "Human Resource Configurations, Intellectual Capital, and Organizational Performance." *Journal of Managerial Issues* 16 (3): 337–360.

Zuber-Skerritt, O. 2005. "A Model of Values and Actions for Personal Knowledge Management." *Journal of Workplace Learning* 17 (1–2): 49–69.

CHAPTER 12

Adams, G., and B. Lamont. 2003. "Knowledge Management Systems and Developing Sustainable Competitive Advantage." *Journal of Knowledge Management* 7 (2): 142–154.

Anantatmula, V. 2007. "Linking KM Effectiveness to Organizational Performance." *Vine* 37 (2): 133–149.

Butler, T., and C. Murphy. 2007. "Understanding the Design of Information Technologies for Knowledge Management in Organizations: A Pragmatic Perspective." *Information Systems Journal* 17 (2): 143–163.

Cabrera, A., W. Collins, and J. Salgado. 2006. "Determinants of Individual Engagement in Knowledge Sharing." *International Journal of Human Resource Management* 17 (2): 245–264.

Cappellin, R. 2003. "Territorial Knowledge Management: Towards a Metrics of the Cognitive Dimension of Agglomeration Economies." *International Journal of Technology Management* 26 (2–4): 303–325.

Carlucci, D., B. Marr, and G. Schiuma. 2004. "The Knowledge Value Chain: How Intellectual Capital Impacts on Business Performance." *International Journal of Technology Management* 27 (6–7): 575–590.

Carrillo, J., and C. Gaimon. 2004. "Managing Knowledge-Based Resource Capabilities under Uncertainty." *Management Science* 50 (11): 1504–1518.

Chen, M., and A. Chen. 2005. "Integrating Option Model and Knowledge Management Performance Measures: An Empirical Study." *Journal of Information Science* 31 (5): 381–393.

Christakis, A., and K. Bausch. 2006. *How People Harness Their Collective Wisdom and Power to Construct the Future.* Charlotte, NC: Information Age.

Cooper, L., R. Nash, T. Phan, and T. Bailey. 2005. "Learning About the Organization via Knowledge Management: The Case of JPL." *International Journal of Knowledge Management* 1 (1): 47–66.

Davenport, T., R. Thomas, and S. Cantrell. 2002. "The Mysterious Art and Science of Knowledge-Worker Performance." *Sloan Management Review* 44 (1): 23–30.

Delone, W., and E. McLean. 1992. "Information Systems Success: The Quest for the Dependent Variable." *Information Systems Research* 3 (1): 60–95.

———. 2003. "The DeLone and McLean Model of Information Systems Success: A Ten-Year Update." *Journal of Management Information Systems* 19 (4): 9–30.

Frydman, R., and M. Goldberg. 2007. *Imperfect Knowledge Economics: Exchange Rates Risk.* Princeton, NJ: Princeton University Press.

Geisler, E. 2000. *The Metrics of Science and Technology.* Westport, CT: Greenwood Press.

———. 2007. *Knowledge and Knowledge Systems: Learning from the Wonders of the Mind.* Hershey, PA: Idea Group.

Gray, P., and A. Durcikova. 2005. "The Role of Knowledge Repositories in Technical Support Environments: Speed versus Learning in User Performance." *Journal of Management Information Systems* 22 (3): 159–190.

Guo, Z., and J. Sheffield. 2008. "A Paradigmatic and Methodological Examination of Knowledge Management Research: 2000 to 2004." *Decision Support Systems* 44 (3): 673–688.

Hall, D., and D. Paradice. 2005. "Philosophical Foundations for a Learning-Oriented Knowledge Management System for Decision Support." *Decision Support Systems* 39 (3): 445–461.

Hammer, M., D. Leonard, and T. Davenport. 2004. "Why Don't We Know More about Knowledge?" *Sloan Management Review* 45 (4): 14–18.

Hansen, M., M. Mors, and B. Lovas. 2005. "Knowledge Sharing in Organizations: Multiple Networks, Multiple Phases." *Academy of Management Journal* 48 (5): 776–793.

Heisekaner, T., and J. Hearn, eds. 2004. *Information Society and the Workplace: Spaces, Boundaries, and Agency.* London: Routledge.

Kincaid, H. 1996. *Philosophical Foundations of the Social Sciences.* New York: Cambridge University Press.

Kleist, V., L. Williams, and G. Peace. 2004. "A Performance Evaluation Framework for a Public University Knowledge Management System." *Journal of Computer Information Systems* 44 (3): 9–16.

Kulkarni, U., S. Ravindran, and R. Freeze. 2006. "A Knowledge Management Success Model: Theoretical Development and Empirical Validation." *Journal of Management Information Systems* 23 (3): 309–347.

Lapre, M., and L. van Wassenhove. 2001. "Creating and Transferring Knowledge for Productivity Improvement in Factories." *Management Science* 47 (10): 1311–1325.

McGrath, F., and C. Parkes. 2007. "Cognitive Style Fit and Effective Knowledge Reuse." *International Journal of Knowledge Management Studies* 1 (3–4): 484–496.

Mu-Jung, H., C. Mu-Yen, and Y. Kaili. 2007. "Comparing with Your Main Competitor: The Single Most Important Task of Knowledge Management Performance Measurement." *Journal of Information Science* 33 (4): 416–434.

Murphy, T., and M. Jennex. 2006. "Knowledge Management and Hurricane Katrina Response." *International Journal of Knowledge Management* 2 (9): 52–66.

Newell, S., J. Huang, R. Galliers, and S. Pan. 2003. "Implementing Enterprise Resource Planning and Knowledge Management Systems in Tandem: Fostering Efficiency and Innovation Complementarity." *Information and Organization* 13 (1): 25–42.

Nidumolu, S., M. Subramani, and A. Aldrich. 2001. "Situated Learning and the Situated Knowledge Web: Exploring the Ground beneath Knowledge Management." *Journal of Management Information Systems* 18 (1): 115–150.

Poston, R., and C. Speier. 2008. "Knowledge Management Systems Usage: Rating Scheme Validity and the Effort-Accuracy Trade-Off." *Journal of Organizational and End-User Computing* 20 (1): 1–15.

Quaddus, M., and J. Xu. 2005. "Adoption and Diffusion of Knowledge Management Systems: Field Studies of Factors and Variables." *Knowledge-Based Systems* 18 (2–3): 107–115.

Rezgui, Y. 2007. "Knowledge Systems and Value Creation." *Industrial Management & Data Systems* 107 (2): 166–182.

Shin, M. 2004. "A Framework for Evaluating Economics of Knowledge Management Systems." *Information & Management* 42 (1): 179–196.

Skok, W., A. Kophamel, and I. Richardson. 2001. "Diagnosing Information Systems Success: Importance-Performance Maps in the Health Club Industry." *Information & Management* 38 (7): 409–419.

Small, C., and A. Sage. 2006. "Knowledge Management and Knowledge Sharing: A Review." *Information Knowledge Systems Management* 5 (3): 153–169.

Stein, E. 2005. "A Qualitative Study of the Characteristics of a Community of Practice for Knowledge Management and Its Success Factors." *International Journal of Knowledge Management* 1 (3): 1–24.

Verworn, B. 2006. "How German Measurement and Control Firms Integrate Market and Technological Knowledge into the Front End of New Product Development." *International Journal of Technology Management* 34 (3–4): 379–389.

Vinsonhaler, John, and Jan Vinsonhaler. 1995. "Using a Knowledge System to Document and Evaluate Faculty Productivity in a College of Business." *Journal of Education for Business* 70 (6): 337–344.

Wei, C. et al. 2002. "Design and Evaluation of a Knowledge Management System." *IEEE Software* 19 (3): 56–61.

Wing, L., and A. Chua. 2005. "Knowledge Management Project Abandonment: An Exploratory Examination of Root Causes." *Communications of AIS* 16 (4): 723–743.

Wu, J., and Y. Wang. 2006. "Measuring KMS Success: A Respecification of the Delone and McLean's Model." *Information & Management* 43 (6): 728–739.

Chapter 13

Allary, S., and C. Holsapple. 2002. "Knowledge Management as a Key for E-Business Competitiveness: From the Knowledge Chain to KM Audits." *Journal of Computer Information Systems* 42 (5): 19–26.

Dalkir, K. 2005. *Knowledge Management in Theory and Practice.* New York: Elsevier.

Geisler, E. 2000. *The Metrics of Science and Technology.* Westport, CT: Greenwood.

Lusiguan, S., S. Wells, A. Shaw, G. Rowlands, and T. Crilly. 2005. "A Knowledge Audit of the Managers of Primary Care Organizations." *Medical Informatics and the Internet in Medicine* 30 (1): 69–80.

Messier, W. 1997. *Auditing: A Systematic Approach.* New York: McGraw-Hill.

Rubenstein, A., and E. Geisler. 2003. *Installing and Managing Workable Knowledge Management Systems.* Westport, CT: Praeger.

Skyrme, D. 2001. *Capitalizing on Knowledge: From e-Business to K-Business.* Boston: Praeger.

Sullivan, P. 2000. *Value-Driven Intellectual Capital: How to Convert Intangible Corporate Assets into Market Value.* New York: Wiley.

Tong, T. 2005. "Ten Steps toward Effective Knowledge Audits." *KM Review* 8 (3): 5–6.

Wright, W., N. Jindanuwat, and J. Todd. 2004. "Computational Models as a Knowledge Management Tool: A Process Model of the Critical Judgments Made During Audit Planning." *Journal of Information Systems* 18 (1): 67–94.

Chapter 14

Ackerman, M., V. Pipek, and V. Wulf. 2002. *Sharing Expertise: Beyond Knowledge Management.* Boston: MIT Press.

Bloom, H. 1995. *The Lucifer Principle: A Scientific Expedition Into the Forces of History.* New York: Atlantic Monthly Press.

Brown, H. 2007. *Knowledge and Innovation: A Comparative Study in the USA, the U.K., and Japan.* New York: Routledge.

Burnett, S., L. Illingworth, and L. Webster. 2004. "Knowledge Auditing and Mapping: A Pragmatic Approach." *Knowledge and Process Management* 11 (1): 25–37.

Ericsson, K., N. Charness, P. Pettovich, and R. Hoffman, eds. 2006. *The Cambridge Handbook of Expertise and Expert Performance.* New York: Cambridge University Press.

Ericsson, K., and J. Smith, eds. 1991. *Toward a General Theory of Expertise: Prospects and Limits.* New York: Cambridge University Press.

Gray, C. 2008. *Managing Knowledge and the Small Firm.* New York: Routledge.

Guyer, P. 2008. *Knowledge, Reason, and Taste: Kant's Response to Hume.* Princeton, NJ: Princeton University Press.

Huseman, R., and J. Goodman. 2007. *Leading with Knowledge: The Nature of Competition in the 21st Century.* Thousand Oaks, CA: Sage.

Jensen, W., W. Steenbakkers, and H. Jagers. 2007. *New Business Models for the Knowledge Economy.* London: Ashgate.

Jennex, M., ed. 2007. *Current Issues in Knowledge Management.* Hershey, PA: Idea Group.

Land, S. 2008. *Managing Knowledge-Based Initiatives: Strategies for Successful Deployment.* New York: Butterworth-Heinemann.

Liebowitz, J. 2008. *Making Cents Out of Knowledge Management.* Lanham, MD: Scarecrow Press.

———. 2009. *Knowledge Retention: Strategies and Solutions.* Boca Raton, FL: Auerbach.

Malhan, I. 2008. *Perspectives on Knowledge Management.* Lanham, MD: Scarecrow Press.

McAdam, H. 2008. *Business Improvement: Integrating Quality, Innovation, and Knowledge Management.* New York: Routledge.

Melvor, R., M. Mulvenna, and P. Humphreys. 1997. "A Hybrid Knowledge-Based System for Strategic Purchasing." *Expert Systems with Applications* 12 (4): 497–512.

Mutch, A. 2008. *Managing Information and Knowledge in Organizations.* New York: Routledge.

Nerkar, A., and N. Paruchuri. 2005. "Evolution of R&D Capabilities: The Role of Knowledge Networks Within a Firm." *Management Science* 51 (5): 771–785.

Nonaka, I., R. Toyama, and N. Konno. 2000. "SECI, BA, and Leadership: A Unified Model of Dynamic Knowledge Creation." *Long Range Planning* 33 (1): 5–34.

Osterich, M., and B. Frey. 2000. "Motivation, Knowledge Transfer, and Organization Forms." *Organization Science* 1 (5): 538–550.

Scarbrough, H. 2008. *The Evolution of Business Knowledge.* New York: Oxford University Press.

Sidhu, R. 2008. *The Ambidextrous Organization: The Strategic Management of Learning, Knowledge, and Innovation.* New York: Routledge.

Skillicorn, D. 2008. *Knowledge Discovery for Counterterrorism and Law Enforcement.* Boca Raton, FL: CRC.

Wallace, D. 2007. *Knowledge Management: Historical and Cross-Disciplinary Themes.* Westport, CT: Libraries Unlimited.

Wiig, K. 1997. "Knowledge Management: Where Did It Come From and Where Will It Go?" *Expert Systems with Applications* 13 (1): 1–14.

Yolles, M. 2008. *Organizations as Complex Systems: Social Cybernetics and Knowledge in Theory and Practice.* Charlotte, NC: Information Age.

CASE 1

Bali, R., G. Cockerham, and C. Bloor. 1999. "Changing Organizational Culture for Successful MIS Implementation: A Case Study." *Proceedings of the 6th International Conferences on Advances in Management,* Baton Rouge, Louisiana, July.

Bower, M. 1966. *The Will to Manage.* New York: McGraw-Hill.

Boyatzis, R. 1998. *Transforming Qualitative Information: Thematic Analysis and Code Development.* Thousand Oaks, CA: Sage.

Haller, G., et al. 2007. "Integrating Incident Reporting into an Electronic Patient Record System." *Journal of the American Medical Informatics Association* 14 (2): 175–181.

Harrison, R. 1972. "Understanding Your Organization's Character." *Harvard Business Review* (May–June).

Hofstede, G. 1994a. *Cultures and Organizations: Software of the Mind, Intercultural Cooperation and Its Importance for Survival.* London: HarperCollins.

———. 1994b. "Management Scientists Are Human." *Management Science* 40 (1): 4–13.

Institute of Medicine. 2001. *Crossing the Quality Chasm.* Washington, DC: National Academy Press.

Kavale, G. 1996. *Interviews: An Introduction to Qualitative Research Interviewing.* Thousand Oaks, CA: Sage.

Kroeber, A., and C. Kluckhohn. 1952. *Culture: A Critical Review of Concepts and Definitions.* New York: Vintage Books.

Lewin, K. 1952. *Field Theory in Social Science.* London: Tavistock.

Lundberg, C. 1985. "On the Feasibility of Cultural Intervention." In *Organizational Culture,* ed. P. Frost et al. Newbury Park, CA: Sage.

McAuley, J. 1994. "Exploring Issues in Culture and Competence." *Human Relations* 47 (4): 417–430.

Porter, M., and E. Teisberg. 2007. *Re-defining Healthcare.* Boston: Harvard University Press.

Schein, E. 1990. "Organizational Culture." *American Psychologist* 45 (2): 109–119.

———. 1996. "Culture: The Missing Concept in Organization Studies." *Administrative Science Quarterly* 41: 229–240.

Smircich, L. 1983. "Concepts of Culture and Organizational Analysis." *Administrative Science Quarterly* 28: 339–358.

Williams, A., et al. 1993. *Changing Culture: New Organizational Approaches.* London: Institute of Personnel Management.

Case 2

Andriessen, D., and C. Stam. 2004. "The Intellectual Capital of the European Union." Centre for Research in Intellectual Capital, INHOLLAND, University of Professional Education, de Baak, Management Centre VNO-NCW. www.intellectualcapital.nl/artikelen/ICofEU2004.pdf.

Bossi, A., Y. Fuertes, and C. Serrano. 2001. "El Capital Intelectual en el Sector Público." http://ciberconta.unizar.es/LECCION/cipub/cipub.htm.

Edvinsson, L. 2003. "IC Entrepreneurship for Knowledge Capital as the New Source of Wealth of Nations." www.wspiz.pl/~unesco/articles/book3/tekst2.doc.

Kaplan, R. and D. Norton. 1992. *The Balanced Scorecard: Translating Strategy into Action.* Boston: Harvard Business School Press.

Marti, J. 2003. "CICBS: Cities' Intellectual Capital Benchmarking System." www.terra.es/persona17/jm_viedma/publicaciones/CICBStrad.pdf.

Mello, S., F. Cohen, and P. Oliveira. 2003. "Avaliação de capital intelectual das páginas web das assembleias legislativas brasileiras." Monografia apresentada ao curso de Pós graduação "lato sensu" do Instituto de Educação Continuada, Belo Horizonte. www.almg.gov.br/bancoconhecimento/monografias/Monografia%20-%20capital%20intelectual.pdf.

Queiroz, A.B. 2003. La Medición del Capital Intelectual en el Sector Público. Tese (doutorado), Universidad de Zaragoza, Faculdade de Ciencias Económicas y Empresariales. Orientadora: Lourdes Torres Pradas.

Santos, L., L. Amaral, and M. Rodrigues. 2005. "Avaliação da presença na Internet das câmaras municipais portuguesas 2003, UMIC–Agência para a Sociedade do Conhecimento, Lisboa." www.osic.umic.pt/publicacoes/PresencanaInternetdasCamarasMunicipais.pdf.

Serrano, A., F. Gonçalves, and P. Neto. 2005. "Cidades e Territórios do Conhecimento, Um novo referencial para a competitividade." Associação Portuguesa para a Gestão do Conhecimento, Edições Sílabo.

Stewart, T. 1997. *Intellectual Capital: The New Wealth in Organizations*: New York: Bantam Books.

Sveiby, K. 1997. *The New Organizational Wealth: Managing and Measuring Knowledge-Based Assets.* San Francisco: Berrett-Koehler.

Case 3

Belobaba, P. 1989. "Application of a Probabilistic Decision Model to Airline Seat Inventory Control." *Operations Research* 37 (2): 183–197.

Binney, D. 2001. "The Knowledge Management Spectrum: Understanding the KM Landscape." *Journal of Knowledge Management* 5 (1): 33–42.

Davenport, T., D. De Long, and M. Beers. 1998. "Successful Knowledge Management Projects." *Sloan Management Review* 39 (2): 43–57.

Earl, M. 2001. "Knowledge Management Strategies: Toward a Taxonomy." *Journal of Management Information Systems* 18 (1): 215–233.

Garud, R., and A. Kumaraswamy. 2005. "Vicious and Virtuous Cycles in the Management of Knowledge: The Case of Infosys Technologies." *MIS Quarterly* 29 (1): 9–33.

Netessine, S., and R. Shumsky. 2002. "Introduction to the Theory and Practice of Yield Management." *INFORMS Transactions on Education* 3 (1): 34–44.

Voelpel, S., M. Dous, and T. Davenport. 2005. "Five Steps to Creating a Global Knowledge-Sharing System: Siemens' Sharenet." *Academy of Management Executive* 19 (2): 9–23.

Zander, U., and B. Kogut. 1995. "Knowledge and the Speed of Transfer and Imitation of Organizational Capabilities." *Organization Science* 6 (1): 76–92.

CASE 6

Davenport, T. 1994. "Re-Engineering: Business Change of Mythic Portions." *MIS Quarterly* 18 (2): 112–123.

Enthoven, A. 1993. "The History and Principles of Managed Competition." *Health Affairs* 12 (1): 25–48.

Kongstvedt, P. 1993. *The Essentials of Managed Care.* Baltimore: Aspen.

Simon, H. 1997. *Models of Bounded Rationality.* London: Macmillan.

Wickramasinghe, N., S. Choudry, and E. Geisler. 2007. "Bionanotechnology: Its Applications and Relevance to Healthcare." *International Journal of Biomedical Engineering and Technology* 1 (1): 41–58.

Wickramasinghe, N., and J. Schaffer. 2006. "Creating Knowledge-Driven Healthcare Processes with the Intelligence Continuum." *International Journal of Electronic Healthcare* 2 (2): 164–174.

Wolper, L. 1995. *Healthcare Administration.* Baltimore: Aspen.

Zuboff, S. 1988. *In the Age of the Smart Machine.* New York: Basic Books.

CASE 7

Heier, H., et al. 2005. "Siemens: Expanding the Knowledge Management System ShareNet to Research and Development." *Journal of Cases on Information Technology* 7 (1): 92–108.

CASE 8

Wickramasinghe, N., and J. Schaffer. 2006. "Creating Knowledge-Driven Healthcare Processes with the Intelligence Continuum." *International Journal of Electronic Healthcare* 2 (2): 164–174.

Index

About the Authors

Eliezer (Elie) Geisler is Distinguished Professor at the Stuart School of Business, Illinois Institute of Technology (IIT) and Director of the IIT Center for the Management of Medical Technology. He holds a doctorate from the Kellogg School at Northwestern University. Dr. Geisler is the author of over 100 papers in the areas of technology and innovation management, the evaluation of R&D, science and technology, knowledge management, and the management of healthcare and medical technology. He is the author of several books, including *Managing the Aftermath of Radical Corporate Change* (1997); *The Metrics of Science and Technology* (2000), also translated into Chinese; *Creating Value with Science and Technology* (2001); *Installing and Managing Workable Knowledge Management Systems* (with Rubenstein, 2003); and *Knowledge and Knowledge Systems: Learning from the Wonders of the Mind* (2007). He consulted for major corporations and for many U.S. federal departments: Defense, Agriculture, Commerce, EPA, Energy, and NASA. Dr. Geisler is the co-founder of the annual conferences on the Hospital of the Future, and the Health Care Technology and Management Association—a joint venture of over one dozen universities in ten countries. He serves on various editorial boards of major journals. Dr. Geisler founded and was editor of the information technology section of the *IEEE Transactions on Engineering Management,* and was a founding co-editor of the *International Journal of Healthcare Technology and Management.* His current research interests include the nature and metrics of technological innovation and knowledge, and knowledge management in complex systems.

Nilmini Wickramasinghe researches and teaches in several areas within information systems including knowledge management, e-commerce and m-commerce, and organizational impacts of technology with particular focus on the applications of these areas to healthcare and thereby effecting superior healthcare delivery. She is well published in all these areas with more than seventy referred scholarly articles, several books, and an encyclopedia. In addition, she regularly presents her work throughout North America, as well as in Europe and Australasia. Dr. Wickramasinghe is the U.S. representative of the Health Care Technology Management Association (HCTM), an international organization that focuses on critical healthcare issues and the role of technology within the domain of healthcare. She is the associate director of the Center for the Management of Medical Technologies (CMMT), a unique research-oriented center with key research foci on knowledge management, healthcare, and the confluence of these domains and holds an associate professor position at the Stuart School of Business, IIT. Dr. Wickramasinghe also is the editor-in-chief of two scholarly journals: *International Journal of Networking and Virtual Organisations* (IJNVO; www.inderscience.com/ijnvo) and *International Journal of Biomedical Engineering and Technology* (IJBET; www.inderscience.com/ijbet), where she was also the journal's founder.

For Product Safety Concerns and Information please contact our EU
representative GPSR@taylorandfrancis.com
Taylor & Francis Verlag GmbH, Kaufingerstraße 24, 80331 München, Germany